WITHDRAWN
UTSA LIBRARIES

Risk Strategies

For Lou, Georgie and Robbie

May you continue to take the right risks

Risk Strategies

Dialling Up Optimum Firm Risk

LES COLEMAN

GOWER

© Les Coleman 2009

All rights reserved. No part of this publication may be reproduced, stored in a retrieval system or transmitted in any form or by any means, electronic, mechanical, photocopying, recording or otherwise without the prior permission of the publisher.

Gower Applied Business Research
Our programme provides leaders, practitioners, scholars and researchers with thought provoking, cutting edge books that combine conceptual insights, interdisciplinary rigour and practical relevance in key areas of business and management.

Published by
Gower Publishing Limited
Wey Court East
Union Road
Farnham
Surrey
GU9 7PT
England

Gower Publishing Company
Suite 420
101 Cherry Street
Burlington
VT 05401-4405
USA

www.gowerpublishing.com

Les Coleman has asserted his moral right under the Copyright, Designs and Patents Act, 1988, to be identified as the author of this work.

British Library Cataloguing in Publication Data
Coleman, Les, Ph.D.
  Risk strategies : dialling up optimum firm risk.
  1. Risk management.
  I. Title
  658.1'55-dc22

ISBN: 978-0-566-08938-1 (hbk)
       978-0-566-08939-8 (ebk)

Library of Congress Control Number: 2009927957

Printed and bound in Great Britain by
MPG Books Group, UK

Contents

List of Figures		*vii*
List of Tables		*ix*
Preface		*xi*
1	Introduction	1
2	Nature and Sources of Corporate Risk	15
3	Why Organizations Take Risks	27
4	Decision Making and Risk	43
5	Impact of Risk on Shareholder Value	73
6	Enterprise Risk Management	79
7	Financing Risk: Insurance and Asset-liability Management	101
8	Managing Risks in Financial Operations	119
9	The New Function of Chief Risk Officer	129
10	Governance and Ethics	139
11	National Risk Strategy	163
12	Management of Corporate Crises	177
13	Lessons from the 'Great Risks'	199
14	Summary and Conclusions	215
Selected Reading List		*225*
References		*233*
Index		*247*

List of Figures

Figure 1.1	Model of firm risk	2
Figure 2.1	Sources of firm risk	16
Figure 2.2	Reduction of point-source corporate risks	21
Figure 2.3	Evidence of increased firm-level strategic risk	22
Figure 2.4	Institutional ownership of US securities	25
Figure 3.1	Prospect theory	29
Figure 3.2	Risk-sensitive foraging	30
Figure 4.1	Decision making paradigm	46
Figure 4.2	Accuracy of uncertain judgements	49
Figure 4.3	Decision making under risk as a real option	56
Figure 4.4	Predictability of systems	62
Figure 4.5	Trends that collapse dramatically	63
Figure 6.1	Financial optimization of risk management	93
Figure 6.2	Integrated risk evaluation and management	94
Figure 6.3	Risk map	96
Figure 7.1	Pay-off line from insurance	109
Figure 8.1	Banking risk map: Operational loss events by exposure and frequency	122
Figure 10.1	Risk governance	142
Figure 10.2	Critical risk management questions	148
Figure 10.3	Relation of executive compensation to performance	150
Figure 13.1	HIH Insurance Stock Price and S&P Rating	211
Figure 14.1	Type I and II errors in risk judgements	217

List of Tables

Table 1.1	Dell Inc case study: Nature of firm risks	6
Table 1.2	Principal risk management techniques	12
Table 2.1	Model of the drivers, controls and measures of firm risk	18
Table 2.2	Annual frequencies of global disasters and catastrophes	19
Table 3.1	Risk-related questions	28
Table 3.2	Mini case studies: Overconfidence and risk taking	36
Table 3.3	Outcomes of common management strategies	36
Table 3.4	National bank risk record	40
Table 4.1	Examples of tangible real options	54
Table 4.2	Risk management using options to defer action	57
Table 4.3	Projected drivers of change	59
Table 4.4	Scenario planning example: Retail petrol supply	65
Table 4.5	Environmental conditions promoting risk and poor decision making	67
Table 4.6	Quick risk quiz	67
Table 6.1	Taxonomy of firm risk	85
Table 6.2	Tangible and intangible risks	87
Table 6.3	Foreword to the Australian standard on risk management	97
Table 7.1	Signs of relationships between economic indicators and finance risks	115
Table 8.1	Incidence of operational risks	122
Table 8.2	Distribution of operational risks by number of banks and value of loss	123
Table 9.1.	Generic key risk indicators	135
Table 11.1	Examples of national risks	164
Table 11.2	Failures in prediction of national risks	166
Table 11.3	Model of national risk management	169
Table 12.1	Examples of corporate crises in Australia	178
Figure 12.1	Taxonomy of crisis types	179
Table 12.2	Australian corporate crises 1990 to 2001	181
Table 12.3	Chaotic sequencing of crises	184
Table 12.4	Plan B	186
Table 12.5	Rules of Crisis Management	193
Table 12.6	Crisis checklist: Key questions for any crisis manager	196
Table 13.1	Some recent 'Great Risks', successful and not so	200

Preface

Risk across finance and management is a theory-free zone. The nearest parallel is medicine in the Middle Ages, when physicians were aware of surgical techniques and medicines that worked. However, they did not know why, nor could they explain the frequent failures; and they were impotent in the face of systemic illness. Today risk managers face much the same situation: they know of techniques that can reduce risks such as audits, controls and procedure guides. Nevertheless, they can rarely anticipate, much less prevent, serious man-made disasters such as strategic blunders, managerial scams and corporate crises. Nor is there a recognized framework to guide optimization of firm risk.

Although risk management has logged many successes, a significant barrier to further improvement is the absence of a comprehensive knowledge framework. The motivation for this work is to fill part of that gap with an outline of the nature and sources of risk in firms. The objective is to set out a body of risk knowledge to support its management, in much the same way that our understanding of human physiology and the physical sciences supports modern medical and engineering techniques, respectively. This is best achieved by linking knowledge from multiple disciplines – especially engineering, finance, management and psychology – to the scientific method of observation, hypothesis, prediction and experimental tests to develop a theory of firm risk. This book is a little about why risk should be managed, but far more about the genesis of risks and the tools available to manage it strategically.

As author I have a simple contention: firms have an optimum risk level, and creatively managing risk to dial up or down the right level is critical to maximizing shareholder value. Three words establish my paradigm. First it is about *strategy* with the meaning given by Sun Tzu who wrote in *The Art of War*: 'Strategy is the great work of the organization. In situations of life or death, it is the Tao of survival or extinction.' Risk management is a branch of strategy, and is the continual fight against every firm's truly deadly foe. A second aspect of my framework is that it seeks to establish techniques to *leverage* risk at the enterprise level with the intent to shape the whole organization: thus there is a strong focus on approaches with sweeping impacts. The third key word is *CFO*: the discussion recognizes that CFOs are increasingly being charged with managing the full range of enterprise risks across a firm, and that the framework of finance offers many relevant and useful techniques that can meet the broad objective of corporate risk management.

Surprisingly for a field as old as risk management, the concept of risk theory is very much in its infancy. Thus it is obvious that practitioners lack useful tools: even in the world's best companies, risk management is pretty naive, relying mechanically on checklists and anecdotal advice. Moreover, except for high reliability organizations and a few sophisticated multinationals and financiers, corporate risk management is rarely integrated across business units. As the need for a better theory of risk has become clear, the subject has emerged to become one of the hottest topics for industry. There is huge scope to develop risk's body of knowledge to meet the needs of management.

Shareholders should ask why their companies do not better integrate risk management. Everyone should ask why academia does not kick start this process.

The stimulus for this work came from the general manager of a bank who asked for advice on how she could make her staff more willing to take risks. My answer to her clear question is a theoretical, empirical and case-based framework that helps senior executives dial up the right level of risk in their organization. The aim is to overturn risk management as checklists or market instruments that work from the bottom up against specific hazards or risk sources, and replace this with tools that can be applied in a strategic manner to address hazards at the enterprise level. The latter arise out of deep seated risk parameters that are specific to each firm, ranging from operational processes through managerial traits to firm policies: each is amorphous and thus hard to control. So a new, systemic approach is required to tackle firm risks. This is particularly important because – even though traditional risk management techniques have proven immensely successful against identifiable point sources of risks such as workplace accidents – there has been no reduction in the frequency of enterprise level risks such as corporate crises and industrial disasters.

Much of my material has come from a research curiosity about business risk which I developed via a circuitous route. After studying engineering, I spent 20 years in industry dealing with risk on a daily basis. First in a series of line jobs in underground mines, transport fleets and call centres; then in planning and finance management roles. This background informed my Ph.D. thesis, which examined why some managers take risks whilst others stand motionless like – as my American friends say – deer trapped in a car's headlights. The topic has interested others, and this book – whilst designed to inform senior executives – supports the course *Risk Strategies* which I developed for fourth year undergraduate students at the University of Melbourne. Academics wishing to teach a similar course should contact me for a copy of lecture materials. Whilst this book is not meant as a textbook, references are provided to give comfort to readers and starting points for deeper study of topics.

I owe many debts of gratitude. To the University of Melbourne for a home to pursue my hobby of research, especially into risk; to Professor Rob Brown for supporting this goal and encouraging me to develop its academic rigour; to Professor Paul Kofman who has provided consistent support; to honours students in *333-405 Risk Strategies* who have been enthusiastic guinea pigs, strident debaters and unfailingly interested; and to family, colleagues and friends around the world who have provided immeasurable support, stimulus and encouragement. Of course the usual disclaimer applies.

Les Coleman
The University of Melbourne

CHAPTER 1

Introduction

There is no future without risk.
    Swiss Re (2004: 5), *The Risk Landscape of the Future*

He either fears his fate too much or his deserts are small,
Who dare not put it to the touch to win or lose it all.
    James Graham (1612–1650), Scottish general

In introducing one of finance's most important papers, William Sharpe (1964: 425), recipient of the 1990 Nobel Prize in Economics, wrote:

One of the problems which has plagued those attempting to predict the behaviour of capital markets is the absence of a body of positive microeconomic theory dealing with conditions of risk.

From a slightly different perspective, Lubatkin and O'Neill (1987: 685) wrote: 'Very little is known about the relationship between corporate strategies and corporate uncertainty, or risk.' Although these and other authors have illuminated their topic, there is still no comprehensive theory of firm risk. This work is designed to help fill part of that gap.

In firms, `risk' is not one concept, but a mixture of three. The first is what might occur: this is a hazard and can range from trivial (minor workplace accident) to catastrophic (explosive destruction of a factory); it is the nature and quantum of a possible adverse event. The second component of risk is its probability of occurrence: for some workplaces such as building sites, the chances of an accident may be near 100 per cent unless workers watch their step. The third element of risk is the extent to which we can control or manage it. Trips are largely within individuals' control. But what about destruction of the workplace? Avoiding that is perhaps only practicable by forming some judgement about operations and standards, and keeping out of facilities which look lethal. To further complicate risk, these elements can be overlain by environmental influences, and the way risk is framed or presented.

Although risk does not have a theoretical place in corporate strategy, it is intuitively obvious that its influence on firm performance is such that it should be an important factor in decision making. Every year, for instance, it seems that a global company is brought to its knees in spectacular fashion by an unexpected event: Barings Bank and Metallgesellschaft, Texaco and Westinghouse, Enron and Union Carbide are huge organizations that were pushed towards (or into) bankruptcy by strategic errors.

Even without a disaster, corporations are extremely fragile: the average life of an S&P 500 firm is between 10 and 15 years (Foster and Kaplan, 2001); and the 10 year survival rate for new firms which have listed in the US since 1980 is no more than 38 per cent (Fama and French, 2003). Company fragility seems to be rising. Of the 500 companies that made up the Fortune 500 in 1955, 238 had dropped out by 1980; in the five years to

1990, 143 dropped out. Thus the mean annual 'death rate' of the largest US companies rose from 0.2 per cent in 1955–1980 to 5 per cent in 1985–1990 (Pascale, 1990). My own research has shown that out of 500 companies in the S&P 500 Index at the end of 1997, 129 were no longer listed at the end of 2003 due to mergers (117 firms), bankruptcy (7) and delisting (5): the annual death rate was 4.3 per cent.

Risk is so pervasive and important that its management offers the prospect of great benefit. To set the scene, Figure 1.1 shows my model of firm risk and its key working assumptions. In brief, observable corporate outcomes – such as profitability and risk – are impacted by relatively stable structural features of the firm that are largely determined exogenously (such as size, ownership and operations); and by more fluid strategic factors that are largely endogenous (such as markets, products and organization structure). These factors, in turn, are shaped by the influences of Politics, Economy, Society and Technology (PEST), and by competitors, consumers and the investment community. External pressures encourage firms to change their tactics and strategies and thus induce moral hazard; and performance – particularly below an acceptable level – can feed back to induce changes in strategy. This is a resource and knowledge-based view of the firm, with risk as a key variable in determining shareholder value.

This framework will be followed in developing a body of theory behind firm risk, and showing how it can be managed strategically to add value. The figure gives a new perspective

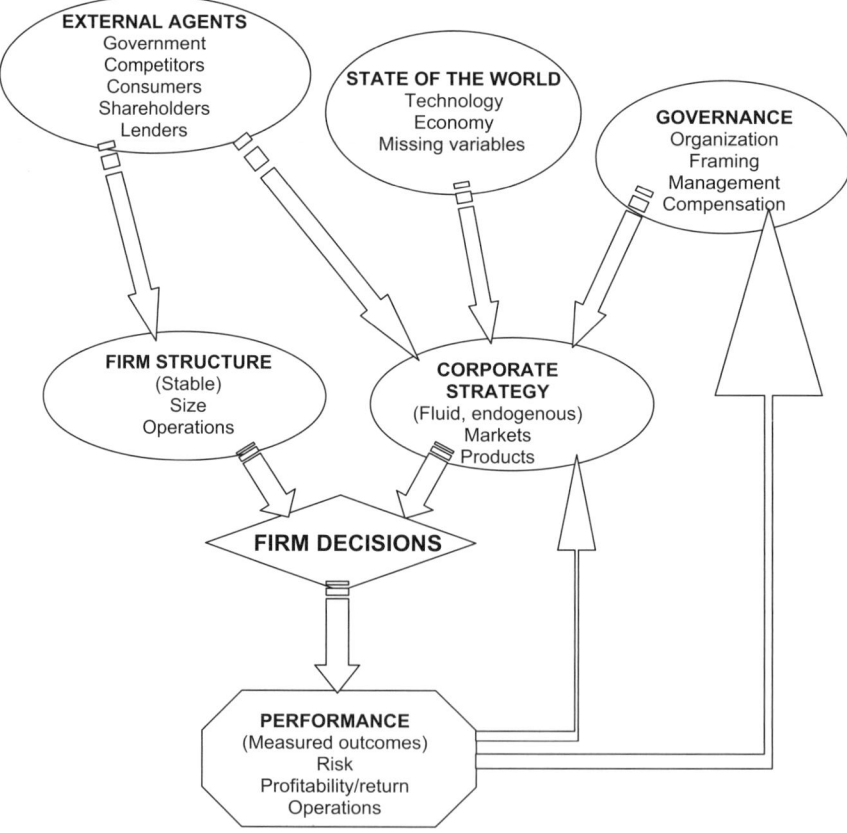

Figure 1.1 Model of firm risk

to corporate performance with its contention that risk and return are determined by a set of common underlying factors in the firm's structure and strategy. This explains the conventional assumption of a direct causal link between risk and return, which seems true across most disciplines. The model here goes further, however, in proposing that risk shares the same drivers as other performance measures, including returns. As we will see, this makes any return-risk correlation spurious because each arises independently from shared underlying drivers. Most importantly, this negates a common management and investor assumption that taking greater risk will lead to higher returns.

The concept of risk throughout the book is *firm risk*. Although measured in different ways, it is a probability measure that reflects the actual or projected occurrence of unwanted or downside outcomes that arise from factors that are unique to a firm or a group of firms. Thus it excludes systematic risks that arise from market-wide factors, such as recessions or equity market collapse. Firm risk incorporates idiosyncratic risk (sometimes called non-systematic or diversifiable risk) from finance which is the standard deviation of returns that arise from firm-specific factors and can be eliminated by diversification. Firm risk is also measured by loss in value, and by the frequency of incidents that contribute to value loss.

The analysis combines the perspectives of corporate finance and corporate strategy, and uses 'risk' with its dictionary meaning as the possibility of an adverse outcome. This is the way that risk is understood by managers, and also by key observers such as the Royal Society (1992) which defined risk as 'the chance that an adverse event will occur during a stated period'. However, we will see that the exact definition of risk is not critical because its various guises – operational risk, downside risk, variance in accounting measures of performance, and so on – are correlated (as would be expected from Figure 1.1).

The topic of corporate risk is important economically. I agree with Micklethwait and Wooldridge (2003) that the world's greatest invention is the company, especially as companies generate most of the developed world's wealth and produce most of its goods and services. Understanding how risk acts on their output offers the promise of a quantum improvement in economic performance, which – in keeping with Sharpe – has languished without explanatory theory.

Risk in firms is the downside of complex operations and strategic decisions: modern companies run a vast spectrum of risks, with many of such magnitude as to be potential sources of bankruptcy. Because the nature and quantum of risk shift along with changes in a firm's markets, technology, products, processes and locations, risk is never stable or under control, and hence is challenging to manage. Fortunately, though, risk shares many of the attributes of other managerial concepts that focus on value, including knowledge, quality and decision efficiency. Improving any one of these often improves the others, so risk management is a powerful tool in improving firm strategy and performance.

Conventional risk management techniques assume that companies face two general types of risk. The first is operational and arises in the products and services they produce, and within their organization and processes. These risks are managed mechanically using audits, checklists and actions that reduce risk; the best approaches are broad ranging and strive for *Enterprise-wide Risk Management* which DeLoach (2000: xiii) in a book of that name defined as:

> *A structured and disciplined approach: it aligns strategy, processes, people, technology and knowledge with the purpose of evaluating and managing the uncertainties the enterprise faces as it creates value.*

The second type of risk that companies face is financial and is sourced in the uncertainties of markets, and the possibility of loss through damage to assets. These are typically managed using market-based instruments such as insurance or futures.

This leads to four approaches to managing business risks that were first categorized by Mehr and Hedges (1963): avoidance; transfer through insurance, sharing or hedging; retention through self-insurance and diversification, and reduction through Enterprise Risk Management (ERM). These techniques have proved immensely successful in relation to identifiable hazards – such as workplace dangers and product defects – which might be called point-sourced risks. As a result of tougher legislation and heightened stakeholder expectations, the incidence of these risks has fallen by between 30 and 90 per cent since the 1970s. Conversely the frequency of many firm-level strategic risks – crises, major disasters, corporate collapses – has risen by a factor of two or more in the same period. This suggests that conventional risk management techniques have reached a point of diminishing returns: they are effective against point-sourced risks, but unable to stem the steady rise in strategic risks.

Despite this, corporate risk management remains unsophisticated. For a start, finance and management experts have little interest in any cause-and-effect links between risk and organizations' decisions. Finance ignores risks that are specific to an individual firm on the assumption that investors can eliminate it through portfolio diversification, and thus 'only market risk is rewarded' (Damodaran, 2001: 172). But this argument is not complete. For instance, market imperfections and frictions make it less efficient for investors to manage risk than firms. Secondly firms have information and resources that are superior to investors and make them better placed to manage risk. Third is the fact that many risks – particularly what might be called business or operational risks – only have a negative result and are not offset by portfolio diversification. Risk management should be a central concern to investors, and exactly this is shown by surveys of their preferences (for example, Olsen and Troughton, 2000).

Similar gaps arise within management theory which rarely allows any significance to risk and assumes that decision making follows a disciplined process which defines objectives, validates data, explores options, ranks priorities and monitors outcomes. When risks emerge at the firm level, it is generally accepted that they are neutered using conventional risk management techniques of assessing the probability and consequences of failure, and then exploring alternatives to dangerous paths (Kouradi, 1999). Systematic biases and inadequate data are rarely mentioned; and the role of chance is dismissed. For instance, the popular Porter (1980) model explains a firm's performance through its relative competitive position which is an outcome of strategic decisions relating to markets, competitors, suppliers and customers. Risk has no contributory role, and is dismissed by Porter (1985: 470) as 'a function of how poorly a strategy will perform if the "wrong" scenario occurs'. Oldfield and Santomero (1997: 12) share a similar view: 'Operating problems are small probability events for well-run organizations.' Even behavioural economics that has recently been applied to firm performance (for example, Lovallo and Kahneman, 2003) generally only attends to the shortcomings of managers' cognitive processes. This, however, completely ignores the huge amount of effort that most firms and managers put into risk reduction.

Another important weakness in risk management is that theory and practice are largely blind to the possibility that managing risks can lift returns. As a result sophisticated risk management practices are uncommon in firms. An example is the archetypal risk machines of banks and insurance companies. Neither considers the full spectrum of business risks being faced by their customers and shareholders: both look to statistics and certainty, rather than what can be done to optimize risk, and concentrate on either risk avoidance or market-based risk management tools. Thus an otherwise comprehensive review of risk management in banking by Bessis (1998) devoted just a few pages to operational risks.

Corporate risk management is equally weak, largely because it tends to be fragmented. Take, for instance, a typical gold mining company, whose most obvious exposures are operating risks to real assets. Control is achieved qualitatively, through some combination of reduction, retention and sharing that becomes a reductionist process of loss prevention. Responses are managed by health and safety professionals, through due diligence by senior management, and via inspections by employees and auditors. Staff are trained like craftsmen through an apprenticeship and rely on tacit knowledge because the firm's operating risks are often complex, hidden and uncertain.

The miner also faces another set of risks that affect its capital structure and cash flow, but they are managed quite differently. A treasury expert will quickly identify and quantify them, accurately estimate costs associated with alternative management strategies, and make clear recommendations on tactics. Well-recognized quantitative tools are portfolio theory, real options and risk-return trade-offs. These risk managers have formal training, apply explicit knowledge and use products as tools for risk management.

Shareholders, however, do not distinguish between losses from a plant fire or from an ill-balanced hedge book. They know from bitter experience that badly managed business risks can quickly bring down even the largest company. HIH, One Tel and Pasminco were well-regarded firms with blue riband directors that failed due to weak risk management. BHP, Fosters, Telstra and other firms did not go broke, but have destroyed billions of dollars of shareholders' funds through poorly judged risks. Risk should be managed holistically, not in silos.

An important trend which we develop at length in the next chapter is that strategic risks – crises, major disasters, strategic blunders – are becoming more common, with growing impacts on shareholder value. A good example is shown in Table 1.1 using the example of one-time market darling Dell Inc. In the year to August 2006, as the Dow Jones Industrial Average rose, the share price of Dell fell 45 per cent after the company's profits dropped, market share slipped and criticisms became widespread about neglect of customer service. In the following months the company was hit by the largest ever electronics product recall, a probe by the SEC into its accounting practices, and the threat of suspension following late filings of financial reports. A stream of executives left and company founder Michael Dell was forced to defend the CEO before firing him in January 2007 and dramatically resuming the position of Chief Executive.

Recurring crises of the type that enmeshed Dell are occurring under three sets of pressures. One is the growing complexity of systems: economies of scale, integration of manufacturing and distribution systems, and new technologies have more closely coupled processes so that minor incidents can readily snowball into major disasters. The second cause is deregulation and intense competition which have forced many firms to take more strategic risks in order to secure a cost or quality advantage. Given executives' poor decision-making record, an increase in the scale and frequency of strategic risks leads to more disasters.

A third contributor to more frequent strategic risks is corporate re-engineering and expanding markets, and the need to maintain returns in an era of low inflation. As

Table 1.1 Dell Inc case study: Nature of firm risks

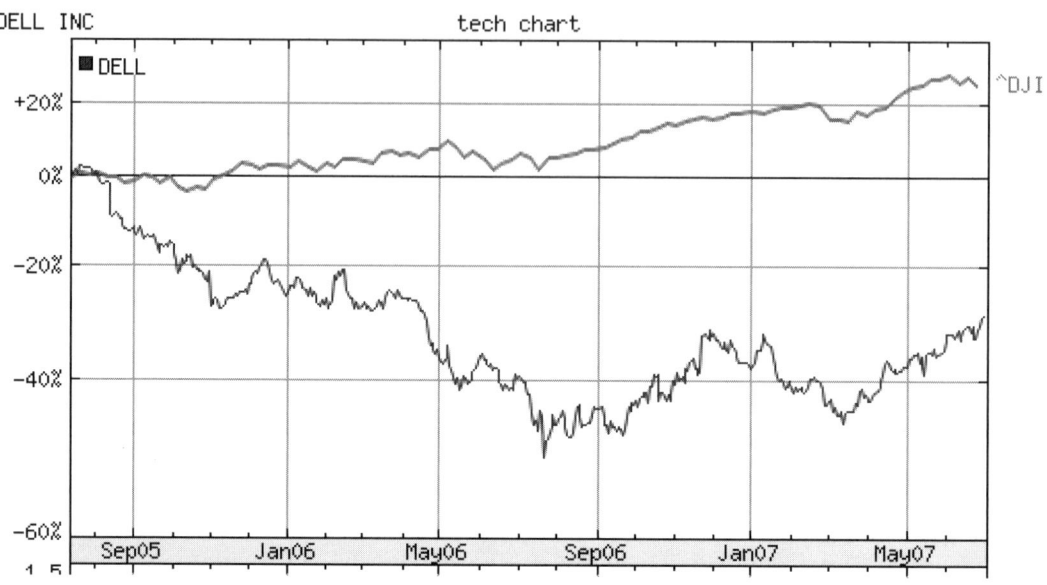

July 2006	Profits slump Drops behind HP as leading US PC manufacturer
7 August 2006	Article in *Barron's* starts: 'Is Dell at death's door?'
August 2006	Recalled 4.2 million PC batteries in largest electronics product recall
	Announced SEC had been probing accounting practices
September 2006	Postponed analysts briefing
December 2006	NASDAQ advised in breach of listing requirements due to late filing of accounting reports
19 December 2006	CFO resigns
31 January 2007	Michael Dell steps back in as CEO

society and industry become networked, intangibles such as knowledge and market reach become more important and so usher in new exposures. Moreover, areas of innovation involving environment, finance and information technologies tend to be technically complex and enmeshed in their own jargon, which promotes yuppie defensiveness that deters even the most interested outsiders from exploring their risks. Too many high-risk areas and processes in firms fall by default to the control of specialists (often quite junior ones) because senior management – which is best equipped to provide strategic oversight – is unable to meaningfully participate in the evaluations involved.

The confluence of these and other contributors to strategic risk explains why conventional risk management techniques have reached a point of diminishing returns: they can be effective against point-sourced risks, but are unable to stem the steady rise in firm-level risks. In short, conventional risk management techniques are simply inadequate to manage contemporary risks, and a new paradigm is required for risk management. That in a nutshell is the rationale for this book.

With 'risk management' so popular as a buzzword, it is timely to consider what it actually is. The concept was first introduced into business strategy in 1916 by Henry Fayol. But it only became formalized after Russell Gallagher (1956) published `Risk Management: A New Phase of Cost Control' in the *Harvard Business Review* and argued that 'the professional insurance manager should be a risk manager'. As new technologies unfolded during the 1960s, prescient business writers such as Peter Drucker (1967) garnered further interest in the need for risk management, and it became so obvious that US President Lyndon Johnson could observe without offence in 1967: 'Today our problem is not making miracles, but managing miracles. We might well ponder a different question: What hath man wrought; and how will man use his inventions?'

Inside firms, elements of risk management emerged in the goals of planning departments, and its philosophy was fanned in students of operations research and strategic management. But not until the early 1980s did risk management became an explicit business objective. Then neglect evaporated with a vengeance. In a popular book *Against the Gods*, Peter Bernstein (1996: 243) argued: 'the demand for risk management has risen along with the growing number of risks'; Daniell (2000: 4–5) agreed: 'We are now living in a world of rising risk and increasing volatility. Everywhere we seem to encounter increasing and intensifying risk … Poor management and lack of leadership have unnecessarily increased risks.' Since reading these works it has intrigued me that neither author felt the need to offer evidence to support their contention. Certainly they would have had difficulty in finding relevant data as its absence is one of the most prominent gaps in our understanding of risk. Perhaps they simply assumed that we are in what Ulrich Beck (1992: 12–13) called the *Risk Society* where risk is a key trait of modern life:

The productive forces [of modern industrial society] have lost their innocence in the reflexivity of modernization processes. The gain in power from techno-economic 'progress' is being increasingly overshadowed by the production of risks.

As risk management became better codified, it established core processes of observation (hazard identification), extrapolation (what could happen) and judgement (the likelihood of occurrence). Moreover it proved immensely successful in reducing point-sourced risks in virtually all aspects of our personal and business lives. Every well-run organization can claim credit for contributing to this remarkable transformation by pointing to efforts made in recruiting and training, risk identification and procedure development, approval processes and exceptions reporting, and so on.

Significantly, though, traditional risk management has been focussed on individual sources of risk. By pigeon holing risks, each has been tackled alone with little heed to systems and how they might form and interact. Risks are not managed strategically in light of firms' full exposures to markets, investments, operations and processes. This has led to two paradoxical features of risk: most corporate disasters now come from either conscious decisions or well recognized risks; and most serious process failures involve well-studied technologies and 'old' risks such as fires and explosions. Management had either neglected or ignored the risk being run (which is typical with financial and strategic disasters), or did not appreciate the potential for a succession of small risks to trigger catastrophe (typical of operational and marketing disasters).

When such catastrophes do occur, the contributing factors are evident with hindsight, and this leads to post-audits using a process called root cause analysis. As the name suggests, it looks not just at what happened, but why: what were the underlying causes that can be identified and managed better in the future? The technique involves a systematic process to identify each human or system deficiency that led to an adverse outcome, and thus eliminate factors that may precipitate a future adverse event. It is analogous to the nursery rhyme (usually attributed to Benjamin Franklin, but probably a much earlier proverb) warning of the outcomes that are inevitable in the relentlessly logical progression of events:

For want of a nail the shoe was lost
For want of a shoe the horse was lost
For want of a horse the rider was lost
For want of a rider the battle was lost
For want of a battle the kingdom was lost
And all for want of a horseshoe nail.

A similar perspective comes in the domino theory of Heinrich (1959) which argues that accidents are part of a chain of events involving characteristics of the victim and environment, a human error that leads to emergence of a hazard or unsafe act, followed by an accident and possible injury. He believed that 98 per cent of accidents were 'avoidable'.

This perspective can build a compelling case for the predictability of catastrophes. Bazerman and Watkins (2004), for example, describe the 9-11 terrorist attacks on New York and Washington, Enron's $US93 billion collapse in 2002, and other shocking events as 'disasters you should have seen coming'.

In the case of September 11 they document (page 21) a series of clear warning signs through escalating attacks on the US by *al Qaida* after the 1993 World Trade Centre bombing; and growing 'evidence that Islamic terrorists intended to use commercial airlines as weapons' including a foiled plot in 1995 by an *al Qaida* linked terrorist group to crash an Air France jet into the Eiffel Tower.

There were also 'gaping holes ... in airport security' that led to clear and strident warnings from reputable, independent observers. In testimony during 1996 to the House Subcommittee on Aviation, Assistant Comptroller General of the General Accounting Office Keith Fultz reported:

The terrorists' threat in the United States is more serious and extensive than previously believed ... Nearly every major aspect of the [nation's aviation security] system – ranging from the screening of passengers, checked and carry-on baggage, mail, and cargo as well as access to secured areas within airports and aircraft – has weaknesses that terrorists could exploit.
Available online at www.gao.gov/archive/1996/rc96251t.pdf.

Security in September 2001 was the responsibility of the airlines which – in a highly competitive industry – predictably took every possible action to contain their costs. Proposals such as those of the GAO to introduce tighter security standards were actively resisted by airlines, and the regulator charged with supervising airport security – the

Federal Aviation Administration – was slow to enforce existing regulations, much less introduce new ones. Looking back it seems fairly obvious why 9-11 occurred.

On the other hand, the support of root cause analysis for recurring 'predictable surprises' has a number of serious deficiencies. It is reductionist: part of the process, for instance, involves charting the chain of contributing events, which inevitably assembles a pattern that fits the data and its sequence. In fact, though, this only explains *how* something *could* have happened, not why. The other defect in conventional analysis of risks and incidents is that it can all too easily identify what philosopher Arthur Koestler (1972) termed 'confluential events' where complex outcomes arise from essentially unconnected parts. Even though the pieces seem to fit, they may not actually have done so in the lead up to disaster.

Illustrations of how seemingly 'obvious' facts do not fit together ahead of time can be seen in the occurrence of major events such as wars. In the case of the First World War, many historians (see, for example: Tuchman, 1962) paint a clear picture of steadily escalating German militarism that ultimately led its leaders to engineer a strike against encircling powers of Britain, France and Russia. The inevitability of this conflict was, however, far from self-evident *before* the War, and an excellent illustration of this is provided by Sir Norman Angell, later a member of the British Parliament and recipient of the Nobel Peace Prize, who wrote shortly before the Great War's outbreak (Angell, 1912: viii–x):

> *[Traditional views of military power] belong to a stage of development out of which we have passed ... Military power is socially and economically futile ... International finance has become so interdependent and so interwoven with trade and industry [but] political and military power can in reality do nothing for trade ... The diminishing role of physical force in all spheres of human activity ... has rendered the problems of modern international politics profoundly and essentially different.*

In short the economic interdependence of modern states means that military aggressors suffer equally with those they defeat and starting a war is economically illogical. Thus war between the world's major economies was unthinkable in 1912. It should have been even more unthinkable in 1938–9.

More basically, every accident, disaster, collapse that involves man-made or human-operated equipment, facilities or processes inevitably stems from human error. Each followed a wrong decision by a person who failed to correctly locate, maintain or operate whatever proximately contributed to the loss. This failure can be explained simply as a moment of inattention or an error by a normally reliable individual. Conversely it can be given a systematic cause such as poor recruitment and training which put the wrong person in a critical position; heavy workload and inadequate support so the person was hampered in making the correct decision; or external pressures, including moral hazard, that promoted error. If an operator makes a mistake because he was tired, hung-over or day-dreaming, is that operator error or a systematic problem?

Sadly the extent of the explanation of any incident is all too often related to its scale, not its real cause. The death of larger-than-life Princess Diana cannot involve a drunken driver and illegally high speeds, but must be due to a conspiracy involving MI5 and Prince Philip. Just 19 men with few resources could not possibly wreak the destructive horror of September 11. Loss of a shuttle and seven photogenic astronauts cannot be due to a single engineer's misjudgement, but must involve all of NASA and much of Congress. Only the combination of mafia, Cuba and oil barons could explain a modern Presidential assassination. Pearl Harbor was such a disaster that it must have been orchestrated by President Roosevelt, and could not be explained by the inability to translate, piece together and act instantly on a huge volume of captured Japanese intelligence. This kind of thinking has surrounded so many incidents that the BBC developed a series entitled 'the Conspiracy Files' [transcripts are available at http://news.bbc.co.uk/1/hi/programmes/conspiracy_files].

Bazerman and Watkins (2004: 35–39) also conjoin the magnitude of a disaster and its causes by suggesting a variety of systemic causes of 9-11, including the apparent unwillingness of those with authority to act on risks that should have appeared obvious. They argue that an important contributor was cognitive biases such as positive illusions that downplay risks, a heavy discount for future costs, reluctance to change and a myopic focus only on immediate problems. This leads to a natural tendency to defer pre-emptive actions that are certain to bring an unpleasant reaction – legislation by Congress, higher airline ticket costs – when they are directed at threats whose occurrence is highly uncertain. In social terms this is what Thurow (1981) called the `zero-sum society' where change brings both winners and losers, but the costs of any policy action tend to be concentrated whereas the benefits are diffuse. These factors militate against alignment of decision frameworks and lead to active protest by highly motivated opponents of change – which are especially likely to emerge in the case of imposed solutions – that can paralyze steps to reduce risks, particularly those associated with public goods.

In the case of 9-11, the criticisms above miss two key points. The first is whether it is ever realistic to safety-proof a system as complex as that of aviation across the US. Certainly it had gaps: every passenger during the 1990s had tales of security incompetence. But – absent huge expenditures – could the gaps really ever be closed? Or would there always be unsafe operations and hence casualties, just as there are in other transport modes such as road and rail? Intuitively it seems a daunting challenge to eliminate risks from people who are prepared to die and can hide themselves amongst the millions of passengers who fly each year out of scores of major airports. At the least, tightening security to detect the few terrorists would impose cost, delay and a flood of false alarms that may be quite unacceptable. This, of course, is Perrow's (1984) argument that some complex systems simply cannot be made safe and hence accidents are 'normal'. Even if the cause of a specific incident can be traced to system-wide problems, this is hardly helpful. Vague, sweeping generalizations – `the system failed us' – may satisfy a public seeking easy explanations, but they do little to prevent recurrence of the problem.

The second issue is whether it would ever have been realistic to anticipate the specific chain of events leading to 9-11. Certainly most of its core elements – including the tactics and targets – had featured in previous terrorist plots; and the scenario was chillingly laid out by Tom Clancy (1994) in the thriller *Debt of Honor* which ends with a commercial airliner flying into Washington DC's Capitol Building and wiping out the US President and political leadership. However, it is one thing to know a broad-brush method (that is, hijack an airliner and fly it – or force the pilots to fly it – into an attractive target), and quite another to anticipate the many possible signs in advance of one specific attack and stop it. Moreover many novels contain plots against government and national symbols, so *al Qaida's* attack could have taken numerous forms. So, are post-audits simply being wise after the fact as they effortlessly connect events in hindsight that could not have been anticipated? A caution on the impracticality of predicting disasters comes from studies of frauds which show that half are detected by accident and another quarter are reported by 'disgruntled lovers'; relatively few are picked up by audit and management (Comer, 1998: 11). If this figure is even remotely true, it bodes ill for the prospects of pre-emptive risk management.

Because risk management can never eliminate every adverse consequence, it must accept the restriction of doing no more than keeping as many as possible within acceptable levels. This 'unmanageable' aspect of risk is an important issue because severe risk outcomes have crippling costs for firms. Material risks of major loss that cannot be avoided mean that every organization needs to face up to and acknowledge the risks it runs, and scope out what could occur and how the resulting situations could best be managed. There can be little doubt that management and control of risk is the most important challenge in business today (Kendall, 1998).

With the scene now set, let us consider the objectives of this book in terms of closing gaps in the theory of risk and its management.

The first involves an understanding of the psychology of human behaviour and the dynamics of organizations. An important assumption is that as much as half of corporate risk taking can be attributed to the characteristics and behaviour of firms and their managers. This is termed risk propensity, and I am convinced that understanding behaviour is critical to managing risk.

A second goal is to apply modern theories and techniques that have proven successful in managing financial risks to management of the full range of risks attached to firms' real assets and business operations. Options theory, for instance, has much to offer risk managers. As examples: insurance can be considered as a put option; and risk affects decision making because high uncertainty increases the value of any optionality and defers commitment. Another approach is to analyze firms as systems whose risk is related to their entropy; or as collections of assets that behave as a portfolio. In related areas, joint ventures can be seen as leverage and there are optimum return-risk trade-offs from diversification.

A third gap lies in the way risk is treated by different disciplines, most prominently that they ignore other contributions to the topic. First there is very limited exchange of knowledge: most modern insurance textbooks have little on finance, whilst most corporate finance texts have little on firm risk or even insurance. Most texts on business risks have little on either insurance or finance. Similarly organization and strategy theory sees risk management as a *process* dominated by checklists and due diligence with a firm-specific focus, whereas financial risk management is all about *products*, particularly insurance and market-based instruments.

In bridging this last gap, I seek to accelerate what Culp (2002: 9) sees as a 'confluence of risk management and corporate finance' in the last decade. Despite a lack of formal integration, risk management and corporate finance are becoming more strongly linked at the business level. Every firm's capital structure is path dependent and a function of its history, especially investment decisions, judgements about capital market moves and operational performance; this means that any firm's risk is interwoven with its historical decisions. A strong rationale for more closely linking corporate finance and risk management is that designing a firm's capital structure without recognizing its risk profile will lead to sub-optimal outcomes for both.

Intuitively the integration of risk management and corporate finance should be easy because they are fungible. Consider a firm that wishes to actively manage its risks. It can adopt one of the standard strategies of avoidance, transfer and insurance, or retention and reduction. However, as shown in Table 1.2, each of these strategies has economic consequences that are identical to those of financial risk management products.

The most flexible risk management strategy is retention, in which the firm accepts a particular risk as an inherent part of day-to-day operations. Many firms consciously or unconsciously retain much of their risk because the alternative is too hard and has limited financial benefit. From a process perspective, retention acknowledges the difficulty in identifying all risks, quantifying their costs, and insuring or transferring each one. To compensate for the risks they are retaining, firms build organizational slack in the form of additional controls, inspections and specialist response capability that can cope with any risks that emerge. This self-insurance is economically equivalent to retaining a flexible balance sheet so that new equity or debt can be issued to cushion the costs of uncertainties.

Insurance is another flexible risk management strategy and is economically equivalent to debt. Each involves an annuity to meet the payout from a specific risk, either by offsetting the cost after the event by drawing down debt, or prepaying the cost of expected exposures through insurance premia. That is one reason why companies with large or unquantifiable risks – such as R&D, mining and technology firms – have low gearing: they build up as much slack capacity as possible to cope with a serious loss.

Similarly transfer of risk is economically equivalent to securitization or hedging. Consider a company that outsources a hazardous or polluting process such as tanning, and pays a premium to isolate itself from any unwanted exposures. This eliminates risks and locks in returns, just as a bank might securitize a portfolio of loans, or a gold company might sell its production forward.

Even though these strategies may be economically equivalent, they do have significant differences after taking into account factors such as taxation and timing. In the case of

Table 1.2 Principal risk management techniques

Strategic Risk Objective	Economic Consequences	Management Perspective	Finance Perspective
Avoid	Opportunity costs of foregone strategy	Preclude	Zero-weighting
Transfer	One-time cost to avoid contingent event	Sharing (Joint Ventures) Outsourcing	Hedging Securitization
Insure	Annuity to payout contingent event	Insurance	Debt
Retain	Write-off costs of contingent event	Self-insurance	Asset liability management Diversification
Reduce		Enterprise risk management	Equity

insurance and debt, for instance, insurance is a prepayment for loss that is immediately deductible from taxable income; whereas debt represents a payment that is delayed until the event and only then becomes deductible as interest expense and depreciation. Moreover the impacts can differ according to tax regime. Equity, for instance, can be a less attractive store of wealth under a classical tax regime where dividends are subject to double taxation.

Perhaps the major difference between the management and finance perspectives on risk management is in their operational aspects. Financial risk products effectively separate risk management from operations, and they have a more directly quantifiable impact on firm value.

Summary of the Book's Contents

This chapter has introduced the topic of managing firm risks by establishing an analytical framework and providing descriptions of key terms. The remainder of the book proceeds as follows.

The next four chapters provide a theoretical basis for risk management by describing the causes, processes and consequences of risk taking. Chapter 2 discusses the nature and sources of firm risk showing the links between different concepts of risk and how they can be traced to a firm's structure and environment. Chapter 3 discusses the behavioural and structural factors that lead managers and companies to take risks, and how this is growing under moral hazard imposed by government regulation and shareholder expectations. Chapter 4 examines the processes of decision making that incorporate attitudes towards risk and which can lead to more or less risky outcomes. It also provides a framework for decision making under uncertainty. Chapter 5 discusses the rationale for dialling up the right level of organizational risk to increase shareholder value.

Four chapters then set out different tools for managing risk. Chapter 6 covers conventional risk management techniques, most of them combined under the concept of enterprise-wide risk management, and Chapter 7 follows with an introduction to the concept and role of a Chief Risk Officer (CRO). The next chapter looks at financial techniques to manage risk, principally insurance and asset-liability management, whilst Chapter 9 discusses risk that arise in financial operations and how they can be managed.

Chapters 10 and 11 address strategic aspects of risk management. They first examine the risk consequences of ethics and governance in companies; and then take a high-level perspective by considering risk at the national level.

The next two chapters address practical issues with a detailed treatment of crisis management and a number of case studies to draw lessons from well-known risks. The book closes with a summary of its key themes and conclusions.

CHAPTER 2

Nature and Sources of Corporate Risk

Like matter, risk cannot be destroyed. It can only be changed from one form to another.
Clarke and Varma (1999: 417)

This chapter introduces the nature and sources of risk: the topic's what, when and why.

The definition of our subject – *risk* – is far from clear, and the literature has long seen risk in multiple guises. Codification accelerated after Knight (1921) drew the distinction between fundamental uncertainty and probabilistic risk, but modern capital markets theory is virtually alone in treating risk as a probability measure related to uncertainty in security returns. Managers, for instance, take a much broader view: they do not distinguish between financial and operational risk, and think of risk with its dictionary sense as the possibility of an adverse outcome.

A contributor to imprecision in risk's definition is that not everyone sees the same event as a risk: particularly where the outcome is a zero-sum, one party's adverse result is their counterparty's win. The division between win and loss is clear in investment; and it can also be true in matters such as litigation and legislation. Other risks, however, are heavily tilted one way: it is hard to see many winners after earthquakes or hurricanes wreak their havoc, or when a company lurches into bankruptcy.

Further imprecision comes because of the many sources of risk. A useful division is that of finance which thinks of systematic risk as factors that similarly affect all economic entities or market assets; it can only be managed by market timing. Firm-specific risk (also called idiosyncratic, diversifiable, non-systematic or business risk) arises from factors that are unique to each firm or sector. Thus the Capital Asset Pricing Model (CAPM)[1] explains expected returns as a function of systematic risk which is proportional to the covariance in returns between the security and the market (beta), and diversifiable factors (alpha and the error term) that are unique to each security.

This work examines *firm risk* which is the possibility of loss to a particular firm: it combines the finance concept of non-systematic risk with managers' concern at downside loss. These risks arise through firms' selection and operation of resources, including assets and people; their accumulation of knowledge and resulting strategies; and a variety of exogenous and endogenous shocks.

Risk follows its dictionary definition as a hazard or exposure to mischance (*Concise Oxford Dictionary*), and matches the way that risk is viewed by managers (March and Shapira, 1987) and investors (Olsen and Troughton, 2000). Thus risk is a probability

---

[1] Capital Asset Pricing Model (CAPM): $R_{i,t} = \alpha_i + \beta_i . R_{m,t} + \varepsilon_{i,t}$; where $R_{i,t}$ is the return from security i during period t; $R_{m,t}$ is the corresponding return from the market; and α_i and β_i are constants.

measure, and is quantified *ex post* from actual experience such as the frequency of operational incidents or variance in share prices. Risk propensity is a complementary *ex ante* measure of expected risk equal to a firm's willingness to accept the possibility of loss. This can generally be quantified only by proxies such as investment choices and strategic decisions such as gearing. Risk management is an action or strategy that deliberately changes either the probability of a risk or the quantum of resulting loss. In summary, risk for us is a probability measure calculated from the frequency of different types of unwanted events.

Figure 2.1 illustrates the ways that corporate risks arise.

Although risk lacks a strong theoretical place in corporate strategy, studies have shown that business risk is important at the firm level. For instance, Rumelt (1991) analysed risk or uncertainty in US company profits as measured by their variance and found that around half was explained by firm-specific factors (and only 16 per cent by industry-specific factors). The endogenous nature of firm risk was confirmed by Palmer and Wiseman (1999) who found that at least 20 per cent of organizational risk propensity is explained by managers' risk attitudes, and relatively little by external factors such as industry structure. This is consistent with evidence that analyses of organization performance which are blind to risk have little ability to explain real-world organization performance. For instance, a meta-analysis of the Porter competitive model by Campbell-Hunt (2000) found it has 'very limited explanatory power'.

A challenge for development of an integrated approach to risk management is that the many different measures of firm risk are generally treated as mutually exclusive. This lack of consistency in risk's definition is taken so seriously by scholars that it has been described as a 'fundamental methodological challenge' (Ruefli, Collins and Lacugna, 1999: 167–168).

Intuitively, though, one would expect that the risk outcomes of any system – such as a firm – are noisy functions of its fundamental parameters. Thus it is not surprising

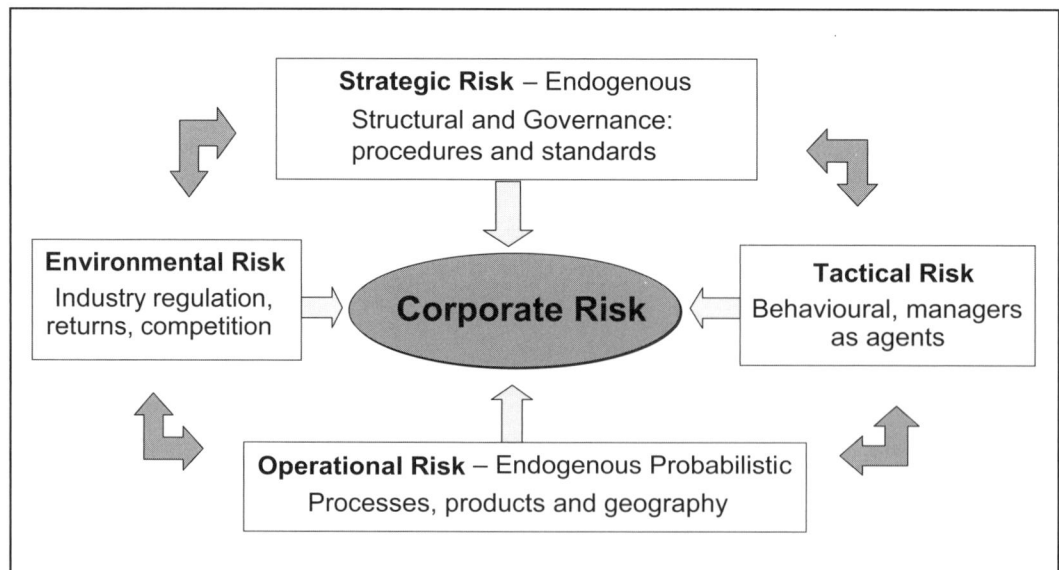

Figure 2.1 Sources of firm risk

to find statistically significant linkages between qualitatively different measures of firm risk, which in turn are similarly related to independent variables such as firm size and historical performance and dependent variables such as financial results. Exactly this is revealed in a number of studies (for example, Miller and Bromiley, 1990; and Palmer and Wiseman, 1999) that variously defined risk using accounting returns, analysts' forecasts, share prices and operational results. The significance is that risk – howsoever defined – is related to other measures of risk, largely because each is determined by common latent risk variables.

Despite evidence of intuitively obvious links between virtually all firm risks, they are still treated differently within most organizations. Risks with an impact in the workplace typically have point sources: they are amenable to reductionist analyses and mechanical elimination and are handled by safety specialists or auditors. This contrasts sharply with risks that might threaten an organization's viability such as complex systems failures, major financial or legal improprieties, or industry restructure: these are handled at senior management levels by planning and finance groups. The split management of risk also arises because risks that impact low in the organizational hierarchy tend to be less complex.

This leads to two quite different types of risk that impact at distinct levels in a company. One involves firm-level business or strategic risk that has three sources. The first is systematic and common to all, or at least many, firms; these risks arise in community norms and macro trends such as industry attitudes, legislation, environment, business philosophy, ethics and stakeholder expectations. Firm-level risks are also caused by structural features of the firm such as governance, operating standards, organization structure, recruiting and training, and resources and competences. The third source of firm-level risks is strategic and tactical decisions by management.

Lower down in the firm, a qualitatively different type of risk arises in a more narrow, largely mechanical, set of factors that are specific to a particular resource or decision such as the firm's balance sheet structure and its choice of technology, process, product, market and employees, and how they are organized and managed. These are *point-source risks* that can be individually identified and managed.

Table 2.1 categorizes principal firm-level and point-source business risks, with their principal drivers and management controls, and measures. Even so, it can sometimes be hard to distinguish between firm-level and point-source risks. Consider the risk of default that comes from elevated gearing levels. This can occur in an era of low interest rates, and thus be systematic; or gearing can be lifted as a deliberate policy by individual company managements and be firm-specific. A similar example relates to risks from natural disasters: storm frequency and intensity may have systematic impacts, as does the escalating cost of assets that might be damaged; but building in higher-risk areas such as mountains and along coastlines brings a more specific impact.

Another example is workplace safety, which is rapidly improving because of systemic factors such as tougher legislation, higher expectations of safety, a better informed workforce and improved technologies. Other reasons, though, will be more specific such as safety standards and practices in individual workplaces. For instance, ExxonMobil Corporation, the world's largest company, has a vision of workplaces in which 'Nobody Gets Hurt' that goes well beyond compliance.

Even users of similar technologies face different risks. Consider the nuclear power industry where the technology is relatively well known and highly regulated. Although each

Table 2.1 Model of the drivers, controls and measures of firm risk

Locus	Fundamental Drivers	Controls (Exogenous and endogenous to firm)	Indicators
Firm-Level Business Risks			
Economic environment	Demography Technology Entrepreneurship	External analysts Boards Lobbyists	Failure rate of companies
Political environment	Investment Government policy	External analysts Electorates Boards	Stability: election outcomes, wars, terrorism
Financial markets	Investment Hurdle returns	External analysts Boards	Shareholder returns
Natural disasters	Probability		Insured losses
Agency problems	Manager incentives Manager hubris	Legislation Shareholder activism External analysts	CEO tenure Corporate scandals
Competitive environment	Industry legislation Competitor activities Technology and innovation	External analysts Boards	Industry concentration
Strategy	Human capital Scope	Boards Stakeholders Advisors	Relative ROCE Competitive position
Point-Source Business Risks			
Operations	Processes Market regions Assets	Legislation Codes of conduct Procedures Knowledge	Crises Accident rates Environmental quality
Finance	Debt, credit policy Market attractiveness Competitive position	Creditors Financial markets and investors	Default rate Relative profitability
Compliance	Operations Organizational culture	Knowledge Governance Audit	Legislative breaches Reputation

plant will have a set of systematic risks that are associated with the technology and industry and so are common across most plants, risks will also respond to plant-specific factors. An example of the latter comes from a study of US nuclear power plants which showed that higher reliability was associated with higher prior earnings by the plant's operator (Osborn and Jackson, 1988). Thus a nuclear plant's risk is lower if its profitability is high.

Thus firm risks are determined by broad industry factors including legislation and community attitudes, the strategies and positioning of each firm, its business practices including risk management, and agency factors such as governance, incentives and culture.

What is Happening to the Nature and Frequency of Corporate Risk?

It is a truism across disciplines that empirical measures are key to effective management. This includes management of risks, where good data are essential to inform policy makers, leaders of public and private organizations, and risk and safety professionals. Whilst individual organizations can rightly consider their risks are a unique product of internal processes, they need to be alert to overall exposures to avoid myopia, and should incorporate population-based data to provide the 'outside view' (Lovallo and Kahneman, 2003). Thus it is appropriate to develop some conceptual framework about general trends in the frequency of corporate risks as a guide to systematic drivers.

Let us start by quantifying risk at the global level using data on corporate crises and man-made disasters provided by Swiss Re (2007 and earlier years) in its annual paper entitled *Natural Catastrophes and Man-made Disasters*. Table 2.2 summarizes Swiss Re's recent data. Since the mid 1990s, annual insured costs have fluctuated in the range $US (2006) 10–110 billion, with an annual average of $US6 billion for man-made disasters and $US26 billion for natural catastrophes (largely storms, earthquakes and floods).

Table 2.2   Annual frequencies of global disasters and catastrophes

	Man-made Disasters		Natural Catastrophes	
	Number	Value ($US'2006 Billion)	Number	Value ($US'2006 Billion)
1995	141	3.6	136	21.2
1996	176	6.1	130	11.4
1997	171	4.3	125	6.4
1998	160	4.8	126	19.2
1999	148	7.3	141	34.6
2000	168	5.0	128	9.7
2001	162	28.0	123	12.6
2002	147	2.6	133	13.7
2003	161	2.9	143	18.1
2004	229	3.6	119	47.6
2005	256	6.6	152	103.6
2006	213	4.0	136	11.8
2007	193	4.4	142	23.2
Average	179	6.4	133	25.6

While natural disasters cause the most damage (whether measured as insured loss or loss of life), the frequency of man-made disasters is higher and has significantly increased from around 75 per year in the 1970s to about 180 since 1995 (an unspecified portion of the increase follows better reporting, especially from developing countries).

Given that insured losses from man-made events are a significant business issue, it is surprising that the academic literature has treated them lightly; and – by studying them as individual cases – adopts an observational, rather than empirical or strategic, bent. Most studies of corporate crises assume they are infrequent and complex, often unique, events. Thus the emphasis is on avoidance through sound risk management, and flexible response through robust crisis management plans. As a result, risk management studies are concerned with the mechanics of crises: best practices in crisis plans and management teams, and summaries of learnings from well-publicized crises. As Loosemore (1999: 9) noted succinctly: '[the crisis literature] has been dominated by the search for improved strategies of prevention and anticipation.' It is rare to see a strategic perspective on disasters.

Although empirical studies of man-made disasters are desirable, a pronounced difficulty is that good data on the frequency of corporate crises and other disasters are hard to find. Reporting is not uniform, definitions are not standardized, and publicity is avoided because corporate reputation dominates experiential learning. Trends are hard to identify because secrecy biases frequencies down; but tougher external scrutiny promotes more accurate reporting over time and introduces an upward bias in the trend.

Thus there is only limited information on the frequency and consequences of man-made disasters. In frustration at these data gaps, I conducted my own analysis and published two articles in the *Journal of Contingencies and Crisis Management* entitled 'The Frequency and Cost of Corporate Crises' (2004) and 'Frequency of Man-made Disasters in the 20th Century' (2006). Analysis supporting these studies pointed to a fascinating trend: some time around 1979 corporations entered a period of high instability; since then, their strategic firm-level risks have been rising, even though operational point-source risks have been steadily falling.

Graphical depiction of these changes is striking. Starting with point sources, two excellent examples of US experience are provided in the Figure 2.2. Panel A plots the frequency of reportable injuries and illnesses amongst workers in all private workplaces in the US and so is a broad measure of occupational safety. There has been a dramatic fall in the frequency of industrial accidents and illnesses in the last few decades, with the 2007 figure less than half that of the early 1990s. This decline is even more striking given that the measure would naturally be biased up as gaps in reporting have been closed by increasingly vigilant regulators.

Panel B reports the risks associated with one of today's most important technologies, commercial aviation and shows the frequency of fatalities per 100 million aircraft-miles. This is another indicator of a point-source risk and its decline has been even more dramatic: the trend fatality rate of US commercial aviation in 2007 was one twentieth of that in 1987.

The rates of decrease in these two risk indicators are matched by declines in many other point-source risks. Continuing with US data, the following risks have at least halved since the 1970s: the number of fires (Karter, 2003: Figure 1); road fatalities (Bureau of Transportation Statistics, 2005); and the incidence of criminal offences per resident, including assault, rape and robbery (Bureau of Justice Statistics, 2006). As an overall

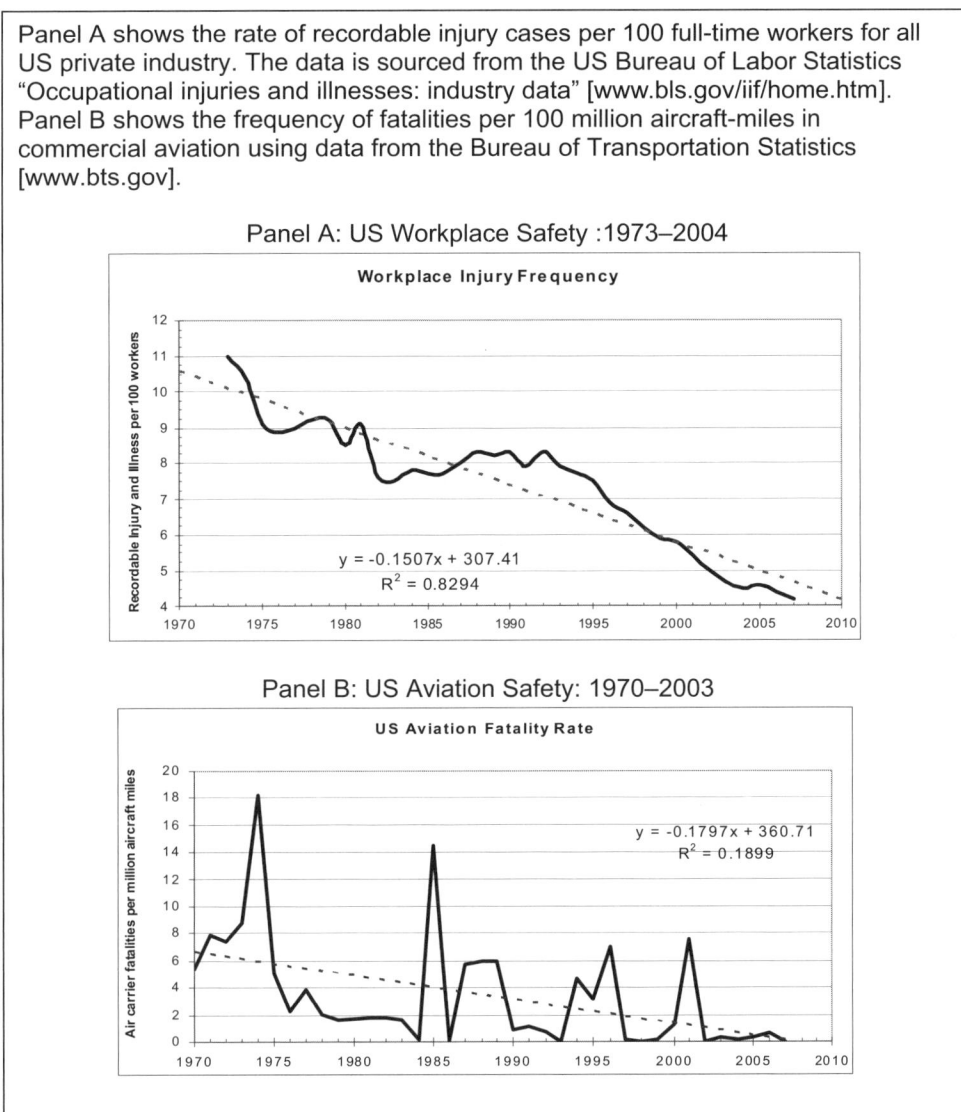

Figure 2.2 Reduction of point-source corporate risks

measure of declining risks to property and person, insurance premia have grown more slowly than GDP since the 1970s (Swiss Re, 2005a).

Moving onto firm-level strategic risks, Figure 2.3 shows that they rose as dramatically as point-source risks fell. Panel A summarizes data on the frequency of man-made disasters in developed countries since the 1960s from the database compiled by the Center for Research on the Epidemiology of Disasters. A good contemporary example is the explosion of ammonium nitrate at a fertilizer factory in Toulouse, France in September 2001. This had the strength of a 3.2 magnitude earthquake, killed 29 people and injured 400, left a 50 metre deep crater, and caused damage for kilometres. Such man-made disasters had been rare events prior to the 1970s; then a chemical spill at

> The top panel shows the number of man-made disasters recorded each year in OECD countries using data from EM-DAT (2005). Panel B is a 12-month moving average of the annualized volatility of all listed US firms relative to volatility of the firm's industry [derived from http://kuznets.fas.harvard.edu/~campbell/data.html].

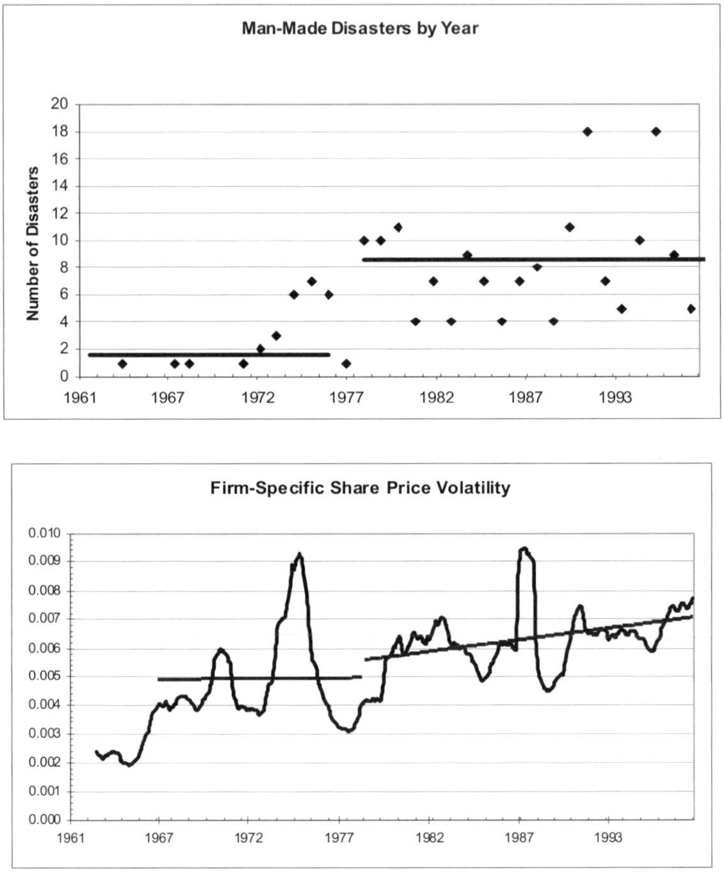

Man-Made Disasters by Year

Firm-Specific Share Price Volatility

Figure 2.3   Evidence of increased firm-level strategic risk

Seveso in 1976 made this Italian town a byword for industrial accidents, and 2 years later came the first year ever to record more than ten man-made disasters in OECD countries (EM-DAT, 2005). The frequency of these complex events grew exponentially last century, so that the current rate is about five times that before the mid 1970s (Coleman, 2006a).

The lower panel takes a different perspective on firm-level risks and uses data prepared by Campbell, Lettau, Malkiel and Xu (2001) who decomposed the return on listed US stocks between 1962 and 1997 into market, industry and firm components. The chart shows volatility in firm returns, which has increased three-fold since 1979. Given that the major component of firm returns is movement in share prices (which are the firm's expected cash flows discounted at a risk-adjusted rate), increasingly common shocks to firm value can be attributed to higher strategic risk.

The rates of increase in these two risk indicators are matched by rises in other firm-level strategic risks. For instance, the corporate default rate has roughly trebled in the last 25 years (Standard & Poor's, 2004); the mean tenure of chief executives has fallen by a third in the last decade (Lucier, Schuyt and Tse, 2005); and the frequency of corporate crises in the US has increased by a quarter in the last decade (Institute for Crisis Management, 2005).

A neat depiction of the reality of the simultaneous rise of firm-level strategic risks and fall of point-sourced risks is provided by the US Transportation industry. The average volatility of transportation firms' share prices – and hence the risk or uncertainty to shareholders – has increased slightly since the 1960s, even though the safety of individual transport modes – as measured by the frequency of fatalities standardized for changing use – has improved by orders of magnitude for aviation and by a factor of at least three for surface transport (US Census Bureau, various years). This gives the counter-intuitive result that the risk to transport users has plummeted, but investors face higher risk from holding transport stocks.

Drivers of Diverging Firm Risk

In summary, the previous section reported a pronounced divergence between measures of corporate risk after the late 1970s, with dramatic falls in the rates of point-source risks and rising incidence of strategic risks. What caused these changes?

The fall in point-source risks is relatively easy to explain. Industry was a dangerous black box in the early 1970s. Rachel Carson (1962), Ralph Nader (1973), the Club of Rome (Meadows, Meadows, Randers and Behrens, 1974), and a raft of other authors made a convincing case that the operational model of most firms was severely flawed. As it seemed that these risks could be directly reduced by technology and legislation, few voters (who were also employees, shareholders or consumers) questioned the need to establish Environmental Protection Agencies, give tougher powers to industry regulators and introduce new legislative controls to improve the safety of products, workplaces and industrial activity. The first Environmental Protection Agency and Occupational Safety and Health Administration were established in the US in 1970, and similar bodies were quickly formed in other developed countries. Legislation acted synergistically with steadily rising stakeholder expectations to mandate safer, less risky operations. At the level of individual risks – workplace accidents, aircraft crashes, product contaminations, process failures – there was a huge improvement, and most individual processes, products and technologies are up to an order of magnitude safer now.

It is not as intuitively obvious why firm-level strategic risks rose during the same period. However, the argument here is that conditions supportive of higher strategic risks began forming in the late 1960s and early 1970s with the spread of inherently unsafe technologies, globalization and economic instability following the first oil crisis. Then an abrupt change in corporate risk was catalyzed in 1978–9 when reformist governments in Britain, the US and elsewhere introduced legislation that reshaped economic conditions, namely deregulation, privatization and retirement savings. These formed a watershed for corporate risk, with such profound long-term consequences that – compared to the 1970s – individual firms are now several times more likely to suffer a serious slump in their share price, and technological disasters are now five times more likely to occur.

The US *Airline Deregulation Act 1978* was the first significant deregulation for 50 years and ushered in a series of changes in industries as diverse as energy, financial services, transport and utilities. Privatization began in Britain in 1979 when the Thatcher Government sold its shares in British Petroleum and then gradually disposed of interests in other State-owned industries. By 1999 proceeds from privatization by governments around the world had exceeded $US750 billion.

Tax incentives to promote retirement savings were the other important policy change and spurred growth of the mutual fund industry. First introduced with the United States Revenue Act 1978, they quickly took hold and 401K plans had become common by 1981. Most of these retirement savings were placed in the hands of professional investment managers in mutual funds with the result that fragmented small shareholders were replaced by far fewer, much more powerful investors. As only the most successful investment management firms can prosper, they placed pressure on companies to lift their returns.

These changes had synergetic effects which transformed the two most important factors that promote corporate-level strategic risks: competition and profit targets. Privatization regenerated whole industries – particularly energy, telecommunications and utilities – that have now become glamour sectors. Sell-offs by government were followed by deregulation which broke down barriers to entry in these industries and many others, especially finance and transport. Firms had previously been conservative and slow changing, which stymied innovation; and their industrial environment was predictable and often controllable. But tougher competition forced them to lower costs of production or differentiate their products, and made industries unpredictable.

Over and above these changes was the wide spread of technology. Perhaps the best indicator is the business application of personal computers which began in 1977 with sales by Apple, Commodore and Tandy. Within a year, half a million personal computers had been sold in the US alone. Continuous advances in technology since then have brought a stream of totally new products such as mobile telephones and DVDs, and totally new processes such as robots and gene splicing. In addition, rising wealth gave consumers more discretionary expenditure, so they were no longer restricted to staples, but could switch demand across a range of goods and services of different characters and quality. Imported cars and foods began to compete with travel and entertainment.

Intensified competition slashed margins across the board from aviation and banking to textiles and water supply. With unpredictable environments and new, nimble competitors and fickle consumers, firms lost control over their industry. Tougher competition and demands from investors for higher returns meant that firms must continually regenerate their internal environment to survive, and so large strategic decisions and fluidity in operations became essential. This is a corollary of the snide comment by Nobel laureate Sir John Hicks (1935: 8) that 'the best of all monopoly profits is a quiet life'.

Figure 2.4 illustrates the impact, and plots the proportion of equities owned by institutions along with profits before tax of US corporations. Prior to 1978, investment institutions were of limited significance, and only about a quarter of listed equities were held by mutual funds and various retirement funds. But after legislation was introduced to encourage retirement savings, institutions became increasingly important to US investors and their control of listed securities doubled to well over 50 per cent today. Competition between funds to deliver superior performance that would attract new investors placed

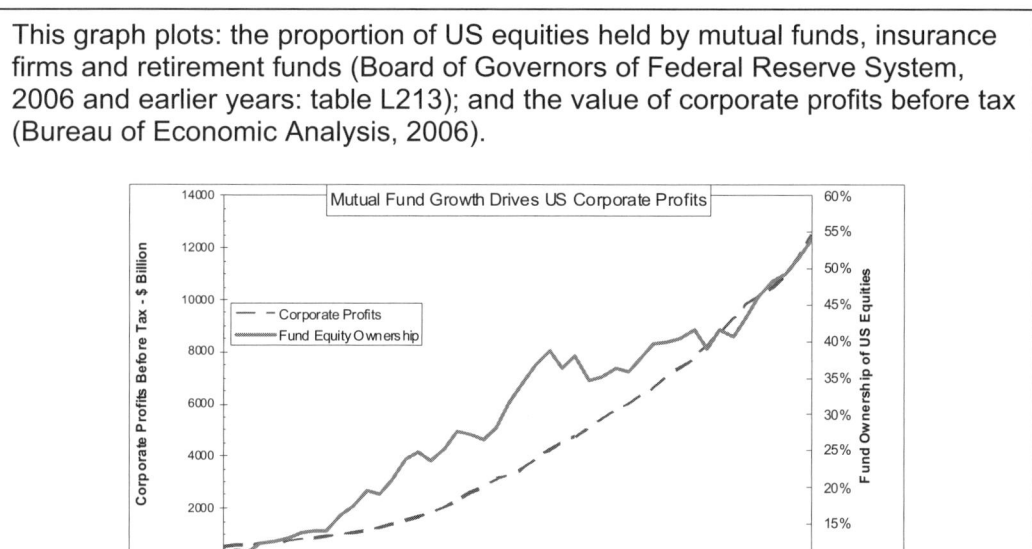

This graph plots: the proportion of US equities held by mutual funds, insurance firms and retirement funds (Board of Governors of Federal Reserve System, 2006 and earlier years: table L213); and the value of corporate profits before tax (Bureau of Economic Analysis, 2006).

Figure 2.4 Institutional ownership of US securities

continuous pressure on companies to improve their profitability. Thus corporate profits rose in lockstep with fund assets.

Changes after the late 1970s forced firms to take an increasing number of more complex decisions, and an inevitable outcome was a deteriorating record of risk-taking by corporations. The inevitability arises from the dismal record of managerial decision making: half of all decisions are wrong (Nutt, 1999), and – as discussed in the next chapter – this rises above 70 per cent for major strategic decisions. Quite simply, many firms have not learned to manage their dynamic environment, and crises, disasters and strategic blunders have become increasingly common.

Empirical evidence to support this argument comes from studies demonstrating how exogenous shocks – particularly deregulation and more intense competition – change industry environments. For instance, because regulation has been used in many industries as a form of stabilization, deregulation typically leads to greater competition; and risk propensity changes in line with industry concentration. Moreover, firms in deregulated industries become free to respond to external developments, and hence are more likely to be spurred to action by shocks. Although the impacts of deregulation can take time to emerge and often persist for a decade or more, concentration of the industry through merger activity is common, and frequently proves the prime driver of more intense competition.

In summary, the analysis above leads to a simple conclusion: technological innovation and increased wealth destabilized industry environments after the early 1970s. Later that decade came a raft of politically mandated regulations which were designed to spur economic growth. These moves acted together to increase competition and lift the performance expected of all firms. The future became less certain and virtually uncontrollable, and forced firms to make more frequent and further reaching strategic decisions. Because many such decisions prove wrong, firm-level risks rose. Thus technology, governments and consumers had sweeping impact by inducing firms to take on additional risks: in short, they imposed *moral hazard* on corporations.

It should be no surprise that sweeping economic, technological and societal changes have ushered in an era of higher strategic risks. Such leaps, of course, are the core assumption behind most theories of development which see evolution as marked by punctuated equilibrium, gales of creative destruction and the like. Moreover, a standard paradigm in finance and other disciplines is that increased return or reward is inevitably accompanied by elevated risk. This led scholars from many disciplines to conclude that a more prosperous society is inherently more risky (for example, Beck, 1992; and Lupton and Tulloch, 2002), just as shown above.

Conclusion

The key conclusion of this chapter is that regulatory oversight and internal corporate governance processes are proving inadequate to ensure effective control of modern industrial risks.

In recent decades most developed countries have implemented comprehensive approaches to risk management that rely on the combination of government regulation and market forces. The complexity of modern systems and processes and pressures to reduce bureaucratic control have promoted self-regulation, on the assumption that people inside any industrial process are best able to manage it responsibly. Self-regulation has been applied to processes as complex as corporate governance, market operations, registration and supervision of professionals, and operating safety. Firms have also established internal corporate governance guidelines to ensure that the standards of their operations exceed compliance requirements of regulations and that they meet the expectations of stakeholders.

However, the exponential growth in disaster frequency, particularly from hazards where industry has extensive experience such as fires and explosions, suggests an obvious conclusion: contemporary regulation and corporate governance are simply inadequate to manage modern industrial risks. In particular, self-regulation all too often degenerates into deregulation and proves quite inadequate. Perrow (1984: 3–4) has been proven right:

> *The characteristics of high-risk technologies ... suggest that no matter how effective conventional safety devices are, there is a form of accident that is inevitable ... Most high-risk systems have some special characteristics ... that make accidents in them inevitable, even 'normal'. This has to do with the way failures can interact and the way the system is tied together.*

Clear empirical evidence of the rising frequency of man-made disasters in industrialized countries points unequivocally to the need for a new risk management paradigm. The principles and practices of both regulation and corporate governance need to recognize that serious risks are now becoming more common. Obviously this is a key justification of the new risk management paradigm that is a theme of this book.

With this background to firm risks, let us turn to an analysis of how they arise.

CHAPTER 3

Why Organizations Take Risks

It seems to be a law of nature, inflexible and inexorable, that those who will not risk cannot win.

John Paul Jones (1747–1792), Naval hero of the American Revolutionary War

This chapter turns to a simple question: what is it about managers and companies that leads them to take risks? The first part of the chapter addresses manager's risk propensity, whilst the second part examines why companies take risks. The motivation for this review is that around a quarter of firm risk taking is due to managers' choice. Understanding why managers take risky choices is fundamental to dialling up the required level of firm risk.

Before starting it is important to acknowledge that the treatment of risk here flies in the face of advocates of value-free decision making who assume that it follows a disciplined process which defines objectives, validates data, explores options, ranks priorities and monitors outcomes (Kouradi, 1999). This clinical approach assumes that risk is neutered using conventional techniques of assessing the probability and consequences of failure, and then exploring alternatives to dangerous paths.

However, my perspective is different in asserting that many decisions simply do not follow the textbook description. This contention is motivated by studies that unequivocally reject the empirical validity of normative models of decision making. For instance, 'facts' often do not influence decisions, which prove to be heavily influenced by heuristics and biases, and the decision maker's personality and history. Decision makers also place their own interpretation or frame on the materials before them and make a unique choice.

There is a rich literature in psychology that uses people's responses to questions to assess their personality, including risk propensity. Examples are set out in Table 3.1, and these and similar questions are combined into many questionnaires that rate individuals' risk propensity.

Whilst quizzes indicate individuals' attitudes towards risk, how do such attitudes arise? Why do some people climb mountains whilst others lounge on the couch? The balance of this chapter reports the findings of studies that examine the drivers of risk, starting with consideration of two key concepts – Prospect Theory and risk-sensitive foraging – that explain many of the differences between people and firms in their risk propensity.

Prospect Theory

Prospect Theory (PT) is one of the most successful concepts in the social sciences. It was developed in a truly seminal paper by Nobel laureate Daniel Kahneman and his brilliant collaborator Amos Tversky (Kahneman and Tversky, 1979) which has become one of

Table 3.1 Risk-related questions

Attribute	Question	Source
Tolerance of ambiguity	Many important decisions are based on insufficient information	Budner (1962)
Need for achievement	I set difficult goals for myself which I attempt to reach	McClelland (1961)
Need for risk	I would like to undertake an interesting experience even if it is dangerous	Keinan (1984)
	I like to play it safe	Pennings (2002)
	In general, I am less willing to take risks than my colleagues	
Instrumental risk taking	To achieve something in life one has to take risks	Zaleskiewicz (2001)
Level of decision maker's control	Risk is higher when facing situations we do not understand	
Impulsivity	I've not much sympathy for adventurous decisions	Rohrmann (1997)
Susceptibility to boredom	I become bored easily	
Interpersonal competitiveness	I have always wanted to be better than others	Griffin-Pierson (1990)
Sociability	I am calm and relaxed when participating in group discussions	Robinson, Shaver and Wrightsman (1991)
Achievement motivation	Successful people take risks	Austin, Deary and Willock (2001)
	I prefer to work in situations that require a high level of skill	Casssidy and Lynn (1989)
Locus of control (external – importance of chance)	When I get what I want it's usually because I'm lucky	Levenson (1974)
	Risky situations can be made safer by planning ahead	
Type A personality	I regularly set deadlines for myself	Williams and Narendran (1999)
	Compared to the average manager, I give much more effort	
	If I play a game (e.g. cards) I prefer to play for money	Zaleskiewicz (2001)
Life satisfaction	I have gotten more of the breaks in life than most of the people I know	Robinson, Shaver and Wrightsman (1991)
Competence	In general I am very confident of my ability	Robinson, Shaver and Wrightsman (1991)
Locus of control (external – powerful others)	My life is chiefly controlled by powerful others	Levenson (1974)
Egalitarian preference	Everyone should have an equal chance and an equal say	Robinson, Shaver and Wrightsman (1991)

the most cited papers in economic science; and then updated to Cumulative Prospect Theory (Tversky and Kahneman, 1992). These papers constitute a descriptive model of decision making under risk, and argue that people derive value or utility from changes in wealth relative to a reference level, rather than from absolute wealth levels. Decision makers weight alternative outcomes by dynamic factors which are related to cumulative experiences, and are independent of absolute monetary values.

Figure 3.1 illustrates PT and shows its classic features of: a convex curve for losses evidencing risk embrace as decision makers see little difference in outcomes as losses escalate; greater sensitivity to losses than equivalent gains as the curve is steeper in its left portion with a more rapid drop in value per unit loss; and a concave curve for gains where individuals are risk averse and place no value on potentially higher gains. This non-linearity in probabilities means that lower probabilities are overweighted, whilst people underweight moderate and high probabilities. As a result, except close to the reference level, decision makers are relatively insensitive to differences in probability and outcome between events which are commonly encountered. The S-shaped curve is an amalgam of ideas. Economists generally assume that marginal utility falls, so that each increment in wealth has less value and hence utility functions are concave. By contrast, psychologists think in terms of diminishing sensitivity to loss that leads to risk seeking over losses and a convex utility function.

Under PT, decisions come in two stages. The first, editing phase simplifies the range of possible choices, often as decision makers eliminate obviously inferior possibilities to shape a realistic set of alternatives: this becomes the source of a number of behavioural anomalies. The second, evaluative phase chooses the optimum alternative. An important feature is that value is measured by changes in wealth, rather than absolute levels (which harks back to older concepts such as 'happiness is relative'). Effectively decision makers frame a transaction in light of its expected impact on their wealth relative to a reference level, and then choose. This is quite different to utility theory in which decision makers rely on probability and absolute values to identify the choice with the highest utility.

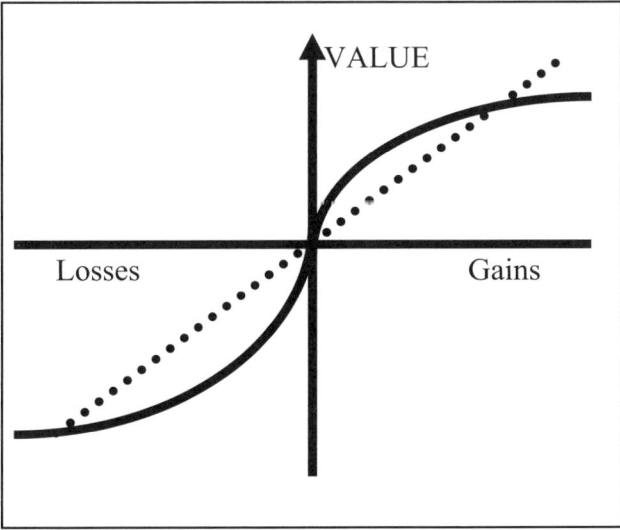

Figure 3.1 Prospect theory

Because PT explains choices that do not match the predictions of normative or utility theory, it has been widely advocated as a practical means of explaining decision making. In economics PT underpins behavioural finance, and it has also found supporters further afield. For instance, Schultz (1997: 2) suggested it as a useful tool in war planning to provide 'a means to determine [an adversary's] mind-set in terms of risk ... It should facilitate predicting enemy reaction to a selected course of action'.

The key idea embodied in PT – that decision makers take more risks when facing losses than when facing gains – has been proven true in animals, humans and organizations. The implication is that risk propensity is not fixed, but shaped by circumstances, particularly changing endowment.

Risk-Sensitive Foraging

A practical model in understanding changing risk propensity in managers and firms comes from animal studies and is best explained using the Figure 3.2 suggested by Smallwood (1996). The proposal is that an animal can choose between two foraging strategies, which – for simplicity – have the same expected outcome, but sharply differing variances. The first option which is shown as a solid line has low variance and means the animal is relatively certain of the result, irrespective of its own skill or environmental pressures. The second option shown as a dashed line has much higher variance and a wider range of possible outcomes.

Risk-sensitive foraging assumes that animals choose their foraging strategy in light of food needs. Consider, for instance, that the solid vertical line shows the amount of food that is the minimum acceptable outcome or required result: the animal is best served by a low-variance risk-averse strategy as there is scant probability of not meeting its needs. However, as the animal's food needs rise and the vertical line moves to the right, the acceptability of a risk-averse strategy declines until the only choice for survival is to embrace the risky, highly variable strategy.

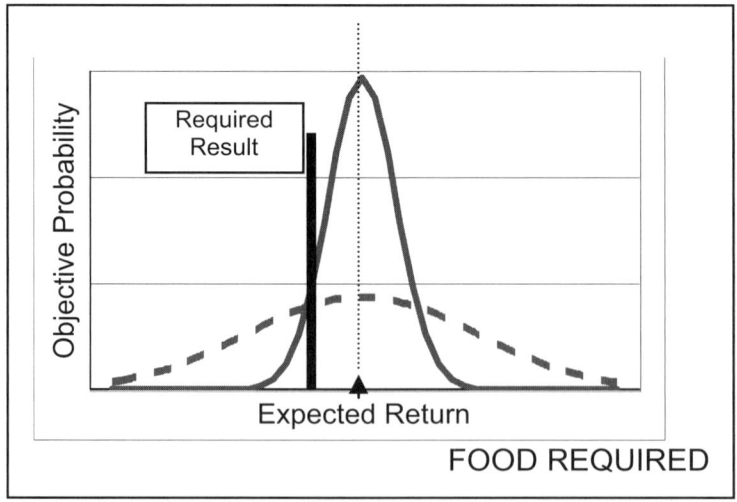

Figure 3.2 Risk-sensitive foraging

Animals' risk sentience was exemplified for me in a breakthrough experimental procedure where Caraco et al. (1990) established birds in a laboratory habitat, and taught them to choose between two feeders that dispensed grain at a constant rate over time. However, one feeder always gave one grain, whereas the other produced either two or zero grains. The birds were risk averse when food was adequate and temperatures warm, and chose the certain single grain feeder. The researchers then lowered the temperature in the laboratory, which threatened the birds' survival. The birds proved to be risk sensitive as their state changed, and preferred the risky zero-or-two grain feeder as food supplies became more critical. Another study by Smallwood (1996) of birds preparing to migrate for the winter found they were risk embracing until they reached maximum body weight and then became risk averse.

Observations such as these show that animals prefer risk aversion when the expected outcome is above the required result, and this is evidenced by their choice of a low variance, relatively certain strategy. Conversely when the required result is greater than the expected outcome, the only chance of achieving an acceptable result is to shift to the risky course with high variance. Risk-sensitive foraging clearly shares much in common with PT as it explains how risk propensity rises as wealth (food) falls below a reference (survival) level. We shall also see that it can explain the behaviours of organizations.

Why Do Managers Take Risks?

The influence of risk propensity on decision making can be expressed simply. Managers who are risk embracing are attracted by a relatively high potential payout; and those who are risk averse require a positive risk adjusted return. This is the normative, or objective, view of risk taking, and is well covered by the subject of decision science. In addition there is the subjective, or descriptive, view of decision making in which managers use their intuition and take account of qualitative expectations, are biased by prejudice (including prejudgements) and emotion, and are influenced by the way the decision is presented.

This section follows the descriptive approach and looks in detail at why managers' risk propensity varies and how biases affect their risk taking. Given the many behavioural anomalies that are known to affect managerial risk propensity, to provide some structure they are grouped under five headings: decision makers' characteristics (especially demography and personality) and perception; reference levels; mental accounting and the assumption of mean reversion; the longshot bias or overconfidence; and the desire for immediate gratification. The discussion below draws heavily from Coleman (2006b), and covers the subject of behavioural finance, which now has an extensive literature, with surveys provided by Barberis and Thaler (2003), Camerer (1995), Kahneman (2003), Rabin (1996) and Ricciardi (2004). Shefrin (2001) has collated some of the most influential papers. A caution that the topic has not really progressed much for decades is the excellent survey by Slovic (1972).

DECISION MAKER CHARACTERISTICS AND PERCEPTION

Studies of real-world decision making have shown that up to a quarter of the variation in individuals' risk taking is explained by personality factors. According to Trimpop (1994), risk takers are psychologically flexible. They have a history of successful risk taking, tolerate ambiguity, seek novel experiences and rapidly respond to stimuli. They are described as adaptable, adventurous, aggressive, informal, optimistic and sociable. Risk takers have a need to be better and faster, and agree with statements such as 'I set difficult goals for myself which I attempt to reach'; they are typical Type-A personalities.

A variety of relatively stable personal traits affect risk propensity. Byrnes, Miller and Schafer (1999) conducted a meta-analysis of 150 studies to compare male and female risk taking and found that the proportion of women accepting any risk is an average of 6 per cent less than the proportion of men offered the same choice. The general consensus from other studies is that increasing risk propensity is linked to higher income and education. Risk takers are likely to be younger, single, and in a professional occupation (Grable, 2000); they also exhibit multiple risk behaviours and so are more likely to pursue dangerous occupations and sports, and adopt risky personal habits such as smoking and reckless driving.

Nationality plays a role in risk taking and studies suggest the following ranking from risk averse to risk embracing: Southern Europe (Greece, Portugal), Japan and Korea, Latin America, Middle East (Israel, Saudi Arabia) and West Asia (Turkey), Western Europe, Scandinavia, Australia, North America and East Asia. When overconfidence is measured as the decision makers' estimated probability of being correct minus their demonstrated accuracy, Asian decision makers tend to be more overconfident than those in Western nations.

An explanation for the mechanism whereby personality determines risk propensity is the proposal by Lopes (1987: 275–6) that:

> *Risk-averse people appear to be motivated by a desire for security, whereas risk-seeking people appear to be motivated by a desire for potential. The former motive values safety and the latter, opportunity … Risk-averse people look more at the downside and risk seekers more at the upside.*

Significantly, this mental schism is consistent with physiological evidence from Magnetic Resonance Imaging (MRI) studies which examine humans at the molecular level. These found that different parts of the brain – and hence different decision criteria such as emotion or logic – are used when decision features vary. Other studies detected a 'switch' in the brain that alternates decision maker perspective between the optimistic, big picture and a cautious, detail focus.

Most decision makers overestimate their skill, placing themselves in the top quartile of performers (Kruger and Dunning, 1999; and Svenson, 1981). This is true even with uncontrollable events, and leads to the illusion of control in which people are more willing to take a risk when they have a competence through relevant skill or knowledge, or when they are able to exercise some control over the outcome.

A well recognized influence on decision making is bounding, where individuals are simply unable to access or process all available information. Economically, this implies that the costs of gathering additional knowledge about a decision are not expected to provide a reasonable return. This leads people to overgeneralize from limited data, rather than committing resources to collect and analyze a more statistically robust sample. They also overweight personal experience and striking observations such as crises, highly publicized incidents and freakish calamities. Another bounding-related decision bias is to require less information to support expectation of a desirable event than to conclude that an undesirable event may occur. Thus recent experience carries more weight than population-based distributions, and – because of self-framing – is especially likely to be overweighted when it supports a preferred outcome.

Because of bounding, decision makers have poor estimates of the true distribution of decision events. Obtaining certainty through proper sampling imposes delay during which opportunities can evaporate; and it is intellectually demanding to remember and process additional data. In amusing fashion, Miller (1956) put a limit of seven on humans' recall capacity. Although this might seem overly restrictive, it actually gives an estimate that the decision maker can be 75 per cent confident is within about 25 per cent of the distribution's true mean[1].

Through the affect heuristic (where 'affect' has its meaning from psychology of an associated feeling or emotion), people mentally tag objects and events with positive or negative feelings or emotions. This creates an inverse relationship between risk and benefit which sees selection of preferred or liked outcomes. Decision makers' mental images of events can override facts and thus overstate the subjective probability of a favourable or dreaded event and understate the probability of an unwanted event; thus prediction becomes linked to outcome preference. These biases can be particularly strong in the face of new problems. An oft-cited example concerns the comment by famous economist Irving Fisher who – just days before the 1929 stock market collapse – opined that 'stock prices have reached what looks like a permanently high plateau'. The subsequent loss of most of his wealth showed he was actually talking about what he hoped would happen, not necessarily what was probable.

This becomes what Tversky and Kahneman (1971) termed the *law of small numbers* that leads to overweighting of recent experience or data and underweighting of longer-term evidence and the population distribution. This can lead to the not infrequent situation where graphic 'eyewitness' reports turn out to be exaggerated and overdramatized. What happens is that the reporter's powers of observation are truncated: stress, danger and uncertainty combine to heighten the use of heuristics, and the most powerful in a time of little data is the availability bias. All but the most experienced observers seize on extreme observations and worst cases because they are the most memorable, and then extrapolate. The unfamiliar sight of even one dead body and a rat can be reported as 'thousands of casualties' and 'plagues of rats'. A good example of this occurred in the immediate aftermath of Hurricane Katrina's destruction of New Orleans in 2005 when the media reported that 'there were at least six murders and 12 rapes' among evacuees in the Super Dome. Subsequent investigation showed only one suspicious death and no evidence of the widely reported mayhem (Carr, 2005).

Decision makers become more risk averse when limits are placed on them; similarly they do not like ambiguity, and so will avoid outcomes with unknown probabilities. These bounds can be reduced and risk taking promoted by providing an excess of data. For instance Yates (1990) discusses the Oskamp Study where psychologists were asked to read a patient's clinical history, build up a personality profile, and then answer questions about his condition and indicate their confidence in the answer. The test was carried out in four stages as subjects were given progressively more information about the patient. Whilst the accuracy of the answers changed little through the study (roughly 30 per cent correct), the psychologists' confidence almost doubled. Thus the doctor who is able to ask

---

[1] Under a binomial distribution, the confidence interval attached to any estimate (or its associated level of accuracy) is given by $\pm z \sqrt{\frac{p*(1-p)}{n}}$ where p is the probability of an outcome, n is the size of the sample, and z corresponds to the level of confidence. Assuming two tails, at the 75 per cent confidence level z = 1.2; for n = 7 and p = 0.5, the confidence interval is ± 0.227 or 22.7 per cent.

many questions of a patient or the stock analyst of a CEO and thereby gain contextual information may only be lifting their confidence, not the accuracy of the prediction.

When facing choices involving future events, decision makers place greater weight on the outcome and benefits, with relatively less weight on the costs and probability of occurrence. This is consistent with optimism, goal orientation and inherent unpredictability of details such as impediments and probabilities. It also incorporates recognition of optionality: why sweat the small stuff when the whole situation may change? Other factors that influence the relative weight that is placed on success and failure include the affect of each outcome, and role of skill. Thus when decision makers face a distant outcome or one where their skill can control the risk, they focus on the benefit and its affect. Conversely when the outcome involves a near-term consequence or possibly large loss, decision makers focus on the risk involved.

An important corollary of the assumption that decision makers' risk propensity leads them to focus on different decision parameters is that they do not have a continuous utility function as assumed in many standard decision models.

REFERENCE LEVELS

Another group of transient influences on decision makers' perspective are reference levels: these establish breakeven points for success/failure adequate/inadequate and can be markers of abrupt shifts in risk attitudes. Reference levels encompass the essence of risk-sensitive foraging which is that decision makers alter their risk preference around a satisficing level, or endowment which meets requirements at the time. This means that risk propensity is high when endowment (food for animals, wealth for managers or firms) is inadequate to sustain the decision maker; however, when endowment is adequate and survival is probable, a lower risk strategy is preferred.

An important element of risk sensitivity is loss aversion. Because losses can have serious consequences, any loss is valued more than an equal gain, and the disutility of any loss relative to the same gain increases with the size of the loss. In other words, the pain of any loss relative to the equivalent gain is directly proportional to the amount, and inversely proportional to risk propensity. This is most obvious in laboratory studies where decision makers are offered a variety of choices (Schneider and Lopes, 1986): as the size of the potential loss increases, people increasingly prefer a low risk outcome.

Reference levels can also serve as an anchor. For instance Lovallo and Kahneman (2003) point out that executives typically begin a decision with a forecast outcome, often prepared by a sponsor of the proposal. Whilst decision makers will adjust their expectations in light of anticipated bias by the sponsor, this is generally not enough. So the reference anchor ensures an overly optimistic assessment of the outcome. This is consistent with studies of decision makers' forecasts which show that their 'error bars' are far too narrow: actual outcomes frequently fall outside the range of possibilities, even when experts are involved (Camerer, 1995).

MENTAL ACCOUNTING AND MEAN REVERSION

The third group of influences on decision makers comprise mental accounting and the assumption of mean reversion.

Thaler (1985) developed the concept of mental accounting in which decision makers apportion their wealth, knowledge and other resources into discrete and non-fungible mental accounts. In economic terms this leads consumers to overweight sunk costs and current, cash outlays. But it also leads to a number of behavioural anomalies. For instance, recent experience becomes important because it provides a personalized sampling of outcomes and changes endowment relative to the satisficing level: thus sequential outcomes have synergetic impacts on risk propensity and hence on decisions.

The net result is that people place more emphasis on the consequences of decision outcomes than on their probabilities. Thus decisions involving risk turn on expectations of how alternative outcomes will impact endowment, rather than on probabilities of the outcomes. This explains why a number of studies find that the facts of a decision are frequently ignored.

Another important decision influence is the assumption that means reversion will apply unless there is reason to believe otherwise. This assumption of mean reversion exerts Bayesian influences so that successful decision makers expect a run of wins to be followed by losses, and – in the absence of overconfidence – will tend to become less risk prone; whilst unsuccessful decision makers expect a turn for the better and can become more risk prone. This gives rise to the gambler's fallacy where decision makers believe that a run of identical outcomes in unbiased events (red or evens at roulette, or favourites in a horse race) is more likely to be followed by a reversal (that is, black, odds, outsider). A clear example of mean reversion is the disposition effect, or tendency for investors to sell assets that have risen in value in preference to those that have made a loss.

LONGSHOT BIAS IN DECISION MAKERS

A challenging feature in understanding how to control strategic errors that contribute to risks is evidence of overconfident behaviour by managers who prefer low probability outcomes that cannot be justified by their statistical record. In gambling this is known as the longshot bias, and one of its best-known examples in management relates to acquisitions where Roll (1986) argued that managers of acquiring firms are over-optimistic in the valuation of targets and over-confident in their ability to monetize potential merger synergies. Selective analysis that induces a level of overconfidence bordering on hubris explains why firms overpay for acquisitions and – through the winner's curse – suffer poor returns. This overconfidence in managers is part of a pattern which psychologists term self-enhancing biases (see Table 3.2). According to Rabin (1996: 50):

> *We are over-optimistic regarding our health and other aspects of our life; we feel we are less vulnerable to risk than others; and we are more responsible for our successes than we are for our failures. We think that we are superior to others in all sorts of ways: we are better at controlling risk, better drivers and more ethical.*

The long-term consequences of such misjudgements were appreciated by Charles Darwin (1871: 3) who wrote that 'ignorance more frequently begets confidence than does knowledge'.

Table 3.3 shows a range of common firm strategies that have high rates of failure including acquisitions, research and development projects, company formation, mineral exploration, new product launches, quality programmes and senior executive

Table 3.2   Mini case studies: Overconfidence and risk taking

It is sometimes suggested that overconfidence is equivalent to underestimating risk. Two cases amplify this point.

Aircraft Fatalities A Report by Australia's Civil Aviation and Safety Administration [16 June 2006 available at www.casa.gov.au/media/other/06-06-16pilot.pdf] into a fatal aircraft crash in July 2005 at Mount Hotham in south-eastern Australia warned:

External or self-imposed pressure can be strong enough for pilots to deliberately place themselves, their aircraft and their passengers in danger when safer alternatives are available. Pressures of time, or of costs, pressures from passengers expecting to get to their destination, or merely the desire not to 'lose face'; any and all can lead to fatal errors of judgement.

In some cases operating crew may also attempt non-standard procedures because they mistakenly believe they are safer than the approved, and legally mandatory, procedures – descending below cloud or 'shooting for the hole' in cloud in order to become visual, or following pilot-preferred landmarks rather than the published waypoints. Furthermore, successful outcomes of previous similar deviations can lull pilots into a false sense of security.

National Australia Bank traders and culture An article in The Australian [11 June 2004] on illegal forex options trading which was headed 'NAB disaster blamed on subculture' reported observations from the corporate watchdog APRA:

'No amount of controls will stop a recalcitrant trader or anyone else really determined to break the rules … This happened because the bank's rules were not taken seriously and because a counter-culture developed.'

Table 3.3   Outcomes of common management strategies

Decision Setting	Success Rate
R&D projects that: meet their expected market share achieve financial success	20 per cent 27 per cent
Drugs that return cost of capital	30 per cent
Information technology (IT) projects that come in on-time, under budget with promised functionality	16–25 per cent
Proportion of major transportation projects where cost estimate is met	14 per cent
Probability of making an economic mineral discovery from a typical exploration budget: Australia (1955–1985) Canada (1945–1979)	 28 per cent 35 per cent
Proportion of mergers and acquisitions with a positive financial outcome	17–40 per cent
Ten year survival rate for new firms in USA listed since 1980 manufacturers between 1963 and 1982	 < 38 per cent 20 per cent
New product launches	< 20 per cent
Proportion of quality programmes that achieve tangible improvements	< 33 per cent
Survival rates for electronics joint ventures	16 per cent
Proportion of externally hired Presidents of US firms that survive 4 years	36 per cent
Sources, respectively: Davis (1985) and Palmer and Wiseman (1999); Nichols (1994); The Standish Group (1995) and Whiting (1998); Flyvbjerg, Holm and Buhl (2002); Mackenzie and Doggett (1992) and Mackenzie (1981); KPMG (1999) and Henry (2002); Fama and French (2003) and Camerer and Lovallo (1999); Roskelly (2002); Harari (1993); Park and Ungson (1997); and Ciampa and Watkins (1999)	

recruitment. There is clear consistency in these poor results from common business strategies as none differs significantly from their mean of 25 per cent. The table can be extended with many other examples. For instance, studies have found overly optimistic biases in cost forecasts, including construction costs in the energy industry (Merrow, Phillips and Myers, 1981); and across a variety of industries (Statman and Tyebjee, 1985). Looking beyond corporate decisions, financial investments are equally risky strategies. For instance, retail fund managers cannot outperform market averages; and their relative performance is not improving (Gruber, 1996). And it is not just in the private sector where common strategies consistently fail: two-thirds of the 37 missions to Mars have failed, often dismally (MacLeod, 2004).

It is an intriguing puzzle why managers regularly adopt high-risk business strategies even though the population-based probability of their success lies in the range 15–40 per cent. As the average firm has just one chance in four of achieving success from a risky initiative, only top quartile performers can expect a positive return.

DESIRE FOR IMMEDIATE GRATIFICATION

A further striking feature of risk-taking behaviour is the preference of managers (like other people) for immediate gratification. Although management and finance assume that elapsed time is the only factor separating the same decision now and in the future, actual behaviour reflects a bias towards immediately achieving a desirable outcome. This effectively underweights risk probabilities and accepts high opportunity costs. It is equivalent to use of a higher discount rate for costs than benefits, which is consistent with behavioural evidence (Sagristano, Trope and Liberman, 2002).

This leads to a preference for investments with high early payouts, and a delay in cost-saving projects including risk management where the benefit is an intangible opportunity cost. A more familiar example is the way that people overweight the enjoyment of a distant event such as a ski trip and underweight its costs including the long drive and queue for entry and tickets; this gives rise to the familiar lament that 'it seemed like a good idea at the time'.

FRAMING

Although personality and experience determine people's inherent attitudes towards risk, their perception is particularly important to decision making. Framing, for instance, involves presenting identical data with a different emphasis, which shifts a decision maker's expectation of the outcome. The result is that different presentations of identical data (threat or opportunity; possible loss or probable gain) elicit different responses from the same individual. Thus a positive frame that projects gains will induce greater weighting for a successful outcome. Stylising a decision as low-risk will gain more broad-based support, especially from risk intolerant executives; whereas focussing on its upper bound is more attractive to risk seeking executives. Decision makers consistently prefer a risky alternative which is framed as an opportunity over one framed as a threat; and take more risks when facing a loss than when facing a gain. They also place their own frame on a decision by editing the materials to be analyzed through instinctive perception of the costs and benefits of each outcome.

Framing can also complement a natural aversion to extremes and a preference for 'normal' choices. This leads to the common experience (not infrequently abused in unscrupulous opinion surveys) that people tend to cluster their preferences or decisions around the middle of a range, irrespective of whether it makes objective sense or not. Simply adding an outlier value to a survey can markedly shift respondents' apparent preferences.

A positive application comes from the suggestion by Pablo, Sitkin and Jemison (1996) that framing can be used to establish organizational risk levels by modifying the attitudes of executives who are involved in planning and implementing major decisions. They propose that measuring performance against outcomes and rewarding success will increase risk taking; whilst forcing adherence to process and providing minimal individual incentives promote risk aversion.

In brief, the way a proposal is presented will shape its appeal. Risk-seeking executives tend to overweight opportunities: they focus on projects with high payout and pay less attention to difficulties that may bring the outcome below the upper bound. Conversely, risk-averse executives overweight the worst-case outcome and divert effort towards minimizing ambiguity, diversity and threats: they perceive a higher level of risk attached to any venture.

Why Do Companies Take Risks?

A recurring influence on firm risk propensity is recent performance, which – in conformance with PT and risk-sensitive foraging – means that risk taking increases when actual or expected performance drops below a satisficing level. Most results suggest that firms are more likely to take risks when facing a loss than when facing a gain.

Fiegenbaum and Thomas (1988) made a detailed study of the financial results of companies in 47 US industries during 1960–79. They chose the industry median return on equity as a reference level, and found that the risk:return relationship was negative below the reference level and positive above it. Better performing firms have lower risk and a positive relationship between risk and return; whilst poorer performing firms embrace higher risk and have a negative risk:return relationship. We return later to this idea of a concave or ∩-shape return envelope, which is consistent with two decision-making populations sharing different risk attitudes.

Similarly Singh (1986) studied 64 medium to large North American firms using a questionnaire and publicly available data. Risk taking was measured with questions about biases towards innovation, debt, R&D and high risk-high return investments; competitive pressure was evaluated by questions about costs, marketing and prices. Results showed that risk taking had a statistically significant negative relationship with return on net worth, which justified Singh's simple, but compelling, argument (page 582): 'poor performance triggers risk taking'. More speculatively: 'firms, when faced with poor performance, would undertake decisions that only further their decline'.

Gambles seem particularly common in desperation. For instance, an editorial in *The Australian* newspaper [17 April 2003] discussed events leading up to the $5 billion collapse of HIH Insurance:

> *The company was destroyed not by hard times or bad luck but by [its executives'] reckless disregard ... for the well-being of anybody but themselves ... The way [they] contributed to*

the company's demise was ... [that] they kept on trying to shore it up with desperate deals, all designed to provide HIH with the cash flow and capital that it needed to survive. The fact that they were gambling, literally, with the future of ordinary Australians does not appear to have bothered or even occurred to them.

It is not just firms that take risks to avoid failure. For instance, in his analysis of the massacre of Israeli athletes at the 1972 Munich Olympics by Middle Eastern terrorists, Reeve (2000: 40) argued that:

[Palestinian Liberation Organization Chairman] Arafat knew Fatah could not afford to keep losing supporters. He seems to have felt that he had no choice but to give tacit approval to the use of blatant terrorism.

Reams of academic research were summed up in the comment of legendary Australian Rules Football coach Kevin Sheedy [*The Australian* 21 May 2003]: 'I have a theory that when things are toughest, you take your biggest risk.'

Structural features of firms also impact their risk propensity. Reuer and Leiblein (2000) found that downside risk or the probability of below target performance is lower for larger firms and those with lower levels of slack resources and fewer international joint ventures. This matched the findings of a study of the risk attitudes of oil explorers in the 1980s which found that risk aversion was directly related to size: large companies tended to be more risk averse (Walls and Dyer, 1996).

Organization can prove an important structural influence on firm risk propensity. Consider the CIA and FBI which are two of the world's pre-eminent decision makers under risk. Kessler (2003) described how CIA Director John Deutch:

Diminished its effectiveness by creating a risk-averse atmosphere ... Deutch imposed a rule requiring special approval before a CIA officer could recruit a spy who was not an upstanding citizen ... The extra hassle of obtaining approval meant many CIA officers simply avoided anyone with a history of problems.

Similar examination of FBI processes found that Director Louis Freeh was personally averse to technology, and his refusal to have a personal computer sent a powerful anti-technology message to the organization. Thus as the war against terrorism grew fierce earlier this decade, the CIA was short of appropriate agents; and the FBI had inadequate technologies.

This experience is frequently seen in corporations, too. For instance, Sykes (1994) describes the driving paradigms and analytical weaknesses that led to a wave of corporate collapses in Australia in the late 1980s and early 1990s. Burrough and Helyar (1990) provide a similar explanation for the near simultaneous US experience.

An important implication of evidence that firm risk responds to inherent structural traits and slowly changing determinants is that the risk propensity of a firm – and often the frequency that it experiences adverse outcomes such as crises – is relatively stable. Firms develop their own risk profiles as an outcome of factors that are specific to recent performance, manager attributes, the firm's traits such as size and a range of exogenous factors. Up to about half of a firm's risk propensity is determined by relatively stable factors, and this matches tenets of Chaos Theory, in which systems do not approach equilibrium nor decay to instability but remain within a region that is defined by an attractor. This leads to the suggestion that organizations are chaotic, and their inherent characteristics act as attractors that confine risk-related performance to a particular space: even though a firm's risks are unpredictable, they tend to be bounded within a region (Dolan and Garcia, 2002). It is easy to envisage this arising in the way that organizations socialize the risk propensity of their decision makers and form a unique culture that establishes the framework which determines risk outcomes. At its most obvious level, this renders some firms as chronically risk prone, whilst others operate without incident even in the most hazardous and complex industries.

Firm risk propensity is also shaped by more transient factors, especially recent performance and near-term outlook. It has been shown that historically poor performance promotes risk taking, and companies are more likely to take risks when facing a loss than when facing a gain. Gambles seem particularly common in desperation, even in the finance industry, based on inherent traits, particularly managers' behavioural biases and attributes, relative performance and firm characteristics such as size.

This, of course, explains why some firms can spend long periods lurching from one crisis to the next, even as all but identical firms operate without incident. An excellent example of this in Table 3.4 shows where one of Australia's largest firms – National Australia Bank – faced a series of seemingly independent but debilitating, crises over years.

Table 3.4 National Bank risk record

National Australia Bank (NAB) is Australia's third largest listed firm and during recent years has faced a debilitating series of crises and strategic errors. Some of NAB's worst risk outcomes are shown in the following table; they covered litigation, operations, regulatory breaches, accounting errors and failed investments.

July 2000	$32 billion lawsuit for breaking commitment to commercialize the AUSMAQ systems platform
September 2000	ACCC launched legal action for price fixing of card fees
September 2001	Wrote off $3.9 billion against Homeside Lending Inc in Australia's (then) second largest write-down
January 2004	Rogue traders lost around $300 million on foreign exchange options, followed by Board turmoil
December 2004	IRA robbery of $65 million from subsidiary Northern Bank
February 2006	$4 billion error in Annual Report caused trading halt
July 2008	CEO Stewart forced into early retirement are revealing shock $830 million write-down of US subprime mortgages

NAB's chronic problems are typically blamed on 'culture'. But how is a bad culture established? Presumably it starts with the Board which sets poor governance standards, recruits an inappropriate CEO, provides the wrong incentives and approves poor strategies. The culture then flows down to the design and management of the organization, and the establishment and monitoring of controls and leading indicators of risks. Finally managers' decisions are translated into actions involving investments, products and contractual agreements, which – when poorly judged or implemented – lead to bad outcomes.

In this way, 'culture' is the outcome of policy decisions and risks that arise from deliberate actions. But why is it that NAB encountered all these problems, when ANZ Bank had none, even though it operates in the same industry, with all but identical processes, and is headquartered only a few blocks away from NAB?

Conclusion

Risks from biases in corporate and managerial decisions can be attributed to a small number of relatively narrowly focussed factors such as managerial hubris and overconfidence, as well as organizational structure. This reductionist approach can lead to the assumption that risks are fungible, so they can be controlled by generic strategies such as enterprise-wide risk management and post-audited mechanically using techniques such as root cause analysis.

My perspective sharply challenges that view. First it shows that firms face two distinct types of risk – low-level point-source risks and more complex firm-level strategic risks – and these risks are changing along quite different trajectories. The drivers are exogenous factors – such as regulation and technology – that have significantly changed firms' risk propensity and are likely to continue.

The second point is that – although low-level risks are under control – this is not true of strategic risks. Traditional risk management techniques have had a natural focus on point sources of risk, whose seriousness has fallen under the scrutiny of auditors, workplace inspectors, safety and quality regulators, and authors of procedural guides. However, their skill in eliminating simple, tangible risks is of little relevance to the control of intangible and more complex risks. It seems that the concept of 'normal accidents' proposed by Perrow (1984: 3) has been proven right and 'no matter how effective conventional safety devices are, there is a form of accident that is inevitable'. With a well-established nexus between risk and reward, it should be no surprise that an increasingly prosperous industrial base has become more risky. The surprise is that the dichotomous development of risks – towards higher firm-level risks and lower point-source risks – has been scarcely recognized.

Although traditional regulatory oversight and internal corporate governance processes have been very successful in reducing point-source risks, they are simply inadequate to manage contemporary firm-level strategic risks. The increase in corporate risks in recent decades points unequivocally to the need for a new risk management paradigm, which calls for a quantum leap in corporate risk management practices. Corporate governance needs better procedures to optimize managers' decisions.

CHAPTER 4
Decision Making and Risk

The essence of ultimate decision remains impenetrable to the observer – often, indeed, to the decider himself ... There will always be the dark and tangled stretches in the decision making process – mysterious even to those who may be most intimately involved.

President John F. Kennedy (Allison 1971: vi)

Human nature ... changes but slowly, if at all; and human nature under stress of danger, not at all

Basil Liddell Hart, *Thoughts on War* (1943: 219)

According to the 'father of modern management' Peter Drucker (1979): 'Executives do many things in addition to making decisions. But only executives make decisions. The first managerial skill is, therefore, the making of effective decisions.' Unfortunately, though, poor decision making is a characteristic of most organizations, and – in light of growth in their strategic risks discussed earlier – is one of the great firm risks. The subject of this chapter is risk management by improving decision making under uncertainty.

Paul C. Nutt (1999: 75), Professor of Management Sciences at Ohio State University spent two decades studying business decisions across organizations in North America and concluded that 'half the decisions in organizations fail'. Perhaps not surprisingly he pointed to structural defects in the decision making process as the cause:

These failures can be traced to managers who impose solutions, limit the search for alternatives, and use power to implement their plans. Managers who make the need for action clear at the outset, set objectives, carry out an unrestricted search for solutions, and get key people to participate are more apt to be successful. Tactics prone to fail were used in two of every three decisions that were studied.

Before discussing the role of risk in decisions, it is worth pondering an important point: what decisions involve risk? In truth, almost every decision is about risk: each requires a choice between competing alternatives, and brings failure if an incorrect choice is made. Sometimes, however, the consequences are trivial. But other wrong choices – ranging from investments to business partners – have far more serious consequences, and these are the ones that need optimization.

Complicating guidance on processes that should be followed when making risky decisions is that retrospective evaluation of any decision is impractical because only the result of the chosen alternative is known with certainty. Other choices may appear better with hindsight, but nobody can ever know what would have actually happened had one been pursued. There is, then, no point in saying that some course of action was a bad choice, no matter how poor or unexpected its results. The outcome of other choices may not have been better, perhaps worse. One can never know. Thus decision processes are permanently surrounded by uncertainty.

This chapter examines the interaction between decisions and risk by setting out theoretical elements of decisions, and then introducing practical decision-making tools including real options and strategic foresight. It is directed at decisions which are: non-routine and hence cannot rely on extrapolation or heuristics; significant in that they commit a firm to strategic pathways and investments that require resources which are large and result in material gains and losses; and are multi-faceted, requiring assessments of external factors including competitive dynamics and strategic objectives.

Models of Decision Making Under Risk

Management textbooks treat it as axiomatic that decision makers follow a disciplined process which defines objectives, validates data, explores options, ranks priorities and monitors outcomes. Risk is rarely mentioned. Biases and inadequate data are even more rarely mentioned, and the possibility that such non-quantified factors may intervene is dismissed in the quip by McClelland (1961: 211): 'The gambling known as business looks with austere disfavour on the business known as gambling.'

However, a number of studies have undermined the empirical validity of normative models of decision making. One challenge is that many decisions do not seem to be influenced by the 'facts'. This has been confirmed in studies which found that the strongest influences on managers' risk propensity came from contextual factors such as a history of successful decision making and positive framing of the problem.

An excellent example of the irrelevance of facts is given by Fair (2002) who tracked the US S&P 500 futures contract between 1982 and 1999 to identify moves of greater than 0.75 per cent within any 5 minutes, which is about seven standard deviations above average. He found 1,159 moves, and then searched newswires at that hour but found that 90 per cent had no identifiable cause. Risk perception is clearly very ephemeral.

Although troubling, it is hard to resist the counter-intuitive conclusion that managers pay little heed to the content of a risky decision. Depending on their own unique perspective and the decision context, they look to the future, virtually independently of the stated facts, and make their decision.

This explains the dichotomy that can emerge between senior executives and analysts following difficult decisions. The executives – including political leaders – choose policies, goals and broad strategies in light of qualitative factors, frequently judging intuitively with sentiment similar to the Queen of Hearts: Decision first, analysis later. This contrasts sharply with the quite different approach of analysts (particularly those operating after the event) who form their judgements using quantitative inputs. This is why the recommendations of experts – everyone from Planning Departments to the CIA – are often neglected: not because they are wrong or of no merit, but simply because they are not relevant to decision making. Pillar (2006: 15), for instance, wrote: 'In the wake of the Iraq war, it has become clear that official intelligence analysis was not relied on in making even the most significant national security decisions.' The author found this 'disturbing', but it should not be a surprise. Quite simply, important decisions involve far more than fitting together selected pieces of a jigsaw to build an obvious conclusion.

The intuitive, qualitative and quantitative elements of decision making have been combined into models that can be crudely divided into three by their principal driver: the psychological, behavioural or empirical attributes of the decision and its associated risks.

Psychology sees feelings and emotions as significant to decisions. For instance, Zaleskiewicz (2001) believed risk taking is strongly influenced by decision makers' motives. He describes *instrumental risk taking* as goal oriented in seeking future profit, and – as a deliberate, cerebral process following expected utility type analysis – is directed at achievement. Examples are education and retirement savings. *Stimulating risk taking* is arousal oriented, with a desire for immediate excitement which is independent of the outcome. This kind of risk taking is non-cognitive, almost reflexive, and driven by sensation seeking. Typical examples involve adventure sports.

The second model follows Raiffa (1968, page xx) for whom decision makers are 'Bayesians or subjectivists [who] introduce intuitive judgments and feelings directly into the formal analysis of a decision problem. [Decisions incorporate] a decision maker's preferences for consequences, attitudes towards risk, and judgments about uncertain events.' This is consistent with evidence that managers do not select risk-neutral, or even risk-weighted, outcomes as would be expected from rational investment decisions.

The third model sees decision makers as objectivists whose choices are based on objective reality, best estimates and expected values. Decisions follow a logical process of data collection, analysis and synthesis to rigorously present alternatives for consideration. They see little room for subjectivity in decision making, save to warn that it can confound results. This is the school of thought termed *decision analysis* which grew out of the ideas of operations research and the scientific approach to management (Taylor, 1967), and secured wide support during the 1970s. It provided a formal language and clarified the basic assumptions behind any decision, and brought transparency to an otherwise complex process.

Whatever the model, decision makers clearly are subject to two sets of influences. The first is endogenous: what they believe and choose to incorporate in their decision framework, and how they process the decision stimuli to make a choice. The second set of influences on decision makers are exogenous and arise from environmental factors that can modify risk propensity; and from the inputs of experts and stakeholders who seek to shape decision paradigms and data.

Decision Processes

As few outcomes cannot be explained with hindsight, sufficient information is available about virtually every event so that it *could* have been predicted. Thus the challenge to decision makers is to obtain and analyze relevant data and choose the appropriate outcome. This task, however, is Herculean in proportion: virtually every conceivable event is surrounded by data, analysis, commentary and opinion, often on a huge scale. Much of it, of course, is conflicting; not only in terms of indicated conclusion, but also the framework and mechanisms underpinning the nature and future course of the event.

Moreover decision settings are quite unstable because decision makers both act on their own decisions and respond to others' actions. This is what investor George Soros (1994) termed his Theory of Reflexivity where systems with thinking participants are not passive because they set up a two-way feedback mechanism between reality or actual events and participants' thinking and expectations. In markets, for instance, participants' bias can override the fundamentals which are supposed to determine prices. Similarly as demonstrated in the Hawthorne Effect by Elton Mayo (1933), merely observing behaviour or turning on a television camera can change it. Reflexivity means that social systems such as organizations and markets have a significant component of indeterminacy. It is hardly surprising to find that normative models of decision making which ignore human or social factors such as biases and behavioural pressures are usually ineffective, as are approaches adapted from the physical sciences which rely upon total separation between events and observations.

Figure 4.1 depicts the problem. A decision maker faces a huge universe of data which must be filtered to be manageable, and then processed through their own personal paradigm that is unique for its knowledge and competencies. The result is that a shared problem with a readily available dataset will lead to differing individual conclusions. When these conclusions relate to the future they cannot, by definition, be wrong as there is no valid yardstick to judge them against. It is only with the effluxion of time that they prove to be accurate or not.

All this establishes a challenging dilemma for managers facing complex decisions. Without being glib, the solution is to pursue a disciplined approach and adopt some failsafe heuristics.

Discipline comes from ensuring decisions are made within a sufficiently comprehensive context. The first step is to define and frame the issue. This is followed by identification of mechanisms driving each decision input, and objectives the decision should meet. The final goal is to set out the range of possible responses and establish their relative costs, benefits and achievability. Once this broad context is established, data can be collected, alternatives ranked and a choice made.

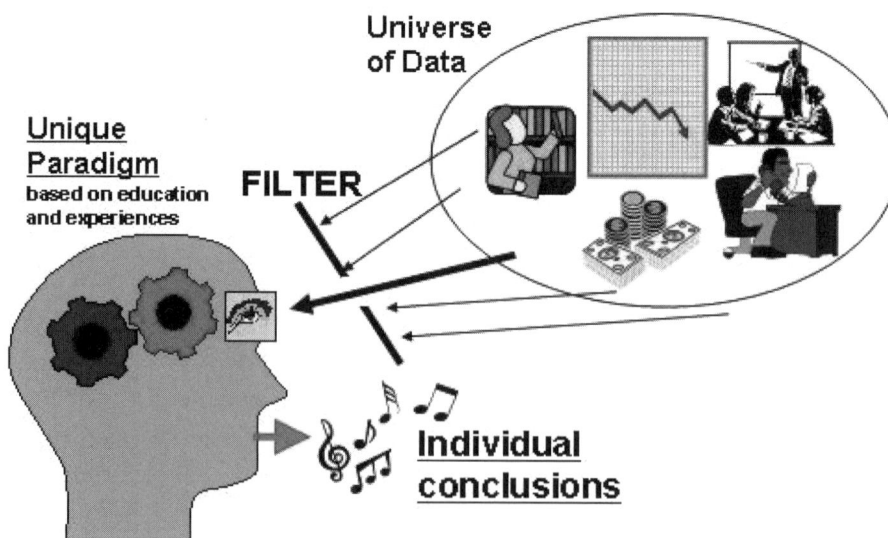

Figure 4.1 Decision making paradigm

Maintaining discipline through these steps, though, is far from simple. Today's powerful databases and analytical tools seduce decision makers into skipping the qualitative steps that define the decision's context. This is reinforced by the practical difficulties involved in identifying and researching every possibly relevant element. This leads to the all-too-familiar case of decision makers unquestioningly relying on a context developed by others. Too often it is but a small step to go from observing that experts best understand the basics of a decision to concluding that experts are best able to manage all aspects of the decision, including policy and strategy. Experts typically have deep-vested interests around their topics of expertise; and their specialist skills do not of themselves bring an understanding or prudent attitude towards the decision's context and consequences. Guarding against framework myopia is a key element in decision making.

Decision makers, then, should pursue several strategies. The first recognizes that it is far easier to establish data than context, and hence resources should be consciously directed towards analyzing the environment surrounding any issue. A second response accepts that third party reactions are critical to any decision's outcome and seeks to anticipate them through formal means such as focus groups and less formal judgements of informed observers.

A good structure for decision making involves Six Sigma which targets measurable improvements to business and financial results by a quantitative focus on customers and strategy. It takes a project-level perspective, insists on metrics and has aggressive targets. This approach is useful in ensuring that forecasts are not driven by biased assumptions but are developed from a valid empirical base.

Decision heuristics can provide a compass that points towards optimal solutions, perhaps by providing greatest benefit to key stakeholders such as customers and employees, or which meet preferred standards in relation to core values such as ethics, quality and safety. Clearly qualifications to this goal are required, especially the need to preserve shareholder value. But, unless managers' decisions benefit customers and other stakeholders, future returns are unsustainable.

Given that risk arises in our lack of knowledge, specifically our inability to predict the future (Coleman and Casselman, 2004), let us focus on techniques to obtain knowledge about the future.

Event Probabilities and Decisions Under Risk

Repeated studies have made it obvious that the effectiveness of decision making and hence of risk taking is constrained by a number of tangible influences. Most obviously essential information can be unavailable, particularly about the future. Decisions are constrained when set in complex environments that are subject to change. There are also limits to decision makers' resources, both data availability and cognitive capability. Inevitably decisions cannot be optimized because there are physical limits on the ability to gather and process all information in a timely fashion. Because decision makers are boundedly rational, they constrain options and follow heuristics – or rules producing automatic responses such as risk aversion – to streamline complex decision making. In addition, there are important, less tangible influences, such as personality, biases, framing and personal motivations ranging from money to prestige. As a result few managers can implement the ideal decision strategy.

An important source of error in decision making is to ignore the frequency of occurrence of the event being predicted. Consider the example of a non-destructive quality control test of items from a production line that is known to give 5 per cent false positives (that is, only 95 per cent of items reported as defective actually are faulty) and 5 per cent false negatives (that is, 5 per cent of items passed are actually defective). If 1 per cent of the items are faulty, what is the probability that an item tested randomly and rejected is actually defective? Superficially, the test is 95 per cent accurate, so the answer is 95 per cent.

Reality, though, is quite different. Assume that 10,000 items are sampled: on average 1 per cent or 100 will actually be faulty. But only 95 of these defective items will be identified; and the other five will be falsely reported as satisfactory. Out of the 9,900 non-defective items, 5 per cent or 495 will be reported as defective. Thus 590 items will be reported as defective, but only 95 or 16 per cent of them will actually be defective. This gives less than one chance in six that a randomly chosen item which is tested as defective actually is faulty. Thus a test that is 95 per cent accurate is only correct 16 per cent of the time!

This example is generalized in the accompanying box in Figure 4.2 and has a number of decision implications. The most important is that a test which is required to be (say) 75 per cent accurate in order to facilitate effective judgement must have an error rate that is no more than about a third of the probability of the event (that is, q:P $\leq$ 0.33). This is because the accuracy or reliability of the test depends not just on the test itself, but also on the frequency of the event. For events with a low frequency (everything from earthquakes and species extinction to corporate collapse and global disasters), judgements need to be extremely accurate to have any value.

Thus to have reasonable confidence in any prediction of an unusual event such as company bankruptcy or a market meltdown, the predictor must have a very impressive capability. This, of course, is at the root of derisory comments such as 'Economists have predicted ten of the last two recessions.' From the box, though, given that recessions occur less than once every decade in developed economies (that is, $P \approx 0.1$), economists' forecasts of recession are about 70 per cent accurate.

The risk-assessment literature in a number of scientific disciplines terms this the 'base-rate effect'. It means that – when the probability of an unwanted event is low – even an accurate test can give so many false positives that it is completely useless. In a typical study, Smith, Lonsdale and Fortune (1999) examined a highly reliable system used for weed risk assessment in Australia which is 85 per cent accurate in determining whether an imported plant will become a weed. But – as the rate at which plants become weeds is only about 2 per cent – the probability of correctly detecting a potential pest is just one in ten. The typical conclusion of such studies is that policy makers should ignore evaluations about what will happen following pests' introduction. The most effective risk management strategy to control imported pests is to wait until an introduced species shows signs of becoming a pest and then eradicate it; or – given that this proves impossible on occasion – ban all importations because none can be confidently identified as safe.

This decision framework explains a recurrent feature of decision making which is that people place minimal reliance upon probability calculations in making judgements. It also explains broad evidence that many decision makers – even those with seemingly appropriate training such as educators and doctors – have great difficulty in interpreting the true nature of seemingly trivial choices: they routinely mis-evaluate probabilities.

Assume an event has a probability of occurrence of P, and prediction has an error rate of q. For N events: what proportion of predictions will actually occur?
The outcomes can be modelled simply. Of N events:
- PN will occur; but q.PN of these will not be predicted.
- (1-P)N will not occur, but q.(1-P)N will be predicted

The outcomes are shown in the table below

Actual Outcome	Predicted Outcome	
	Occurrence	Non-occurrence
Occurrence	(1-q).PN	q.PN
Non-occurrence	q.(1-P)N	(1-q).(1-P)N
Total	P.N + q.N - 2 q.PN	2qP.N + N − q.N − P.N

Thus the probability that a predicted outcome will actually occur is equal to:

$$\text{Probability of Correct Prediction} = \frac{(1-q)P}{P+q-2qP}$$

This is shown graphically below. The horizontal axis shows the value of P, or probability of an event's occurrence; and the vertical axis shows the error rate of the test, q. The lines show various probabilities that a prediction proves true [in Bayesian terms this is Pr(Occurrence|Predicted Occurrence)].

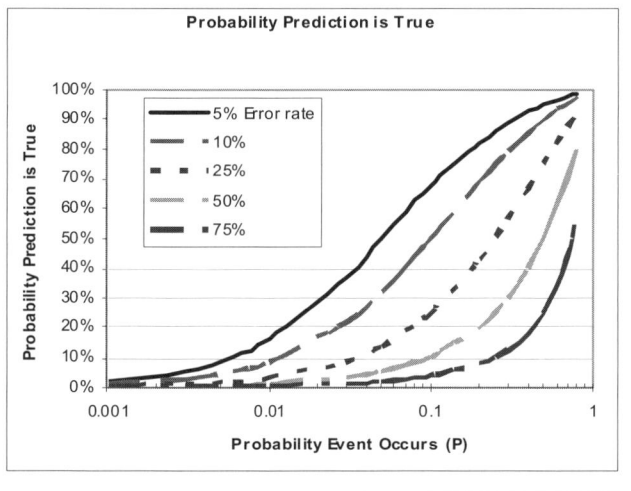

Figure 4.2 Accuracy of uncertain judgements

The tendency to misunderstand the statistically obvious is most clear in the gambler's fallacy and hot hands, which are, respectively, the beliefs that that occurrence of an event outcome (for example, win by red, heads or horse number one) lowers or increases the probability of a reoccurrence in an identical, independent event. Although the roulette ball has no memory, many gamblers credit it with cognitive skills. But there are myriad examples of our inability to properly assess probabilities.

Consider meeting a friend overseas in front of your favourite painting, which recently occurred to me whilst admiring a Renoir portrait at the Musée d'Orsay in Paris. What are the odds of this happening? Impossibly low is what most people say at first. But the real question is: what is the probability of meeting someone you know whilst holidaying overseas? My own experience – confirmed by a show of hands in several classes – is around 30 per cent. Most of us travel with one or more companions during particular seasons to popular destinations and then spend our days in or close to tourist attractions. It should not be a surprise to encounter someone we know.

Risk is the same. The probability of a comet striking a factory is impossibly low. But the probability that one of a firm's plants will be damaged by some impact – truck, flood, windstorm or heavenly object – in a decade is probably quite high.

Another amusing example of misunderstood probabilities has built up around the US television game show *Let's Make a Deal* which was hosted by Monty Hall (Gigerenzer, 2002: 217–223). Contestants were given a choice between one of three closed doors: two doors had a goat behind them, whilst the third had a car. When the contestant has made their selection, Monty Hall follows a formula and opens one of the other two doors to reveal a goat: contestants are then offered the chance to change their selection. Most contestants and observers believe that switching or staying have the same expected outcome: a 50 per cent chance of winning the car. Thus a columnist in *Parade* magazine who argued that staying won only a third of the time, whilst switching won two-thirds of the time was bombarded with critical letters, amongst them a college professor blustering: 'As an educator, I find your column reprehensible …'

In truth the best strategy is to switch. Assume that the car is equally likely to be behind any of the three doors. Selecting a door at random offers a one in three chance of selecting the car: there are two chances in three that it is behind one of the other two doors. When Monty Hall opens a door, he does not change the odds: there are still two chances in three the car is behind one of the doors that the contestant did not choose. If the allocations are unbiased and selections are random, one contestant in three will correctly choose the goat, and switching loses. But in two of three cases where the contestant chooses a door with a goat behind it, Monty Hall opens the other door that always reveals a goat and so switching will result in choosing the car. Thus switching gives two chances in three of winning a car; and staying gives just one chance in three of winning a car.

The confusion arises because the contestant is not facing a random choice between two doors, which would occur, for instance, if Monty Hall reallocates the car and the goat behind the two remaining doors after the contestant makes a selection. Rather the choice is subject to a variety of external influences that moderate the 50:50 odds. In this case there is a precondition in the shape of an earlier random arrangement. Hence one choice is twice as likely to succeed as the other.

A recent review by Fernandez and Piron (1999) concluded that – providing Monty Hall follows fixed rules, like a blackjack dealer, and the only decision maker is the contestant – then it is clear that contestants should always switch doors. They closed with rhetorical flourishes: 'Why have so many people, including mathematicians, come to such different conclusions about the Monty Hall problem? One possibility is that the concept of conditional probability is poorly understood. Another explanation is that the precise game being played has not been articulated clearly.'

The Monty Hall problem is just one example of how decision makers misunderstand probabilities, and hence risks. One trap is to define risk too narrowly. It seems that humans and laboratory rats 'homogenize probabilities' and narrow distributions by underestimating high probabilities and overestimating low probabilities (Real, 1991). A further contributor to possible miscalculation of probabilities is that the mean value of a skewed distribution such as acquisitions or dividends on horses probably appears higher than it actually is because the memorable success is overweighted. Thus we can allow distant risks to loom large whilst we overlook the familiar. A person who dreads the tiny risk from a comet's impact can be blind to the germs and mites in their bedroom. Alternatively institutional memory can be allowed to promote blindness so that individuals or institutions can do no wrong and their risks are 'untouchable'.

But the key take-away from base rates, chance encounters and the Monty Hall game show is that decision makers routinely mis-estimate probabilities because they ignore prior facts. This leads to a type of decision process that is called Bayesian after an eighteenth-century clergyman and amateur scientist. The starting point involves Bayes Theorem (Beach, 1997) which is defined by the following expression:

$$P[H|E] = \frac{P[H] * P[E|H]}{P[E]}$$

In words this says: the probability of an event H given the occurrence of event E is equal to the probability of event H, times the probability of event E given the occurrence of event H, divided by the probability of event E. This expression is useful because it allows validation of probabilistic data presented in a form that is different to population statistics. Adopting this approach is essential in sequential decisions where there is useful information available from the outcome of similar previous decisions.

A significant number of risky decisions occur sequentially, for instance: credit approvals in a bank, commodity trades in a Treasury, cycles in a manufacturing plant or launches of a space shuttle. One of the important reference levels, or ledgers of mental accounting, is the risk associated with each successive decision: that is, the decision maker's estimate of probability or risk is dependent on outcomes of similar previous events.

Consider a manager who is contemplating a risky strategic decision and knows that the population-based probability of its success is 0.25. They have previously made five such decisions and two proved right, and so they believe that their success rate is at least 40 per cent. Are they right? In Bayesian terms the manager's question becomes: given that the mean success rate of similar decisions is 25 per cent and two out of my last five decisions were right, can I rely on an expected future success rate of at least 40 per cent? This can be expressed as follows:

$$P[P\ Success = 0.40|\ Two\ out\ of\ five\ successes]$$
$$= \frac{P[P\ Success = 0.40] * P[40\%\ successes|P\ Success = 0.40]}{P[Two\ out\ of\ five\ successes]}$$

Assume that the manager is 60 per cent certain their success rate exceeds 40 per cent, so P[H], is 0.60. To calculate P[E|H] and P[E], assume the event outcome follows a binomial distribution of either success or failure. In the case of P[E|H], the postulated mean is 0.40, and hence standard deviation is [$\sqrt{0.40*(1-0.40)}$=] 0.49; in a sample of five decisions, the sample mean is 0.40 and the probability of achieving two successes is 50 per cent. P[E], the probability of two out of five successes based on population outcomes, has a population mean of 0.25 and standard deviation of 0.43, which gives a probability of 34 per cent of two successes in a sample of five.

This gives: P[P Success = 0.40|Two out of four successes] = 0.60*0.50/0.34 = 0.88. In words, there is an 88 per cent probability that the manager's true success rate is 0.40 given their two successes. Thus – after the run of successful outcomes – the manager can confidently conclude that their real success rate is more than the 0.25 average of their peers, with around 90 per cent probability that it is close to 40 per cent.

Real Options Framework for Decisions Under Risk

Options are a familiar concept in finance: they are contracts which give the right to buy or sell an asset at an agreed price and are enforceable at the option holder's discretion. In gambling terms, options allow their holder to wait until the race has been run, or the wheel has stopped spinning before deciding either to bet their stake or pass. But, like every form of insurance, options are expensive: for instance, the premium or cost of an option to buy or sell a share at the current price any time in the next year typically costs between 5 and 15 per cent of the share price, depending on its volatility.

Since at least Merton (1977), it has been common to think of other financial products, particularly equity and debt, as options. Thus equity represents a call option over a firm's assets, and has an exercise price equal to outstanding debts: pay off the debt and you own the assets. Shareholders will exercise this option when the value of the firm exceeds the face value of the debt or a lower negotiated payout. Similarly debt is effectively a put option to liquidate the company: shareholders put the firm's debt to its lenders by defaulting on loan agreements, lenders take any assets and shareholders forfeit their equity. Shareholders will exercise this option and default on the loans when the value of the firm is less than the face value of its debt.

It quickly became clear that many managerial decisions incorporate option-like features. Most obviously, the decision maker can determine whether and when various components of the decision will be implemented (which is equivalent to exercising an option) and also often obtains price protection. This led to development of the concept of 'real options' (first used by Myers, 1977) where the value of an untraded or non-financial asset can be priced as an option when its return or payoff is a function of the price of an underlying asset, and the decision maker has flexibility to modify the asset's return through delay, expansion or abandonment. This pattern occurs with many strategic decisions because they typically incorporate a series of steps – identify, analyze, rank, select, implement, operate and expand or terminate – that each incorporates the choices to delay, modify or cancel in light of additional information; this optionality can persist for decades in long-lived projects.

Real options monetize the advantages of being able to modify a decision's progress, reduce uncertainty surrounding it through acquisition of knowledge, and take advantage of volatility in its value. In a nutshell, real options increase the value of a sunk investment in a non-financial asset such as land or intellectual property if the owner has flexibility to decide whether and when to develop, use or dispose of the asset. As traditional present value analysis does not incorporate these possible additional cash flows, it may not accurately compare the relative values of a set of opportunities. Thus pricing the benefits of optionality – particularly the sensitivity of a project's value to new information – can lead to better decision making.

At the heart of advocacy of real options is the concept that being able to keep one's options open has value for its flexibility or *optionality*. As this thinking crystallized, there was a flurry of activity, with many articles and several books appearing under the title *Real Options* (see Reading List). These consider that assets in place are actually real options which can be developed or utilized in different ways and timeframes as circumstances change.

Real options have been most effectively applied to fallow assets that require expenditures for their development, and are particularly applicable to patents or mineral deposits. Thus a mining lease over a gold deposit or a pharmaceutical patent can be turned into marketable products (gold bullion and drugs, respectively) by building a mine or manufacturing plant. If the lease or patent is considered as a call option, then the present value of the income stream from the product's sale is equivalent to the market price of the underlying asset, and the development cost is the strike price of the option. Real options have been used to value assets as diverse as oil fields (Paddock, Siegel and Smith, 1988), gold deposits (Tufano, 1998), patents (Bloom and Van Reenen, 2002) and football players (Tunaru, Clark and Viney, 2005).

Despite the hype of advocates of real options, managers who tried to use this new tool quickly became frustrated at its complications and excessive flexibility. This is not surprising as a moment's thought shows that virtually every decision involves optionality. Purchases can be sold, plans rearranged, and even 'binding contracts' are subject to *force majeure* or can be bought out. Managers in an uncertain world recognize that there is value in delay and flexibility so they can rebalance strategy: their decisions had always been intuitively biased towards maximum flexibility. For instance, a manager who needs to acquire land for a new project will tend to defer the decision if possible, and will be tempted to buy more land than needed if this can be done cheaply. Thus many managers found little merit in real options valuations and they did not gain favour.

A second problem has been the difficulty in estimating the volatility of the option, which often proves the most difficult step. Most descriptions of how to value real options insist that 'prices of traded financial securities are *always* [original emphasis] used ... for valuation of illiquid corporate assets' (Arnold and Shockley, 2002: 83). However, the volatility of a real option is a function of the uncertainty of the cash flows associated with the asset during the period they are discounted back to a present value. Unless volatilities of the asset value and the security price are comparable, then the latter cannot be used as a proxy for the former.

Consider the mining lease on a gold deposit as a real option to extract its contained reserves. Theory says the option value of the deposit is a function of the volatility of gold bullion prices. In practice, though, gold miners simply do not have the ability to instantly liquidate their real option in the way that can be achieved by the holder of a financial option. For instance, if gold prices doubled overnight, the holder of a call option on bullion could immediately crystallize the benefit. By contrast, the best the owner of the gold mine could achieve is to sell any unhedged production forward (which has a limit due to liquidity restrictions and operational uncertainties) or suffer the delay and cost of increasing production capacity. This points to the critical defect in valuing real options using financial options techniques which is to equate gold fragments deep in the earth to 'paper gold' that is easily traded.

Analyses of resource stocks show that real options valuations are well above those of the market, which, of course, is why advocates of real options lament that traditional valuation techniques are too conservative. Whilst this is not so important for investments that trade in an informed market, it does caution strongly against following suggestions that a real options approach should be used to value assets that do not have an established market (for example, Paddock, Siegel and Smith, 1988).

Although real options have limitations, their current neglect is unfortunate as they do have practical application when the holder enjoys the right to exercise a contractual agreement. This is amplified by Table 4.1 that gives a variety of examples of real options. Insurance, for instance, can be thought of as a put option, which is contingent on the occurrence and outcome of an insurable event such as fire or flood damage. In the event of damage covered by insurance, the insurance company pays the loss in value less a deductible (this is further discussed in Chapter 7).

Applying real options thinking to managerial decision making explicitly provides the ability to manage business risks by limiting their downside and weakens the influence of sunk cost in decision making. Rational decision making is all about optimizing *future* cash flows: the only value of historical expenditures or efforts is in their current realizable value. It is all too human, though, to have a preference for assets and choices that are familiar or personalized. Managers, then, can persist with an apparently failing strategy because of factors such as a vested interest in its success or misplaced expectations.

Real options impose a useful discipline on decisions with uncertain outcomes where the state-variable is the actual (that is, uncertain, *ex post*) outcome of the decision; and also provide a useful framework to analyze risks and their management (Triantis, 2000). For instance, the ability to defer risk management is an effective call option over the

Table 4.1 Examples of tangible real options

	Option Type	**Option Premium**	**Strike Price**	**Market Value**
Undeveloped mineral deposit	Call	Lease cost	Project development cost	NPV of contained minerals
Patent	Call	Acquisition cost	Project development cost	Discounted cash flow from sale of product
Operating lease	Call	Net cost of lease vs. buy	Written down value of asset	Market value of asset
Lease renewal	Call	Nil (?)	Market rental less costs of relocation	Market rental
Insurance	Put	Insurance premium	Deductible	Insured loss
Self-insurance	Put	Balance sheet reserve	Market value of insured asset	Insured loss
Term life insurance	Put	Insurance premium	Nil	Value of insured life

action: it need not be taken until some point in the future when the cost (that is, strike price) has fallen relative to the benefit (that is, market value). This gives the manager the opportunity to take advantage of uncertainty, and recognizes that risk management might become easier in future when there is more time or money, the outcome improves through a better result or lower cost, or there is less pressure from competing activities. With a difficult or unpleasant task that is not time critical such as cultural change in an organization, giving up smoking and implementing difficult risk management initiatives, there can be reward for procrastination. Delay can be driven by optimism; but it is also a form of natural hedging where time might reduce the cost of action; whereas deciding now removes all optionality and can reveal error.

The negative is that inaction can open up the possibility of loss or failure that could otherwise have been avoided: deferring a decision involves the risk that markets or circumstances will deliver a less desirable outcome than immediate action. If the risk is unmanaged, it is equivalent to *writing* a put option over the risky outcome, so that its cost must be borne by the decision maker. Thus delaying risk management is equivalent to writing a put option over the potential risk: the costs of risk management are avoided giving a certain positive saving which is equivalent to the option premium, but costs following any loss will need to be paid out. Conversely acting now to reduce risk protects the decision maker's position against an adverse future development, and locks in *ex post* returns.

Two real-options decision strategies can be used to manage the risk of inaction. The first is to consciously do nothing, on the basis that – just as most options expire worthless and hence justify not taking an outright position – most risk management strategies without an obvious benefit can never be justified. This, of course, provides an immediate return in the form of expenditure avoided by continuing to accept the risk. A second strategy is to offset adverse outcomes that might arise from an unmanaged or residual risk. This can be achieved contractually through insurance or service contracts; or operationally by putting in place mechanisms to contain unwanted consequences.

This perspective provides a rational explanation for a rich literature of case studies that points to inaction by managers so that risk level becomes higher than optimal: firms accept unmanaged risks that all too frequently lead to damaging outcomes. These attitudes regularly involve large, respected, well-regulated firms in high-technology environments such as NASA (Starbuck and Milliken, 1988) as well as more mundane operations. They cannot be attributed to ignorance or myopia, and so this risk-taking behaviour needs to be explained in rational terms.

Figure 4.3 uses a real options framework to examine the payouts from different risk management strategies. On the left is an uncovered decision that has some risk: the payoff equals the *ex post* return. To the right is a 'risk-managed' decision where a risk management programme has been put in place to eliminate or contain a risk: the downside is capped by paying a premium to eliminate the risk or to cover it by using insurance or hedging. Thus most of the upside is captured, but the maximum *ex post* loss is limited to the risk premium. The motivation, of course, is regret avoidance. The result is that real options allow the decision maker to capture most upside and reduce most downside to give a double benefit to shareholder value. They are an excellent risk management tool.

The significance of this depiction is that – by adopting a risk management strategy – the decision maker has effectively purchased a put option which will offset most of the cost of an adverse future outcome.

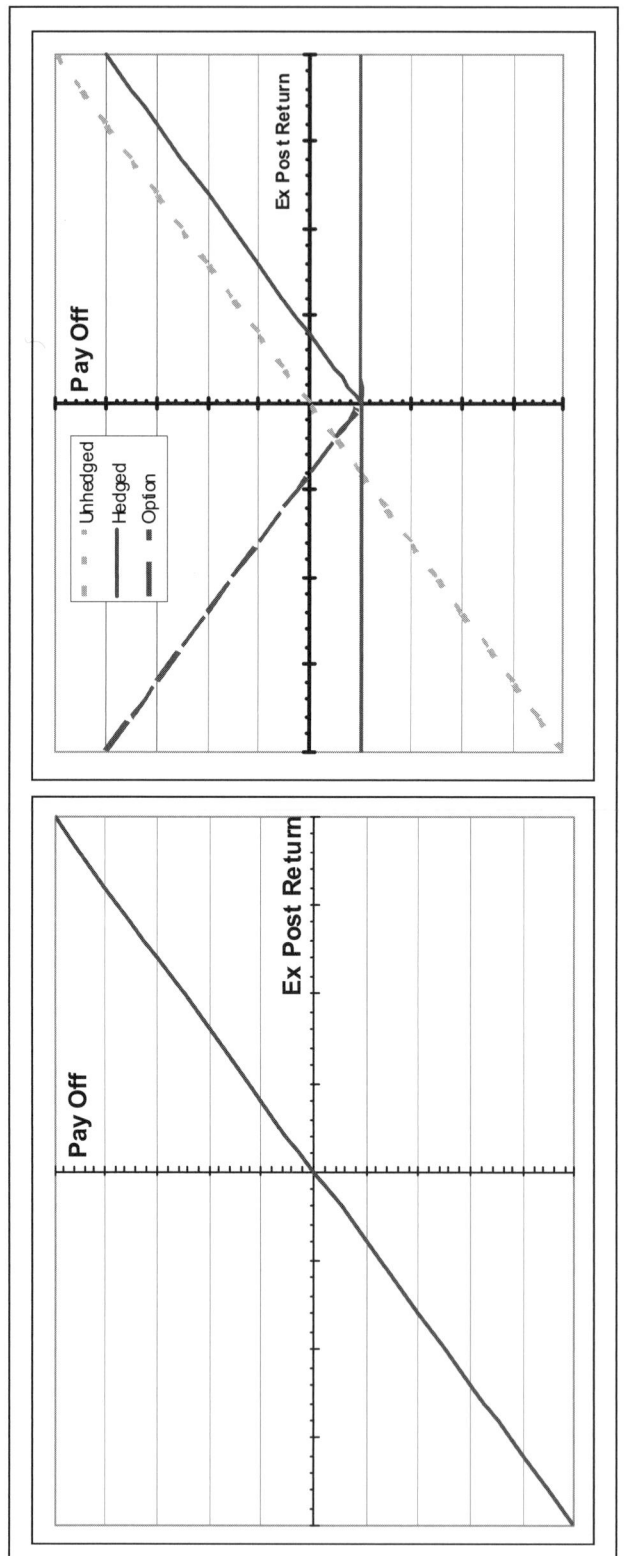

Figure 4.3 Decision making under risk as a real option

Table 4.2 shows several examples of risk management strategies that contain optionality, or embedded real options. The latter enable decisions to be taken in stages, or deferred until uncertainty is removed. In the case of risk management, this means waiting for evidence that an event appears increasingly likely and then taking pre-emptive action; or else waiting until the event has occurred and mitigating its effects.

Table 4.2   Risk management using options to defer action

Locus/Type of Risk	Risk Minimization	Optional Risk
Equipment failure	Preventative or scheduled maintenance	Repair after failure
Product development	Invest in R&D	License or acquire new technologies as needed
Market entry	Establish own operations	Use agent or joint venture

An excellent example of how optionality can be applied to risk management is airline security which is a topic of great interest at the time of writing. Risk managers know that terrorist hijackers are prepared to die and that they have access to explosives which are virtually undetectable. Moreover hijackers comprise a few in many millions of travellers. Thus there is a huge cost involved in preventative strategies such as passenger screening because of the required resources, and the delay and passenger inconvenience, especially in the case of false positives. These strategies, however, will almost certainly fail to detect determined hijackers. An alternative is to implement targeted passenger screening such as profiling, and use the saved resources to manage hijackers who will inevitably board aircraft through air marshals and damage mitigation such as bomb proofing cargo holds. This strategy of passive risk management has already been accepted as the optimum solution in most heavily trafficked public facilities, such as sports grounds, office buildings and railway stations. These implement only coarse screening of entrants, and minimize risk through security-based architecture that makes buildings more resistant to damage, and incorporates built-in security measures such as improved natural lighting, optimized barriers, direct line of sight to sensitive areas, evacuation paths and so on.

In summary, a real options framework for risk management integrates financial strategies across a firm so it can select risks to preferentially leverage. Merck, for instance, used this approach and decided to hedge some financial risks – particularly foreign exchange exposures – to ensure that it retained spare capacity to take risks in value-adding areas such as research and development of new drugs. By hedging operating cash flows they are able to maintain spending plans (Nichols, 1994). This is in marked contrast to Mobil Corporation's relatively unhedged position in the 1980s: when oil prices fell, so did the firm's cash flows and its investment spending. This applied to all Mobil subsidiaries so that its retail subsidiary – Montgomery Ward, which was a net consumer of oil and so benefited from lower prices – cut back on investment at a time when its competitors were expanding.

Strategic Foresight

Many decisions are made in a context where conventional wisdom about the present, or what might be called the shared contemporary paradigm, holds true. This can be within a near-term timeframe – say the next year or three – where current trends and conditions will largely persist. Or it may be where little change is expected. Consider, for instance, staples such as food, clothing, furniture: so little about them has changed in millennia that a modern family dinner table would hold few surprises for ancient Phoenicians. Similarly, most contemporary transport modes would be familiar to people from 1920. Despite a lot of hype about rapid change, many designs and channels of delivery of important products and services – including housing, health care, transport, education, social welfare and employment – have changed little in decades, if not centuries. In the case of such stable frameworks, it is safe to assume incremental change and follow a normative decision model.

Conversely, other areas will be buffeted by significant change which must be factored into decision making. A useful technique here is *strategic foresight*, which is a convergence of strategic planning, future studies, organization development and technology planning. The aim is to bridge the conventional contemporary paradigm to a model of what critical factors could look like a decade or more ahead. This enables decisions to comprehend future conditions, and sensitizes decision makers to future risks.

Table 4.3 summarizes a number of views on major drivers of future change. The column headed *Strategic Foresight* sets out drivers developed by Marsh, McAllum and Purcell (2002); the key issues driving business come from Dauphinais (2000); the next column is from a McKinsey 2006 survey of executives on global trends they expect to have impact through to 2015 (Davis and Stephenson, 2006); whilst the far right column is my view.

Such changes usher in a new environment that must be factored in to decisions. But how can a useful view of the future be developed given forecasters' poor record? Extending Arthur C. Clarke's conclusion that 'most erroneous forecasts are due to a failure of imagination or failure of nerve,' a trend or event that has the potential to disrupt the contemporary paradigm will have several essential components.

The first is that it must make sense. In most cases, this means that the idea, product or trend has occurred somewhere else. Whilst it is overly simplistic to assume that California leads much of the world by 3 to 5 years or that mid-ranging developed countries such as Australia, Canada and Sweden move in synch, that is not a bad starting point. It is also important to remember that demand will not emerge without a clear need and justification, and often a change in thinking.

Further requirements are the availability of complementary products and an obvious need. A good example is the skyscraper which was impractical without electricity infrastructure that could power lifts and lights, and was not needed until cities grew with the move from employment in agriculture and manufacturing to services and offices.

Changed thinking can need a catalyst to create a sense of urgency that weakens instinctive resistance. Typically most people benefit from the *status quo*: they understand existing technologies and processes, are familiar with their ground rules, and have reached accommodation with their implications. Changing the paradigm means relearning, and possibly losing wealth or status that has been accumulated: for anyone who has come to terms with the conventional paradigm, there is risk and cost associated with change.

Table 4.3   Projected drivers of change

	Strategic Foresight	*Business Issues*	*McKinsey*	*Coleman*
Political	• Instability from pollution and resource depletion		• Centres of economic activity shift profoundly • Big business comes under increasing scrutiny	• Regional dynamics • Sustainable business processes
Economic	• Knowledge as value adding	• Knowledge management • Shareholder value	• Public-sector activities balloon • Natural resource demand grows, with strain on the environment • Non-traditional business models flourish	• Falling commodity prices • Implacable competitiveness
Technological	• Digital revolution and ubiquitous chips • Biotechnology	• Innovation • E-Business • Disruptive technology	• Connectivity transforms the way people live and interact • Management becomes more scientific	• Critical mass of technologies
Social	• Social division based on digital literacy • Globalization	• Growth • Organization • Globalization	• Consumers grow and age • Global labour strategies become essential • Economics of knowledge change	• Rise of individualism • Output focus
??	Unexpected events			• Factor X

It is common to encounter people who are unwilling to accept even the possibility of change, such as Jeserec who is a character in Arthur C. Clarke's (1952: 29) novel *The City and the Stars* and 'did not merely believe in stability; he could conceive of nothing else'. Such conceptual blocks or behavioural biases are probably at the heart of statements such as that in 1943 by IBM Chairman Thomas Watson that he could only foresee a world market for five computers; or the oft-repeated (but probably apocryphal) proposal by some Congressmen to close the US Patent Office around the end of the nineteenth century because 'there was nothing left to invent'. Hubris, fear and sloth are just some of the barriers to accepting the need for change, or even its possibility. Another is that the trade-offs involved in achieving large changes are so risky that doing nothing can seem an attractive option. That is why many strategies consciously eliminate continuation of the status quo, as advocated in the business cliché that Cortez' first act on reaching the New World in 1519 was to 'burn the boats'.

Culture is a particularly important barrier to change. According to Foster and Kaplan (2001), companies fail because of cultural lock-in. This involves a gradual stiffening of decision making as control systems and mental models that are shared within the firm – its core concepts, beliefs and assumptions, cause-and-effect relationships, inherited wisdom – are bureaucratized, converge and become outmoded. Lock-in dampens a company's ability to innovate or shed fading activities, renders it unable to change even in the face of clear threats, and brings deteriorating performance. Quite often it becomes simpler to change the people than restructure an organization.

There are many examples of firms that suffer cultural lock-in or market neglect. A few years after Peters and Waterman (1982) published *In Search of Excellence* about America's best-run companies, *Business Week* ran a cover story 'Who's Excellent Now?' [5 November 1984] which pointed to failure by a number of formerly excellent companies to keep up with changes in their markets, especially Atari, Delta Airlines, Digital Equipment, Hewlett-Packard and Texas Instruments. In an important pointer to discussions in Chapter 10 on governance, the article blamed the companies' strategic shortcomings on poor organizational structures and processes.

In many cases, then, change needs a catalyst, and these come in many forms including new technologies, individuals, crises, consumers and competitors. Examples, respectively, at the national level are nuclear weapons, Chancellor Hitler, the 1930s Depression, protest groups and globalization. At the level of firms they include the PC, Henry Ford, collapse of Enron, fast food demand and Dell's distribution model.

Technologies are a major source of change as they not only create their own demand but shape what is possible. For example, after the 1960s, cheap shipping promoted global trade in commodities and encouraged concentration of plants. The drive towards integration was born, and – in quick succession – Boeing's 747 cut travel costs, and toll-free telephone numbers and tumbling communications costs made it easy to service wide regions. Geography appeared redundant, and regional and global links formed in everything from computer and telecommunications systems to recruiting and foodstuffs. This is a clear example of how technology promotes convergence of processes, and so eliminates distribution chains and intermediate storage. The results impact the business model of every industry that does not directly supply its manufactures and services to end users; and link potentially incompatible processes by bringing together previously unmatched systems, markets and cultures.

It is a commonly accepted fact that half or more of the capital invested by developed countries in the last decade has been directed at new technologies. To date the results as conventionally measured by productivity statistics have been modest. We are yet to exploit the critical mass of technologies which has been created in many sectors by the huge investment in home and office IT, and through a global network of cheap communications.

This untapped technology-in-place from past investments represents a vast resource that is capable of being leveraged at low incremental cost (the technique engineers graphically term 'debottlenecking') to be much more productive and facilitate centralization and unprecedented flows of information. This will yield huge synergies because network productivity has a power relationship to its number of components. Using experience of past technologies, greatest benefit is likely to come from innovative combinations: a period of intense innovation is likely! This will see: inherently risky processes become more automated and on larger scale; and increasing interest in undertaking ambitious projects (particularly in old technologies such as buildings and bridges) which inevitably are more vulnerable.

Many economic, demographic and social changes promote implacable competition which flows into relentless focus on output, drive for lower costs and greater productivity. This inevitably renders organizations more complex and vulnerable. Reorganization, regionalization, globalization and other euphemisms for corporate re-engineering all result in a reduction in resources and thus a loss of expertise, back-up and redundancy. Thus virtuous circles – such as America's new economy of the late 1990s – can turn vicious if expectations are not met.

A common catalyst for change – even in sectors that are not rapidly evolving – is the opportunity to simplify or expand the scope of a useful service. Incorporating mobility, for instance, transformed industries as diverse as entertainment (portable TVs, radios, DVDs) and communications (mobile phones and wireless technologies).

Declining cost structures as production moves up the cost curve are another catalyst for change and have consistently accelerated market penetration. For example, a popular explanation for rapid growth of electronics is Moore's Law, which says that semiconductor performance will double every 2 years without any increase in costs. Comparable change has been wrought by evolution of the Boeing 747 which has kept long-haul airfares constant in nominal dollars since its introduction in 1970; and by technology which steadily reduced the real cost of most commodities, despite some spikes such as that during 2003–2008.

An important driver of change is markets which can quickly resolve gaps that emerge between actual and potential performance. To keep up, firms must see themselves as a revolving portfolio of products and services at various stages of development, which requires research and a formal process of product creation and destruction. With this in mind, Pascale (1990) opens his book *Managing on the Edge* with the line: 'Nothing fails like success' and goes on to argue that 'great strengths are inevitably the roots of deadly weaknesses'. Good examples of marketing success that led to failure include IBM which was brilliant at mainframes, but failed to see the PC; and Encyclopaedia Britannica which had a brilliant intellectual product, but failed to see that parents wanting to help their kids had begun to buy a PC instead of an encyclopaedia which is about the same price. In this context, the Nike slogan – 'To stay number 1 you have to train like you're number 2' – has considerable decision-making merit.

Just as markets are change catalysts, so are their rules. Deregulation, for instance, has been a powerful contributor to change in industries as diverse as aviation, transport, communications and financial services.

A useful framework to evaluate external threats is the Porter (1985) five forces model of industry returns. This sees industry dynamics as shaped by the bargaining power of suppliers and consumers; the costs of entry and the threat of substitutes; and the nature of competitive rivalry. Another common approach is to look for potential changes by brainstorming using some version of PEST, which considers significant catalysts for change under political-economic-social-technological headings. It can be extended using ethics-environment-legal-demographics and so on to build acronyms such as STEEP, PESTLE and STEEPLED.

When attempting strategic foresight, it is necessary to think about the requirements for any system to be amenable to meaningful predictions. First it must be defined and closed: a process that is not understood and quantified and is open to multiple forces will behave erratically and cannot be realistically predicted. It is virtually impossible to predict systems that are complex or chaotic such as weather and currencies, or which experience a rapid pace of change which D'Aveni (1994) calls hypercompetitive markets. Second the number of elements being predicted must be small enough to ensure homogeneity of response; and they must fit within a reliable causal model, for which there is valid data.

Figure 4.4 develops these points to show degrees of forecastability.

An example of a system that is frequently the subject of forecasting is human population. This is probably feasible for local and national populations which are generally well defined with good models and data. But it proves much more difficult to forecast population at the global level and estimates need to be built up from smaller components. Another system that does not lend itself to forecasting at any level is currency: that is because the number of variables impacting on most currencies is so large and their affect so variable that they prove impossible to forecast.

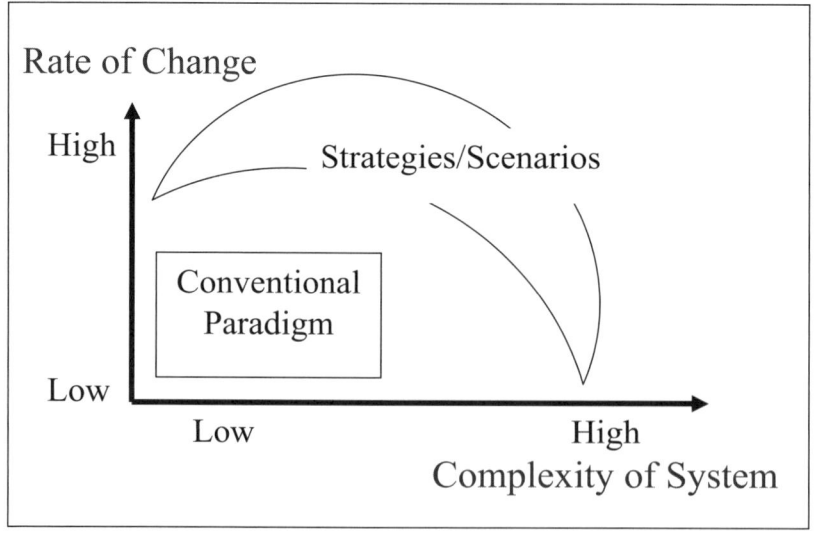

Figure 4.4 Predictability of systems

Figure 4.5 shows two examples of systems that are subject to varying patterns of change and predictability. The left chart shows the US birth rate during the last century and the right chart shows the winning distance in the Olympic Hammer Throw. Each was stable for an extended period, then experienced major discontinuity, followed by resumption of a constant value. The US birth rate was relatively stable above 24 per 1,000 population until 1960 when it slumped below 16 within a decade. After changing little since the first Games, the winning hammer throw distance went from 60 metres in 1952 to over 80 metres after 1980. Arguably each system suffered an unpredictable shock that was facilitated by commercialization of a new drug: contraceptives and steroids, respectively. Evidence of the latter came at the Beijing Olympics where the silver and bronze medallists each tested positive for testosterone. These are graphic examples of systems that are not subject to simple extrapolation and statistical analysis, and epitomise the difficulty in predicting complex systems: inevitably this uncertainty brings risks.

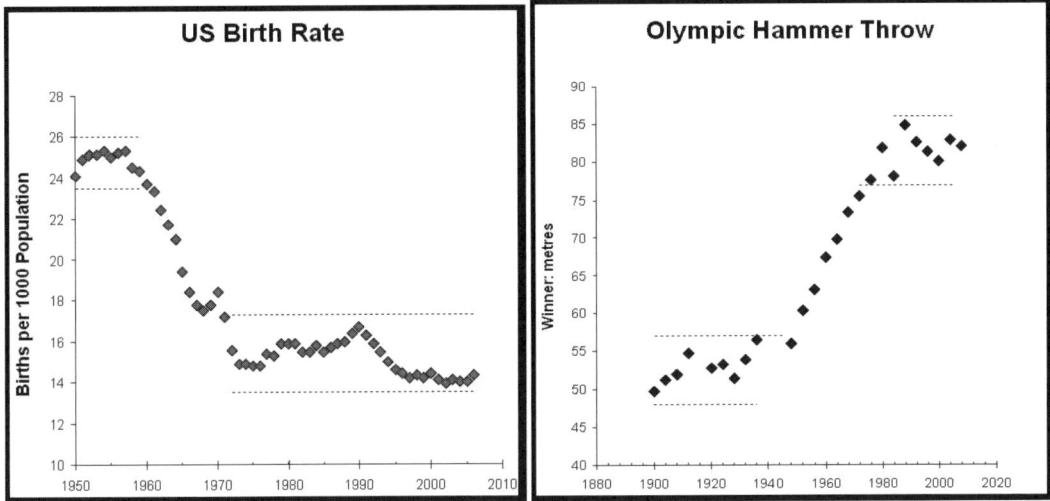

Figure 4.5 Trends that collapse dramatically

Examples such as these show the difficulties in forecasting paradigm shifts, as each needs: a clear justification; adequate support in terms of sponsors and complementary products and services; at least one viable model or product; and a market. The important feature in each case is that the utility provided by the implied major change makes economic, personal and social sense. This explains a common feature of many failed forecasts – particularly of the rate of take-up of new technologies and products – which is to concentrate only on the capability of the product and ignore weaknesses in its utility and functionality.

One of the rare retrospectives of popular forecasts is by Steven Schnaars (1989) who provided three guidelines when evaluating paradigm shifts: avoid technological wonder; ask fundamental questions; and stress cost-benefit analysis. This prevents being trapped by over optimistic advocates of the ability and probable success of technology; and helps debunk forecasts that represent prevailing orthodoxy, rather than fact. And because imprecise knowledge can encourage use of blunt instruments with sweeping impacts and unexpected consequences, sensible guidelines ensure adequate data are collected and avoid harebrained schemes.

This suggests another approach to forecasting – particularly in contemplating risks – which is to think in terms of *effect* rather than cause. For instance, any firm can identify a vast number of low-probability risks that form a noisy background of hazards. These include everything from terrorist attack to computer failure. Although each is individually improbable and does not justify a tailored response, there are so many possibilities that at least one is likely to occur. This can be true of business risks as diverse as regulatory change, competitor attack and development of new technologies and products. Sensible strategy builds generic responses that can manage the almost certain occurrence of one of these low-probability background risks.

In summary, decisions need to suit the times and recognize they are a changin'. That is why people and firms with the knack of reading change always appear to be in the right place with the right product offerings.

Scenario Planning

A useful tool in making decisions in risky and uncertain environments is scenario planning. This is a relatively structured process which involves development of coherent 'stories of the future' using a combination of nine steps (Ringland, 1998):

1. Define the scope of the analysis, and tease out the focal issue or key decision.
2. Develop data on the decision, covering factors such as industry size, competitors, substitutes, policies, technologies, profitability.
3. Identify key trends using PEST or STEEP, Five Forces, competitive analysis and other models of how the area of decision operates.
4. Understand the drivers of these trends, and rank them by importance.
5. Bring drivers together into scenario themes.
6. Reduce the number of scenarios to two, often giving them descriptive names.
7. Elaborate the story behind each scenario; check for consistency and plausibility.
8. Identify the issues arising.
   - Does the organization have adequate competencies?
   - What contingency plans need to be made?
   - What no-regrets actions can be taken?
9. Think of scenarios as a 10-year journey, and develop milestones of what should be seen along the way as each scenario unfolds.

Table 4.4 provides an example of scenario development using the retail petrol industry as an example.

Scenario planning is useful in industries and firms where uncertainty is high relative to managers' ability to predict or adjust. These can be rapidly changing environments, those subject to disruptive change such as a government policy shift, or facing a potential crisis such as Y2K or chronic natural disasters. Other applications arise where costly surprises have occurred in the past following market disruption by new products or competitors, or arrival of disruptive technologies.

Table 4.4   Scenario planning example: Retail petrol supply

First Step: Identify key drivers and outlook

Key Forces

- Demand: Cars *Travel distance* Fuel economy
- Quality: environment and engine technology
- Location of demand changes
- Internal and international trade
- Price of crude oil: petrol price elasticity; taxes
- GDP: petrol consumption is economically sensitive

Underlying Drivers

- Standard of living: cars, travel
- Environmental expectations: emissions
- Engine/vehicle technology: substitutes
- Internal migration

Second Step: Develop scenarios and list their implications for strategy

Scenarios

- *Green Death*   Strong environmental pressures, perhaps driven by climate change, which reduce demand and lift taxes, encouraging substitutes
- *Raging Fire*   Continuing rise in living standards and dispersion of ageing population to lifestyle locales with strong demand growth (silver birds)

Implications

- *Green Death:* competencies in alternatives and policy lobbying; new lower cost business model under restructuring and strong competition
- *Raging Fire:* capacity expansion, improved logistics, upgrade customer buying experience

Secondly, scenario planning can kick-start corporate regeneration, where the quality of strategic thinking is low, and no one thinks outside the box. The result is to challenge conventional wisdom and scope out a different future for staid industries, which might include aviation, hotels and manufacturing.

Superficially the technique is attractive, but it has a number of deficiencies. Scenarios can degenerate so that they just incorporate 'conventional wisdom' or underpin existing planning assumptions. Insistence on 'logical scenarios' and 'consistent stories of the future' assumes a level of forecasting ability that is usually lacking and can narrow perceptions to a single evolutionary path, so the results are blind to many, low-probability issues, some of which will almost certainly occur.

Decision-making Environment

The decision techniques discussed above are complex and demanding of resources. They really only need to be used in risky environments. Considerable work has been done on developing checklists and other measures so that external reviewers such as auditors can identify potentially risky settings. One way is to look for complex processes which:

- are based on assumptions rather than empirically-based extrapolations of established causal relationships. 'Trust me, it will work' is not a good justification;
- represent high-cost innovations. Products that are expensive find it more difficult to attract customers; projects and investments that are more expensive are inherently more complex;
- lack a clear value proposition. Support from customers or other stakeholders is hard to elicit in the absence of clear benefit or utility from any change or innovation;
- move beyond established frameworks. The development of a system is most likely to occur along established trajectories, and expectations that 'this time is different' are usually unmet. New business models that have not incorporated pilot testing are at high risk of failure: thus fast-finishing seconds often do better than leaders. That is why it is said that nobody makes money on a new industrial development until the first two owners have gone broke; and why many successful new technologies, including PCs, video recorders, mobile phones, and digital cameras, did not take off until the second or third version was introduced;
- resist disruption in the face of emerging catalysts for change. When regulation, markets, technology, consumer preference or competitors' strategy change, then inaction is unwise. Similarly asymmetries in information, quality or return are the physical equivalent of arbitrage opportunities and will eventually be closed.

A second approach recognizes that the environment around a decision shapes its risks, and Table 4.5 lists indicators of potentially weak decision making using material prepared by the Board of Governors of Federal Reserve System (1997). Strategic evaluation of environments identifies settings where caution is required, or risk management resources should be preferentially directed. This can serve as a checklist of attributes that are indicative of a setting that promotes risky situations or poor decisions.

Another environmental assessment tool is in the `Quick Risk Quiz' in Table 4.6. This involves eleven questions with yes-no answers that have been linked to poor risk outcomes. Around 70 per cent of organizations with a score of four or more are likely to experience a crisis in any 3 years (Coleman, 2006b). This shows that risk-prone companies are in industries which are regulated, uncompetitive, technologically advanced and not responsive to consumer needs. Companies which experience crises have structures and processes which contain the seeds of major problems. They undertake many complex activities, and this sets them up for strategic failures from a wave of knock-on impacts that can cascade through process systems. Crisis-prone companies produce finished products and so any failure means they face immediate customer impact. They also have offshore investments which are common sources of crises because of control and reporting difficulties.

Given the influence on risk of company strategy and goals, it is not surprising that companies that are crisis-prone have Boards which lack expertise, and have weak management structures through not recruiting the best candidates. Apart from structural factors, companies create crises by promoting a pressure-cooker atmosphere with demands for results and repeated cost-cutting programmes. This inevitably leads to instability;

Table 4.5 Environmental conditions promoting risk and poor decision making

Environmental Factor	Contribution to Elevated Risk
Anxiety for income	Pursuit of earnings overrides sound investment criteria
Compromise of investment principles	Investments do not meet established criteria, possibly due to stakeholder influences, anxiety for income, biased compensation and competitive pressures
Incomplete record keeping	Financial decisions are not properly documented, including gaps in supporting analysis
Failure to document contractual arrangements	Sales or contracts are negotiated without full documentation or approvals
Inadequate scrutiny of routine processes	Familiarity breeds contempt
Excessive optimism	Allows known weaknesses or risks to be downplayed in light of optimistic expectations about outcomes
Ignoring warning signs	Failure to monitor or heed forward indicators of risks, such as increased frequency of minor losses or defects
Lack of supervision	Inadequate involvement of management in initial decisions, and monitoring of ongoing operations
Technical incompetence	Staff lack the skills and experience in operations
Overextended resources	Resources – human, capital and financial – are inadequate to meet the needs of ongoing operations
Internal competition	Compromises procedural requirements

Adapted from: US Federal Reserve (1997) *Branch and Agency Examination Manual*

Table 4.6 Quick risk quiz

Think about whether your organization:	
1. Is in a regulated industry	Yes/No
2. Has many complex activities	Yes/No
3. Has direct investments offshore	Yes/No
4. Produces finished consumer goods or services	Yes/No
5. Has a high level of internal competition	Yes/No
6. Has implemented repeated cost-cutting	Yes/No
7. Cuts corners to get results	Yes/No
8. Is expanding rapidly	Yes/No
9. Has a Board with expertise in all areas of operations	Yes/No
10. Has an ethical approach to business	Yes/No
11. Appoints best candidates as managers	Yes/No

Scoring Questions 1–7: 1 for 'Yes', 0 for 'No';
Questions 8–11: 0 for 'Yes', 1 for 'No'.

but can also induce a climate of corner cutting, and tolerance of low standards in product quality and performance.

The aim of these thumbnail sketches is to establish simple measures of organizations' risk propensity. They suggest that firms encounter unwanted outcomes because they tolerate or establish risky environments, rather than failing to eliminate risk sources. This, of course, traces risks to strategic and organizational-level factors, rather than point sources. The implication of structural and environmental factors as sources of risk is that firms can experience crises because of their strategies and processes, rather than an absence of good risk management practices. Companies which minimize their exposure to crises take practical steps to monitor problems through product quality reviews and attention to brand and reputation protection; and they are more likely to have appropriate policies and contingency plans in place.

Stakeholder Influences: Managing Experts

Experts play important roles in decisions. The first is that they add to perceived control over the decision and this is especially valuable to risk-neutral decision makers. Second they support due diligence and can be an important justification for executives' decisions.

Many people, however, have poor experience of experts. Lord Salisbury, who was Britain's Secretary of State for India during a troubled period in 1874–8, wrote somewhat bitterly: 'No lesson seems to be so deeply inculcated by the experience of life as that you should never trust experts' (Cecil, 1921).

Sadly for decision makers, this is borne out by empirical studies of experts' ability which reveal that expertise is generally lacking. For instance, Colin Camerer (1995) sought to determine the accuracy of experts' forecasts by examining 100 studies that were supported by observable data such as test scores, medical examinations and financial ratios. The consistent finding is that simple regressions using historical data beat the experts. He concluded: 'The *only* [his emphasis] documented exceptions to the general conclusions that models outpredict experts are a few kinds of esoteric medical diagnosis.' Bolger and Wright (1994) identified 40 studies of expertise, and similarly found only six groups of experts which evidenced good judgement, including racetrack tipsters. Even though there are plentiful incentives for expertise amidst the complexity of markets, most evaluations of experts' performance in the economics and finance literature conclude that a coin remains a competitive forecasting tool (Cochrane, 1999).

A similar picture is painted by Yates (1990) who found that physicians, psychologists and stock analysts could do no better than simple naive strategies; only weather forecasters consistently display skill.[1] Another study of forecasts of political developments found

---

[1] Many readers may not share this conclusion, especially as the American Meteorological Society (1991) admits that meteorologists can only display 'considerable skill' in forecasts of up to 12 hours; beyond then their ability decays so rapidly that meteorologists have only 'slight to marginal skill' in forecasts beyond four days. However, Soll (1996) provides an intuitive rationale to support their ability by pointing to forecasters' large sample sizes, and quite specific goals; and the fact that short-term weather patterns persist and respond consistently to a small number of parameters. In fact the accuracy of weather forecasters is consistent with discussion in Chapter 4 on Bayesian decision making. Most weather forecasts address high probability outcomes such as sunshine on most days and regular rainfall, so even a modest level of accuracy can give reliable judgements.

that experts 'were only slightly more accurate than one would expect from chance,' and tartly concludes (Tetlock 1999: 335):

The now voluminous literature on judgemental biases and errors raises doubts about the capacity of even highly motivated professionals to perform the types of information-processing tasks that rational-actor models regularly posit that people routinely perform ... This largely cognitive-psychological literature casts doubt on our ability to draw sound causal conclusions from complex arrays of data.

A good survey of expertise comes from a pioneering analysis which reviewed environmental impact assessments that had been developed for major development proposals in Australia, and compared their predictions against actual results. Over half the outcomes fell outside the range of 0.5 to 2.0 times the prediction, and the study concluded that the mean accuracy of predictions was 44 per cent (Buckley, 1991).

It seems that the few groups of experts who do display expertise are either dealing with events that enjoy a higher probability of occurrence (such as short-term weather forecasting); or they are individuals with special skill that enables them to see through noise (and, for example, diagnose rare diseases) or else to understand complex, non-linear environments and identify conditions where linear relationships have broken down.

Whilst a comprehensive evaluation of the ability of experts is beyond my scope, there is strong evidence that those in most disciplines are not able to add value to simple models. If 'experts' are so likely to be wrong, a process to manage them is necessary.

What can be done? First demand validation. When computer graphics can show Forrest Gump shooting the breeze with President Johnson, non-experts need independent verification and reasonableness checks of core data and assumptions. Apart from healthy scepticism, it helps to fall back on common sense. This is a tool evolved by humans over aeons to gain an evolutionary edge and we should not be shy to use it. Decision makers also need independent evaluation of the mechanisms underlying predictions. Independence, here, is characterized not just by the absence of direct pecuniary interest, but also by a willingness to consider multiple outcomes and not doggedly pursue a single path. Stand alone thinking is essential against the moral suasion of herds.

As the future is the murkiest of all brews, its management demands the hubris of hunches to balance risk and uncertainty. The best approach starts by defining expectations from science, knowledge and technologies; establishes practical approaches to risk evaluation; and continually applies reasonableness checks. Peers should review proposals, taking into account sponsors' track record, especially failures! Sensible management of experts gives them clear directions about what problems and questions need solving. Post audits of proposals ensure schedules and budgets are adhered to by kicking the pace along when work stalls; and they help pick out proven performers and knowledge gaps.

When communicating risks there is an important role for ethics and transparency. Any hint of bias, secrecy or cover-up gives instant credibility to conspiracy theorists, and leads to policy gridlock. Experts need to set out their key premises: what they know about the issue and areas of uncertainty; other possible effects; and the financial and technical assumptions behind alternative responses. Unfortunately too many experts have traded ethical standards for an adversarial climate and a culture of winning irrespective of the merits of their position. Experts need a morality that guides them to appreciate the social ends that are served by their training and skills.

A data risk that experts can introduce into decisions involves what Bazerman (2006: 2) calls self-serving bias. Judgements that are actually shaped by self-interest will be justified on seemingly unbiased criteria: 'the expectation of objective judgment ... is unrealistic... One of the most important subjective influences on information processing is self-interest. People tend to confuse what is personally beneficial with what is fair or moral.' This is particularly important in evaluating advice from individuals or groups that have an interest in a decision's outcome. This, of course, incorporates the role of advisors where decision risk is encapsulated in the caution of Comer (1998: 8) that: 'If you do risky deals, don't be surprised if you are exploited.'

Firms face growing influence from private sector agents, particularly financial institutions such as mutual funds and the private regulators of financial markets and systems. This gains significance as these agents are also influencing governments: taxation of dividends and share buybacks, for instance, is increasingly responding to the preferences of mutual funds; and government reform of the financial system often follows lobbying by major firms in the financial markets.

Pressures can be strong from corporate advisers who use their knowledge and privileged positions to encourage high-risk strategies such as acquisitions (Lewis and Zalan, 2004). Given that Boards typically rubber-stamp proposals by chief executives, CEOs and their advisors effectively make most strategic decisions. This promotes a significant agency problem in that managers and advisers will rationally pursue their own self-interest, which – because decision, risk and remuneration are separated in firms – can lead to a clash between shareholder and manager interests. In addition, CEO contracts and option packages can encourage restructuring activity; and advisors reap disproportionate benefits from large transactions. Thus it can be in the interests of CEOs and advisers to promote asset churning, often coyly termed deal flow. Finally skill in major transactions is a preserve of advisors, but it can provide career enhancement for CEOs. Thus the asymmetry in knowledge – of transaction execution between advisors and CEOs, and of transaction risks between Boards and CEOs – can promote poor decision outcomes.

There is no doubt that we need the help of experts to identify, control and mitigate the unwanted consequences of our growing knowledge. We need them, too, to help develop policy which buys flexibility, control, correctability and insensitivity to error. But expertise needs ethics to be really useful. In particular, experts need to be clear about what assumptions they rely upon, what evidence has been excluded and the level of accuracy in their forecasts. Managers' practical foresight sees strategy, communications and understanding as essential. They know that every trend interacts in a complex fashion with many other developments, and forecasts err because of preconditioned learning, lack of experience and complementary developments. Although managers may not be as technically knowledgeable as experts, their experience is valuable given that all parties lack adequate information.

Conclusion

A major problem with normative decision analysis is that virtually all data and evidence are coloured by judgement and opinion. Thus 'facts' are not, and can easily be ignored; nor are 'experts', and they, too, should frequently be ignored. Given the imprecision in decision processes, how can firms guard against the risks inherent in decision making? Four techniques are useful.

The first is to be aware of the environment. Most advocates of a particular choice suffer from sponsor's bias; and – although their audience inevitably makes some adjustment for the assumed bias – the projected outcome acts as an anchor, and estimates retain a favourable bias. Thus test projections against population-based estimates and zero-base evaluations by independent experts (including peer reviews); and conduct other reasonableness checks such as estimates of outcomes based on flawless execution, execution by the leading competitor and historical execution by the firm (Lovallo and Kahneman, 2003).

A second technique to improve decisions around uncertain events is to construct an outcome tree which lists each possible outcome and shows factors that could influence their various probabilities. A variant is to work backwards to the outcome by developing hypothetical descriptions of why a particular decision failed. For example, a firm might be planning to invest $1 billion in a new oil refinery to supply south-east Asia. Teams would be told that the decision failed, with each given a different reason: the construction process was flawed; output did not meet specifications; the refinery proved unprofitable. Teams are then asked to explain why. Because people are better able to identify patterns in hindsight, this perspective can provide powerful insights into potential risks (Kleindorfer, Kunreuther and Schoemaker, 1993). And it is easier to find flaws when analysts are committed to seeking out sources of weakness.

A third technique is to use scenarios, or stories of the future which are integrated depictions of plausible outcomes that must hang together and be logical. Scenarios have the effect of providing diversity to options under consideration. The same result can be achieved by inviting dissenting experts from outside to provide input, or using participants in the decision to debate for and against the alternatives.

The final technique is feedback. Decision makers can be given quick feedback by independent critiques of their projections (whether from population data, experts or prospective hindsight), through training in decision processes, from analyses of comparable past decisions, and from their own performance.

To conclude, President Kennedy's observation at the start of this chapter is prescient: decision making and risk taking are archetypal examples of the application of tacit knowledge: some rules can be taught and some techniques can be learned; but success involves such complex judgement across multiple areas (decision criteria, choice options, relevant data, future developments and execution techniques) that skill in risk choices is hard to transfer.

The implication is that some individuals will be good judges of risk; and some settings will promote value-adding risk taking. Managers and investors, though, should be aware of the corollary that some individuals and settings will be marked by poor risk taking! They need to take into account that most serious failures occur through systematic biases in judgement, rather than criminal or dishonest behaviour and acts-of-god.

CHAPTER 5
Impact of Risk on Shareholder Value

Great deeds are usually wrought at great risks.
    Herodotus, 5th century BC Greek historian, *The Histories Book 7*, Chapter 50

The policy of being too cautious is the greatest risk of all.
    Jawaharlal Nehru (1889–1964) to the Indian Parliament

Risk management is an important goal for firms. It avoids loss in shareholder value from damage to property and other assets, business interruption and liabilities to third parties. It is also an important consideration in strategy by ensuring that the right level and type of risks are taken. In fact, dialling up the right level of risk is a core firm competency. Thus the world's largest mining company, BHP Billiton, told investors in 2001:

> *What we invest in and how we collect our portfolio has an implication on that risk profile ... In terms of the capital approval process [we ask] what is the risk profile of this project? Is that too much risk for us to be able to deliver on our other corporate promises? ... The way we manage risk is really through the strength, flexibility and diversification in the portfolio.*

Given that so many firms devote considerable resources to risk management, this chapter evaluates its justification.

Prior to Modigilani and Miller (1958), the structure and financial policy of firms including risk optimization were important to investment (see, for instance: Meyer and Kuh, 1957). In later times, however, the assumption of perfect capital markets has rendered decisions independent of financial structure and policy. The irrelevance theorem states that capital structure – including risk protection – cannot create value. A tenet of modern portfolio theory is that value in a firm is created solely by optimized investments and efficient operations: no value can be added on the liabilities side of the balance sheet, nor by managing risks.

The argument above requires significant broadening for three reasons. The first is that firm-specific risk has become more significant to investors, and is now the predominant source of their risk. The second point is that market imperfections mean that firms can often manage financial risks more effectively than shareholders. Thirdly, of course, is strong evidence that shareholders generally welcome the fact that managers spend considerable time and resources on managing risk.

Consider each in turn.

Does Risk Matter?

There seems little doubt that variance in returns of individual stocks – and hence the riskiness of individual firms – has risen in recent decades. The trend was first identified in the US market by Malkiel and Xu (1997), and then confirmed by Campbell et al. (2001) (and others) who found that variance in the firm-specific component of stock returns has roughly trebled since 1962. This change could only come from an increase in the variance of shocks to cash flow or discount rate, or decreased covariance between the two shocks. The authors suggested a number of possible reasons including company structures that were more focussed and less diversified; changes in the inherent volatility of stocks, perhaps due to listing of firms earlier in their life cycle; compensation of executives through stock options which leads them to follow strategies that increase stock volatility; changes in patterns of information flow so that the volume of price sensitive data is greater, more lumpy or arrives earlier; and herding amongst institutional investors which now control most firms.

This result prompted a flurry of papers designed to test whether idiosyncratic or firm-specific risk has any ability to explain variations in security returns. Although this represents a revisiting of an old conclusion (dating at least to Fama and MacBeth, 1973) that firm-specific risk cannot explain returns, it was justified given the qualitative change in risk.

Whilst debate continues on whether and why firm risk may have risen, it is clear from materials in Chapter 2 that firms face an increasing probability of encountering a crisis or major incident, especially arising from poor strategic decision making. Risk management is a growing problem.

Intuitive Benefits of Risk Management

Further justification for effective management of firm risks arises because markets are imperfect and shareholders do not have unfettered access to financial risk management products and tools.

For a start, managers have greater knowledge than shareholders about the quantum and nature of their firm's risks, and so are better placed to optimize them. Consider, for instance, risk from changes in market prices such as interest rates or commodities, and which companies can eliminate through hedging. Shareholders cannot know the size and timing of commodity revenues and foreign currency cash flows, nor the nature of offsets that come from natural hedges such as debt. In addition the presumed risk management techniques available to shareholders – such as diversification and hedging – can only diversify dividend (or perhaps earnings) streams, and not fluctuations in cash flows; nor can they match the risk reduction that comes from the co-insurance effect following corporate restructures that increase scale. Thus firms have a greater capability for financial risk management than investors.

In other cases firms are better placed to manage risks than shareholders because market imperfections mean that risks have frictional or transactional costs. One cost is imposed by progressive tax systems where firms with volatile income can suffer a tax drag due to asymmetrical treatment of losses and gains. Even where tax is symmetrical – as in Australia – differences in timing between tax losses and the offsetting credit have a present value impact. Another risk-related cost that cannot be managed by shareholders is the possibility that managers in higher-risk firms can be deterred from investing in projects with attractive risk-adjusted returns because of cash shortfalls, or because they are averse to accepting further risk.

The third rationale for risk management by firms is that shareholders gain value through reduction of pure risks. These are often termed insurable risks, and – whilst exposing the firm to income volatility – only offer the chance of loss; examples are storm damage, fire or theft. These risks form a subset of business risks, including strategic errors. Managing pure risks does not have a symmetrical impact on returns as it limits downside risk whilst retaining exposure to favourable upside changes. Considerable value can be added by managing these business risks which directly reduce the probability of some left tail events.

A particularly fearsome left tail event is 'financial distress' which arouses concerns from creditors about the possibility of default or bankruptcy. As firms approach bankruptcy, they suffer diminution in reputation as a supplier, customer and employer; management is distracted; and the value of assets steadily erodes. Again firms are better placed than shareholders to manage this risk.

A different intuition on the benefits of risk management comes by adopting the conventional assumption in finance that a firm's value is equal to its expected future cash flows discounted at an appropriate risk-adjusted rate. The discount rate reflects total risk to the firm's cash flows, which is the sum of market risk and diversifiable risk. Given that firm value changes with either expected cash flows or the discount rate, and risk can alter both parameters, firm risk has multiple impacts on shareholder value. Changes to a firm's risk propensity will alter its strategy and make activities more or less likely to produce a loss. Because the shift in risk propensity changes operations, it also alters the level of expected returns. A second impact on value comes when the expected cash flows become more or less certain, and so the discount rate is changed to reflect altered uncertainty around expected returns. Reducing downside risks lifts expected returns and lowers the discount rate giving a double boost to shareholder value.

The link between corporate returns and risk arises in the cost and uncertainties that are associated with strategic risks. Failures, crises and incidents have direct costs and divert management attention, and so reduce profits and thus returns. In addition, risk raises uncertainty over future profitability and creditors require a premium to support risky companies. Higher borrowing costs further reduce earnings.

Elsewhere in this book (Chapters 4 and 7), options have been proposed as a useful tool in managing and pricing risk. Given that the value of an option is directly related to its volatility, when shareholder equity is considered as a real option over the firm it might appear that risk management lowers the volatility of income and so will reduce firm value. However, risk management does not change the expected values of the asset's future income, nor does it reduce the inherent uncertainty associated with an asset's cash flows. What it does achieve is to introduce – often at a cost as an insurance policy, or with hedging when the market is in contango – another component to the *firm's* income which can make it smoother. Thus the risk associated with the firm's total cash flows will fall, even though there has been no change to the risk of cash flows expected from the underlying assets. To the extent that lower risk to cash flows reduces the cost of capital, risk management should increase the present value of expected future cash flows. Thus risk management – even within a real options framework – can add value.

Do Shareholders Prefer Risk?

Managers clearly favour an active programme to manage risk given the time and resources spent on it. But what about shareholders? Evidence is that they, too, welcome effective risk management. For instance, a survey of 314 professional money managers (68 per cent of them Chartered Financial Analysts) by Olsen and Troughton (2000: 26) found that:

> *Professional investors rated downside risk, as represented by the chance of incurring a large loss or failure to meet a target, as a dominant dimension of risk ... [They] rated uncertainty about the true distribution of possible future returns as a close second in importance. Variability of return, as measured by standard deviation or beta, received ratings of only slightly to moderately important. The chance of earning a large gain was considered to be unimportant.*

Thus effective management of firm risk has become as important to investors as to managers.

Further indication that shareholders expect effective risk management comes from studies that value firms' risk management programmes, particularly hedging. Hedging can build in a price 'premium' which has been calculated at around 5 per cent for foreign exchange hedging (Allayannis and Weston, 2001) and as high as 14 per cent for US airlines that hedge fuel costs (Carter et al, 2003). The general consensus is that the hedging premium can be significant; and risk management offers value to investors[1].

In summary, effective management of risk has many attractions. It increases the value of a firm, and meets an objective that shareholders cannot achieve themselves. Avoidance of badly chosen risks indicates stronger strategy development, reduces costs of failure and probably indicates good governance. It seems that good risk management brings fewer shocks to firm earnings and reduces expenses: thus lower risk translates into higher returns.

The Relationship between Risk and Return

The discussion above that reducing risk lifts returns is totally inconsistent with the standard assumption in many disciplines that return is directly linked to risk, whether or not the latter is considered to be uncertainty in earnings or an operational measure. This is a longstanding perspective, dating back at least 25 centuries to Herodotus as expressed in his quotation at the start of this chapter. Let us now examine the evidence that higher risk brings higher return, which is a corollary of the standard assumption of constant risk-adjusted returns across alternative strategies.

The first systematic study of firm-level risk and performance was conducted by Bowman (1980), with such striking results that they became known as the *Bowman Paradox*. His analysis found that more profitable companies had lower risk, as measured by variability in profits. This has been confirmed in subsequent studies, most particularly with consistent evidence that safe, incident-free operations are the most profitable

---

1   On the other hand, a number of studies have found no significant value impact from hedging (for example, Jin and Jorion, 2004; and Bartram, Brown and Fehle, 2004).

whether it be nuclear power plants (Osborn and Jackson, 1988) or airlines (Noronha and Singal, 2004).

Despite the common assumption of a positive return-risk link and any intuitions, empirical studies variously find that it is insignificant, significantly positive and significantly negative, and Scruggs (1998) provides an interesting table summarizing the disparate results.

One way that the positive, neutral and negative links between risk and return could be reconciled is if return has a concave relationship with risk. This is not a new idea and was proposed in an early edition of *Dictionary of Political Economy* (Higgs, 1926: volume III, page 224):

> *The classes of investments which on the average return most to the investor are neither the very safest of all nor the very riskiest, but the intermediate classes which do not appeal either to timidity or to the gambling instinct.*

More formally, Walls and Dyer (1996) and other authors have found a concave, ∩-shaped relationship between operational risk and return. The same concave relationship is evidenced by a number of datasets including Harvey (1995) who published data for more than 800 listed stocks in 20 countries; and historical returns and variance for different asset classes published by Bernstein (2000) and Georgiev, Gupta and Kunkel (2003).

This could arise is from the nature of the two variables' distributions. Consider, for example, evidence that many investors will pay too much (that is, more than the expected future cash flows discounted at an appropriate risk-adjusted rate) to acquire a security with the potential for very high returns. This is the classic 'longshot bias' in which risk-loving gamblers pay more for high-dividend runners, or longshots, than can be justified by their objective probability of winning. These gamblers value skew, or even the small chance of a large payout. The same is true of managers and investors who – as discussed in Chapter 3 – frequently adopt strategies that have only one chance in four of financial success. Investors who bid up the price of high-risk securities will reduce their return and establish a negative relationship between returns and higher levels of risk. In combination with the conventional assumption of a positive relationship with return at lower levels of risk, this leads to the concave return-risk link.

This refutation of the conventional finance assumption that return and risk have a positive, linear relationship is not, of course, the first time that relatively old scholarly contributions have been found to retain immediate currency.

Conclusion: So, Does Risk Impact Shareholder Value?

Material set out in this chapter is consistent with the behaviour of shareholders, including professional investors. They expect that firms will manage risks, not only to reduce unwanted outcomes but also the consequent adverse impact on value and – more proactively – to dial up the right level of strategic risk. Thus there are substantial theoretical benefits from sound risk management programmes and they are an important management responsibility.

The intuitive conclusion that risk impacts shareholder value implies that risk management can add value, and that its level or intensity can be determined using conventional decision analysis. Thus risk management becomes a strategic process in which risks are eliminated, managed or accepted according to their relative costs and benefits and with the objective of adding shareholder value.

Although intuition and evidence show that risk does impact shareholder value, the relationship is neither simple nor linear. In particular, evidence of a boomerang return-risk relationship has important implications for management of risks. It means that increasing risk beyond the point of maximum return is not rewarded and will progressively reduce the expected return. This indicates that a firm or portfolio with the highest expected return will have a median level of risk; any change is particularly unfavourable when incorporating a higher level of risk because the expected return falls as risk rises.

A second implication comes from the fact that a firm or portfolio has an optimum level of risk. Consider a firm whose risk is beyond that which delivers maximum return: if the firm's management reduces its risk level, investors will see both an increase in return and a reduction in risk. This confirms the intuitive belief that managing firm risk is of benefit to stakeholders, and makes implementing strategies that dial up the optimum level of risk an important management responsibility.

Moving beyond the nature of the return-risk relationship brings even more complex trade-offs. For example, Drucker (1967) argued that there were some risks that a firm cannot afford *not* to take; by implication, understanding a risk and being able to eliminate it does not mean that the firm should do so. Certainly it is naïve to believe the cliché that risk brings its own reward. But risks that are well judged and well implemented have long been seen to add significant value. Clarke and Varma (1999: 414) argue: 'If corporate managements could manage risks better, avoid catastrophes and achieve above-normal returns, a company's stock price would soar.'

This opens up a range of approaches to risk management: ignore risks; passively manage them using policies and formulaic approaches; actively manage risks to match strategy to risk type; and seek to use risk as a profit generator to add value. Thus risk management has become so important that it should be a core component of corporate strategy and the direct responsibility of a senior executive. We discuss risk management and the important role of a Chief Risk Officer (CRO) in the following chapters.

CHAPTER 6
Enterprise Risk Management

A cunning fellow is man ...
He has a way against everything,
And he faces nothing that is to come
Without contrivance.

Sophocles (441 BC), *Antigone*

Conventional management of risk is a reductionist process that makes loss prevention its core objective. According to Emmett J Vaughan (1997: 30) in his classic text *Risk Management*:

Risk management is a scientific approach to dealing with pure risks [i.e. situations which involve only the possibilities of either loss or no loss] by anticipating possible accidental losses and designing and implementing procedures that minimize the occurrence of loss or the financial impact of losses that do occur.

In keeping with this book's objectives of dialling up the right level of risk, this chapter will take a broader approach. It starts with an introduction to the principal risk management techniques and then concentrates principally on a holistic approach to managing risk, namely *Enterprise Risk Management* (ERM).

Conventional Management of Risk

Risk management is not a new concept, and – since a pioneering outline by Mehr and Hedges (1963) – there have been four conventional approaches: avoidance; transfer through insurance, sharing or hedging; retention of core risks through self-insurance; and reduction.

Risk avoidance involves the simple decision not to allow a particular risk to emerge. It involves refusing to accept any level of a particular exposure, and brings the opportunity cost of closing off strategic alternatives. Firms generally avoid risks that are not part of their strategic plan, not valued by shareholders, or not expected to provide return that compensates for the risk.

A variation is to minimize the amount of a particular risk. This is typical in investing where an individual may accept the benefit of a high-risk asset class such as hedge funds or emerging markets, but commit only a small portion of the portfolio, perhaps a few per cent.

However, when this is done by a business – say by running a dangerous process on a pilot scale – the rationale needs to be fully explored because the business is exposed to liability merely from its participation. If the process is highly risky, then failure will result in significant damage, even if it occurs on a small scale. Thus the qualitative risks associated with a full-scale plant are being accepted, but the benefits are not being achieved. A typical example of this middle ground is Australia's experimental nuclear reactor at Lucas Heights in New South Wales which is too small to provide the power generating benefits of fission, but retains most of the risks.

A second technique to reduce risks whilst retaining exposure to their benefits is to transfer part or all of them to a party that is more able or willing to accept the exposure. This can be achieved through sharing the risk as occurs with a joint venture, or contractually transferring future costs and exposures using insurance, or another financial instrument, or through an operating agreement, such as occurs with outsourcing. The intuition behind risk transfer is that there are advantages in correctly allocating a firm's business risks so they are managed by the party with the optimal competencies: thus correctly apportioning responsibility for risk means that its management is achieved at least cost.

Risk transfer and retention enable different parties to select risks where they have a comparative advantage. Thus firms will retain risks which are essential to their business model and vision, or where they have particular expertise. An oil production company, for instance, would not hedge away its exposure to oil prices; nor would a construction company hedge against cost overruns. The former risk is core to the firm's mission, whilst a construction company is best able to manage the potential costs from project overruns. Conversely an airline may not want exposure to oil prices, and many firms do not want exposure to financial markets; so they transfer these risks. Other parties may have superior information gathering capability in relation to particular risks and are able to use this to manage them more effectively. A good example is in cooperative marketing and purchasing arrangements, including cartels for commodities, where price risk can be optimally managed.

When risks are transferred, their nexus with returns is broken and parties to the transfer bear disproportionate shares of risk and return. Similarly broken is the nexus between the costs of an adverse risk outcome and the ability to control its occurrence. At the extreme a party can accept much of the risk even though it does not have control or receive appropriate return. Breaking the risk-return nexus can also change the behaviour of the originator of the risk and its acceptor; and bring complications to the parties' relationship that lead to less efficient risk management (Doherty, 2000).

Agency costs, or the *principal-agent problem*, are associated with the world's greatest invention – the joint stock company (Micklethwait and Wooldridge, 2003) – and arise because the principals (shareholders in the case of a firm) bear all the risks, whilst an agent manages them and may not always act in the best interests of the principals. In the context of the previous chapter, an agency problem arises when managers focus too much on the possibility of financial distress and investment failures which bring costs to them through loss of reputation and employment, and – increasingly these days – personal liability. Thus it is in the interest of managers to reduce income volatility and the probability of financial distress, because this augments the value of their position. This will not result in optimal risk propensity if, for example, managers forego more risky investments, especially those that have a highly attractive risk-adjusted return.

Moral hazard is a potential agency problem that arises when the owner or operator of an asset transfers its risk to another party and so has a lessened incentive (financially, if not morally and legally) to minimize risk exposures; inaction, complacency and carelessness may ensue. Moral hazard occurs after the risk is transferred, and involves opportunistic or selfish behaviour by the party controlling the risk. The severity of moral hazard is compounded when the party bearing the risk has no control over (perhaps not even any ability to observe) actions that may affect the risk.

The impacts of moral hazard can be sweeping. Sometimes it is passive by removing a barrier or penalty for risk. This is the effect of insurance because it transfers the cost of loss or damage away from the party who owns or operates the insured items to a party with no direct control over how they are used. On other occasions moral hazard can be more active and promote risk. For example, the ability of taxpayers to deduct interest expense from their income encourages them to borrow more than they otherwise would and hence take more financial risk.

Sometimes moral hazard operates perversely. Consider industry regulation. When it is weak, industry is left to self-regulate which generally does not work well. At the time of writing, China is regularly in the news because its regulatory framework has not kept pace with its manufacturing expansion and Chinese consumer products ranging from toys to pet food and toothpaste have been recalled in their tens of millions. Loose regulation encouraged firms to take risks so that China could be the world's fastest growing economy for decades. At the other extreme, overly strict regulation can induce complacency within the regulated bodies and make tightly regulated industries – ranging from banks to nuclear plants – relatively high-risk activities. Thus both weak and strong regulation can lead to excessive risk.

Adverse selection arises from information asymmetry about a return:risk trade-off, so that the party transferring the risk does not share all relevant information with the risk's recipient. This is sometimes known as the 'lemons problem' (Akerlof, 1970) and induces risk recipients to suspect that all the risks they are taking on are worse than average, on the assumption that they would not be transferred otherwise.

Tackling such conflicts in managers is an objective of many employee incentive schemes which are designed to optimize risk management by avoiding penalties associated with agency costs and adverse selection. Managing the risks from moral hazard must induce principals to behave responsibly; whilst managing risks from adverse selection requires lemons to be weeded out or differentially priced. We shall see later that these are major concerns for insurance companies.

Costs of avoiding risk and problems with their transfer mean that the most common technique used by firms to manage their risks is retention. Retained risks are of three types. The first includes risks that are unique to the firms' business model and valued by shareholders. Mining companies, for instance, will typically retain exposure to commodity prices.

The second type of risk forms part of a firm's operations – what might be called core risks – so that it is best placed to manage them. These range from operational risks in processes and plants to marketing and credit exposures, and are typically well recognized and subject to optimizing strategies. The third type of risk is retained casually by firms, with little analysis of their implications. These risks may not even be recognized, much less optimally managed, and so contain significant exposures.

Current thinking on managing business risk is strongest in encouraging tools that control known risks and is evidenced by James Bond who opined in *Goldfinger*: 'Once is happenstance. Twice co-incidence. Three times enemy action.' This wait-and-see approach is weak in identifying newly emerging risks, and in quantifying their probability and consequences. The reason why is obvious: new risks involve what *will* happen, and their management relies upon forecasting, prediction and modelling without data. As future events are unknowable and not amenable to scientific rigour, their nature, probability and consequences simply cannot be quantified.

Reduce Risk: Enterprise Risk Management

Reduction is the fourth approach to risk management and the subject of the balance of this chapter. The modern approach is holistic and entitled ERM, and takes a very broad approach by breaking down silos between operations, treasury, audit, insurance and so on and seeing 'risk' for a firm as anything that could adversely impact its assets or cash flows. It combines conventional risk reduction techniques such as loss prevention with natural hedging and the law of large numbers.

ERM is described by DeLoach (2000: xiii) as:

A structured and disciplined approach: it aligns strategy, processes, people, technology and knowledge with the purpose of evaluating and managing the uncertainties the enterprise faces as it creates value. 'Enterprise-wide' means an elimination of functional, departmental or cultural barriers. It means a truly holistic, integrated, forward-looking and process-oriented approach is taken to manage all key business risks and opportunities – not just financial ones – with the intent of maximising shareholder value for the enterprise as a whole.

Another definition by COSO (2004) is that:

Enterprise risk management is a process, effected by an entity's board of directors, management and other personnel, applied in strategy setting and across the enterprise, designed to identify potential events that may affect the entity, and manage risk to be within its risk appetite, to provide reasonable assurance regarding the achievement of entity objectives.

Whatever definition is used, the hallmarks of ERM are to see risk positively as a vehicle that can increase shareholder value; and to employ ERM to integrate the firm's overall risk profile.

Moving to ERM is demanding. Fragmented approaches need to be integrated, even though risks may remain independent of one another. Culture needs to change. Attention needs to shift to a new set of strategic, firm-level risks. Senior management needs to support and monitor the redefined risk environment because ERM – like quality and knowledge management – needs to be built into every significant managerial decision. The changes need to be communicated cogently to investors and other stakeholders.

The challenge of ERM is that 'risk' is generally uncertain, almost always in the future and often in dispute: it is easy to defer consideration. Addressing this challenge means that risk management needs to have the right motivation, perspective, goals and support. The right balance needs to be struck between prudent response to probable loss events and wild depictions of improbable, dire occurrences (it is no better to be a Cassandra than a Chicken Little[1]). ERM involves teasing out actual and potential causes of significant loss of shareholder value, particularly strategic risks and other exposures that cannot be covered by insurance.

Modern risk management understands which factors are critical to success, and which could trigger disaster. Not surprisingly the most useful elements of risk management are the most difficult, and the process will always be a black art. Best risk management ensures sufficient controls are in place to eliminate serious error. It strategically attacks risks by analyzing and prioritizing them from the top down so that proper balance is struck. It asks probing questions: what can go wrong? What would the costs and consequences be? How could we solve it?

Best practice companies clearly establish who is responsible for managing risks, and against what criteria. They maintain processes that independently audit business units, and report performance against key outcomes; have adequate skills and understanding of their systems and standards; and have codes of conduct which are observed and enforced. They have well trained and vigilant groups which promote active evaluations: not just tick-and-flick checks that test whether approvals and procedures have been followed, but post audits of key investments and other decisions, and peer reviews of business unit performance. These are conducted with sufficient maturity to ensure that good risk management is rewarded; and breaches and errors result in positive lessons for the future rather than a climate of fear.

This more sophisticated approach to risks – pro-actively managing, instead of ignoring, them – is like other forms of insurance and has a cost by imposing controls on existing operations and constraints on new ventures. However, control systems are only as good as the integrity, ethics, skills and authority of people, and the reliability of other resources involved. Short of exorbitant cost, even the best embedded controls provide only partial assurance against risk and failure. This type of consideration requires broadening of the return-risk trade-off to a triangular interaction between risk, return and the actual and opportunity costs of risk management systems and controls.

Striking the right balance is a key management responsibility. It is best conducted with discipline such as the following seven-step process:

1. Recognize the existence of risk.
2. Understand each risk's mechanism and its probability of occurrence.
3. Provide motivation to institute controls.
4. Establish a framework which sets a target for the ideal risk mix.
5. Develop tools for managing risks which are appropriate to their probability of occurrence and consequences.
6. Implement a risk management system.
7. Monitor results and regularly revisit the strategy.

Consider each step in turn.

---

1   Cassandra is a figure from Greek mythology who was able to foretell the future but – because of a curse by Apollo – nobody believed her predictions. Chicken Little comes from a fable of uncertain origins about a chicken of that name who is eating lunch one day under a tree when an acorn falls on her head and she rushes around telling everyone that the sky is falling.

STEP 1: RECOGNIZE RISKS

The key to developing a comprehensive, but meaningful, catalogue of risks is to first establish their framework. Listing risks without context weakens understanding of their causes and consequences and can be blind to potential control strategies. The framework seeks to understand the firm and covers industry, organization and processes. Analysts ask questions such as: what can happen? How? What is new or ill-understood? What risks are embedded? Recognition of risks enables their management to be assigned to individuals and products that are best placed to optimize the response.

As discussed earlier, risk recognition is an inherently difficult concept, especially when risk sources are buried in complex processes whose inter-relationships are hard to identify. It is obvious in finance, for example, where derivatives have earned the reputation of being risky, perhaps even evil. Thus auditors are all over Treasury transactions. But there can be just as many risks in mundane operations. For example the common business activity of closing a sale can involve: breaches of legislation relating to restriction of competition or consumer protection; financial loss from mis-pricing or poor credit; fraud; exposure to product liability suits, even if the product is misused; and so on. So before we spend time on strategies to control risks, it is worth identifying what they can look like.

It seems trite to observe that risks are most evident in hindsight. But this makes the point that it is easier to recognize the chain of occurrences that would precipitate an event, rather than extrapolating potential developments beforehand. Risky events can literally be invisible until they occur because they are imprecise, diffuse or hinge on precursors.

A useful strategy to take advantage of what is called the *hindsight effect* is to work backwards from a generic or hypothetical risk: how could we become subject to a law suit? What would trigger a product recall? The most effective approach to identifying potential new risks takes a plausible (not necessarily proven) risk and examines possible drivers. The choice of outcome is important as a major weakness of root cause analysis and other retrospective risk evaluations is they are blind not only to future risks but existing risks that have not emerged due to effective control systems including managers' expertise or serendipitous interventions. When risks are contained by controls, continued preventative mechanisms can appear redundant and lead to their relaxation or removal. My favourite example is to jokingly suggest taking traffic lights away from any intersection where there has not been an accident. This attitude is not so fanciful as it has been proposed as an explanation for the *Challenger* space shuttle disaster (see: Starbuck and Milliken, 1988): NASA took each successful shuttle launch as evidence that risks were lower than it had feared and so relaxed its controls. Similarly the absence of a major shipping accident in the Alaskan port of Valdez saw the relaxation of safety precautions and reduction of emergency response capability that ultimately contributed to the occurrence and severity of the *Exxon Valdez* oil spill (see Chapter 13).

Developing a comprehensive listing of possible risk outcomes requires thinking from different perspectives. The typical approach to determining potential risks is a checklist to facilitate brainstorming, such as Table 6.1 which broadly categorizes different risks using a top-down view.

Another perspective on risks is to divide them into specific categories according to type and location. One set is tangible because it is measurable or affects tangible assets. These risks arise from internal sources related to the company's operations, products, structure

Table 6.1   Taxonomy of firm risk

Firm-Level Strategic Focus	Financial Risk	Operational Risk
Investment	• Financial Markets: commodities, interest rates, exchange rates	• Consumer markets • Technology and processes
Organization structure	• Balance sheet	• Staff
Competition	• Price	• Market share • Product range
Assets	• Liquidity • Counterparties (credit and settlement)	• Property, plant and equipment • Security, safety (including third parties)
Employees	• Theft • Cost	• Availability • Training • Safety, industrial relations
Regulation	• Fines	• Contractual
Intellectual property (competencies)		• Data and knowledge • Processing systems (IT)
Stakeholders	• Shareholders	• Employees • Customers • Suppliers • Community

and management; and from external sources related to the economy, the marketplace's legal framework, and the state of the company's industry(ies). Other sources of loss are natural events ranging from storms to earthquakes; risks that are related to customers such as credit and market; operations that might involve accidents, product liability, fraud and malpractice; finance risks in markets and liquidity; and compliance risks. Fortunately tangible risks can generally be identified in advance by use of inspections, checklists and so on.

Another set of risks is less tangible and – although often identifiable – is far more diffuse and imprecise. These arise in intangible assets and include employee skills and competencies, customer and supplier contracts and relationships, brands and patents, intellectual property and knowledge, market reach and process knowledge. In short they comprise the fruits of successful strategic decisions and the proven ability to make good future decisions. In addition they reflect the huge synergies that modern firms gain from asset integration though linking regions and networks. A measure of the importance of intangible risks is that the market capitalization of companies in major equity markets is now several times the book value of their assets: this means that an average firm's intangible assets comprise as much as 75 per cent of its value (versus around 50 per cent in the 1980s).[2] Now that intangibles comprise a significant portion of shareholder value, managers must tackle previously irrelevant risks. A major source of loss is in intangible assets and process integrity.

Examples of tangible and intangible risks are shown in Table 6.2.

Firms must now consciously manage three sets of intangible risks they could previously ignore.

The first of these relates to organization. All but the smallest firms must choose a structure, typically built around products, customer types or regions. This maximizes productivity, but – by considering only organization objectives and norms – opens up a variety of risks. For instance, a strong head office requiring extensive reports and answers to myriad follow-up questions may be run by a handful of staff but require an army in branch offices. Moreover it can compartmentalize information and opportunities along lines that do not necessarily correspond to the integrated, regional framework that is expected by customers. Within the organization there is a set of human risks that relate to right person-right job, culture and ability. This is a function of recruiting the right competencies, training the right skills, and setting an environment where individual capability is maximized. Given that employee surveys typically elicit the response that employees are working below their capacity, there is great potential to add value by programmes that utilize everyone to the maximum.

Perhaps the most significant risk in organizations and operations involves culture. Huntington (1993), for instance, has argued that: 'The dominating source of conflict [in global politics] will be cultural.' He supports this by pointing out that civilizations and their cultures differ for fundamental, longstanding reasons; the interactions between cultures are growing as the world becomes smaller; globalization is weakening nationality and lifting consciousness of culture as a defining characteristic; and shared cultures are promoting regional blocs. If this is true, there will be a roll back of American (and perhaps Western) culture outside of North America and Europe, with huge risks in the markets and organizations of global firms.

A second aspect of culture relates to the mores, principles and heuristics of an organization. The litmus test is the simple question: when an employee faces a new problem or issue, what criteria will be used to resolve the way forward? Will they include self-interest or profit; safety or speed; quality or expedience? Is near enough good enough? Consistent responses to these questions lead to predictable firm behaviour that has led to the concept of firm reliability in the organizational behaviour literature. An organization with high reliability has internal processes, operations, culture and external relationships that establish a high probability of reliable, incident-free operations even when using the most complex and risky technologies (La Porte, 1996). These low-risk firms are characterized by clear objectives, appreciation of the risks and economic benefit

---

[2] An alternative view is that *people* now comprise a much larger proportion of a firm's value than its physical assets. However, the relevance of people turns on the nature of their knowledge. They are of little value *per se* if their knowledge is explicit and can be codified in customer lists, procedure guides and manuals, or can be bought in as the expertise of engineers, marketers and designers. People only add value if their knowledge is tacit and is unique to the individuals through their innate skill ('brilliance') or slow-to-accumulate expertise ('experience').

Table 6.2   Tangible and intangible risks

	Source	Risk exposure
Tangible	Natural events	• Assets and staff • Supply chain
	Political and social environment	• Legislation • Operations
	Customers	• Market • Credit
	Products	• Quality • Price • Demand
	Operations	• Accidents • Product liability • Fraud and malpractice
	Finance	• Revenues and costs • Liquidity
	Compliance	• Reputation • Diversity
Intangible	Structure Organization	• Risk propensity • Right person-right job
	Community	• Constraints • Cultural limits/rubbing points
	Technology	• Breakthrough, opportunity
	Competitors	• Breakthrough • Drive for change/lower cost
	Knowledge	• Strategy gaps, errors
	Skills and competencies	• Knowledge
	Strategy	• Insufficient information or analysis • Model mis-specification
	Reputation	• Innovation • Competitive strength

of their activities, very high technical competence, stringent quality assurance, rewards for identifying error and high levels of organizational slack.

The second set of intangible risks relates to strategy gaps, particularly from insufficient information and analysis. Environments with inadequate or rapidly changing knowledge are both high risk: the ability to manage within such settings is a function of knowledge that has already accumulated and continues to be collected. This makes information and intelligence gathering an important corporate competency.

However, information about the future is uncertain and itself a source of significant risk. A good example came in the early 1980s when demand in Japan rose for commodities – especially iron ore and coking coal – and the Japanese Steel Industry (JSI) reacted aggressively to avoid cost escalation by manipulating markets to promote overdevelopment. The Japanese Ministry of International Trade and Industry (MITI) produced forecasts of growth in future demand for steel in Japan that proved wildly inflated and supported development of massive overcapacity for production of raw materials, especially iron ore, coal and natural gas in Australia, Canada and South Africa. According to Koerner (1993): 'Contractual and purchasing strategies which were used [by JSI] to initiate mining developments in Queensland and western Canada appear to have resulted in destructive competition between firms, state governments and the two supplier nations.' So even while commodity demand in Japan and elsewhere boomed, prices collapsed.

Just as information is a risk, so, too, is the wrong analytical framework or model. An interesting example is offered by analyses of stock market behaviour based on data obtained from the US market. Although this provides a long-term database going back to the start of the nineteenth-century, it was a period during which the US market rose from zero share of the global equities market to around half today. This represents a considerable survivorship bias, which means that conclusions based on historical behaviour of the US market may not be generalizable, either to other markets or future periods. Dimson, Marsh and Staunton (2006) suggest that survivorship bias is so pervasive that the foundations of much finance theory may be based on unrepresentative empirical evidence and hence provide mis-specified models. Relying on the theory and projections of such models is risky.

Another indicator of the need to be open-minded at the early stage of risk assessment is provided by statistically significant links between markets and a variety of natural phenomena including phases of the moon, sunshine and weather, especially rain. Other surprising links have a human basis, including the Presidential stock market cycle and the barriers to market moves posed by memorable numbers such as Dow 10,000. Further statistically proven influences on markets are more difficult to explain including Friday the 13th and daylight saving, whilst the capability of the winner of the Super Bowl to predict the course of US stock prices seems clearly spurious (Maturi, 1993). The point, though, is that a risk exists if enough people believe in it!

This concern is not confined to finance as many non-financial risks boil down to uncertainty in the appropriate business model. Initiating a new activity brings in knowledge risk. Model risk is present whenever a decision relies upon an assumption about the future. Data risk occurs when reports from the media, market researchers, financial groups or other bodies are relied upon in decision making. The intangible risks of decision making and strategy development are important enough to warrant the extended discussion on decision risk in Chapter 4.

The third set of intangible risks relate to another party's unexpected breakthrough or hitherto hidden agenda. Corporate Pied Pipers can no longer make any product to any standard with confidence that someone will buy it. Markets are changing, not always because of need or with justification as changes can be agenda driven, subject to disruptive technologies, or follow malfeasance. Thus risks arise from: a new discovery which threatens markets, costs or revenues; the development of a complementary process; a legislative initiative; or the spillover of an event in another sector. One topical example is global warming that could have impacts far removed from consumers of fossil fuels.

An important, barely visible wave of risks comes from technology which can often remain ill-understood for lengthy periods and expose us to unknown or ignored perils. A good example is radiation where time has cut the safe exposure level by 95 per cent since it was first regulated in 1952. It is immaterial whether new technologies prove dangerous because of their sponsors' enthusiasm, lack of accountability or greed. Poor understanding or acknowledgement of their merits seem chronic. Technology also increases what is possible and creates its own demands which can be slow to emerge (for example, fax machines). Technology's risk is greatest when knowledge of it is restricted, and this can only be mitigated over time by the free flow of information. A significant complication in the management of technological risks is that few are ever fully developed as demonstrated by regular breakthroughs in even the most ancient of technologies. Good examples of old technologies being modernized include brewing and wine making, food manufacturers that now make space foods, and the regular smashing of sailing records.

Conversely the steady development of new technology has cuts risk through better communications, the ability to impose tighter controls and improved understanding of hazard drivers. Thus the total risk from technologies continues to fall. Technology also lowers costs, with excellent examples in the cost of a personal computer and an air fare from Australia to Europe, both of which have remained at about $A2,000 for decades, despite huge improvements in their quality and utility.

A consequence of modern economic and social realities is that organizations are forced to embrace change. Many which fail the test show telltale signs of growing risk. They might have a dominant chief executive with a short tenure who wants results at all costs. They may lack a robust culture which enforces management integrity and ethical values; or lack a good controls environment, reporting systems, and informal communications network which allows whistles to be blown without career damage.

Ambitious objectives and demand for the new reshape previously risk-free processes. For example, imposition of unreasonable objectives often triggers failures as evidenced by the increasing number of accounting frauds which are directed at improving reported results instead of the more traditional theft.

It is clear that every firm's most important intangible asset is its competency in risk management. However, it is worth stating that change has always been with us and today's shifts – in communications, finance and not much else – can be over-hyped by a media which reports it as uniquely new instead of yet another breaker in the near endless set of transforming waves that come each generation, or so.

STEP 2: UNDERSTAND RISK'S MECHANISMS AND PROBABILITY

Few significant events occur in isolation. Take the example of war (which has all the components of business risk and strategy writ large) and a seemingly isolated incident such as the shock sinking within a few hours in December 1941 of the British battle cruisers *Prince of Wales* and *Repulse*. They were found by a wandering formation of Japanese aircraft and became the first capital ships to be lost to air attack. One reading is that this was a one-off tragic event. Another comes from an interesting analysis by Middlebrook and Mahoney (1977: 79–81) who trace its roots back through decades of differences between the combatants in their training, armament selection, planning and choice of military strategy. Substantial research and investment enabled Japan to execute such an attack whilst Britain's tactics left its capital ships vulnerable. The attack was part of Japan's ambitious and well-shaped plans to capitalize on its attack on Pearl Harbor and within 150 days achieve a vast Greater East Asia Co-Prosperity Sphere stretching from the Russian border to Burma and New Guinea:

> *The scale and boldness of the proposed Japanese attacks can only be described as breathtaking ... But the Japanese, by daring and skill coupled with a savagery that their national code encouraged but which the rest of the world found loathsome, were to prove capable of achieving most of these aims.*

It is not easy to anticipate such a sweeping event (which Kuhn, 1970 would accept as a new paradigm), but it gives a good example to be heeded by managers seeking to understand the mechanisms and probability of abrupt catalytic changes. Most obviously they need broad questions. What is the range of possible outcomes? What would limit them?

With the focus of risk management on activities under the firm's control, it is not uncommon to overlook external dependencies and risks. Thus another broad-ranging question involves reliances, especially in complementary processes. Who, for instance, worries about their waste removers, public utilities or postal services; and the practices of firms which have taken on outsourced services such as cleaning and security? But each offers risks – not least to reputation – unless their operations meet desired standards of performance in relation to the environment, health and safety, customer service, ethics and so on. The solution is for firms to think in supply chain terms of the risks that might be embedded in the goods and services they purchase.

Apart from external service providers, many organizations effectively outsource some tasks that they keep in house. Information Technology (IT) or systems activities are typically consigned – figuratively, if not physically – to a remote area of the organization and not included in core strategic considerations. This is a serious error given the almost complete dependence of modern organizations on IT efficiency, and the frequency and serious consequences of failures of IT investments. Few managers dispute the common observation that it is rare for an IT project to come in on time, under budget and with the promised functionality. This makes it surprising that many firms are unwilling to force standard project management techniques on IT investments.

The opposite of a reliance is the assumption that no other party will see the same developments, nor pounce on the same opportunity. Of course, this happens all the time as fast food outlets seem to cluster like defenceless wagons, and consultants and financial advisers drive companies like sheep from one management must-have to another. At the heart of this risk is what Lovallo and Kahneman (2003) termed 'competitor neglect' in which firms underestimate the potential of competitors to disrupt markets and their business model.

An important feature of risks is the degree to which they are independent. Although financial risks are typically considered to be related, this can also be true of business risks. Consider a company that owns a fleet of vehicles that it leases to customers. At one extreme the frequency and severity of isolated vehicle accidents are independent of one another, and so the firm can calculate its exposure using statistical analyses. On the other hand, the way the company attracts and evaluates customers may introduce systematic biases; so may the choice of vehicle and the way the fleet is maintained. For instance, the risk profile of a company with a fleet of sports cars that advertises in lifestyle magazines is likely to differ fundamentally from that of a firm with mid-size domestic cars that advertises in local newspapers. Moral hazard and adverse selection can make random risks systematic.

Another good example of an external driver of risk can be seen in circadian rhythms, where accidents have a pronounced pattern of occurrence across the working day and week. For instance, the frequency of industrial accidents is twice as high between 4.30 pm and 6.30 am as it is during normal working hours (Folkard, Lombardi and Spencer, 2006); and CEO sudden deaths – which are most commonly due to heart attack or stroke – typically occur during the evening and early morning, and often at weekends (Boari et al., 2007). Managers need to take such factors into account in designing shift systems and staffing, and in establishing outside hours emergency response capabilities.

The probability and consequences of risks depend on mitigation practices. In the case of new processes, prudent over-projection of risk is appropriate to set a floor, rather than a ceiling or long-term estimate. The degree of over-projection of the risk of a new process should be proportional to the level of experience with sources of the risks.

Finally the nature and environment of risks are regularly changing, so that what is not a problem today can loom large tomorrow. Think of diseases and tyrants which come and go, along with transient crises such as the Millennium Bug. This can render judgements of risk time-varying. For example, in late 2000, a number of long-haul airlines came under fire for what the media called 'economy class syndrome' which is the occurrence of blood clots (Deep Vein Thromboses or DVTs) amongst passengers in cramped seating for long periods. The airlines pointed out that their in-flight magazines had long carried appropriate advice to stretch during flights; but consumer groups and legal firms sensing a class action demanded more. British Airways was the first to crack and began printing warnings on its tickets shortly after New Year. Where uncertainty holds sway, the range of risk is wide and perspective gives varied answers, so that risk evaluation reflects the views of the analyst!

Although this process of understanding risks can be easily described, the components are just as easily jumbled, and this inevitably yields an unsatisfying result. A good example is the Millennium Bug where a trillion US dollars was spent on avoiding a hazard (collapse of the world's computer systems when 2000 dawned) which had zero risk of occurrence, as proven by the absence of problems in countries, including much of Asia, which ignored the problem.

STEP 3: MOTIVATION TO CONTROL RISK

Risk management involves committing effort and resources now to avoid an uncertain future event. This can be hard to justify, and actions to tackle risks can lack motivation and urgency.

Any manager seeking motivation for active risk management need only read how US giant Proctor & Gamble (P&G) lost over half of the $US200 million principal on a 5 year interest rate swap during a few months in early 1994 (Myers, 1995). P&G had expected interest rates to fall or remain stable, whereas they rose rapidly. P&G sued the bank that brought it the complex derivative and argued that it did not understand how its value would shift as interest rates changed. But the analysis points out that the 'risk strategy' was in fact a huge gamble as the loss arose from a combination of 'zealous bank marketing and a dangerous willingness to believe that markets can be beaten'. P&G had lost sight of the reality that 'the culture of Wall Street has always been one of *caveat emptor* ... Unless there is a fiduciary relationship when you deal with an investment banking firm, the costs of ignorance are borne by the client'.

Significantly the P&G derivatives loss shares a feature common to many disasters: it occurred during a relatively routine operation within an apparently well-controlled area of an apparently well-managed company. Somehow, though, a huge corporate risk was taken on. Perhaps it was unwitting, especially without senior approval. More likely, though, overconfidence or gambling induced actions by a risk taker with little heed for the cost if their judgement proved faulty. Given the sequence of similar derivatives losses that unfolded during the 1990s, it seems that few firms had proper scrutiny and controls in place in this rapidly growing finance area. New, ill-understood derivatives proved irresistible.

The most obvious motivation to control risks is to reduce their financial impact: this, of course, involves a cost-benefit analysis, because – no matter how a risk is managed – there will be some cost involved. Intuition suggests that risk management inevitably reaches a point of diminishing returns, where the residual risk is so small that no effort is justified in further reduction. This can be illustrated as per Figure 6.1. The cost of reducing risks – the mitigation cost – typically has a diminishing payout so that it rises more rapidly as remnant risks decline; similarly the potential payout or cost following a risk – the exposure – will decline more slowly after lumpy high-cost risks are eliminated.

The net is that risk management can be optimized *financially* by reducing risks until the cost of further reduction exceeds the benefits, which means ignoring risks to the right of the 'optimum' proportion, and simply allowing them to run their course. Naturally this needs to be balanced by non-financial criteria. In particular – as we discuss in Chapter 10 on risk communication – there can be a strong reaction from stakeholders when firms knowingly run risks that are too expensive to mitigate. Injury or other damage can subject the firm to angry criticism and large damages awards from judges and juries.

STEP 4: ESTABLISH RISK APPETITE

This is what politicians mean when they demand of each other: `how much ticker do you have?' The answer is unique to each individual and organization and is affected by:

- physical constraints, particularly the nature of an organization (charity vs. hedge fund);
- legal issues such as acts, articles, constitution, financial covenants;
- what is acceptable in terms of type of quantum of risk;
- the balance between costs and exposures.

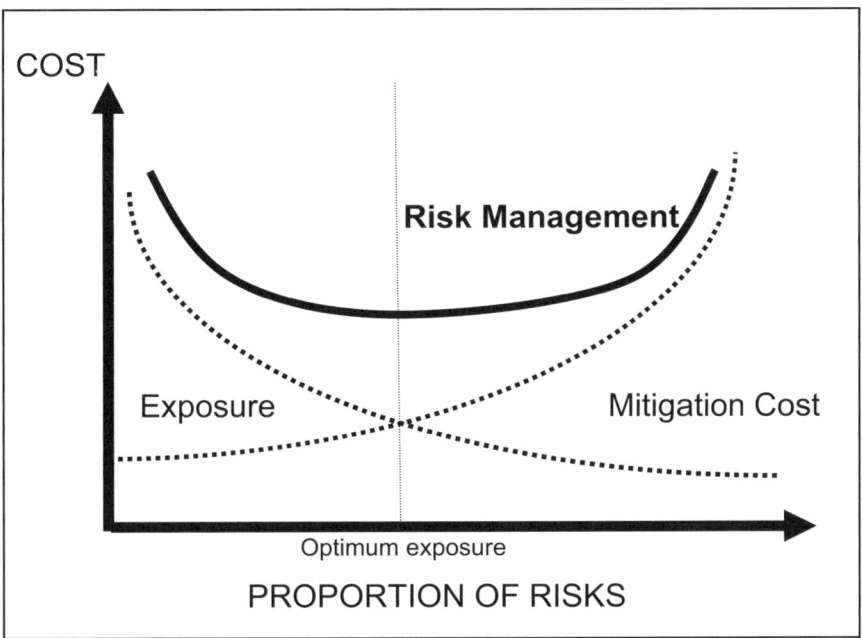

Figure 6.1   Financial optimization of risk management

The ultimate question underpinning strategic risk management is whether the return expected from the activity is appropriate given the risks involved. If the risk-adjusted return is too low, why should the risk be run? Jawaharlal Nehru highlighted the balance required when he used a speech to the Indian Parliament to admonish timid supporters: 'We are prepared to take risks, but intelligent risks. The policy of being too cautious is the greatest risk of all.'

In business, reducing risks benefits community, lenders, directors and management; whereas increasing well-judged risks often only benefits shareholders. Dialling up the right level of risk without disadvantaging other stakeholders is a key management responsibility. Establishing a firm's risk appetite is the strategy that dials up the optimum level of risk.

STEP 5: DEVELOP SYSTEMS FOR RISK CONTROL

A key objective of this book is to treat risk as a systematic topic, and set out techniques that manage it holistically. This is easier said than done as it requires *systems* for risk management, rather than processes or products. Moreover, the effectiveness of any system depends on the nature of a risk, especially the ability to control it, which is a complex function of industry and process, expertise and natural hedges.

The starting point is to recognize lessons from the big corporate disasters which can be boiled down into a few key elements:

- understand the business environment;
- bundle risks into self-controlling groups;
- establish 'no-go' zones and report breaches;

- watch moves in cash;
- report meaningful measures;
- send clear messages;
- reward desirable behaviours.

Steps such as these will help provide an environment where risk management is part of the culture. They also establish the concept of a risk chain (Young and Tippins, 2001) that sees risk analysis, evaluation and management as a series of intertwined steps, much along the lines of Figure 6.2 (that was suggested by Walker, 2001). The idea is to place systems for risk control within a wide-ranging framework that encompasses each of the organization's key aspects (social, operational, legal and so on) and then narrows the analysis to examine specific sites and events and identifies potential risks in terms of who or what can be impacted, and the type and quantum of exposure. This enables the analyst to determine the sources and contributors of loss; and hence calculate probabilities and impacts. Mitigation systems can be put in place; and finally, of course, outcomes can be post audited.

An important aspect of any risk management system is how an organization is structured and how its tasks are framed. We have already seen how risk is higher when procedural controls are light and when activities are framed as low risk with high

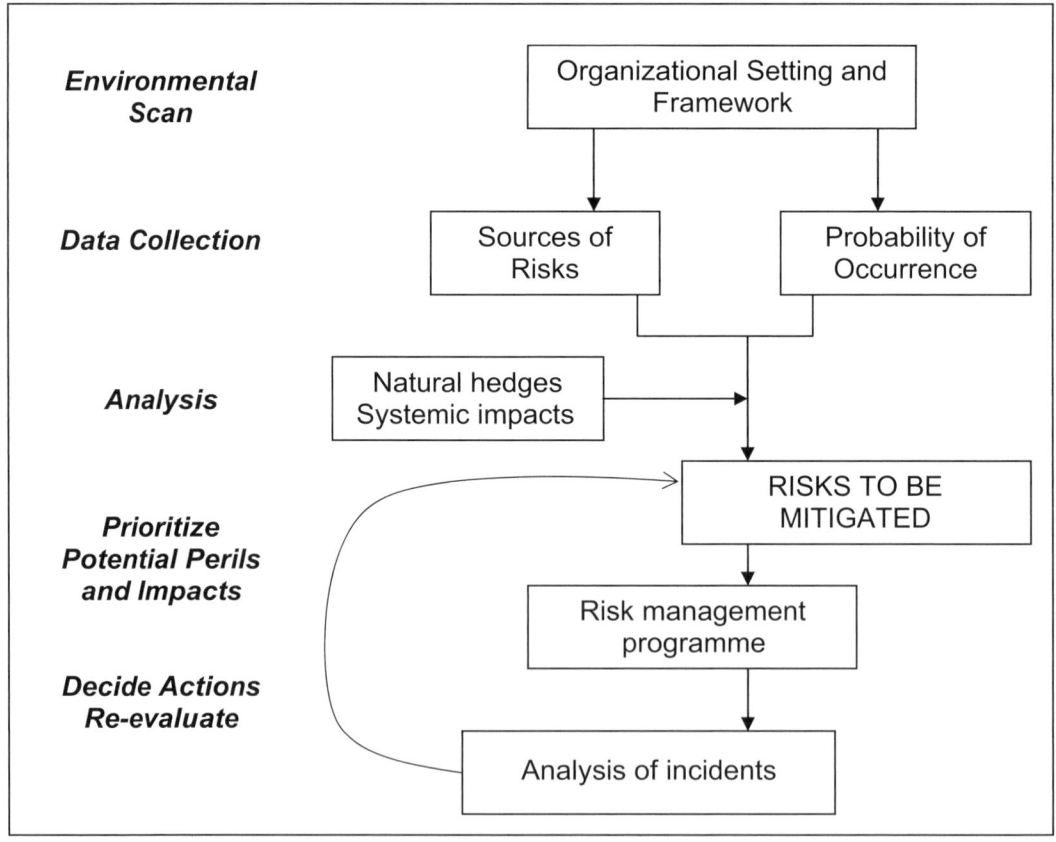

Figure 6.2 Integrated risk evaluation and management

expected returns. Risk is higher, too, when results are measured and managers are paid for performance. This makes it important to properly design the physical structure around high-risk activities and risk management processes, particularly: the resources, reporting and processes associated with the activities; and the extent of their integration.

A consistent contributor to risky environments is inadequate resourcing, oversight and controls. Moreover, when high-risk activities are isolated from moderating influences (including freedom of expression by whistleblowers) the environment can become complacent or even fatalistic about bad outcomes. NASA, for instance, is sometimes accused of treating as normal risks that would be unacceptable anywhere else. On the other hand, oversight is impractical when it becomes too close to its target operation. This has been shown repeatedly in large financial losses such as the collapse of Barings Bank where audit or back office groups were not kept independent of traders.

In terms of framing, consider a training department. Although the broad objectives may be similar for training of new recruits by an insurance company and security provider, the latter is inherently far more risky if it involves skills in self-defence and use of firearms. The objectives or tasking of the two training departments will differ significantly, shift their relative risk and demand quite different controls, monitoring and safety objectives.

Yet another trade-off in establishing a risk management system involves the choice between human-based and system-based controls. A common safety system on machinery is an interlock so that two inconsistent actions cannot be taken simultaneously. Thus a machine may be inoperable unless a safety guard is in place; and a process will be automatically terminated by a circuit breaker such as a 'dead man' control if it moves outside acceptable parameters.

Other automated risk controls can be completely passive. Security protection can be achieved through bars on windows, crash barriers, fencing and walls. Public facilities – such as sports grounds, office buildings and railway stations – are now designed so that the contours of the structure dissipate the shock from bomb blasts and minimize injury. In fact there is a whole new subdiscipline emerging of security-based architecture that seeks to make buildings more resistant to damage, and safer for occupants.

Other risk controls, though, rely solely on humans. A good example is medicine, where – despite dramatic increases in the cost and complexity of processes in recent decades – the principal strategy behind management of modern medical risks remains reliance on the centuries-old technique of human checks. The industry fails to fully utilize available risk management techniques – even such basic features as standardization – despite evidence that its labour intensive approach is so prone to failure (Lanham and Maxson-Cooper, 2003). Reliance on human checks constitutes an embedded source of high, chronic risk that represents a significant opportunity cost.

Conversely, building a culture of safety and risk awareness within staff can be a cost-effective way of identifying and eliminating risks. Similarly integrating occupational health and safety with industrial relations will reduce accidents and illness frequency.

STEP 6: IMPLEMENT A RISK MANAGEMENT SYSTEM

Implementation steps should be obvious. They cover the correct organization structure, the right balance between controls and costs, and adequate resourcing, especially training and reporting. It is clear that risk management must be systematic and the strategy must be continually revisited. This can be facilitated by a risk map such as shown in Figure 6.3 that plots out actions. For those that are potentially serious, a broad-capability response needs to be put in place to counter serious consequences for a large number of improbable events. For low probability events without serious consequences, the best response is to manage them as part of a broader ERM system.

In the case of high-probability events, there is justification for tailored response. Those that are serious should be eliminated, or – if that is not practicable – avoided. Frequent events with less serious consequences need to be addressed by process improvements that are inherent in ERM.

Risk management systems can be creative too, and an attractive strategy for many risks is to physically isolate them, particularly in the case of risks with large potential consequence. Thus it is common to see industrial plants concentrate together, or explosives factories sited in a remote location. An analogous strategy is to quarantine financial risks. This was employed by the companies involved in Australian lead mining and smelting – North Broken Hill Peko Limited and CRA Limited – which formed Pasminco Limited in mid-1988 as the entity to hold all their lead mining and smelting activities. Thus North and CRA shareholders effectively shed any financial liability for health and environmental problems associated with a century of profit taking from their extensive lead operations. A similar strategy has been followed by firms that sold their tobacco-related business. For example, in 1995 Kimberley Clark spun-off its subsidiary that supplied materials to cigarette manufacturers, and a year later American Brands (which had changed its name in 1970 from American Tobacco) spun-off its tobacco manufacturing business.

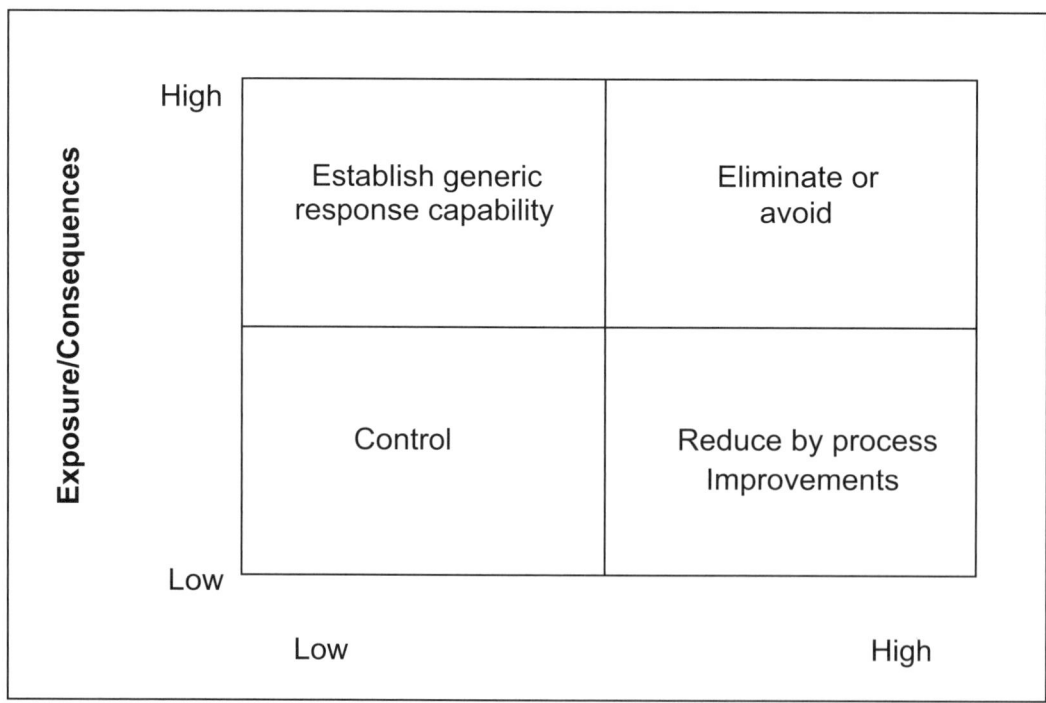

Figure 6.3   Risk map

STEP 7: CONTINUALLY REVISIT THE STRATEGY

As risks and their environments change and migrate, risk management is not static. An ongoing evaluation includes:

- Key Risk Indicators (KRIs);
- post audits of investments and other risky decisions;
- root cause analysis of incidents;
- zero-based re-evaluations of risk management.

AS/NZS 4360: 2004 Australian/New Zealand Standard Risk Management

Those looking for detail on ERM should refer to the Australian Standard AS 4360 which stands out as a beacon of lucidity in an increasingly cluttered and imprecise field; it is widely cited around the world as a practical guide to risk management. Its foreword is shown in Table 6.3.

AS 4360 is designed as 'a generic guide for managing risk … [that] may be applied to a wide variety of activities, decisions or operations'. Its foreword is set out in the accompanying box and provides an excellent summary of risk management. The Standard

Table 6.3 Foreword to the Australian standard on risk management

> Risk management involves managing to achieve an appropriate balance between realizing opportunities for gains while minimizing losses. It is an integral part of good management practice and an essential element of good corporate governance. It is an iterative process consisting of steps that, when undertaken in sequence, enable continuous improvement in decision making and facilitate continuous improvement in performance.
>
> Risk management involves establishing an appropriate infrastructure and culture and applying a logical and systematic method of establishing the context, identifying, analyzing, evaluating, treating, monitoring and communicating risks associated with any activity, function or process in a way that will enable organizations to minimize losses and maximize gains.
>
> To be most effective, risk management should become part of an organization's culture. It should be embedded into the organization's philosophy, practices and business processes rather than be viewed or practiced as a separate activity. When this is achieved, everyone in the organization becomes involved in the management of risk.
>
> Although the concept of risk is often interpreted in terms of hazards or negative impacts, this Standard is concerned with risk as exposure to the consequences of uncertainty, or potential deviations from what is planned or expected. The process described here applies to the management of both potential gains and potential losses.
>
> Organizations that manage risk effectively and efficiently are more likely to achieve their objectives and do so at lower overall cost.

is accompanied by a companion document HB 436 *Risk Management Guidelines* with details and advice on implementing a risk management strategy. They identify seven main elements in the risk management process.

The first is *Communicate and consult*. This process informs and engages stakeholders, establishes a consultative team and communications plan, and promotes ownership of the risk management strategy.

The second is *Establish the context*. This defines the environment around the risks, both external (industry, regulation, stakeholders and firm SWOT) and internal (culture, competencies and vision, mission, values). It sets boundaries to the risk management process, and defines the type of risks to be managed.

The third is *Identify risks*. This follows a structured process (checklists, brainstorming, data mining) to list risks that might happen, and their causes and loci.

The fourth element is *Analyze risks* which 'is about developing an understanding of the risk'. It involves assessing probability and consequences, and the relevance of existing controls. Analysis is both qualitative and quantitative, and makes use of scenarios and sensitivities.

The fifth is *Evaluate risks* which involves ranking risks for response.

The sixth element is *Treat risks*. This develops a range of options, which broadly divides risks into those to be retained and those to be reduced; then prepares treatment plans.

The last is *Monitor and review* which is an ongoing process that updates the risk management plan as circumstances change and experience is gained.

Special Case: Low-Probability Risks

A theme that runs through discussion in the past few chapters is that the occurrence of low-frequency events – such as major risk outcomes – can sometimes be impossible to predict. Thus even the most accurate forecast will lead to too many false positives, where risk managers are able to credibly identify many low-probability events, but know that most will not occur. Their consequent reluctance to be seen as overreacting results in a most undesirable response: action does not seem to be worth taking against recognizable risks, so that hindsight renders many disasters as 'predictable surprises'; and a major loss brings overreaction as barn doors are slammed tight (which is why armies and risk managers always appear to be training for the last war or disaster).

The concept of predictable surprises is dismissed in a lengthy discussion in Chapter 1, but it also seems that the approach of ERM – research, identify and eliminate risks – may not be appropriate for low-probability risks as it spreads resources thinly in anticipation of improbable occurrences. It may be preferable to adopt a different strategy by evaluating the *consequences*, rather than the causes, of low-probability risks and putting in place a coping, rather than control, mechanism. To some observers this may appear an admission of failure, and akin to old style end-of-pipe environmental controls which tackled unwanted by-products such as emissions rather than engineering clean processes. Just such an approach, though, has been adopted by banks to manage their operational risks: establish an equity buffer that is capable of securing deposits in the event of loss. Given that commercial banks are – arguably above all firms, save insurers – pre-eminent in the business of risk management, their unique strategy for managing business risks may hold lessons for other firms.

Shifting the objective in management of low-probability risks from pre-emption to effective response places a strong emphasis on strategies such as avoidance, monitoring of risk predictors, containment and crisis response. This style of risk management involves anticipating the generic consequences of a wide range of low-probability risks and putting in place appropriate responses, which are typically omitted from strategies built around ERM.

To see how the emphases differ, consider Y2K. In the late 1990s, a number of regulators seemed to have overreacted to this risk and required companies to develop excruciatingly detailed plans to cope with the possibility of extensive computer failures on 1 January 2000. Best practice firms met the regulators' requirements, but used this as an opportunity to develop generic responses to systemic computer failures. Similarly firms that are currently being urged to plan for an outbreak of Avian bird flu may be better off developing a response to widespread unavailability of staff, due to any one of many possible causes ranging from illness through disruption of the transport system to general urban unrest.

Conclusion

ERM represents contemporary best practice in matching firm risk to firm competences and expected returns. It is a holistic and structured process that brings substantial benefits. It offers solutions that fit firm risks.

CHAPTER 7
Financing Risk: Insurance and Asset-liability Management

Bear one-another's burdens.
                                  Saint Paul, *Letter to the Galatians,* Chapter 6, Verse 2

This chapter considers two risk management techniques, namely transfer through insurance and retention through asset-liability management. Importantly these strategies differ sharply from avoidance and reduction as neither impacts the probability of an unwanted event occurring; they merely allocate the financial loss involved.

Insurance[1]

Insurance is a contractual arrangement whereby an annuity in the form of a stream of regular premium payments secures indemnity against a much larger, uncertain loss under specified conditions. Insurance contracts enable financial markets to allocate risks to parties that are best able and/or most willing to accept them. The concept is an old one, originating with the Romans, and modern techniques date to the Fire of London in 1666. Today the global insurance industry collects around $US5 trillion each year in premiums.

The mechanism of insurance involves pooling exposures so that a group shares the costs of losses that are expected by members of the group. The size of the premium paid by each member is determined by an assessment of likely losses; and formation of a group ensures – through the law of large numbers – that premiums cover losses. Insurance does not change the probability or consequences of loss, but provides certainty about how the loss will be financed. The group has a predictable exposure to loss although individual members do not. Thus insurance is most effective with high-frequency events that are statistically independent and have stable probability distributions. The efficiency of the pool – in terms of certainty in its mean risk and hence adequacy of premiums to cover events – rises with the number of participants and independent risks covered by the pool.

The principal type of insurance purchased by firms protects against losses resulting from damage to assets, interruption to business operations, and legal liability to stakeholders and third parties. These are termed property insurance and liability insurance, and they

---
1   Considerable data on the US and global insurance industry is available from the Insurance Information Institute at www.iii.org/media/facts/statsbyissue/pcinscycle/. A good introduction to the insurance industry in Australia is provided in Australian Competition and Consumer Commission at www.accc.gov.au

can have specific purposes such as protection against fire, theft and workers compensation liabilities.

Conventional capital markets theory argues that insurance does not add value because the same result can be achieved by firms or shareholders through diversification (MacMinn, 1987). Similarly economic theory does not support insurance because of its negative expected return (Mayers and Smith, 1982). Conversely insurance is commonly purchased by even the largest companies, and appears to be an important aspect of risk management. Given that the average firm will have a negative expected return from insurance – particularly cover for property damage and liability – it can appear a puzzle why insurance exists.

The dilemma between evidence of widespread purchase of insurance and its theoretical negative impact on firm value is generally resolved by arguing that insurance protects cash flows that managers and shareholders cannot diversify. Thus insurance is a cost-effective strategy to avoid losses that could otherwise threaten bankruptcy, which explains why many firms carry large deductibles on their insurance policies and hence only pay for protection against losses that could result in financial distress. This is given a behavioural spin by arguing that managers who are loss averse overweight large losses and so are prepared to pay to avoid them, whereas insurers tend to be risk neutral. As Zeckhauser (1995: 161) writes: 'Risk aversion swamps informational content.' Even managers who are not affected by behavioural biases will insure losses when they have private information about limits on the firm's cash flows and are aware of specific risks (which gives rise to fears by insurers of adverse selection).

Another benefit of insurance flows to stakeholders who have a concentrated risk that cannot be diversified, such as the firm's managers and creditors. Insurance can also resolve the agency cost when risk-averse managers distort investments away from risky projects, irrespective of their risk-adjusted return. In this way insurance benefits shareholders by promoting prudent risk embrace.

More broadly, insurance can be an important element of corporate governance. When a firm purchases insurance, there is inevitable scrutiny of its exposures and risk management practices. This can lead to more accurate estimation of expected losses, introduction of more efficient risk management, and better understanding of the nature and consequences of underlying risks. When firms face constraints on time and expertise, external review of their risk management adds value, so this is a growing activity for insurance companies which help clients reduce expected losses.

Traditionally insurance has distinguished between two types of risk. The first is pure risk, which is one that has only the chance of loss. Thus the risk to a firm's assets from fire or storm only involves loss; there is no chance of benefit. Conversely speculative risk also has the possibility of gain, such as occurs with the market value of a building. Most insurance relates to pure risks.

Insurance also involves three important concepts that are shared with other areas of finance: moral hazard, adverse selection and agency problems. Moral hazard arises when insurance changes the behaviour of the insured party. A firm that buys insurance may, for instance, cut back on risk mitigation because such expenditures may only result in lower payout by the insurance company. Insurers seek to offset this by imposing covenants on policies (such as minimum operating standards, risk management programmes and use of safety equipment), and by including deductibles so policy holders share part of any loss. However, it is impractical to comprehensively specify and monitor all steps necessary, and thus eliminate moral hazard.

An indicator of the extent of moral hazard was proposed by Zeckhauser (1995: 158) who suggested that 'the number of people suffering a common fate ... [indicates] how much control they had over their fate'. A single house fire can be dismissed as carelessness or arson; but destruction of many residences – such as occurs in bushfires – points to a cause beyond individuals' control. As an aside, this affirms populist politicians who provide relief to people who suffer in a major disaster.

Adverse selection occurs when the insured pool contains a higher than expected proportion of bad risks. This is an inevitable bias given that bad risks will have a stronger incentive to take out insurance because they anticipate a higher expected payout (equal to: probability of loss multiplied by insured amount minus deductible and premiums) than good risks. This can be offset through obtaining full information from firms (such as prior loss history and risk mitigation efforts) in order to isolate bad risks using heuristics and scoring programmes. These bad risks are either excluded from the pool or pay higher premiums.

Agency problems arise when there is separation between the principal who is responsible for meeting the costs of a loss (that is, the insurer) and the agent who takes actions that contribute to, or can avoid, a loss (that is, the firm or its managers). These problems are most common with actions that do not affect the probability of a loss (which is largely a moral hazard) but alter the quantum of loss.

Consider the process involved in making payouts to meet third party liabilities following an insured event such as sale of defective product. Absent a court battle, payments are negotiated between the policy holder and perhaps many affected parties. Thus the existence of a liability is readily established, but determination of the payout is more problematic especially as the policyholder may prefer to make generous settlements when major customers or other important stakeholders are involved. The insurer can only offset this problem and control the quantum of loss by establishing a framework for evaluating payments, sometimes to the extent of participating in negotiations.

Agency problems may also be at the root of refusal by whole industries – for example cigarette manufacturers and carbon emitters such as coal companies – to cease practices that could result in catastrophic payouts. The cigarette companies are always free to terminate their operations, wind up the firm and dispose of assets with any residual returned to the shareholders. Or they can continue in business (retaining the jobs and prestige of their managers) and effectively gamble that losses will not occur, or will be covered by insurance. While this may suit the cigarette firms, neither case is positive for the insurer: termination of operations has a slight negative effect (no potential payout, but loss of premium); whilst continuation of operations has a large potential payout.

Oftimes these problems compound each other. Consider the owner of a petrochemical plant that incorporates processes that – despite its best efforts – are likely to result in infrequent spills of product. Because the spills are inherently uncontrollable, the firm may elect to insure the costs (which exposes the insurer to adverse selection). Once insurance is in place, moral hazard may increase the number and severity of spills. In addition there is a set of agency problems such as the choice the firm faces between thoroughly cleaning up all the damage that occurs following each spill (which will probably reduce operating income) or else deferring clean up and running a small risk of catastrophe (such as offsite migration of the product or groundwater contamination) that will be covered by insurance.

A challenging aspect of moral hazard, adverse selection and agency problems is that each arises from information asymmetry and is expensive to avoid because of the costs of obtaining relevant information and monitoring the policyholder's performance. Even in well-functioning insurance markets, they tend to raise the expected payout and – when these problems become large – insurers simply withdraw from the market.

Given that insurance relies on pooling and large numbers, insurable events have a number of core characteristics:

1. The number of insured entities must be large relative to the frequency of loss. This ensures that the law of large numbers applies to minimize uncertainty in costs borne by the pool. Moreover the expected losses need to be large enough to justify development of a market for coverage.
2. The frequency of expected loss must be quantifiable. Unless the details of loss events are known in advance, the exposure cannot be calculated.
3. The event must be clearly definable and its loss must be financially quantifiable, or else payouts cannot be readily established. Insurance involves a contract that must be able to fully detail risks or perils, the assets covered, and the place and timeframe of insured losses.
4. The loss needs to be uncertain, which means that the distribution of events is random and the pool must contain members who will not suffer loss. Thus events that are inevitable (such as wear and tear) or easily avoided are usually not insurable.
5. Individual losses must be independent, so that there is no concentration of exposures and only a small proportion of the pool is impacted at any one time. Concentration is avoided by diversification across geography, industry and risk types; and by the practice of reinsurance whereby insurance companies pool or sell their exposures to each other. Risk can also be spread across time so that in times of few claims the insurer builds up a reserve to meet spikes in payouts. Typically insurance is not available against non-diversifiable risks, which leads insurers to refuse some types of insurance such as flood and drought or war damage because all members of the pool could be simultaneously affected.
6. It must be possible for the pool to protect against adverse selection whereby a disproportionate number of firms with relatively high probability of loss seek cover, which results in transfer of wealth from low- or average-risk firms to high-risk firms. It is the role of underwriters to avoid taking on bad risks through accurate assessment of the probability of loss associated with each new insurance policy, and – if necessary – imposing additional costs, taking steps to reduce the exposure (for example, through loss-prevention programmes), or refusing to cover firms with a bad loss record.

Firms that decide to take out insurance have a number of important decisions to make, particularly: what risks will be insured? And which insurer will be used?

The decision on which risks to insure can be answered in terms of the character of the risk and the expected loss. Both need to be tested against the firm's risk appetite.

Firms will not insure risks that are a core part of their business. A building firm, for instance, may not buy insurance against cost overruns on construction projects as it has expertise in this area; similarly a manufacturer may not insure against process interruption or defaulting creditors because managing these risks are core competencies. However, both firms may insure against damage to property and plant, product liability suits and workers compensation. The test is whether or not shareholders buy stocks in the firm to secure exposure to the risk, or whether they expect the firm to be insured against such risks.

Firms may choose not to insure against small losses because the costs exceed the expected benefit (to promote loss avoidance, many insurance policies provide substantial reductions in the premium if a significant deductible – or the amount deducted from the loss to determine the payout – is accepted) or they are able to obtain some internal pooling of risk. Conversely they will insure against events which could result in loss that is high relative to the firm's financial capability, even if the event is of low probability.

The process of consciously not taking insurance on particular classes of losses is termed self-insurance. In practice most firms will self-insure core risks and small exposures, but purchase insurance to cover large exposures and risks where they do not have a competency.

In deciding on coverage, a firm should think of insurance as a technique to avoid the cost of a contingent claim, which links insurance, debt and equity. When a substantial loss occurs following an insured event, there is a hierarchy of payments: first the firm pays any deductible; then the insurance company pays to the limit of the coverage; shareholders pay any deficit up to the realizable value of net assets; and creditors pay up to the value of firm liabilities. If these payments are less than the damages caused by the insured event, affected parties including government meet the residual costs. The payments by insurers and affected parties are contingent: that is they only become liabilities when the damages arise. Shareholders and creditors, however, have already contributed capital which is at risk following a loss.

Firms with a large self-insurance programme may establish a captive insurance company, which is a controlled entity designed principally to provide insurance to its owner or a group of owners (including trade associations). This can provide cost-effective insurance because tax benefits are achieved by deducting premiums, but profit that would accrue to an external insurer is retained in-house.

The choice of insurance company involves judgements about the insurer's financial capability, claims processing record and the cost of the cover. Financial capability is most practically evaluated using ratings agencies such as those of Standard & Poor's.

The way that an insurance company pays claims against insurance policies can be important because anecdotal evidence is that unscrupulous insurers can routinely reject claims to avoid payments. Thus it is preferable to have an insurer which has a responsible attitude to claims and is reliable in providing ongoing cover.

Once an insurance liability is crystallized, a process termed loss adjusting is used to quantify the claim. Essentially this requires establishing that the loss is actually covered by the terms of the insurance contract (that is, the insured firm has an interest, and the damaged asset and the causes of damage are covered by the policy) and then quantifying the loss. Policyholders can simplify this process if they hold good records and can clearly document claims.

An example of loss adjustment that can be particularly complicated involves business interruption insurance. Here the insured amount is the net profit before tax that would have been earned if the insured event had not occurred plus costs that must still be met such as payroll. Claims are evaluated by compiling relevant historical accounts (profits, revenues and fixed payments), adjusting them for seasonal factors and changes in business mix, and assessing lost future profit and fixed costs.

Insurance Contracts

Insurance has unique provisions in relation to indemnity, insurable interest, actual loss and subrogation. Most are designed to ensure that the policyholder does not profit from an insurance claim.

Insurance indemnifies only against a specified loss and only for the actual loss incurred. Thus the policyholder must have an economic interest in the insured property: typically this means ownership, but it can extend to third parties through public liability and insurance of mortgages or receivables.

The interest in the property must be insurable so that the policyholder would suffer an actual financial loss if it is damaged or destroyed. This means, for instance, that items can only be insured for market value, and there is no payment for non-financial losses such as grief. This distinction, however, can become blurred. For instance, courts can award costs for pain and suffering or punitive damages to plaintiffs who are impacted by an insured event; whilst neither payment meets the test of financial loss, they are a financial cost to the insured firm and hence payable under its insurance policies.

In the event of damage to an insured asset, the payout is limited to the actual loss suffered, irrespective of the value of the insurance contract. For an asset that is destroyed, this will be the market or replacement value. In the case of business interruption insurance, the payout is the loss of income arising from damage to income-producing assets; and the payout from liability insurance is the amount that must be paid by the policyholder. If an insured firm has part of its loss met by another party, this amount will be deducted from the insurance company's payment.

Insurance contracts typically contain a coinsurance provision whereby the payout is reduced when the cover is less than the value of the asset. Thus if a policyholder purchases cover for only a portion of the asset (which can appear logical given that partial damage is more likely than complete loss and premiums are proportional to cover), then the amount of damages covered by any payout will be reduced in proportion to the amount by which the asset is underinsured.

Subrogation is a provision in insurance contracts that enables the insurer to collect damages from a negligent third party. For instance, if a policyholder's building burns down due to negligence by a neighbouring firm, the insurance company will payout the cost of the building and may then sue the neighbour for the damages.

Insurance contracts will also require full disclosure by the policyholder of any facts that may be relevant to the cover, and payout will be withheld in the event of material non-disclosure.

Costing Insurance

Pricing of insurance is an important consideration. Insurers recognize they face a competitive market and hence must establish a trade-off between the price they charge for cover and their attractiveness in terms of financial strength and claims processing.

Thus weaker firms may have to lower their premiums to attract customers; paradoxically this can accelerate their weakness if inflows from premiums do not match payouts (as demonstrated by the collapse of HIH Insurance in 2001). Similarly firms that cut premiums may impose more onerous selection criteria (to limit adverse selection) and/or establish harsh claims settlement processes to retard and reduce payouts.

Theoretically establishing a price for insurance is straightforward: identify expected payouts for each type of cover; add an appropriate loading for expenses and return, and possibly uncertainty; and establish a rate in terms of cost per unit of cover. The cost of insurance is its premium, which has two components: funds that are pooled to cover payouts following loss; and expenses to cover the insurer's costs.

The payout portion of the premium is related to the loss ratio or percentage of premiums that are expected to be paid out as losses. When a premium is collected, the loss ratio determines reserves which are set aside to cover payouts that are anticipated but not yet paid. The loss ratio is calculated by statistically evaluating the probability of payout in light of historical claims data (the number and cost of claims by all policyholders) and overlaying information specific to the policyholder (accident or claim history, nature of business, risk management programmes).

In practice, there are numerous complexities in establishing premiums.

First the premium needs to be adequate in light of payouts, but not so high that it makes the insurer less competitive. Moreover excessively low rates are as bad as those that are too high as income is inadequate to meet claims. Striking the right balance is difficult as the rate is based on *expected* losses and so premiums are set before the largest component of costs – claims to be paid out – are known.

A second requirement is to equitably share costs across participants in each insured pool, which offers different approaches. The premium can be set as a cost per unit (fixed premium per employee, customer or transaction) or as a proportion of value (such as wages or turnover) and these result in different premia for members of the pools. In addition, the premium should vary between classes of insured in light of their risk (examples include age, gender and location of the insured), but it can be hard to establish equitable boundaries.

The final difficult aspect of setting premia is to minimize moral hazard, agency problems and adverse selection. These may make it desirable to offer incentives such as bonuses to attract lower risks, but this shifts wealth between insured parties and may militate against effective pooling. The solution is creative use of deductibles, incentives and penalties.

More broadly costs of insurance can be impacted by a wide variety of factors such as expectations of policy holders, legislation and legal processes including court awards, insurance markets and risk factors such as changes to weather. With all these variables it is not surprising that annual premiums vary widely, ranging from a low of about 0.15 per cent of insured value for houses to as high as 5 per cent for motor vehicles.

Special Case: Catastrophe Insurance

Arguably most firms should only insure risks that they cannot manage themselves or which would produce losses that threaten their viability. Many of these very large losses are not related to core business, especially damage with systemic causes such as a storm or natural disaster, infrastructure failure or terrorist attack; others include very large payouts following some sort of internal disaster such as plant explosion or major product contamination. Almost by definition, then, firms have a critical reliance on their insurance company in the event of a disaster, which raises the issue of insurers' capability to meet very large payouts.

Catastrophes involve events with insurance payouts above $US10 billion, and the most expensive has been Hurricane Katrina which caused over $US80 billion in damages when it hit the New Orleans region in August 2005; the most costly man-made disaster was the 11 September 2001 terrorist attacks on the US which cost insurers about $US40 billion. Credible modelling suggests there are a variety of single events with payouts of around $US100 million, which is around one third of the equity capital of the insurance industry (Cummins, Doherty and Lo, 1999). Even larger payments would follow worst case cataclysms, such as a severe earthquake in Tokyo which could cost a trillion US dollars or more.

A lot of interest has focussed on the frequency and distribution of catastrophes. These events appear particularly well suited to sophisticated modelling as they can be clearly specified and have good historical data. However, most lie in the right tail of the probability distribution of a large set of much less damaging events. Thus their distribution is not always clear, and their frequency can take on the appearance of randomness.

In addition there is uncertainty about whether the frequency of catastrophes is constant. For instance, many reinsurers (which tend to have concentrated exposure to catastrophes) are intensively researching the issue of climate change given the intuition that warmer temperatures on the Earth's surface imply greater energy available to be absorbed by storms such as hurricanes which could bring more frequent severe events with greater potential damage. Similarly insurers will seek to understand if a sequence of events – such as several large earthquakes or tsunamis in one region – are merely coincidental or are related to some new driving force.

Beyond data, there are two concerns over the insurance industry's ability to meet the costs of a catastrophe. The first is that some policies may not be honoured, resulting in bankruptcy of the insurer and possibly of the insured firm(s). The second is that insolvencies inevitably lead to considerable disruption in all sectors of the insurance market, although this is usually moderated by price increases.

Although these severe, low-probability events are demonstrably important to firms, it is not practicable for the insurance industry to hold sufficient reserves to cover them, and this has brought research interest in techniques to manage catastrophe risk (see for example, Froot and Posner, 2000). Analyses reveal considerable uncertainty surrounding probabilities and costs. For example, premiums for catastrophic losses in the US since 1970 were several times higher than would be expected based on historical losses (Froot, 2001: 554). This suggests either a constraint on the supply side (that is, insurance firms have market power), or that the price of insurance is expected to be higher in the future (perhaps due to changes in cost structures or catastrophe frequency, adverse selection or uncertainties such as patterns of litigation).

Insurance as a Put Option

Insurance contracts are structured so that – in the event that a firm suffers an insured incident – the policy will make a payment equal to damages up to the insured amount less any deductible. Thus the net return from insurance equals the payout less the premium paid to insure the asset.

A moment's thought shows that an insurance policy is economically equivalent to a put option. Just as the holder of a put option on (say) a share can put the share to the option writer if the share price falls below the option's strike price, the holder of an insurance policy can put the insured asset to the insurer if damages pull its value below the insured amount.

The pay-off line for an insurance policy is shown in Figure 7.1, and is identical to that of a conventional put option.[2] Inclusion of a deductible makes the insurance policy out-of-the-money; and it is an American-style option because it can be exercised at any time before expiry (subject, of course, to occurrence of an insured event).

To illustrate the benefits of thinking about insurance as a put option, consider a firm that has Property, Plant and Equipment (PPE) with a replacement value of $US100 million and takes out property insurance for an annual premium of $US100,000 with a deductible of $US1 million. Assuming there is 0.07 per cent chance of total loss of the assets in any year (which is consistent with a premium of 0.10 per cent), the expected payout from the insurance company in any one year is 0.0007 multiplied by $US99 million, or $US69,300; after the premium, this gives an annual expected net return of – $US30,700.

Over (say) a 20 year asset life, the firm will pay insurance premia of $US2 million, even though there is less than one chance in 70 that it will claim for total loss of the assets during that time. Thus insurance seems a poor economic decision.

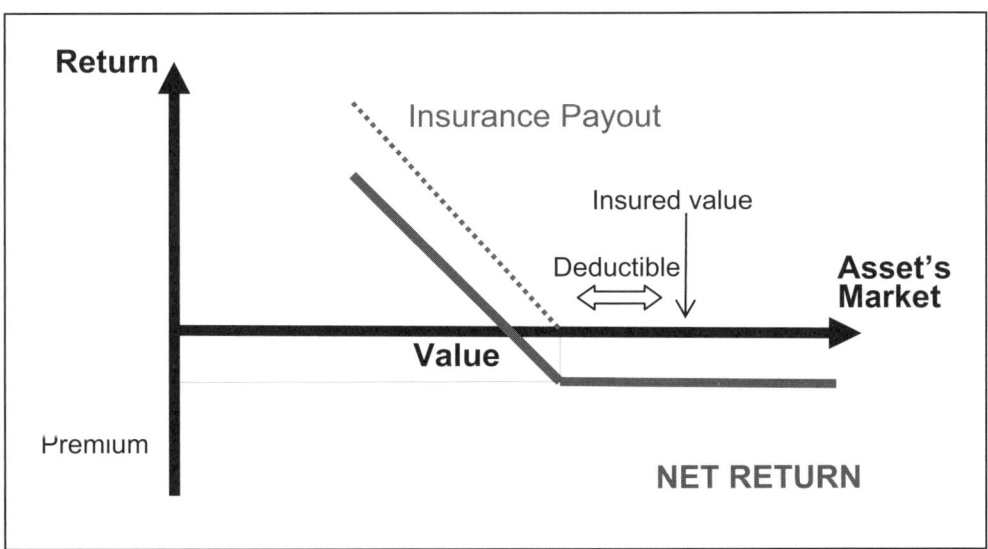

Figure 7.1 Pay-off line from insurance

---

2   A search through representative finance texts did not identify any treatment of insurance as a put option. Note, though, that some authors consider insurance as equivalent to a call option. According to Doherty (2000: 188): 'The payoff [from an insurance contract] ... is exactly the same structure as the payout on a call option.' This is based on a pay-off diagram with 'Size of Loss' along the horizontal axis, so that the payout slopes upwards to the right in the same style as a call option. In most treatments of options, though, the pay-off diagram plots the *market price* of the underlying asset along the horizontal axis as per Figure 7.1.

An alternative options view is that the annual insurance premium gives the firm the right to put its assets to the insurer for up to $US99 million in the event of an insured loss. This put option can be valued using the Black Scholes model which gives a minimum of about $US7.0 million. As calculated earlier, the expected payout from the insurance policy in any year is $US69,300; but when the insurance cover is viewed as purchase of a put option, its value to the firm is about 100 times higher. Although large, this is not surprising given that that the volatility or uncertainty in the possible loss (ranging from nil up to $US99 million) is so high.

What makes the expected cost of cover provided by the insurer so much lower than its value to the firm? Quite simply: pooling. When the insurer writes a portfolio of just 42 policies, the variance in expected payout drops so far that each policy has a value of about $US70,000. From the perspective of the insurance company, it has a pool of policies with low variance and minimal time value: the pool's value as an option is the same as its expected value. Thus the insurance company places no value on policies' optionality, whereas the firm taking out insurance sees it as providing considerable real option value.

Although this is a simple example, it confirms that – despite the negative expected return from insurance – treating it as a real option explains the attraction. Each firm is part of a pool of insured parties, and the expected cost to each party is uncertain even though the pool's payout is relatively certain (assuming the usual care to avoid concentration risk, agency problems, lemons and so on). Removing this uncertainty of individual outcomes has a value – analogous to the time value of an option – to policyholders, and hence makes insurance much more valuable than its expected negative payout.

Although insurance companies are effectively writing put options, providing the risks of individual policies are largely uncorrelated the volatility of the payout is minimal and the portfolio of 'options' have virtually zero time value. This explains why firms will pay more than the expected cost to eliminate non-diversifiable risks, and why insurance companies are so unwilling to cover systemic risks such as flood or terrorism which could involve many high-payout, correlated risks.

Insurance Company Operations

Insurance companies have seven principal activities.

The first is to market policies, which is the public face of insurers and generates the premium income that is essential to fund liabilities. The second function is underwriting which is equivalent to a credit check and involves judging which risks to accept so that applicants' risk matches that desired for the pool. The risk can be established using a range of acceptance criteria (such as requiring installation of a burglar alarm), or by using 'scores' to rank the magnitude of risks (such as by a plant inspection, or a medical exam).

The third function of insurance companies is rate making which involves analysis of actuarial data to establish the risk of the pool and set the premium to be charged. The fourth function is claims management where loss adjusters evaluate and settle claims. This typically involves legal judgements. Moreover it is often the only experience that policyholders have with the insurer and so most firms expend considerable effort to make this a positive experience, which boosts their credibility and strengthens their competitive position.

The fifth function is to manage the insurers' assets, which are usually financial in the form of cash and investments. Although policy premiums go to pay claims, they are paid annually in advance and so are held on average for at least 6 months. In accounting terms, these are a provision for expected claims and termed 'reserves'. Insurers have further assets in shareholders' equity and a surplus that is built up over time to protect against a concentration of claims. These returns are generally not built into calculation of premiums, and so investment can be critical to financial success of an insurer. Naturally they also provide security for policyholders and this can set up tensions where shareholders prefer maximum returns, whereas policyholders prefer maximum security.

The sixth function of insurance companies involves their back office operations, compliance programmes to meet the industry's extensive regulation and other administrative requirements. Their final function is a range of consulting services where the insurance company uses its skills to add value for customers and generate fee income. This can cover research, which is rapidly growing and can be quite extensive as evidenced by Swiss Re's *Sigma* series. Consulting can also include provision of risk management advice to reduce customer costs.

A particular type of firm is the re-insurance company which offers 'insurance for insurance companies'. This sector of the industry generates over $US100 billion per year in premiums and is dominated by a few global firms including Munich Re and Swiss Re.

Re-insurance is transparent to the insured party as it allows the insurer to accept, and then shift, the exposure. By allowing insurance companies to pass off some of their liability, reinsurance balances their exposures and taps the industry's global capacity, which is especially important following catastrophes. Reinsurance also provides an exit mechanism from insurance or a particular line of business.

Asset Liability Management

This section introduces Asset Liability Management (ALM) which has a long history in the archetypal risk machine of insurance companies. This is because the performances of asset and liability portfolios are linked for insurance companies, especially through reserves held to meet expected payouts and reliance on income from investments to meet long-tailed liabilities.

Although ALM has typically been the preserve of liability funders such as insurance companies and banks, it is just as applicable to corporate finance. It is an integrated financial strategy that recognizes interdependencies between components of a balance sheet from events and decisions that impact both assets and liabilities. It encompasses currency, equity and debt, assets and liabilities; and it incorporates an understanding of their quality, maturity and counterparty risks. The objective is not just value maximization, but to ensure the firm has adequate liquidity to meet its needs and that it optimizes financial risks. The strategy aims to provide robust risk management through the business cycle, in light of stakeholder expectations and competitor activities.

Many descriptions of ALM are imprecise, but the core concept involves identifying and closing mismatches or gaps between assets and liabilities. These mismatches can be absolute, such as an excess of liabilities over assets which indicates a funding or liquidity risk. Another mismatch is across time, where a firm has qualitative differences in the duration of its assets and liabilities so that liquidity gaps may emerge in the future. Mismatches can also be relative, so that assets and liabilities have different sensitivities to changes in market prices (commodities, interest rates, exchange rates, inflation) which allow gaps to emerge through the business cycle. ALM manages risks by matching firm liabilities, assets and income: value comes through linking contributors to risk on each side of the balance sheet.

ALM also incorporates off-balance sheet assets and liabilities such as joint ventures or leases, and can be extended to revenue streams. Recognizing mismatches with revenue streams is particularly important when they have embedded linkages either to the economy in inflation-based pricing or to financial markets, especially commodity prices.

ALM is a modelling-intensive technique and lends itself to developing projections under different scenarios of the impacts on target variables such as income, volatility of market-related revenues and expenses, and balance sheet values. A number of software developers have emerged, and there are numerous ALM models available.

ALM strategy can be static, and designed to match assets and liabilities through the cycle. An alternative dynamic approach adjusts strategy in response to changes in financial conditions and cash flows with the objective of optimizing return or value, and risk to them. Dynamic ALM might change spreads as the yield curve shifts, or alter revenues to secure a fixed rate of return. A typical value-driven strategy involves dynamically managing assets through the cycle so that liabilities can be funded, or *vice versa*. Thus the present value, duration and convexity of assets and liabilities will be matched (Shimpi, 2003). All of this makes ALM an integral component of corporate finance, and it usually sits in the Treasury function.

Integrating ALM into Corporate Finance

ALM can be viewed as an integrated financial strategy, linking assets, liabilities and off-balance sheet items to costs and revenues in light of the quality and nature of firm risks. The strategic objective is to minimize financial risks by closing asset-liability mismatches through the business cycle. In particular, ALM optimizes operating risks through ERM and optimizes strategic risks through governance; matches risks in capital structure to other firm risks; and uses risk management products including insurance to balance exposures.

This is completely consistent with the standard objectives of corporate finance which are to optimize deployment of capital resources so as to maximize value; provide capital to support firm exposures, and liquidity to support operations; and optimize risk and financing costs. It recognizes that a firm's operations and strategies determine its risks and these can be complemented by matching financial risks. ALM takes account of contingent capital provided through insurance and the residual level of firm risk after financial and operational risk management.

An advantage of ALM is to specifically link firm risk to corporate finance. Risk management is integral to corporate finance as it affects cash flow uncertainties and capital needs across time; and contributes (especially through insurance) to the level of available capital. A typical example of using ALM to minimize overall risks involves a company with high-commodity price exposure which might prefer to hedge other financial risks whilst minimizing fixed costs including debt.

Although the management of these risks can be embedded in business units (for example, credit may be a part of the marketing or distribution group), the overall exposures are recognized centrally and coordinated. Let us consider how a firm might utilize ALM to shape portfolio composition, liquidity, counterparties and asset funding.

The conventional assumption in corporate finance is that investment decisions should be made independently of the method of financing them. Thus an acquisition or new project should be evaluated in terms of the returns it delivers relative to the risks of that investment; and financing should be an independent firm-wide consideration. In practice most firms link the investment and financing decision to optimize risk: acquisitions, for instance, tend to rely more heavily on debt finance than do built investments.

An essential attribute for ALM to be used in risk management is that business risk can be linked to risk in financial markets. Consider, for instance, an investment in a cyclical sector such as power generation or transport where financial performance will be weakened by economic slowdown. If this project is financed by debt (which tends to rise in cost as the economy slows), then the firm can face compounding risks during periods of economic slowdown that will not be recognized by separating the investment and finance decisions.

A second consideration is that a firm which has minimal diversification may find it desirable to select new investments on the basis of their risk reduction capability, not just for their risk-adjusted returns. Consider a mining company that produces a single commodity such as gold or coal. It faces a range of potential growth opportunities, but may prefer to diversify its asset base through investment in a commodity where it has operational competences but which is not closely related to that of its core business; this might involve copper, rather than silver or platinum, for the gold miner; and uranium or bauxite for the coal miner.

A third link between risk management and corporate finance arises in capital structure, where – because of the relatively high costs of equity – managers prefer debt as a source of additional external finance. As lenders are generally risk averse, particularly to the possibility of bankruptcy, risk management can simultaneously reduce the risk to creditors and accommodate managers' aversion to use of equity for financing. Thus risk management increases the availability of loan capital. Although a firm with a strong balance sheet (that is, low gearing) and stable cash flows (that is, minimal cyclical exposure) can access borrowings when required, a firm with uncertain cash flows finds debt expensive, and needs an ALM strategy to minimize cash flow variations.

Under ALM, if a firm's assets are of inherently high or low risk, then its liabilities can be made less or more or so through debt, and so make the firm more robust to risks. Away from the balance sheet, a firm with large business risks such as R&D or mineral exploration might eliminate other risks to improve its overall stability. Similarly a conservative organization structure improves the firm's ability to withstand business risks.

The innovation here is to combine investment, financing and operating decisions, even though this is generally not advised in primers on investment evaluation. Firms adopting ALM for risk management integrate financial analysis across their balance sheet and allocate capital to projects in light of firm assets and liabilities, not just project-specific risks. Effectively they combine the principal techniques of risk management – which are incorporated in operations, capital structure and financial products – to establish firm-wide objectives and measures of risk.

Hedging

Hedging is a type of diversification that matches separate exposures so that their values move in opposite directions. One approach is financial hedging using contracts that protect against loss in value due to market movements. Typically a physical exposure (either an asset or liability) will be offset by a financial contract such as a forward or option: thus a long physical position can be perfectly hedged with a forward sale so that changes in the values of the two positions are identical, but opposite. Non-financial or natural hedging does not use financial contracts, but balances physical positions so that they net out any changes in value from market moves.

Apart from protecting shareholder value, hedging can be used to avoid an accounting loss, or translation risk. For instance international accounting standards mean that – if a firm has a wholly owned subsidiary in another country – its assets and liabilities must be translated at year end to the parent's currency. If the subsidiary is an integrated part of the parent's operations, then any variation in value due to changes in exchange rate is recognized as income; where the subsidiary is remote from the parent, the variation is offset in a foreign currency translation reserve which is part of the shareholders equity. In either case if the subsidiary is financed by equity (as opposed to local debt that would establish a hedge), there can be significant financial impacts from exchange rate changes. The parent may hedge this exposure, particularly to avoid triggering breaches of loan covenants such as minimum levels of net assets.

Firms have a variety of non-financial hedging techniques that enable them to achieve a low-risk outcome equivalent to that achieved by using financial hedges. These pay to lock in an outcome, or apply natural hedging and tailor strategy or operations to neutralize business risk.

An example of locking in the result of an otherwise risky outcome involves a company with environmentally damaging processes that outsources them to avoid exposures in vulnerable segments of its supply chain. Car manufacturers, for instance, often outsource seat production (which involves tanning) and spray painting. Other examples involve firms that locate their operations to avoid weather risks, which explains why theme parks congregate in population centres along the world's various Gold Coasts.

Natural hedging occurs when firms are able to match the market exposures of their assets and liabilities so that a change in price brings offsetting gains and losses. This effectively integrates operational and financial risk management by evaluating market exposures in light of assets, liabilities and expected revenue streams. A good example is a company that has assets that are economically (or effectively) denominated in foreign currency. This can arise because the assets are located offshore and cannot be relocated, or with assets that produce foreign currency revenues either because that is the international price basis of the goods sold (such as gold or oil revenues) or else the goods and services are sold in foreign currency. To offset currency risks, the company may finance the assets through foreign currency debt: this gives it a hedge against adverse currency moves because – as exchange rates change – the value of the debt moves opposite in direction to the value of the assets or the discounted present value of the company's expected income stream.

An example of this process is given by the international airline Qantas which is a highly geared firm with interest-bearing liabilities not much less than shareholders' equity. Although Qantas reports in Australian dollars (AUD), as approximately a third of its revenue is in currencies other than AUD, according to the Annual Report: 'Cross-currency swaps are used to convert long-term foreign currency borrowings to currencies in which the Qantas Group has forecast sufficient surplus net revenue to meet the principal and interest obligations under the swaps.' Qantas is effectively balancing the currencies of its debt with those of its revenues to reduce foreign exchange risk.

Another type of natural hedging is enjoyed by insurance companies and protects them against ruinous payouts following a major disaster. First they build up reserves over time from which they can make payouts. In addition the publicity following catastrophes combines with many firms' risk aversion to cause re-evaluation of the adequacy of existing insurance cover; this typically results in a surge in new or extended policies and often a tighter market that enables premiums to be lifted. Thus insurers have reserves to withstand payouts from catastrophes that bring new business and higher margins

There are two important considerations in natural hedging. The first is that it usually requires some change in the firm's operations or business strategy, which – of course – is not required when using insurance or other financial contracts. A second consideration is the potential for mis-specification of the mechanisms involved. Consider a firm that is seeking to maximize the use of natural hedges to minimize market exposures. These latter can include interest rates, exchange rates, commodity prices, margins and credit. Table 7.1 shows an example of the signs relating these parameters, assuming that they are principally influenced by economic growth that lifts demand and inflation which leads through to higher commodity prices and interest rates.

Thus a commodity producer can have the prices of its products set in global markets by the balance between growth-driven demand and more diffuse supply, with exchange rates and the costs of its debt responding to domestic economic growth. A domestic manufacturer will pay global prices for its raw materials; but costs, margins and interest rates are set domestically. Natural hedging can obviously be quite complex.

Over and above this, shocks can disrupt financial markets, and changes in prices can feed back into other markets. The classic example of this was the OPEC-driven

Table 7.1 Signs of relationships between economic indicators and finance risks

	Intermediate Impact	Financial Market Impact
Economic growth	+ Consumer/industry demand	+ Commodity prices
		+ Margins
		+ Credit
	+ Inflation	+ Interest rates
		- Exchange rate
	± Balance of trade	± Exchange rate

surges in oil prices in the 1970s that led to stagflation and global recession. On a smaller scale, the cyclical nature of economies means that economic growth can initially lead to higher margins, but then comes a slowdown and reduced demand and higher costs and bankruptcies. Thus firms that wish to reduce financial risks need to consolidate all exposures and then choose the appropriate strategy mix between allocating capital and so foregoing revenue, or paying for the finance solution. Even when the model is appropriately specified, natural hedging strategies will be unsuccessful if markets do not behave as expected.

Diversification

Diversification is achieved through portfolios of assets and liabilities on firm balance sheets that serve the same purpose as those incorporating investments, which is to enable risks to offset each other. The approach is analogous to natural hedging and has two rationales.

The first stems from the concave relationship between return and firm diversification, where returns are highest for firms with operations in several sectors, and lower for firms with few or many segments. Thus diversification becomes a value-adding strategy for firms with a limited range of industry segments or asset types, and those whose risks are correlated (or respond to systemic factors) or have adverse financial consequences that dwarf their revenue contribution (for example, with concentrated assets; or processes that have high cost, even if low frequency, risks). Such firms should think in portfolio terms of the variability of loss caused by inbuilt risks.

This leads to the second rationale for diversification which is as a strategy to reduce volatility in income. Diversification to reduce risk always benefits shareholders when reduction in non-systematic risk is rewarded, or when it can be achieved at a cost that shareholders cannot match. Thus firms should diversify when they can do so more cheaply than predicted by CAPM (which is the best that a shareholder can achieve) or when they can capture market inefficiencies (for example, mis-pricing of risk) that are not available to shareholders.

A good example of how diversification reduces risk comes from acquisitions that diversify shareholder income through economies of scale or scope: the firm generates similar returns for shareholders, but at lower risk. Thus Treynor and Black (1976: 311) suggested that 'managers may be interested in an acquisition because it will give their company more stability'.

Another perspective is to apply diversification to the portfolio of a firm's risks within a risk budget that limits its total risk. This can be quantified as in the Value at Risk (VAR) approach discussed in the following chapter. Alternatively it can be more qualitative so that high risks in one part of the business or balance sheet will be countered by low risk elsewhere. Thus mining companies with a high exposure to commodity prices will limit other financial exposures by adopting low gearing. Some firms achieve risk diversification through their operational strategies. For example, in a discussion of Hollywood's conservatism in relation to the Internet, *The Economist* (23 February 2008, page 75) reported a studio executive as saying: 'Every weekend, we sit on pins and needles watching to see if our films will flop and that doesn't encourage risk-taking in the business as a whole.' The motion picture industry is loathe to make big changes to

Financing Risk

its film distribution system and business model because of the large risk inherent in the rest of its operations.

Liquidity Risks

Liquidity risk is the probability that target gearing is exceeded, either by inadequate cash flow or cyclical factors. As this can lead to unwanted gearing levels or breach loan covenants, it is desirable to smooth cash flows so that excessive debt is not drawn down, and the typical solution is to use natural hedges to balance cash flows in and out. Thus firms will negotiate sales and purchase contracts to match the timing of receipts and payments. Similarly loans will be structured so they are scheduled for repayment at times of projected cash surplus. Dynamic ALM to manage liquidity risk through cycles in financial markets ensures that the present value, duration and convexity of assets are each higher than that of liabilities (Shimpi, 2003), which ensures a surplus of assets, even when yields change.

A more strategic liquidity risk relates to longer-term funding where investment returns are inadequate and capital is depleted. A useful way to think about funding risks is the concept of gamblers' ruin. Firms, like gamblers, face a series of decisions with the possibility of failure: ruin occurs when a run of failures exhausts available capital. The probability of ruin can be determined using the equation below (Geiss, 2006):

$$P_{ruin} = \frac{\left(\frac{1-p}{p}\right)^i - \left(\frac{1-p}{p}\right)^N}{1 - \left(\frac{1-p}{p}\right)^N}$$

where: P_{ruin} = probability of going broke; p = probability of success from each decision; i = initial capital expressed as multiples of the value of each decision; and N is target capital.

Obviously if p<0.5, the probability of ruin becomes certain. If p>0.5 and N→∞:

$$P_{ruin} = \left(\frac{1-p}{p}\right)^i$$

so the probability of continuing in operation indefinitely is equal to the value of:

$$1 - \left(\frac{1-p}{p}\right)^i$$

There are two implications of these equations. First, for a firm to survive the probability of success of each decision, p, must exceed 0.5. This might appear obvious, but the high failure rate of start-up firms suggests that few of their managers have a good understanding of the risks in their business model. The second implication relates to risks associated with the firm's corporate strategy, particularly its financing: the higher the value of initial capital, i, the more likely the firm is to continue indefinitely and/or reach a target size.

Thus: a) a firm cannot stay in business unless it can *guarantee* that the mean probability of financial success of its strategies is greater than 50 per cent; and b) even with good probability of success (for example, $p > 0.67$), the firm needs to have adequate capital ($i = 3.3$ for 90 per cent probability of survival). This, of course, is merely an empirical version of the epigram attributed to Leonardo da Vinci: 'He who wishes to be rich in a day will be hanged in a year.'

Conclusion

ALM in financial institutions deals with market-based assets and liabilities that have well-defined historical data that enable rigorous statistical techniques to match both sides of the balance sheet under a variety of scenarios.

ALM has found less use in non-financial corporations where data is not as comprehensive, and the objective – maximizing return from assets – differs from that of banks and insurance companies, which is to earn a spread between assets and liabilities. ALM, though, has strategic advantages by facilitating integration of risk management and financial strategy. For instance, a large firm may rely on its balance sheet strength and so not hedge or take out insurance. But it will have a very active programme to manage operational risks because of their potential impact on reputation (large firms can be held to a higher standard than smaller firms) and will also expend considerable effort on strategy development because of its strategic risks.

ALM should find application in non-financial firms, particularly as a framework for thinking about corporate finance: how assets and liabilities can be jointly managed to improve returns, optimize capital structure and reduce risk to shareholder value.

CHAPTER 8

Managing Risks in Financial Operations

> *Financial theory, properly applied, is critical to managing in an increasingly complex and risky business climate.*
>
> Merck CFO Judy Lewent (Nichols, 1994: 89)

This chapter is concerned with risks that arise within banks and within the financial operations of other organizations. The most significant risks involve credit and Treasury, but there are financial risks in audit and business systems, and they can loom large during due diligence and in project management. The finance function also incorporates many embedded risks and – although these are usually routine and thus amenable to management by processes and systems – some are lumpy and involve one-off transactions. As this last group of one-off transactions can be technically complex, they have been the source of major corporate disasters.

Bank Risk Management

Banks occupy a unique space in consumer perceptions, and – unlike most important companies – are black boxes to the average customer. This is despite the ubiquity of bank contact points, especially since the spread of electronics put an automatic teller machine on every blank wall. Moreover, bank services are essential to the daily life of individuals and companies, and to their longer-term goals such as home ownership and business expansion. In evaluating banks' risk management strategies, let us focus on business risks, with only limited attention to any risks that banks may take through trading in financial markets.

Bank operations are inherently unstable. The most obvious cause is that their liabilities (which are largely customer deposits) have a much shorter life than their assets (mostly loans). Depositors tend to be reluctant to lock their money away for long periods, and value the ability to withdraw it at short notice. This is in marked contrast to borrowers who want the security of a term loan, and the resulting imbalance is quite marked. In a typical bank, around 70–80 per cent of deposits and other liabilities are due to be repaid within 3 months, whereas almost the same proportion of loans and other assets are not due to be received for at least 3 months.

A second obvious source of risk is that banking's core commodity – money – is a powerful incentive towards deception and theft. Borrowers who need money are motivated not to disclose any weaknesses in their financial position. This information asymmetry – adverse selection or sometimes the 'lemons problem' because the information-poor party may unwittingly buy lemons (Akerlof, 1970) – means that banks run the risk of accepting poor credit risks. Money also contributes to more direct risks whether it is smash-and-grab raids on ATMs, credit card fraud or theft by employees.

Traditionally banks have concentrated on risks from outside that are related to markets and counterparties, particularly borrowers, and tended to be dismissive of endogenous risks agreeing with Oldfield and Santomero (1997: 12) that 'operating problems are small probability events for well-run organizations'. More recently, however, the Basel Committee on Banking Supervision (2001: 94) has become explicitly concerned about operational risk and began actively promoting appropriate management responses.

These bank-specific risks combine with generic business weaknesses to establish a range of banking risks that – for taxonomical convenience – are generally classified under six categories established by the United States Federal Reserve Board: credit, liquidity, markets, operations, reputation and legal compliance (Koch and MacDonald, 2006: 74–98).

Credit risk is the possibility that a borrower will not repay the interest and principal on its loan from the bank as agreed; it arises at the moment when a bank advances a loan and persists until the loan is repaid. Given that income from lending comprises most bank revenue, an important objective of management is to maximize interest income. A typical strategy might be to make loans that attract higher interest rates because there is greater credit risk attached to the security offered (such as the future earnings of a project rather than liquid assets) or to the borrower. The bank might then manage this risk by increasing credit scrutiny prior to loan approvals, monitoring loan performance and developing expertise to help borrowers work through difficulties. In any event, the acceptance of higher credit risk will be evidenced by a relatively higher level of interest income; it may also result in a worse loan loss experience as measured by the amount of loans written off as uncollectible. Forward indicators of expected credit risk include impaired loans where it seems unlikely that all amounts due (interest as well as principal) will be repaid; a rough measure of this is the proportion of loans where interest and/or principal repayments are overdue by more than 90 days (non-performing loans).

Liquidity risk is the possibility that a bank cannot meet its own funding obligations as they fall due, including repayment of deposits to lenders and provision of loans to new borrowers. This risk is minimized by holding liquid securities. However, these have lower yield; and so another strategic objective of management is to minimize the bank's holdings of cash and low-interest bearing securities. Banks that hold a lower level of liquid assets, particularly cash, are increasing their liquidity risk. This is countered by holding capital, which is the surplus of assets over liabilities and measures a bank's uncommitted financial resources which are implicitly available to cover unanticipated costs without impacting depositors (that is, banks' liabilities).

Market risk arises from the possibility of an adverse move in the price of securities (such as bonds, shares and foreign currency) that are held by the bank, either as assets or in a trading portfolio. It is a measure of the probability that bank assets can be monetized and used to repay depositors. Sensitivity to market risk indicates the bank's exposure to capital loss from moves in interest rates, exchange rates and security prices, which can become acute when the duration of assets is not matched to that of liabilities.

Another useful taxonomy of bank risk is the six categories that comprise the US Uniform Financial Institutions Rating system; it rejoices in the acronym CAMELS and refers to: **C**apital adequacy; **A**sset quality; **M**anagement quality; **E**arnings; **L**iquidity; and

Sensitivity to market risk (Koch and MacDonald, 2006: 92). These factors are analogous to measures discussed above, and quantify a bank's ability to meet its financial obligations, principally deposits from customers.

The final group of risks – operational, legal and reputational – are potentially the most serious as they can escalate into crises that threaten a bank's viability. Despite the importance of these risks, they are hard to quantify as there is no standard reporting mechanism, and data are further restricted because it is usually in the banks' interest to minimize knowledge of untoward incidents to prevent copycats or undermining of creditor confidence.

Operational risk is defined as 'the risk of loss resulting from inadequate or failed internal processes, people and systems, or from external events' (Basel Committee on Banking Supervision, 2001: 94). Legal risk includes the possibility that the bank will suffer loss due to failure to comply with industry regulation, because of a successful lawsuit by another party, or from unanticipated liabilities including contractual obligations. Reputational risks result from publicity that damages the bank's image and flows on to its relations with customers and other stakeholders, resulting in loss of income. In recent years the topic of banks' operational risk has attracted increasing attention and there are now a number of good analytical treatments available (see, for instance, Alexander, 2003).

The Basel Committee on Banking Supervision (or BCBS) (2002) has led the management of operational risk and established seven loss event categories: internal fraud; external fraud; employment practices and workplace safety; clients, products and business practices: damage to physical assets; business disruption and systems failures; and execution, delivery and process management. These are further broken up by eight business lines ranging from corporate finance to retail brokerage. Because of a dearth of data, the BCBS polled a range of banks on the incidence of these operational risks and Table 8.1 summarizes results.

The data cover losses from operational risks during 1998 to 2000 as reported by 63 banks for about 37,000 events involving a loss of more than USD/EUR10,000. An indication of the focus on this topic by the banks is that over half the respondents 'reported that their data were not comprehensive for any business line, or were unable to provide information about the degree of comprehensiveness'.

Most of the losses were either external fraud, largely in the retail area, or process failure in trading or retail banking. Although damage to physical assets was unusual (comprising less than 1 per cent of the loss events), it contributed 29 per cent of the value of losses. 'Operational risk losses' are not defined by BCBS, but they appear to include only direct costs, and ignore lost income. The significance of this is shown in 'Business disruption and systems failures' which comprise less than 1 per cent of losses by number and value, whereas anecdotal evidence suggests that design and operational failures of computer systems alone are major problems for banks.

This type of data can be used to highlight risk priorities as per the risk map shown in Figure 8.1. Based on this information, the largest unmanaged risks in banks arise in execution, delivery and process management; damage to physical assets; and external fraud. Although it is tempting to suggest that resources should be directed into these areas, it is also important to ensure that this does not relax efforts in areas that would become high risk without current operational controls.

Table 8.1 Incidence of operational risks

	Internal fraud	External fraud	Employment practices and workplace safety	Clients, products and business practices	Damage to physical assets	Business disruption and systems failures	Execution, delivery and process management
Corporate Finance	* 0.9	* *	* *	* 0.7	* *	* *	0.5 0.6
Trading & Sales	* 0.9	* 0.6	* 0.3	* 1.2	* 0.5	* *	10.3 8.1
Retail Banking	2.9 4.0	36.2 10.8	5.0 3.6	4.5 3.2	0.6 1.1	* *	11.6 5.6
Commercial Banking	* *	3.7 4.2	* *	0.6 2.1	* 16.2	* *	2.0 9.2
Payment & Settlement	* *	* *	* *	* *	* *	* *	2.9 1.4
Agency and Custody Services	* *	* *	* *	* *	* *	* *	2.4 2.0
Asset Management	* *	* *	* *	* 1.1	* *	* *	1.7 1.2
Retail Brokerage	* 1.0	* *	2.1 0.9	1.4 2.6	* 8.8	* *	4.1 1.5
TOTAL	3.5 7.6	43.9 16.1	8.0 5.5	7.1 10.9	0.9 29.0	1.0 0.7	35.4 29.5

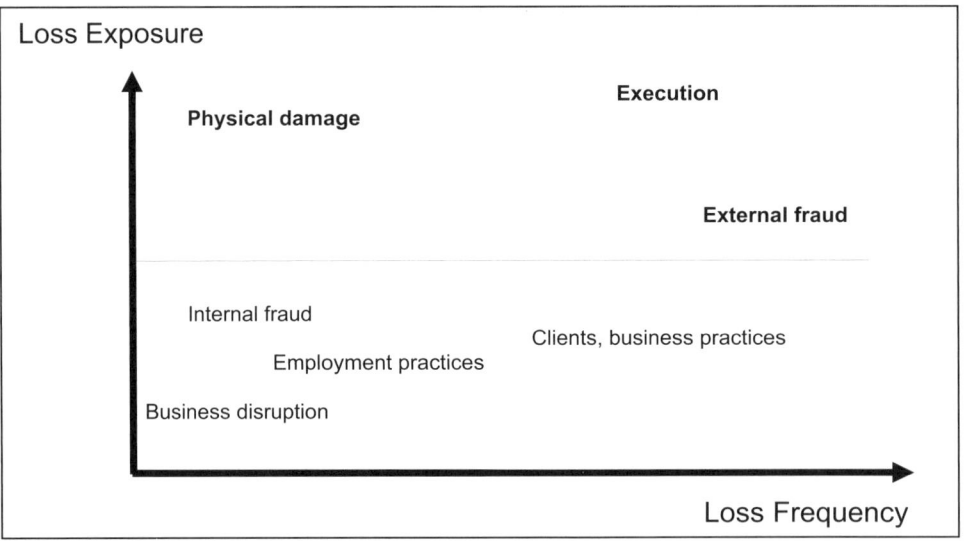

Figure 8.1   Banking risk map: Operational loss events by exposure and frequency

The distribution of bank loss events that were identified by the Basel Committee during 1998–2000 is shown in Table 8.2. Although care needs to be taken as the data are not complete, the banks' experience is highly variable. Half the banks had less than one

Table 8.2 Distribution of operational risks by number of banks and value of loss

Reported Loss Events	Banks – #	Value of Loss (EUR million)	Per cent of Events	Per cent of Total Loss
0–50	16	<0.1	89	14
51–200	13	0.1–0.5	8	11
201–500	6	0.5–1.0	1	5
501–1000	5	1.0–10	1	20
>1001	3	>10	0.2	51

event per week, although almost a fifth had one each day. Losses, not surprisingly, were very skewed: over half the value of all losses came from just 65 events (0.2 per cent of the total) that each cost more than EUR10 million.

Whatever the nature of banks' risks, the principal techniques to manage them are through changes to capital structure or investment strategies (that is, the composition of assets and liabilities), and by taking out some form of insurance, including hedging (naturally and through financial markets).

Banks are intensely aware of the risks they face and respond to expectations by stakeholders for prudent risk management. For instance, explicit discussion of risk takes up at least 10 per cent of the overview of business and financial results in banks' *Annual Reports*. They recognize the disparate nature of risks, which arise across business conditions, competitive forces, regulation, market moves, credit, operations and control systems. In a typical analysis, National Australia Bank (NAB) sees the need for a broad response:

> *Effective management of risk is a key capability for a successful financial services provider, and is fundamental to the Group's strategy. The Group's approach to risk management is based on an overriding principle that risk management capability must be embedded within the business' front-line teams to be effective. This overriding principle embodies the following concepts: all business decisions proactively consider risk; business managers use the risk management framework which assists in the appropriate balancing of both risk and reward components; all employees are responsible for risk management in their day-to-day activities; and risk management is a core competency area for all employees.*

The fact that NAB provides such a comprehensive report on its risks is arguably the response to a series of crises in recent years that have thrown into question its strategic capabilities (see Table 3.4). NAB probably recognizes that provision of information lowers the cost of equity and debt capital because, if it failed to display a comprehensive understanding of its risks, depositors and investors may overestimate the risks that are posed to their own funds and hence require a higher rate of return.

What factors could lead a bank to become so exposed to risk that it fails? As discussed in Chapter 3, firms develop their own unique risk profiles as an outcome of factors that are specific to recent performance, manager attributes, the firm's traits, and a range of exogenous factors. Up to about half of a firm's risk propensity is determined by relatively stable factors. Firm risk propensity is also shaped by more transient factors, especially recent performance and near-term outlook. It has been shown that historically poor performance promotes risk taking, and companies are more likely to take risks when facing a loss than when facing a gain. Gambles seem particularly common in desperation, even in the finance industry.

Competition has also been shown to increase risk, including that of banks. One study of the 140 largest banks in the US found that those with a stronger competitive position (more market power and a more valuable franchise) have lower risk (as reflected in lower interest rates on their deposits) (Keeley, 1990).

Despite banks' awareness of the risks that their depositors face, governments consider banks are incapable of implementing appropriate risk management systems and so heavily regulate the industry. Although it may not always so obvious *what* regulations should be imposed on banks, the variety and significance of their risks make it intuitively obvious that some regulation is necessary (Dow, 1996). Regulation expects some improper conduct by bank managers including fraud, anti-competitive behaviour and incomplete disclosure of information. It assumes markets will fail to monitor and discipline bank risks because incentives to mislead are strong, and few stakeholders have the information or capability to assess the risks of their bank. Regulation ensures the implementation of banking-specific rules of conduct and disclosure, and is generally designed to secure the financial safety of retail customers. It sets up tensions between banks and regulators, which evidence themselves in different perspectives on costs, disclosure requirements and permissible activities.

Counterparty Risk

Counterparty risk occurs in every non-cash transaction as the possibility that the buyer (who accepts a payment obligation) fails to pay in full and on time. It arises when the transaction is agreed and persists until it is settled. Outside financial markets, counterparty risk is typically termed 'credit risk', and is significant for many non-financial organizations and the greatest contributor to bank failures.

Most firms are generally little concerned at the risk of default by lenders and other creditors. An important exception, however, applies to suppliers of critical goods, or contractors on a complex or lengthy project. If the creditor collapses, it can cause considerable delay and disruption, so it is not uncommon to subject selected suppliers and contractors to credit checks.

However, no firm or lender enjoys the same certainty in relation to payments it has not yet received, and a major risk to firms is the possibility of default on payment obligations by counterparties.

Whilst most firms continuously encounter a small proportion of bad debts, this can rise significantly in the wake of an economic slowdown where declining sales push financially weak firms into distress. Although 1 per cent of rated companies fail in the average year, credit risk is highly cyclical and collapses are concentrated 2 or 3 years after a recession. Losses due to creditor default can also be high when the firm has concentrated exposures to cyclical industries such as agriculture or construction, which respectively can suffer a drought-induced slump or collapse of prices following localized over-building. Even when counterparties do not default, generous credit terms or delays in collections can significantly increase working capital and contribute to liquidity risks.

Motives to control credit exposures are clear: poor credit control is a major cause of firm collapse, particularly banks; and credit outstandings – which can be as high as 10 per cent of the firm's assets – add to working capital requirements without earning a return.

Minimizing credit risk requires limits on individual exposures and a portfolio perspective on total exposures. The typical strategy is to diversify credit exposures across sectors, particularly by geography, industry and type of creditor (as measured by stage in the business life cycle, customer mix, management ability and so on).

Another important strategy is to balance credit risk – the historical or expected probability of default – against return. This is generally a sophisticated process in banks where the trade-off is clear. In non-financial organizations, though, the trade-off is often less clear: even if risk can be readily quantified, return is a combination of margin and volume of sales relative to resources required, and can change over time.

In principle, strategies to manage counterparty risks are relatively straightforward: implement a rigorous approvals process using real time, not historical, data (for example, credit bureaux reports); seek adequate security, including bank guarantees, mortgages or pledged assets, prepayments and letters of credit; set credit limits at the lesser of capacity-to-pay and need; and always price credit so that there is a proper balance between the margin and volume of sales and the risk and cost of default.

Credit risk evaluation has become a highly sophisticated process, using a mix of qualitative and quantitative measures. It starts by developing a rating at the country level with stock market performance and interest rates; assesses currency risk in light of foreign reserves, foreign debt and the current account; and projects political stability and the impact of any special factors. Examples of the last include major events such as the Olympic Games and reliance on exports and imports that have cyclical prices. The next step is to evaluate the risk of each industry in light of its regulatory environment, growth, competitive aspects, capital intensity, cyclical position and volatility. An important aspect is the industry's default experience.

After rating the country and industries, firms can then be evaluated in light of key success factors such as management (costs, cash flow, success through cycles), cost structure (relative to competition and in light of scale and efficiency), financial flexibility, strength of brand and franchise, and use of technology. Quantitative evaluations will prefer cash flow measures to equity-based ratios.

Technology is rapidly simplifying credit management processes. Enterprise systems such as SAP integrate credit with order entry and accounting; and there are a variety of providers of credit evaluation and monitoring services. The latter enable appropriate due diligence on customers that can examine all risks including gearing, financial and operational risks; and – by quantifying the risks of each sale – systematically balance risk and return. Systems that report performance (particularly delays in repayments) in a timely fashion enable timely intervention (in the jargon, they help credit managers yell loudly!).

The key success factors in managing credit risk are avoiding concentration, sound approval processes, adequate security and real-time reporting against agreed limits. This points to three important management aspects of counterparty risk: establish standards for loan or credit risks; evaluate the magnitude of counterparty risk; and – when necessary – provide resources to work out counterparty default. The major difficulty in managing credit risk (and the usual contributor to corporate failure) is heavy exogenous influences, particularly the moral hazard that is induced by responding to competitors' approaches. Firms – including banks – that 'buy' market share by relaxing credit standards increase credit risk, possibly for the whole industry.

Treasury Operations

Treasury operations involve the initiation and execution of transactions that support a firm's funding activities. They include a number of related, high-risk activities, including some or all of the following:

- cash receipts and banking, or internal pooling of funds;
- borrowings and repayment;
- stock issues and buybacks;
- currency, interest rate and commodity price risk management;
- large, one-off payments, especially in foreign currencies.

Treasuries have been at the heart of many of the best-known banking and derivatives disasters, which involved non-routine transactions that were complex and/or unique. These features compound risks for two reasons. First the transactions are hard to understand, even for insiders and even many auditors, much less senior executives with approving authority. Those with responsibility for approving the transaction may not appreciate its uncertainties nor be able to monitor any losses that might emerge. Secondly uniqueness brings large fees for the arranger of the transactions, which can establish strong motivations for them to promote risks, especially those for which they are not accountable. It is not surprising that transactions which are difficult to evaluate and monitor are a source of loss.

Minimizing the possibility of unmanaged risks in Treasury operations involves a number of basic steps.

First routinize and automate as many transactions as possible. This is becoming ever easier with improved banking packages, links to enterprise systems such as SAP and increasing electronic interfaces between firms. Ideally transactions should flow seamlessly through initiation, approval and execution without the need for manual intervention.

Technology can automate marking-to-market, or calculating updated valuations of all financial instruments. This is easy for exchange traded securities because fair market prices can be obtained online. However, many complex financial transactions involve packages of securities whose prices depend on changes in spreads and prices that cannot be directly observed. This obviously raises the possibility of error in valuations, including manipulation. Prudent treasuries ensure independent revaluation of non-traded securities on a regular basis.

The third step is to establish an appropriate organization structure and compensation system. Ideally this will involve the appointment of a Treasury head who has a significant history with the firm which makes them a known quantity who has been conditioned to the firm's values; naturally the Treasurer will have sound finance qualifications and experience. It is unwise to compensate Treasury staff on the basis of profitability.

Next place limits on non-routine, manual transactions using clear policies and guidelines. Given that most risks can be managed cheaply and effectively with futures or simple over-the-counter products, management might question the wisdom of using anything other than vanilla financial securities.

Make sure that the organization exercises adequate scrutiny over unique, complex transactions. This is not just a matter of multiple approval signatories, nor approvals outside Treasury. It requires knowledgeable, independent review of each transaction including: its rationale; what exposures are involved; how current market value will be monitored; and circumstances under which the transaction terminates.

The final step is to regularly report Treasury performance and evaluate the integrity of controls. This, too, should be subject to independent review by specialist auditors.

Value at Risk and Risk Budgets

Value at Risk (VAR) is a statistical measure that indicates possible loss at a given confidence level due to market moves within a specified period. Thus a firm may calculate it has a 5 per cent probability that its portfolio of borrowings, commodities and foreign exchange could lose more than $US1 million in a day. Its VAR with a probability of 5 per cent and holding period of one day is $US1 million. The probability cut-off and the holding period are chosen to reflect the firm's risk management philosophy and the turnover of its portfolio (Linsmeier and Pearson, 2000).

VAR is calculated by identifying the components of the portfolio at risk, using historical data to value the portfolio over time, and then developing a distribution of portfolio values, particularly its standard deviation. The portfolio values can be derived day-by-day using actual market prices; or inputting historical data to a Monte Carlo simulation. The history of markets is that their returns are skewed with fat tails (that is, they have more very large moves – especially losses – than predicted by a normal distribution), and this needs to be built into any VAR calculation.

VAR suffers from two major shortcomings. The first is that it uses historical market moves and security correlations: if the future ever proves different, the modelling is irrelevant. This makes the period covered by historical data important lest it miss previous, especially short-lived, relationships from times of different monetary, economic or fiscal conditions.

The second shortcoming of VAR is that its simple nature tends to ignore extreme events. For instance, the 5 per cent cut-off used above means that the firm will experience a million dollar loss every few weeks. Conversely the time between extreme market events is measured in years. This can be partially overcome by using actual events to model losses. Firms may model changes in value of their portfolio that would have occurred around crashes of the US stock market on Black Thursday (24 October 1929) and Black Monday (19 October 1987), or savage bear markets such as that after March 2000 and November 2007. Other events might be oil shocks such as those in the 1970s when oil rose in a virtual straight line from $US2 per barrel in 1973 to $US40 in 1979. This approach – termed '*stress testing*' – gives a realistic picture of what could happen.

The useful aspects of VAR are its simplicity, and that it prices risk as a probability measure: the firm has a 5 per cent chance of losing $US1 million in a day. The latter leads to the concept of a '*risk budget*' where a firm can decide on its maximum VAR and then design an appropriate portfolio. The firm may decide that $US1 million is too much, and implement strategies to restructure its portfolio to reach a lower target level. Providing the modified portfolio is still efficient (in terms of meeting the firm's business and financial objectives, and with an appropriate balance between cost and risk), this is an effective way of managing market risks.

Conclusion

Since deregulation of global financial markets in the early 1990s, there has been an explosion in the range and value of financial products that can be used to manage risks. Many of these are over-the-counter instruments that offer large commissions, and tailored financial solutions: even risk-neutral finance managers can find them useful, although all but the most sophisticated managers will have difficulty in evaluating and monitoring the risks of these complex instruments. There are also risks embedded in day-to-day financial operations because they involve literally all of a firm's activities, particularly counterparty risks. Firms intent on managing enterprise risks should have a strong focus on risks within their financial operations.

CHAPTER 9

The New Function of Chief Risk Officer

If everything seems to be under control, you're just not going fast enough.
Mario Andretti, Formula One World Champion

It is only within the last decade that risk management has become institutionalized. Pressures to enhance its practices intensified in the second half of the 1990s under impetus of disasters that highlighted weak internal controls and lack of regulatory oversight. In 1995 alone, the failure of Barings Bank and closure of Daiwa Bank's US operations provided textbook examples of the consequences of poor risk management. That year the US Federal Reserve introduced its 'Supervision by Risk' framework which moved away from the transaction-based scrutiny of bank soundness and on to checks on how effectively specific risks were being managed. This spread quickly to other countries, and the UK introduced a *Risk Based Approach to Supervision of Banks* in 1998. With growing internationalization of the financial system, the Basel Committee began to more actively promote convergence of banking standards.

During the 1990s the concept of Enterprise Risk Management (ERM) – which is discussed in Chapter 6 – became popular as it blended the top-down approach from banking with an organization-wide perspective. The number of academic articles referring to ERM grew from virtually nil in the mid 1990s to 30, or more in the last few years (Liebenberg and Hoyt, 2003). ERM also fed growing stakeholder expectations for better risk management, typified by the *Turnbull Report* prepared in 1999 by the Institute of Chartered Accountants in England and Wales.

In the late 1990s, stock exchanges in New York and most developed economies became more attuned to the need for enhanced risk management and required listed companies to report their preparedness for Y2K and the steps they had taken to reduce exposure to the Millennium Bug. This was the first time many executives had looked across their companies at a strategic risk, and they were further sensitized to the implications for corporate-wide risk management by the failures of Enron and WorldCom. These developments and others showed Boards a better way to manage risks than just through low-level insurance, audit and occupational health and safety groups. Thus many Boards acted even before the *Sarbanes-Oxley Act* of 2002 whose section 404 requires company Annual Reports 'to contain: (i) a statement of management's responsibility for establishing and maintaining an adequate internal control structure and procedures for financial reporting; and (ii) management's assessment, as of the end of the company's most recent fiscal year, of the effectiveness of the company's internal control structure and procedures for financial reporting'. The US trend soon spread, so that numerous regulators and stock exchanges now set and monitor standards for risk management programmes.

These initiatives not only prompted changes to corporate governance, but also ushered in a more onerous regulatory and reporting framework. The concept of *compliance risk* emerged as a major concern for firms, and many responded by centralizing their risk-related programs. Thus was born the position of Chief Risk Officer (CRO), whose role is relatively simple: provide leadership for ERM, ensure compliance and coordinate risk reporting. The position of CRO was first established in the early 1990s, with Industry folk lore attributing the term to James Lam who was appointed by GE Capital in 1993 to manage credit, market and liquidity risks and put 'Chief Risk Officer' on his business cards (Economist Intelligence Unit, 2005a). Not surprisingly numbers began to explode around 2000. The role has proven most successful in heavily regulated industries such as banking and energy where regulatory risks – losses sourced in existing or prospective regulation – are becoming more significant.

Cynics sometimes suggest that firms are appointing CROs merely to demonstrate they are serious about risk management. Duke Energy, for instance, appointed its CFO as the firm's first CRO in mid-2000 with considerable fanfare and said in a press release:

Duke Energy has named Richard J. Osborne its first chief risk officer (CRO), reflecting the increasing strategic importance of risk management in the rapidly changing energy marketplace. In announcing creation of the position, Duke Energy Chairman, President and Chief Executive Officer Richard B. Priory noted that the company's rapid growth and globalization make effective risk management critical … 'Over the past several years, we have worked hard to build our risk management acumen, discipline and skills, and we have successfully elevated corporate risk management to a source of competitive advantage.'

As discussed in Chapter 13, Enron also made a high-profile CRO appointment and this has since been seen as just a smokescreen, rather than a useful signal of management intent. Enron was probably the archetypal example of a firm that uses appointment of a CRO to signal its commitment to protect stakeholder interests. Its CRO reported directly to the Chief Executive and was theoretically charged with systematic oversight of all Enron's risks and independently monitoring exposures. According to Arthur Andersen partner James DeLoach (2000: 16) who wrote a popular introduction to ERM: '[Enron's] ERM approach represents the state of the art for non-financial organizations.' In reality, of course, there was no integrity to the CRO position at Enron and that firm's risk management processes were a sham deliberately designed to lull analysts.

More positively, considered appointment of a credentialed and empowered CRO can signal the commitment of Boards to effective risk management and its elevation to a strategic level. This is because the CRO is a senior executive and becomes part of the firm's leadership. Consistent with the signalling benefits of a CRO is evidence that firms with higher gearing are more likely to appoint a CRO than equivalent firms with less debt (Liebenberg and Hoyt, 2003). More leveraged firms have relatively higher default risk and earnings volatility, and the CRO may give comfort to creditors.

Important to the CRO role is ensuring it is adequately supported by a team of risk specialists, augmented as necessary by consultants. An active CRO inevitably rolls out an ERM programme, with all its implications for training, data collection, strategy studies and performance evaluation in a brand new area. Good CROs follow Anton Chekhov (1978) and act as if 'the whole organization is their orchard'. And they expand risk management into new areas, incorporate more sophistication into its analysis and add value.

Once a CRO is appointed, an important goal is to manage *regulatory risk*. According to a survey of senior executives by Economist Intelligence Unit (2005a: 8): 'Regulatory compliance emerges as the overriding focus for risk managers today, and will remain the top priority'. A companion study asks rhetorically: 'How did regulation, much of which is designed to reduce business risks, become a source of risk in its own right?' (Economist Intelligence Unit 2005b: 2). The answer is that chronic market failures and the rising incidence of corporate crises have forced legislators and market regulators to respond by imposing more onerous reporting requirements and explicit risk management frameworks. This has come formally through Basel II requirements, the *Sarbanes Oxley Act*, International Financial Reporting Standards and stock exchange guidelines; and less formally through best practice statements by associations representing auditors, directors and investors. Firms now face the paradox of growing risk from regulations that have been designed to reduce risk! Best practice Boards will be aware that much of the potential of an effective CRO is lost by a focus on compliance to the exclusion of strategy.

Even if a CRO is not appointed, most firms would benefit from a centralized role where a compliance manager monitors regulatory requirements and compiles standardized data on risk to meet multiple needs. This is obviously a subset of the tasks of a CRO, as it does not incorporate strategic objectives, nor add any value.

Let us now consider the nature of CROs and their role.

Objectives of a Chief Risk Officer

A key question is how the role of the CRO differs from the risk management responsibilities of the Board. The working assumption here is that the CRO will establish a sophisticated approach to the firm's risk management, and to monitor and report its progress.

The first objective is to provide leadership for ERM. This involves a number of activities, starting with establishing an ERM programme as discussed in Chapter 6.

The next step is to formally integrate all risk management functions, staff and responsibilities across the company within the CRO's group. Unless risk management activities are fully integrated, the benefits of establishing an ERM programme and the CRO role will not be achieved. Bringing all risk activities together enables the CRO to develop policies across the full set of firm risks. This will involve authorities (such as approval limits on transactions and sign-offs on risky decisions), procedure guides (minimum safety standards and training requirements), reporting (positions at risk and incidents or near misses) and inspection frameworks. A centralized group also has the scale to develop and implement tailored training in risk management processes for all staff. This will differ according to function and responsibility, and may incorporate a tiered approach where some staff are made experts in risk, much along the lines of black belts in Six Sigma.

The second objective of a CRO is to coordinate internal and external risk reporting. This is a core CRO function and requires firm-level indicators of outcomes such as milestones for programme implementation, and performance against Key Risk Indicators (KRIs). Setting up firm-level data requires a build-up by business units, and this can assist business units to develop their own risk measures which are incorporated into the firm's process measures.

Independent of any external reporting requirements, the CRO also needs to establish baseline measures of firm performance and indicators of best-in-class outcomes. Accurately measuring risk outcomes is important because setting up a specialist risk function and increasing the cultural awareness of risk will increase reporting and so bias-up the apparent incidence of measures of risk. To properly evaluate the effectiveness of the risk programme requires an accurate baseline; and objectives need to be set against best practice which will typically come from benchmarking. The last can throw up some surprises. My favourite came in a presentation on risk management by the risk manager of a supermarket chain who somewhat shamefacedly reported that their benchmarking showed they had a significantly higher lost time injury frequency than a steel manufacturer. Supermarkets were seen as 'safe' environments and employees eschewed prudent behaviours when lifting, driving and myriad other tasks that can only be made free of injury by the right attitude.

The third objective of a CRO is to ensure compliance with stock exchange and regulatory requirements for risk management, which involves ensuring that the firm's risk management policies and procedures exceed compliance and then enforcing them.

A fourth, more aggressive, objective of a CRO is to better incorporate risk into the firm's strategy and programmes. This would include extending the firm's business plans to specifically incorporate risk management. When this is combined with the CRO's sign-off on risk aspects of major decisions, it is desirable to develop models that demonstrate the impact of risk on business operations, and optimize the return-risk trade-off in strategy development, particularly new investments.

Like any company-wide initiative, extending risk management is expensive, and the decision needs to be supported by demonstration of the value added for stakeholders. Thus the CRO will test their performance against tangible and intangible criteria.

The tangible criteria are relatively clear, and include: declining measures of risks, and at least matching performance of the best competitor; reduced expenses that are directly attributable to risks such as insurance and workers compensation expenses (although much of this is very long tailed with costs associated with accidents that might have occurred a decade earlier); and fewer breaches, 'surprises' and adverse events.

Unfortunately many benefits of better risk management are difficult to measure. These less tangible outcomes cover items such as:

- Closer integration of risk measures into project evaluations and operations. This is an awareness issue that requires employees, especially managers, to see advantages in identifying and managing risks. Thus it involves education and evidence of the benefits of ERM.
- Better matching of risk propensity to decisions. In the workplace it is appropriate to test outcomes against clear, low-risk criteria such as 'nobody gets hurt' or 'fish can swim in our effluent'. Other decisions, though – whether credit approvals, research projects or market innovations – may be expected to fail occasionally; not because mistakes are acceptable, but because some losses are a consequence of better calibrated risk taking.

Perversely an effective CRO may increase awareness of risks, promote increased risk propensity, ensure more comprehensive reporting and bring an increase in the frequency of reported adverse events.

In brief, the CRO position will have four principal roles: strategic evaluation of risks and their optimum management; communication of risk strategy and performance;

administration of the risk management process, including audit and insurance; and participation in crisis management. Clearly this requires a broad set of competencies covering finance and management, engineering and communications; and the ability to innovate, see ahead, clearly communicate complex subjects to different audiences, and garner organizational support for cultural change. Rarely will this range of attributes be held by one person; but this, of course, is not necessary for a CRO who is supported by a team of specialists who posses technical, training and other skills.

Key Risk Indicators

One of the most important roles of a CRO is to provide timely reporting of risks and performance against agreed targets, typically as a set of agreed KRIs.

Most managers are familiar with Key Performance Indicators (KPIs) and this concept has been extended – by the Basel Committee on Banking Supervision (2003b) (BCBS) and others – to the idea of KRIs:

> *Risk Indicators are statistics and/or metrics which can provide insight into a bank's risk position. These indicators tend to be reviewed on a periodic basis (such as monthly or quarterly) to alert banks to changes that may be indicative of risk concerns. Such indicators may include the number of failed trades, staff turnover rates and the frequency and/or severity of errors and omissions.*

Any framework of KRIs needs to include reports of actual outcomes and – because these data are 'backward looking' – also incorporate some leading (or forward looking) indicators that point to current developments that may impact on future risks. These are best communicated through risk maps discussed in the previous chapter that plot exposure against frequency for expected risks or value losses. At a minimum KRIs should incorporate:

1. Actual loss experience. This should be broader than just net P&L impacts and include events that do not have material costs (especially 'near misses' and disruption to customers, employees and operations). Results should be categorized by business line and loss type.
2. The firm's best thinking on risks it faces. This includes anticipated risks (particularly self-assessment such as the 'ten top risks we face') with probabilities and consequences.
3. Value at risk, particularly for financial measures.
4. Firm and industry data on risks, mapped as consequences vs. probability.
5. Milestones that are indicative of scenarios for credible generic risks in terms of consequences and required responses. The implication is that passing a milestone should trigger heightened awareness of this risk.
6. Organizational 'red flags' such as executive turnover; legal or ethical charges; reporting errors; and backlogs in production and accounting.

This becomes particularly important given that most major disasters have been presaged by previous incidents bordering on criminal behaviour.

According to a recent survey of banks, their 'Top 20 KRIs' can be grouped as follows (KRIeX.org, 2005):

i. Organization: staff turnover; employee complaints.
ii. Counterparty/Customer: credit quality; failed trades; client complaints; new accounts; customer attrition.
iii. Internal Processes: inventory (cash) losses; market risk limit excesses; expenses; investigations underway.
iv. Audit and compliance: risk and control self assessment audit scores and issues; compliance breaches.
v. Technology: system downtime.
vi. Criminal activities: theft, fraud (internal and external).
vii. External threats: IT system intrusions; economic indicators.

This kind of analysis lends itself to development of comprehensive sets of KRIs covering potential sources of failure involved in individual transactions. A good example of the many risks involved in a financial deal by a bank or trader is provided by Scandizzo (2005).

How should any firm develop its KRIs? From a Board's perspective, the most important leading indicators of serious strategic risk are poor financial performance and a weak competitive position, management's failure to react in a timely fashion to internal and external developments, and deterioration in the firm's reputation and the occurrence of unacceptable (even if minor) losses of value, particularly criminal actions. These, respectively, indicate factors that could lead to unexpected increase in risk propensity through ambitious strategic initiatives to boost profits, heightened exogenous risks due to a failure to understand the environment, and evidence from counterparties and operational outcomes of a heightened risk environment.

More specifically, KRIs foreshadow potential deficiencies in the firm's supply chain, product quality, compliance, process integrity and operational efficiency.

Developing a set of KRIs will combine generic measures of standard pressure points that affect any organization along with more granular yardsticks that relate to the organization's mission and to its proprietary products and services, processes and plant, finances, and suppliers, customers and employees. Table 9.1 sets out a framework for KRIs.

Is the Chief Risk Officer a `Real' Position?

A number of commentators suggest that the concept of a CRO is inherently flawed (for example, Quinn, 2004). This has a number of bases, including arguments that risk strategy is the core responsibility of the CEO and/or CFO; the role of the CRO is not easily delimited and so sets up turf battles; and the discipline of risk management is too immature to provide adequately resourced staff. The last is not helped by the large number of narrowly trained insurance managers and actuaries who see senior CRO roles as the opportunity to secure attractive promotions.

Table 9.1 Generic key risk indicators

Risk Type	Leading Risk Indicator
Poor financial performance	• Profitability and return relative to benchmarks and competitors • Earnings 'disappointments'
Weak competitive position	• Relative share performance • Loss of market share • Relative performance using financial and operating measures
Management's failure to react in a timely fashion to developments	• Internal – missed financial and operating targets; budget and project overruns • External – 'shocks'
Deterioration in reputation	• Opinion of analysts • Business media reports
Occurrence of unacceptable losses of value	• 'Shocks' to share price • Fines or charges associated with finances (theft) or operations (environment, OHS)
Supply chain	• Inventory stock out • Spoilage/shrinkage
Product quality	• Customer complaints • Quality defects • Customer attrition
Compliance	• Audit
Process integrity	• System failure
Operational efficiency	• Incidents, even when minor
Organization	• Staff turnover • Employee absence • Decline in productivity
Finances	• Credit quality • Working capital

Following the discussion above, it is obvious that an effective CRO will manage a series of complex processes embedded in the firm's operations and provide independent reporting of their effectiveness. This is impractical without two factors.

The first is independence and high-level support. The position should report to the chief executive, and certainly not to the CFO or a line manager. The CRO also needs explicit support from the Board, such as a formal reporting relationship with the Committee responsible for risk management (which may be a Compliance, Audit or Risk Committee, depending on the Board's structure).

The second requirement of a real CRO role is adequate span of control. The CRO should have direct responsibility for (and adequate staffing to manage): insurance programmes, including workers' compensation; security; operational safety and environmental groups; internal audit, covering both financial processes and operations; the ERM programme; risk reporting; and crisis response. The CRO should also be closely involved in evaluation of embedded risk processes such as credit and Treasury operations (including risks arising in financial and commodity markets). In addition, the CRO should formally sign-off on the risk aspects of major projects. Unless the CRO has authority of this magnitude, the role will not secure respect.

Establishing an adequately resourced CRO is a possibly poisoned chalice. The role is very broad, requiring familiarity with all aspects of operations and expertise in a number of new fields (especially information technology and modern industrial processes). The CRO is continually exposed to conflicts over the detailed monitoring and reporting of financial and operational processes, and to reaction emerging from the need to alter the firm's culture. Moreover the costs associated with ERM and the CRO can be large and obvious whilst the tangible deliverables are hard to demonstrate: results of initial cost-benefit analyses can be discouraging.

Above all, the CRO is involved in continuous oversight and reporting of operational activities. This obviously sets up the potential for conflict with line managers. In addition there are practical obstacles in achieving comprehensive data collection and integrating all risk activities, which are principal benefits of a CRO function. Large businesses are characterized by fragmented IT systems, lack of data, invisibility of outsourced or embedded operations, and reluctance to allocate resources now to offset uncertain future events.

Conclusions

The CRO's role has emerged following tighter regulation and reporting requirements in a time of growing sophistication of risk management. Demonstration of its worth comes in: communication of risk performance, including a measure of total organization risks and analysis of previously unappreciated risks; training so that risk awareness becomes a core managerial competency; implementing innovative risk solutions, including use of risk as an investment criterion; and demonstrating value to stakeholders from risk management.

An obvious imperative of the coordinating-type CRO role is that many poor risk outcomes have come from siloing risk management. This conclusion recurs in post-audits such as that of 9-11 where various security bodies – FBI, CIA, NSC – had bits of the puzzle but did not share them. No single body or person had all the parts, and – like things owned in common – these risks were not well managed.

The concept of a CRO is intuitively appealing, but there are practical issues involved in its successful implementation. Whilst none of them weaken the benefits of the position, it does need careful consideration before implementation, except in a few industries – particularly banking – where it is clearly justified by the need to comply with explicit new regulations. But when effectively implemented, the CRO role provides Boards with a new perspective of the nature of risks in the firms' strategies: these insights offer the possibility of significant value additions.

CHAPTER 10
Governance and Ethics

The price of leadership is responsibility.
  Sir Winston Churchill, British statesman and historian (1874–1965)

Fear is our chief safeguard.
  Pericles (495–429 BC) quoted in Thucydides' *History of the Peloponnesian War*.

Given that risk management has always been a core governance function, much of this chapter may appear redundant, but the space is justified on several grounds. The first is the analysis in Chapter 3 which showed that firm-level strategic risks are growing, possibly quite rapidly. Boards are proving unable to control the adverse consequences of their decisions. This alone justifies a new governance paradigm that is better able to manage risk.

The second need for improved governance and corporate risk management arises in the modern business trends of continually accelerating change, with greater possible damage, and increasing uncertainty. Modern breakthrough technologies and tools are increasingly complex, smaller in size and spread their effects more widely and quickly. Thus they contain ever-larger elements of uncertainty in both benefit and risk. To thrive in such climates firms need their leadership to focus on optimal growth and pursue strategies with a high probability of success.

More effective Boards offer the best opportunity for firms to thrive. Certainly managers and all workers have a responsibility to eliminate hazards and take appropriate risks. But they lack the independence of thought and strategic perspective that are essential to properly balance risk, return and the costs of risk management processes. For instance, biases from moral hazard and agency problems can promote suboptimal outcomes in management decisions; and pressure for immediate results and heavy discounting of future costs can defer essential risk management programmes.

Despite the obvious need for Board-level risk strategy, it seems that Boards of even the world's largest companies have a relatively unsophisticated approach to the task. A contributor to this is the tacit demarcation in many firms whereby the Board concentrates on oversight and reporting, whereas management controls strategy and secures rubber-stamp approvals from the Board as necessary. The controls focus of the Board is further exacerbated by tougher regulations and legislation (including Basel II and *Sarbanes Oxley Act*) which promote an emerging compliance culture. There are unfortunate consequences when badly judged risks encounter ineptitude and complacency.

The first is that a myopic emphasis on compliance means regulated matters take precedence. As a result, risk is not managed in an integrated fashion across the company which would see Boards actively balancing risk-return trade-offs in light of costs and opportunities. The second unfortunate implication is that the emphasis on meeting regulatory expectations downplays strategic management of risk.

A third implication of the growing compliance focus of Boards is that they may not exercise sufficient scrutiny over management proposals. Bosch (1995) argued that:

> *Management dominates the board and controls the company with little or no constraint or effective accountability. There is a substantially increased risk that the interests of shareholders will be disregarded and that serious damage may be done to creditors and other stakeholders.*

The need to refocus on strategies to maximize risk-adjusted value for shareholders is clear from a Booz Allen study of value lost in 1,200 large firms (each capitalized at over $US1 billion) during 1998 to 2004. This found that 60 per cent of losses were due to poor strategy, 27 per cent due to operational problems and a mere 13 per cent due to compliance failures. The study concluded 'strategic and operational blunders have caused far greater shareholder value destruction [than compliance failures]' (Kocourek and Newfrock, 2006). This, of course, is consistent with earlier discussion of the high failure rates of even routine decisions, and an even worse outcome for strategic decisions with 70 per cent or more wrong.

A final issue in relation to governance is the changing nature of firm principals, with much greater concentration of ownership following tax incentives to encourage retirement savings. The proportion of US firms owned by managed funds doubled from 20 per cent in 1980 to 40 per cent in 2004 (US Census Bureau 2005: table 825; and 2006: table 1187). Because these more powerful institutional shareholders are better able to influence management, the intensity and sophistication of performance pressures on Boards has changed significantly.

Thus this chapter takes a broad view of the scope of governance (so as to embrace associated topics including ethics and sustainability) but focuses on delivering firm strategies that have a positive risk-adjusted return. This is not to downplay compliance and regulatory issues, but these have already been addressed in discussion of the Chief Risk Officer (CRO).

Governance Defined

Corporate governance is a simple concept: it is the process whereby investors in a firm assure themselves of a reasonable return.[1] This typically means that investors with influence (either through the magnitude of their shareholding or their relations with the firm's Board and CEO) use it to secure appointment of a CEO to run the firm and a Board of Directors to provide oversight. Reporting to other shareholders is generally limited to accounts (financial and literary) of historical outcomes. Most importantly, improving governance is not directed at better processes, but at achieving better outcomes as measured by shareholder value.

For me the objectives and processes of corporate governance are set by the firm, and are not determined by others' agendas. This is encapsulated by Sternberg (2004) for whom governance 'exclusively [involves] ways of ensuring that corporate actions,

---

[1] Note, though, that there are other approaches. Kaen (2003: 1), for instance, starts his book on the topic: 'Corporate governance is about who controls corporations and why.' This is the school that depicts governance as a battle between competing interests.

agents and assets are directed at achieving the corporate objectives established by the corporation's shareholders'. The last are generally assumed to prefer to have the value of their investment maximized, consistent with legislative compliance whilst recognizing that value will not necessarily be optimized by a myopic focus on profit.

At one level, this process seems to be working well in most developed economies (see, for instance, the global survey of governance by Shleifer and Vishny, 1997). The flow of new funds through initial public offerings (IPOs) and other new equity raisings is high, and equities are favoured for the long term by investors, large and small. Shareholders generally seem satisfied with most firms' governance.

On the other hand, there is an emerging volume of criticism that the model is deeply flawed. This comes from academic analyses (for example, Jensen, 2001); sacking each year of at least 5 per cent of CEOs of the world's largest companies; more frequent corporate crises and scandals; and a groundswell of legislation and shareholder activism seeking to alter historical governance practices. It is not helped by egregious examples of poor governance such as the Board of Lehman Brothers which filed for bankruptcy in 2008. Out of 11 directors in 2006, five were aged over 75 years, including an ex Broadway producer and an 82-year-old former actress. Hardly the right stuff to manage one of the world's great risk machines!

Moreover governance is becoming a more important influence on shareholder value. An international survey of institutional investors conducted by McKinsey found they ranked good corporate governance alongside financial performance and most 'had "pulled back" from investing in companies because of their poor corporate governance' (Coombes and Watson, 2002). In terms of this book's objectives, it is interesting that the rationale for change in governance is gravitating around the way that Boards manage risk. Lord Levene, Chairman of Lloyd's, put this succinctly [www.lloyds.com/News_Centre]:

[For Boards] risk management is critical. Companies need to recognise that the risk environment has changed, and they cannot rely on 20th century management techniques to solve 21st century problems.

Influential stakeholders are more strongly emphasizing the risk component of governance. According to Moody's Investors Service (2004), this includes risk management, risk analysis and quantification, risk infrastructure and intelligence. This is what might be termed risk governance and requires:

Involvement of directors (including external and non-executive) in reviewing risk appetites and control effectiveness, directors' awareness of risks, relevance of their backgrounds to assess risks; collective and individual responsibilities of and awareness by executive management on risk matters, integration of risk considerations in budgeting, capital allocation, and determination of capital adequacy; [and] organization, staffing, resources, veto powers and enterprise-wide role of risk management function(s).

Moody's provides details of key risk governance topics as shown in Figure 10.1.

The core elements of risk-driven corporate governance include: the firm's risk appetite and target risk outcomes; a mechanism for incorporating risk into strategy development; an appropriate risk management organization; and timely reporting of risk outcomes.

> **KEY TOPICS in RISK GOVERNANCE**
>
> **1. Risk Governance at Board Level**
> - Extent to which Board (including external or independent directors) is involved in defining risk appetite, control structure and organization
> - Awareness and understanding by Board of risk exposures
> - Mandate and practical workings of Board-level risk and/or audit committees in reviewing risk management and effectiveness of controls
>
> **2. Risk Governance at Executive Management Level**
> - Involvement in risk decisions by executive committee, risk awareness of top management
> - Mandate and practical workings of executive-level risk committees
> - Risk measures and considerations used by executive management in determining capital allocation and overall capital adequacy decisions
>
> **3. Risk Governance – Risk Management Organization and its Influence**
> - Reporting lines and authority of risk management functions
> - Mission of risk control: monitoring/measuring/reporting vs. active management and mitigation
> - Independence/autonomy of risk organization
> - Centralized vs. decentralized risk organization, integrated vs. silo risk control, extent of adoption of enterprise-wide risk management concepts
> - Existence and implementation of enterprise-wide risk management concepts
> - Veto power and forcefulness of risk control/management on new and existing products
> - New product approval procedures
> - Process for the dissemination of risk principles, preferences, risk-taking decision authorities, policies and procedures
> - Steps taken to provide education and training for broader personnel in risk matters

Figure 10.1 Risk governance

The first element – to establish the firm's risk appetite and target risk outcomes – involves quantification of risk objectives; establishing limits on what is desired and what is not; and putting in place a relatively stable organizational framework that explicitly reflects risk management objectives.

The second risk governance objective is to embed risk into strategy development and this needs a formal process covering: standardized risk requirements for management, investments and product design; training on how to evaluate and leverage risk; and criteria to evaluate and reward managers' performance against risk-based performance measures.

Third is to establish an appropriate risk management organization which may be as simple as appointing a CRO to report jointly to the CEO and Board Risk Committee, and providing them with adequate resources and organizational support.

Risk-driven governance involves continuous examination of risk outcomes through timely reporting to all stakeholders, both in quantitative terms (such as through Key Risk Indicators – or KRIs) and as qualitative reports on objectives and process improvements.

These can be combined in more comprehensive documents which are useful in explaining a variety of non-financial outcomes to stakeholders, including risk, safety, environment, R&D and long-term strategy. Many firms now have impressive Sustainability Reports, particularly mining companies and banks.

This can lead to a comprehensive view of corporate governance that incorporates communications to various stakeholder groups, strategy formation, knowledge management and communication within a broad risk framework. The best depiction of this risk governance approach is the interesting framework for risk-biased corporate governance developed by Shell, which – reminiscent of many Enterprise Risk Management (ERM) perspectives – places risk within a governance framework that links it to strategic responsibilities.

Risk governance emphasises linking disparate strategies and functions, so it needs to be alert to unexpected knock-on impacts. When consciously influencing and measuring risk outcomes Boards need to consider a range of possible implications, including undesired impacts. An example of the latter is imposing a requirement for approval on an exceptions basis of decisions that could prove high risk. This might place the onus on decision makers to identify such decisions by extrapolating their risk possibilities, and then obtaining approval from a level of management higher than required by other authority criteria (such as amount of the investment) or from a central risk group. This appears to be a prudent and reasonable policy. However, it contains an implicit message that risk is 'exceptional', which would almost certainly result in either a deluge of exceptions, or an unwillingness for managers to contemplate risks. Either way this policy would make the organization more risk averse. Exactly this happened to the CIA after it adopted a policy which required special approval to recruit suspected or proven criminals as spies. Even though such people were often best placed to provide information, the difficulty in obtaining approval to use them meant that many CIA officers simply ignored their potential, leaving the CIA short of good information (Kessler, 2003).

Institutional reluctance to take the right risks is not an unlikely occurrence. A prominent cover story in the magazine *Business Review Weekly* [17 April 2003] was subtitled: 'Obsessed with corporate governance, company boards are afraid to take risks.' And Chair of CSIRO, the Australian government-funded research body, Catherine Livingstone (2002) pointed to the 'risk paradox' where stakeholders are becoming more risk averse just when greater risk is required to tap increasingly beneficial new technologies.

The final aspect of governance relates to increasingly onerous statutory requirements. This has gone furthest in the US where outrage following the collapse of Enron, WorldCom and other firms catalysed the *Sarbanes-Oxley Act of 2002* (often referred to by the acronym SOX) and related requirements introduced by the Securities and Exchange Commission. These have imposed much stricter corporate governance requirements in areas such as reporting, disclosure and auditor independence; and through making company officers more explicitly accountable for their actions.

Although SOX is not law outside the US, it does apply to foreign companies that have US parents, a listing on a US exchange or a US incorporated subsidiary. Moreover many countries have experienced corporate collapses to rival those that catalyzed SOX: Europe had Parmalat and Vivendi; and in Australia HIH, OneTel and Pasminco collapsed almost simultaneously in 2001. These, too, have resulted in anguished response by legislators and regulators, such as amendments to the *Corporations Act* in 2004 in Australia. It is inevitable that the requirements of *Sarbanes-Oxley* will continue to be felt in boardrooms of many countries.

Governance Principles and Guidance

As a rule, tighter governance guidelines follow scandal. In 1991, for example, London was rocked by two collapses. The first involved the Bank of Credit and Commerce International (BCCI) which became the world's (then) worst financial scandal when it failed following a '$20-billion-plus heist' which included allegations of money laundering, bribery, terrorism and a host of other offences (Beaty and Gwynne, 1993). The second emerged after publisher Robert Maxwell drowned in mysterious circumstances off the Canary Islands when it was revealed that he had been siphoning funds from company pension plans to pay debt. The London Stock Exchange reacted by commissioning Sir Adrian Cadbury to prepare a report entitled *Financial Aspects of Corporate Governance* whose recommendations were widely adopted.

Guidelines typically set out steps that a prudent director can and should take, and most are informed by the publicity surrounding a high-profile corporate collapse or prosecution of a company officer. A good example is the AWA case in 1992 which involved heavy losses from foreign exchange trading, and the judges wrote (Bottomley, 1997: 308–309):

> A Board's functions, apart from statutory ones, are said to be usually four fold: to set goals for the corporation; to appoint the corporation's chief executive; to oversee the plans of managers for the acquisition and organisation of financial and human resources toward attainment of the corporation's goals; and to review, at reasonable intervals, the corporation's progress towards attaining its goals.

Most directors have accepted the court's opinion that 'it is of the essence of the responsibilities of directors to ensure that they take reasonable steps to place themselves in a position to guide and monitor the management of the company'. This, of course, is easier said than done and so a number of documents have been prepared in different countries to provide practical guidance. The most influential statements on what constitutes 'best practices' have been issued by stock exchanges and professional bodies. The Institute of Chartered Accountants in England and Wales, for instance, sponsored the *Turnbull Report* of 1999, which took a risk-based approach to corporate governance. It recommended that boards develop, implement and monitor an effective system of internal control which is designed specifically to protect shareholder interests.

Stock exchanges have also tightened their governance requirements, with a lead taken by the New York Stock Exchange's review of its corporate governance listing standards (NYSE, 2002: 2). This included provisions such as majority independent directors, guidelines on meetings and compensation, audit committee responsibilities, business conduct and ethics, and reporting. Inevitably the lead was followed internationally, so that the Australian Stock Exchange (ASX), for instance, introduced *Principles of Good Corporate Governance* which included provisions such as establishment of a sound system of risk oversight and management and internal control.

Whilst a practical director's manual is beyond my scope, an excellent précis of a director's role is given by Bosch (1995: chapter 6) who proposes that prudent directors will ensure that:

- Board decisions are comprehensively minuted and action items recorded for follow up until satisfactorily completed.
- Policies are established in important areas, particularly those where the firm faces risks. These are reviewed periodically.
- An effective system of internal controls and audit monitors compliance with policies and reports regularly.
- Directors satisfy themselves that they understand the assumptions and processes behind each decision, and that they are reasonable.
- Decisions required of the Board are adequately supported, with sufficient time for evaluation and discussion.
- The Board is regularly and accurately informed of performance against historical and leading indicators of desired outcomes.
- Directors have access to management, firm operations and advice as necessary. Bosch also points to warning signs of potential trouble on Boards, including:
- Information is either late or incomplete, and errors are not reported.
- Major projects are not post audited, particularly those that were unsuccessful.
- The Chairman or CEO is dominant, and there is little cohesion between directors.
- There is evidence of staff discontent, deteriorating results (including share price underperformance) or concern expressed by responsible outsiders (analysts, regulators, ratings agencies and the like).

Boards improve effectiveness by reviewing their collective performance and that of individual members. This can extend to retreats where a dedicated period – such as a weekend in an out of town venue – is set aside with a targeted agenda and directors work with senior management to focus their talents on improving the firm. Directors can also be very useful if assigned the lead in an area of company operations where they have expertise so they can help analyses and shape future strategy. These general objectives can be met by focussing on specific tasks of setting risk propensity, CEO and staff selection, risk reporting, ethics and sustainability, and risk communications. Most obviously, successful governance requires balance between the firm's culture, Board, CEO and internal controls.

Framework for Risk-based Corporate Governance

Most directors ask rhetorically what they can do about risk management as they see themselves as the recipients of management's advice, and restricted to choosing between alternatives put to them. The position is even more difficult when there are a significant number of executive directors (which is the US model) as the latter have the ability to use knowledge gained from their daily involvement in the company to dominate the non-executive directors. Conversely shareholders have a right to expect that experienced (and well-paid) non-executive directors will be wrestling with the future of their investment and affording a measure of protection. So, despite the difficulties, directors need to use their expertise and authority to probe critical aspects of risk management and help strike the right balances. How?

The first step is to get Board composition right. Recruit diverse contributors from different backgrounds, including capable women. Ensure there is enough expertise in key strategic areas – especially technologies and markets – to add value to decision making. Have a productive work ethic and style of operation.

A second step is to insist on familiarity with all plant and processes. Include briefings on risk in operations and reliance on interfaces. Demand answers to key questions: are adequate controls in place? Are people, procedures and systems right?

The third step is to keep risk on the Board's agenda. Regularly revisit the key question: is the organization accepting enough risks of the right type? Fix some absolute performance minima using customer and shareholder-based criteria, and scrutinize breaches (using more carrot and less stick). These could include disabling injury, reported segment loss and product recall. Promote operational audits over areas with critical exposures such as quality, financial integrity and safety.

The Board agenda should include reporting against established early warning measures and KRIs. Directors should establish less formal checks by developing and leveraging linkages with knowledgeable observers (analysts, brokers, journalists), and ensuring insiders can blow whistles in safety.

The final step is to test how well management understands the uncertainties attached to existing and new processes. Demand forecasts of key results and examine the outcomes: good forecasts imply clear management understanding of processes. Watch moves in cash and people. When new strategic directions are chosen (for example, acquisition or new market or process) seek clarification on how they fit with existing assets and competencies; what competitive advantage is obtained; what results are expected (performance, finance, and timelines). Promote internal peer reviews of key decisions and obtain external input.

Responsible Boards should demand strategically-based information such as best and worst likely outcomes, assumptions underpinning strategies, resources used, measures of performance and competitive positions. Directors have a legal obligation to probe along these lines, and – given the huge potential exposures for shareholders – should make it a key part of their duty of care. Although 'corporate governance' and 'due diligence' have come to be viewed defensively in some quarters as providing directors with legal defences against shareholder criticisms and negligence actions, at their best they reinforce shareholder interests and encourage directors to utilize their time and skills on strategy, monitoring performance and validating management decisions.

Targeting Risk Levels

The next step in fostering risk governance is to set a target risk level for the firm. This is a common objective of analysts and Meulbroek (2002: 5), for instance, proposes that: 'Managers of the firm can target specific levels of systematic and total risk. Using risk management techniques, they can amplify or dampen the risk of firm's operations to stabilize it at this targeted level.'

In reality this is quite impractical. Consider, for instance, the efforts of BHP Billiton which is the world's largest mining company. In 2000 it calculated Cash-Flow-at-Risk

(CFAR) – or 'the worst expected loss relative to projected business plan cash flows [earnings after interest, but before taxes, depreciation and amortization] over a one year horizon under normal market conditions at a confidence level of 95 per cent' – at about $0.8 billion. In the year to June 2000, BHP's cash flow was $2.5 billion; just 2 years later it was $4.4 billion; and in 2006 it was $16.5 billion. As a result, BHP's share price rose from under $10 in late 2000 to peak near $50 in mid 2008, after which it quickly lost more than half its value. Market changes completely swamped BHP's risk outlook, and made it completely impossible to understand what caused the resulting uncertainty in share prices.

That is not to say that firms should ignore measures of risk, whether they are financial or operational. But it does caution against a mechanical approach. A number of software vendors provide tools to support calculations of CFAR, which – although of limited value in setting quantitative targets – are useful for understanding relative losses and ranking risk management objectives and alternative investments.

Risk to shareholders is a combination of Value-at-Risk (VAR) and CFAR. VAR is uncertainty in share price that arises from instantaneous shifts in the market, particularly systemic factors such as interest and exchange rates. CFAR reflects uncertainty in the firm's future cash flows due to operational factors (such as costs and production volumes) and commodity prices and other inputs to cash flow calculations. A rise in interest rates will increase the discount factor applied to firm cash flows and hence lower its value: this is VAR. A cut-back in production due to (say) an industrial dispute will reduce expected cash flows and hence the present value of the firm: this is CFAR.

Every firm should understand how risky it is in comparison to the market as a whole and against key competitors. This relative risk highlights possible strategic gaps such as risk propensity that is either too low or high. Firms should also dissect the elements of risk to shareholder value (again in absolute and relative terms) as this shows efforts that are required in relation to specific types of risk, and how strategies should be developed.

Firms should specifically evaluate the impacts of risk management programmes, investments and other strategic decisions on risk levels and risk propensity. This is most obvious as a formal decision on the amount of capital and/or expense that the firm is prepared to risk in achieving strategic objectives. Thus a Board may set a target of (say) 10 per cent real annual growth in revenues (to double in size every 7 years) and decide that it will invest half of its capital programme in aggressive (that is, higher risk) projects to support the growth target. The result is a clear signal of higher-risk propensity and a more open approach to investment proposals. In this way, specific objectives against operational measures are far more effective in setting risk propensity than a vague 'risk target'.

An alternative approach is to monitor the 'cost of risk' which is the value of expected losses plus expenses associated with risk management. These can be tangible with a direct impact on the P&L, such as insurance, risk reduction and financial expenses. Other costs, though, may be less tangible and include the opportunity costs of risks avoided and the expected loss of value from risks being run. This is a useful technique to quantify risk appetite, particularly if it can be compared to competitors' strategies.

Apart from regular KPIs, the Board needs to be alert to emerging risks. Figure 10.2 takes a top-down approach and points out factors that could indicate the need to more closely monitor developments.

> **Critical Questions on Risk Environment**
> 1. What is the firm's risk management strategy (balance between avoid-insure-manage)? What is its strategic risk appetite? What risks are acceptable and what are unwelcome?
> 2. Does the organization have a history of problems (including near misses) or a risk bias?
> 3. Are incentives in place to promote integrity? Think in terms of Five Forces as well as rewards for decision makers.
> 4. What is the 'frame' of the business and operating environment? Consider geography, industry, governance, assets, management objectives, moral hazard
> 5. What is the 'culture' of the business and operating processes? Consider organization, structure, controls, reporting, KPIs; and the psychodemographics of staff (age, background, personality, recruiting) and counterparties
> 6. Is this a new process? If so, how far up the learning curve are operations (training, procedures, routines, predictability).

Figure 10.2 Critical risk management questions

In summary, dialling up the right level of risk is a key management responsibility, and requires balancing the leverage or exposure to:

- markets: product, geography and industry;
- processes: equipment, process, raw materials and manufactures;
- business models: distribution, co-venturers and management systems.

Recruiting the CEO

Firms – like individuals – are boundedly rational, and their managers and other staff cannot consider every possible strategic alternative, nor exhaustively analyze each decision. Thus they use heuristics (mental shortcuts) to identify types of strategy that are likely to gain acceptance. The role of the CEO is to provide leadership for the firm, and as part of this will shape its high-level heuristics: what strategies, including investments, will be supported; and how they will be ranked and approved. The CEO will also set the firm's key performance criteria, and hence what behaviours will be rewarded, and those that will not.

It is no surprise, then, that 'the CEO is the single most important factor in a company's stock price' (Jackofsky, Slocum and McQuaid, 1988). Similarly, the characteristics, behaviour and performance objectives of the CEO are important influences on a firm's risk propensity. At the extreme, failures of corporate governance have been sheeted home by the International Federation of Accountants (2003: 15) to 'dominant, charismatic chief executives who were able to wield unchallenged influence and authority over the other senior executives and board directors'.

For the Board, there are two aspects of the CEO selection process that have strong implications for risk. The first is the inherent risk propensity of the CEO, on the basis that this will be transmitted through decisions to other managers and set the risk profile of the firm. The second risk-related aspect of CEO recruitment is moral hazard that is induced in the CEO, particularly by their background, compensation package and how performance is evaluated.

A key initial decision in recruiting a CEO is whether or not to prefer an internal candidate as they have a lower level of risk propensity. This is because they tend to be socialized to the company, often have wealth invested in its stock, and are more mindful of the implications of their decisions on the firm's counterparties.

Once the pool of candidates is identified, the next step is to identify a skilled manager whose risk propensity matches that desired by the Board. An evidence-based evaluation would use the risk indicators in Chapter 3 to evaluate personality. Does the candidate have personal traits indicative of high risk (male gender, youth, low level of assets, confidence)? Do they display risky behaviours (smoking, adventure sports, risky investments)? Tests of risk propensity come through review of the candidate's record in terms of risk attitudes. Has the prospective CEO: taken risks in business in the past? What level and type? How successful were they? What contributed to success and failures? Does the CEO have a record favouring future risk taking (either recent failures, or a series of successful risks)?

Gender can be important, too. Most obviously because of empirical evidence that women are less likely to take a given risk than men (Byrnes, Miller and Schafer, 1999). It is important to note, though, that such studies do not say that women will not take well-judged risks; and they say nothing about the quality of risk taking. A second impact of CEO gender on strategy has been termed the 'glass cliff' and occurs when women are put into precarious leadership positions (Ryan and Haslam, 2005). A variant of this is the 'daughter syndrome' where women executives are viewed by male supervisors as surrogate daughters and not exposed to the rough-and-tumble of corporate life. In these cases the CEO can be chosen for the wrong reason or not used to their capacity.

Once the CEO is chosen, the Board needs to frame the role and establish a compensation structure.

Framing involves agreeing the firm's principal objectives and how they will be achieved, possibly in a VisionMissionValues (VMV) statement that provides benchmarks or standards against which executives can test decisions. Successful politicians shape election campaigns with simple, clear statements – 'It's the economy, stupid' (Bill Clinton in the 1992 US Presidential election) – and Boards should do the same to keep managers' strategy on point. Corporate reports – whether addressing safety, sustainability or finances – should provide evidence of outcomes against this framework.

Separately the Board should agree strategic and operational objectives with the CEO, and specific goals and action plans. One set of these objectives will relate to shareholder value, particularly expectations in regard to the level and quality of returns. Another is the shape and components of the organization: what are the sources of growth and returns in terms of business sectors and types of strategy? A third area of focus is on the organization and the culture and behaviours of managers, including performance measures to evaluate individuals.

Compensation of the CEO can have several components: one is fixed; another can be related to performance against specific targets; and a third can be more broad and related to corporate results, particularly through grants of stock or options. The importance for risk governance of getting CEO compensation right is clear from many analyses which find strong causal links between compensation and firm investment decisions, capital structure and risk propensity. As shown in Figure 10.3, different compensation components have quite different pay-offs to CEOs and hence exercise different pressures on the risk propensity.

At the extreme where an executive is paid only a fixed salary, there is an incentive to avoid risks that may jeopardize job security; moreover the only way executives can access additional benefits from their employer is through pursuing self-interest in the form of perks. This leads to a compensation package that provides some incentive on the assumption that it will encourage executives to promote shareholder value and be more aggressive, including investment in riskier projects.

Compensation is more likely to have an incentive component when agency problems are greatest: that is when shareholders and Boards must rely more on managers' judgement and skill. Uncertainty in the firm's broader environment – whether caused by competitors, technology, regulation or other factors – can lead to lower profits, higher risk of bankruptcy or increased need to innovate. Uncertainty makes it difficult for boards to direct management and effectively monitor their performance. At the same time, uncertainty increases the opportunity to take strategic initiatives and increases the potential returns: the incentive and need for risk taking rise. Thus uncertain environments promote delegation of responsibility to managers and lead to remuneration with a higher incentive component. In short, the nature of executive compensation responds to exogenous risks faced by a firm.

In theory, compensation systems where the wealth of the CEO and other executives responds to their employer's stock price ensure alignment between the interests of managers and shareholders: it should solve the principal-agent problem. Meeting this alignment objective via stock or options and so directly linking compensation to share prices – rather than (say) accounting results or other performance yardsticks – is also seen as equitable and free of any subjectivity. Despite the attraction of stock-based compensation, it is not always straightforward.

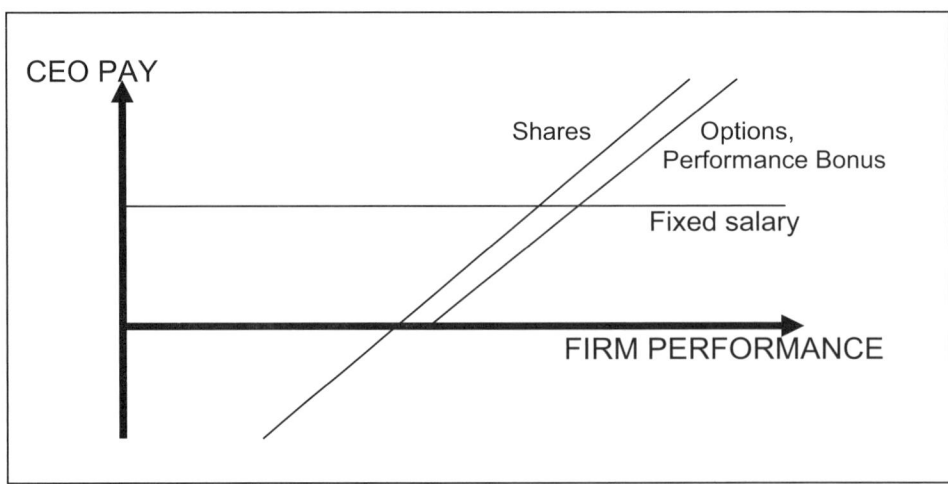

Figure 10.3 Relation of executive compensation to performance

There are differences, for instance, in the nature of incentives provided by shares and options. Shares have a linear pay-off so that managerial wealth rises and falls directly with the share price. This introduces the possibility of loss for managers and – perhaps perversely – can increase their risk aversion. Options, however, have only a zero or positive pay-off: this tends to make managers more risk prone, particularly when their options are out of the money (that is, when the price at which shares can be purchased is above the current share price). A number of studies – such as one involving gold mining companies by Peter Tufano (1996) – have shown that firms whose managers are compensated with shares take less risk than firms where managers are compensated through options. The impact of options and stock provided in CEO compensation packages flows through to corporate finance decisions. For instance, Rajgopal and Shevlin (2002) used a sample of US oil and gas firms to examine the influence of employee stock options on firm risk as measured by exploration and hedging strategies. They found that firms whose CEOs have more options will pursue more risky investment strategies and avoid risk minimization tools such as hedging.

The recent history of executive compensation schemes has shown that putting managers' pay at risk does not necessarily achieve the alignment that was sought by advocates of incentive-based compensation schemes. A large contributor to this misalignment, of course, is that most shareholder wealth is held as shares whereas a large portion of executive wealth is held as options that have quite different payout and drivers. A particular misalignment is to risk propensity, so that stock-based compensation can either raise or lower managerial risk propensity and lead to over- or under-investment in risky projects.

A second misalignment from at-risk compensation schemes is that bonuses calculated from accounting data (as opposed to stock prices) induce managers to manipulate accounting procedures in order to maximize their income. This can involve massaging accruals and – at the extreme – fraud, including falsification of results.

In short, recruiting and motivating the CEO is one of the Board's most important tasks, but it is a process that is fraught with complexity. This is assuming ever greater importance as the role of the CEO changes in the face of demands by shareholders, regulators and other stakeholders for better company performance. Historically they had been tolerant to the extent of complacency of managements that delivered reasonable returns. Now decisions are being reviewed in considerable detail, particularly those that benefit the CEO, senior executives and directors. Thus the CEO has an important role in promoting responsible consideration of how the firm's very purposes are to be met.

Leadership: *Sine Qua Non* of Risk Management

Leadership is a vital factor in risk management. In his delightful biography of one of history's great leaders, Barry Unsworth (1999: 135) paints a grim portrait of Admiral Nelson's incompetent superior, Sir Hyde Parker, who almost brought them both disaster at the Battle of Copenhagen, but Nelson cut through the indecision and obstinacy by famously holding the telescope to his blind eye. Military annals – which concentrate on risky strategic decisions – have many such examples including an observer of the ill-fated Dardanelles campaign of World War I[2] who divided its participants into men who fought like lions and leaders who could not make a decision. The 'lions led by donkeys' metaphor has persisted into modern times as evidenced by the common lament that we honest toilers lack the leadership we deserve, whether the powerless subjects be in business, politics or the professions.

Well-led organizations judge their risks better and therefore encounter fewer problems. Their leaders provide certainty over objectives and responsibilities; impose high standards of integrity, operational performance and ethical values; and strengthen controls and expertise. The essence of leadership is the ability to distil sense and order in the face of uncertainty. Thus its hallmarks are vision and courage, and the ability to evaluate unfamiliar problems and teach their solutions. Leaders construct clear environmental paradigms that good managers can lean on: they modify and reconstruct these business frames as the environment shifts. The leader who exercises good judgement is the best risk manager.

Leaders of organizations of the future will wrestle with individualism (which requires empowerment), increasingly sophisticated demands and technologies (requiring hitherto unanticipated knowledge of consumers and processes), internationalization (requiring a quantum leap in communication skills) and societal changes (to be leveraged). This will demand a management style epitomized by the traits of a clever sheepdog which captures diverse styles and skills; respects creativity; manages more complex markets, resources and risks; copes with emergence of boutique regions and sectors. These leaders will sensibly shape opinion amongst all stakeholders, and build bridges not walls.

Getting the Organizational Structure Right

Zegart (1999: 1) launches her interesting review of America's intelligence agencies with the comment that 'organization is never neutral'. She concluded that alignments of an organization, allocation of responsibilities within it, appointment of staff and access to resources have huge implications for outputs, particularly risk. The often trivial-seeming details of such decisions will set the tone – and hence performance – of every organization. Again a full treatment of organization design and recruiting is beyond my scope, but a number of observations can be made.

First there are two important distinctions to draw between the CEO and the rest of the organization. Obviously everyone but the CEO has a direct supervisor. In addition only the CEO can be equitably compensated on the basis of organization-level performance as everyone else has only partial responsibility.

These distinctions have significant implications for performance. First the formal reports and checks imposed by the CEO will form the core activities of most employees, given the adage that 'what the boss checks gets done'. Because most employees will be rewarded for their indirect contribution to organization performance, a critical choice is the levers that they are asked to influence. Senior employees, too, will expect to gain a significant amount of their work satisfaction from psychic rewards arising out of status, which is often a function of resources given to them whether it be a corner office, larger

---

2   This strategic failure was one of history's most significant as success would have opened up supply lines into Russia prior to the 1917 Revolution and perhaps changed the course of geopolitics in the twentieth century.

budget, more staff or Board attention. This can lead to sometimes-acrimonious infighting which results in suboptimal distribution.

As the mechanics of any organization's operations are usually obscure even to the most interested outsider, efficient design is essential. Procedures and performance expectations should be codified so they can be measured and monitored, and need to be chosen carefully for the messages they send. And, even though organizations theoretically serve shareholder interests, they are created by the shareholders' agents, and can suffer agency problems ranging from sloth to selfish ambition.

A significant component of governance is ensuring organizational effectiveness. Are processes in place, for instance, to appoint the best candidates? Does the organization learn from its experience and take into account external events? Does it continuously improve by throwing up new ideas, including renewal of core processes? Does performance meet the expectations of shareholders and exceed that of competitors? Does the Board understand and effectively oversee key activities, in terms of receiving accurate projections and reports and adding value to strategic decisions?

Because organizations tend to cling to the status quo, change is difficult. However, improvement should always be an objective of governance. Badly functioning organizations harm performance, lead to failed initiatives, and represent a huge opportunity cost. The best tool to ensure appropriate change is independent post-audits of important decisions.

The Biggest Risk of All: Getting Strategy Right

Taking the right number of well-judged risks maximizes shareholder value. Almost by definition, companies which judge risks well are long-lived and – according to Arie de Geus (1997: 12–14) – these companies are:

- sensitive to their environment and keep feelers out, tuning in to what is going on and facilitating timely response;
- cohesive with a strong sense of identity, an idea of community with management priorities focussed on the health of the organization;
- tolerant, especially of activities at the margin (including experiments and eccentricities) which stretch their understanding of what is possible;
- conservative in financing.

Echoing the above, a study by the International Federation of Accountants (2003: 18) found five factors are critical in strategic success:

1. Clarity of strategic objectives and decisions that are consistent and well chosen. Company reports, statements and comments should be aligned with these objectives.
2. Successful execution of strategies and decisions. This requires particular attention to change management.
3. Competency in large transactions, particularly mergers and acquisitions, given that most firm failures involve a failed major acquisition. These typically occurred because too little attention was paid to how much to pay for the acquisition, and inadequate

resources were applied to post-deal challenges, such as blending of systems and culture, restructuring and business optimization.
4. Timely and effective response to new information and environmental changes so that the firm moves with market trends. This could extend to formation of a 'strategy committee' of the Board that updates firm objectives.
5. Effective risk management that includes adequate resourcing of risky strategies and ruthless termination of incorrect decisions.

There can be little doubt that corporate success – whether measured by longevity, returns or growth – is not a function of risk management, but of successful strategic risk taking. Quite simply Boards that seek to maximize shareholder value need to spend more time on risk, specifically factor it into decisions, and probe the firm's risk measures and performance. Unless firm risk is a frequent item of discussion, directors will not become familiar with it; and cannot build the knowledge framework within which to consider decisions.

The first step in developing superior strategy is to draw upon a variety of opinions and options. An interesting perspective is that of an artist as they can lead change: artists who are knowledgeable about latest developments – science fiction writers and filmmakers are good examples – have a way of taking an idea, extrapolating it and putting it into a different, future context. Thus 20-year-old *Star Trek* movies show communicators little different to the latest mobile telephones; and a retrospective of the predictions in '2001: A Space Odyssey' showed that Arthur C. Clarke's 1968 novel had a pretty good record (*The Australian*, 23 January 2001).

The second is to be more tolerant of uncertainty. Point forecasts are foolish in concept: predictions need to be accompanied by estimates of their precision (the size of the error bars) and the reliability of key underlying assumptions. Even though speculation and scenario planning have a high chance of being wrong, their 'stories of the future' are good planning tools.

Third is to recognize that a conclusion can be true even though we do not know all its aspects. This means it is unwise to routinely shoot messengers with bad news, especially as truths do not last. Conversely it is wise to adopt assertive scepticism about claims of crisis given the probability of false positives.

Sadly I do not believe that experts can offer much help in building strategy. As discussed in Chapter 4, their technical knowledge of a subject rarely translates to accurate predictions about its risks and future developments. Generalists who know an issue's broader setting can usually predict its future more accurately than experts who know the issue's substance and not much else. It is lazy to slip from acknowledging that experts best understand the basics of an issue to accepting they are best able to manage it.

Looking ahead, the biggest risk to firms will continue to be poor decision making. Long gone are days when corporate Pied Pipers could make any product to any standard with confidence that someone would buy it. Governments' biggest threat now is from concepts that a small group can leverage through technology into wide support. Individual authority is making life unpredictable for institutions which do not serve the needs of constituents, whether consumers or voters.

No matter how well organizations manage their risks, in the chaotic, results-driven world envisaged in this book, there must be losers. Inevitably winners take nearly all, and so there will be a significant premium attached to good strategic decisions, and to distinctive (perhaps even contrarian) moves. A firm's wealth is of its own choosing through the risks it takes.

Managing Risks of New Technologies and Processes

Nearly all technologies have affected humanity by changing the rhythms of our life and widening the range of achievements. Rousseau may have seen each new discovery as degrading humanity from its original state as a race of happy savages, but new technologies have generally brought collective good (for otherwise they would not be embraced). Where Rousseau got it partly right is in new technologies' unanticipated risks and costs.

A host of factors contribute to the risks of new technologies: sponsors' enthusiasm which shades or ignores risks; unsuspected impacts from (and on) complementary processes; unanticipated applications of the discovery; and so on. When any technology is first launched, there cannot be broad understanding of all its direct and indirect impacts. In short, risk management is impossible. Enough time needs to be bought to gain experience and understand the new technology's implications so that adverse consequences can be brought under control.

History shows that the direct physical consequences of technologies are often well recognized, but side effects take time to emerge. Who, for instance, could have convinced Henry Ford that his car would lead to urban sprawl, drive-ins, the death of drivers, obesity and alienation of people in outer-city suburbs? A sometimes-tempting strategy towards the unknown is act-then-learn. This adopts a real options approach to innovation and values the ability to identify, control and mitigate unwanted consequences. Perhaps the best strategy to manage risks of new technologies and processes is to use time and experimentation to buy flexibility, control, correctability and insensitivity to error.

Firms that intend to introduce (or react to competitors' introduction of) new technologies should heed one of the few retrospectives of innovation by Schnaars (1989) titled *Megamistakes*. He concluded that success in managing the risks of new technologies involves: avoiding technological wonder; asking fundamental questions; and stressing cost-benefit analysis. There is a clear need for better independent evaluation of the risks of new knowledge and technologies in terms of: what benefits will be sought? What costs will be borne? What impacts will not be tolerated?

Communicating Risk

Communication of risk has two aspects: how to comprehensively understand the nature and probabilities of risks; and how to most effectively explain it to stakeholders.

Communication strategy must be shaped by recognition that adverse impacts of risks are shared between stakeholders, whereas their benefits are concentrated with most going to shareholders. Thus thoughtless communication of risks to the community, regulators, lenders and employees will elicit a negative reaction. Miscommunications merely alarm stakeholders. This will be at a cost to shareholders who benefit from well-judged risks. Tensions are inevitable if stakeholders myopically focus on risk reduction because shareholders and their agents are most interested in the optimized trade-offs between risk and return.

A paradox of risk communications is the significant potential for misinterpretation when viewed in hindsight or isolation. In a provocative analysis, US jurist Professor Kip Viscusi (2000: 586) suggests that juries awarded the highest penalties in product liability suits where defendants had conducted risk evaluations and cost-benefit analyses of risk reduction, and decided not to eliminate a known (usually small) risk associated with use of their products. He pointed out: 'This result is the opposite of what would occur if the legal system fostered better corporate risk behavior.'

The same risk of misinterpretation applies to post-implementation audits and analyses of incidents or crises. Viscusi (2000: 567) provides a sober warning to risk strategists:

> *The analysis [following a serious product failure] should highlight shortcomings that can be fixed to prevent future tragedies. The effect of such a frank assessment, however, could be to increase the company's liability ... Companies face a complex Catch 22 situation. If they [do not undertake a] post-accident risk evaluation, they might be found irresponsible for failing to address the risks that caused the accident ... But a frank post-accident report that is shared with the plaintiffs could affect the company's liability for the accident if the report finds fault with the company practices that led to the accident.*

Moreover, if the company fails to produce the report or destroys it, then juries could draw an adverse inference that the report would have been unfavourable.

Although it might be desirable for companies to think systematically about risk and to sensibly balance safety with stakeholders' willingness to pay for it, doing so in a logical manner can be misconstrued as putting a price on safety. This 'misinterpretation risk' means that firms need to be very careful about how they undertake risk analyses; naturally, too, a public commitment to complete safety may be quite imprudent.

The objective of risk communication, then, should be to inform all stakeholders that prudent risk management strategies are being followed, and to demonstrate that their benefits are being achieved, without necessarily disadvantaging any group. Reporting a firm's strategies to manage a specific risk in isolation is fraught with danger, which makes it desirable to integrate risk communications into a broader framework where risk management is just one corporate objective.

Stakeholder Theory

Consistent with broadening communications about firm objectives, a school of thought emerged in the 1960s that management has responsibilities in addition to single-purpose pursuit of shareholder value. This gradually coalesced around the concept of *stakeholder theory* where stakeholders are groups which contribute to the organization's success: this clearly includes shareholders, employees and customers, which comprised the triple bottom line in the 1990s, but it now more commonly incorporates social, environmental and financial accountability. These objectives can be further extended to cover various obligations to suppliers, the local community and even prospective customers and those affected by the firm's externalities (which is effectively everyone in every country in which the firm operates or has impact). Some authors have linked stakeholder theory to concepts such as corporate social responsibility to promote 'sustainable development: economic prosperity, environmental quality, and ... social justice' (Elkington 1998: 32).

A serious mistake made by many opponents of stakeholder theory is to assume that all its proposals are just *culs de sac* that will not add shareholder value. There is no doubt that some are, and others will see little progress for decades. But many topics are consistent with rising expectations of shareholders and other stakeholders, and interface to the sense that core community values should be shared by firms.

Blind application of stakeholder theory, however, ignores the reason why a firm should alter its optimal strategy (that meets legal requirements and maximizes shareholder value) to meet concerns or interests of other parties. At the extreme, implementing stakeholder theory becomes a nonsense as it imposes multiple objectives and perspectives that are required to meet the needs of numerous ill-defined stakeholders. Stakeholder theory without clear objectives and performance criteria is a logical impossibility.

A practical interpretation of stakeholder theory is that it can sometimes be economically beneficial for a firm to modify its optimal strategy to assuage concerns of groups other than shareholders. Consider, for instance, whether a firm should behave ethically, which is a litmus test of ideal community standards. More specifically, even though a firm may be strictly entitled to rely upon the principle of *caveat emptor*, is ethical treatment of key stakeholders – particularly employees, customers and suppliers – in the long-term interests of shareholders? The integrity, reliability and support of these groups are important to firm success. If they can assume that their dealings with the firm are efficient and equitable (and thus do not involve risks from information asymmetry or ruthless conduct) then both parties save the costs and delay of information search and other risk avoidance measures. Directionally this lifts productivity and product quality, minimizes disruptions such as absenteeism and industrial disputes, and reduces risks such as fraud. The resulting trust and loyalty can save further costs in identifying, recruiting and training replacement employees, customers and suppliers; and can facilitate expansion of the customer base. Thus there is a powerful economic argument in favour of ethical treatment of counterparties: quite simply, it widens a firm's bid-ask spread and so lifts profitability.

Concerns at the damage to firm value from unethical practices can be extended to incorporate other qualitatively important topics such as safety and environmental performance. As stakeholder theory gains credibility, it becomes complemented by links between financing, investment and sustainability, and broadens the perspective of good governance to incorporate corporate social responsibility and the quadruple bottom line. This can be integrated into sustainability reporting, which advocates such as CPA Australia say:

Seeks to more closely align reporting, underlying management practices and measures of corporate performance with the notion of sustainable development ... [Thus] decisions explicitly take into consideration the impacts on natural and human capital, as well as financial capital.

This style of governance responds to expanding interest in firm externalities, and provides more information on more topics to more groups. Such comprehensive communications adopt a pragmatic approach to stakeholders: there may not be a strict requirement to address interests of all parties, but ignoring them will adversely impact shareholder value. This richer picture of the firm encourages external parties to contribute and buy in to its strategy. It is also an excellent framework within which to explain a firm's risks.

This broader view of governance is not simple to implement. Taking account of claims by pressure groups, for instance, is fraught with risk because so many of their predictions (and hence proposed responses) have proven wrong over decades. Comprehensive debunking of many 'expert forecasts' is provided by Lomborg (2001) and Coleman (1998). Thus listening to stakeholders requires firms to comprehensively understand issues lest they act unnecessarily. By extension Boards need to take a leadership role in debates – economic and political as well as environmental – about topics that could prevent them from maximizing shareholders' value.

Risk Management as Sustainable Investment: The Equator Principles

Few executives can be unaware of ethical issues. At the formal level, industry and professional associations have ethical guidelines for members; and company VMV statements invariably acknowledge responsibility for ethical treatment of stakeholders. Less formally, political correctness is rampant in most workplaces[3] and various training programmes are designed to stamp out unethical practices.

Firms are now facing many formal and informal requirements to adopt ethical and sustainable strategies. One of the most comprehensive involves project financing which has long been the preferred technique to fund mining and infrastructure projects in developing countries. As many of these developments brought significant environmental, social and economic damage, sponsors of project financing have received increasing scrutiny. In response, a number of banks met in 2002 to establish a framework and incorporate the World Bank's guidelines on environmental and social issues into project financing. This became 'the Equator Principles', and by 2008 over 60 banks had signed on, including ABN Amro, Citigroup, HSBC and Westpac.

According to the Principles, signatories wish:

> To ensure that the projects [they] finance are developed in a manner that is socially responsible and reflect sound environmental management practices. By doing so, negative impacts on project-affected ecosystems and communities should be avoided where possible, and if these impacts are unavoidable, they should be reduced, mitigated and/or compensated for appropriately. [Signatories] believe that adoption of and adherence to these Principles offers significant benefits to ourselves, our borrowers and local stakeholders

Signatory banks will only provide loans to projects that conform to nine principles:

1. Projects will be categorized according to International Finance Corporation (IFC) criteria as category A, B or C which, respectively, are likely to have significant, limited or minimal adverse social and environmental impacts
2. Category A and B projects will conduct a Social and Environmental Assessment that proposes appropriate mitigation and management measures.
3. For projects in countries other than high-income OECD members, the Assessment will demonstrate compliance with: host country laws and regulations; eight IFC standards

---

3 An interesting test of one's own prejudices is provided by the website of Project Implicit: https://implicit.harvard.edu/implicit/demo/index.jsp

relating to working conditions, pollution, community health, resettlement, resource management, indigenous peoples and cultural heritage; and the IFC's environmental, health and safety guidelines.
4. Assessments will include an Action Plan that 'describes and prioritizes the actions needed to implement mitigation measures, corrective actions and monitoring measures necessary to manage the impacts and risks identified'.
5. Assessment processes will consult with communities affected by the project and incorporate relevant concerns.
6. A Grievance Mechanism will facilitate resolution of any concerns at the project's social and environmental performance.
7. The banks agree to: Conduct an independent review of each Assessment to ensure their compliance with the Principles.
8. Incorporate covenants into project financing documentation to ensure each project remains in compliance with the Principles and is decommissioned appropriately.
9. Require borrowers to engage experienced external experts to regularly review compliance.

Each bank adopting the Principles reports its implementation processes at least annually.

The Principles have a number of implications, most of which are consistent with better governance and improved strategic decision making. Of relevance to risk management is frequently asked question number 2 on the website:

Is there a risk management rationale for financial institutions to adopt the Equator Principles?

Definitely. Institutions that adopt the Principles ought to be able to better assess, mitigate, document and monitor the credit risk and reputation risk associated with financing development projects. Additionally, the collaboration and learning on broader policy application, interpretation and methodologies helps knowledge transfer, learning and best practice development.

For borrowers, the Principles require consultation with stakeholders, formal evaluation of project impacts and regular evaluations of performance. These steps should reduce the possibility of crises such as employee or landholder protests and provide indicators of performance against key risks. This largely fits within prudent risk management guidelines and should improve decision making and performance. That is not to say there are no weaknesses in the Equator Principles. For instance, their implementation relies on individual participants rather than a centralized regulator, so that standards and monitoring may not be consistent. Also gaps in application introduce some uncertainty to the borrowers. In addition, of course, the lack of universal adoption by all project financiers means that some project developers can evade the Principles' requirements and perhaps gain at least short-term advantage.

Complementing the Equator Principles is the Global Reporting Initiative which is based in Amsterdam with major industry sponsorship (Deutsche Bank, Ford, Microsoft, Shell) and an international Board from industry, unions, the professions and organizations promoting sustainable development. Its Sustainability Reporting Framework covers economic, environmental and social performance.

Not surprisingly the Equator Principles and Global Reporting Initiative have been used proactively by a number of organizations to strengthen their risk management. Excellent examples are provided by banks such as Citigroup; manufacturers such as Toyota Motor Corporation; and mining companies such as Oxiana Limited, which was the best performing listed stock in Australia in 2005–6 and financed a project in Thailand according to the Equator Principles.

Apart from debt financiers, providers of equity are becoming more demanding of corporate values. Ethical investing, now more commonly called Socially Responsible Investing (SRI), has been around for many years and about 10 per cent of funds under management in the US follow these principles. Contributors insist on philosophical goals, and there is little evidence that SRI funds perform differently to the broader market.

More recently there has been a trend towards 'sustainable investing', whose leading advocate is Generation Investment Management, which is an investment fund started in 2004 by former US Vice President Al Gore (website: www.generationim.com/philosophy/). The fund believes that 'clients are looking for investment management firms dedicated to long-term investing' because they can derive value from firms that are effective in meeting future economic, environmental and social challenges. Generation's philosophy is that:

Investment results ... are maximized by taking a long-term investment horizon because a majority of a company's value is determined by its long-run performance. Sustainability issues can impact a company's ability to generate returns and therefore must be fully integrated with rigorous fundamental equity analysis to achieve optimal long-term investment results.

Finance has generally not been thought of as a driver of ethics and sustainability. However, providers of both debt and equity are becoming more insistent on a range of non-financial performance criteria.

Ethics Does Pay

With non-financial criteria guiding investment of 10 per cent of funds under management in the US (Social Investment Forum, 2006), it appears they offer positive financial benefits for firms. This seems particularly true of ethics in its dictionary meaning as morally correct or honourable (*Concise Oxford Dictionary*). The moral compass for ethical behaviour is the Golden Rule, or seemingly universal principle to treat counterparties as you would like to be treated, which is common in philosophy and religion. The Gospel of Matthew: 'Do unto others as you would have them do unto you'; the Talmud: 'What is hateful to you, do not do to your fellow man'; the Udanavarga: 'Hurt not others in ways that you yourself would find hurtful'; and so on. In business terms, ethics means setting goals beyond legal compliance and value maximization; ensuring a high standard in dealings with counterparties; and not taking advantage of information asymmetry or monopoly bargaining power. It follows the moral heuristic 'do unto other [firms] as you would have them do unto you' (Sunstein, 2005).

The justification is that when firms treat counterparties ethically, the latter will perceive low risk of information asymmetry or adverse selection, with the following financial impacts: customers will not seek to discount prices; suppliers, including employees, will not pad their costs or reduce their quality; investors will not discount the stock's price; and the community will not impose restrictive covenants to protect against externalities from firms' operations such as damage to the environment. The result is a wider buy-sell spread for ethical firms: they can charge higher prices and will pay lower costs.

This leads to the conclusion that even though ethical behaviour may have a cost, it is much less than the cost of ignoring ethics (Chami, Cosimano and Fullenkamp, 2002: 1718). Signals of ethical behaviour attract or repel counterparties depending on what they consider as important, and the firm's ethical standards will influence those counterparties that choose to deal with the firm. Importantly this intuition does not see a trade-off between ethics and financial performance: they are complements, not substitutes.

Conclusion

Strategic risk management is a core element in governance and its demands are being raised through regulatory controls and heightened stakeholder expectations. At the same time, a better educated and more prosperous community has (consistent with moving up the Maslow, 1954, hierarchy of needs) begun to take greater and more informed interest in the conduct of businesses that underpin that prosperity. Business trends make prudently judged and effectively managed risks an integral part of firm success and rising prosperity.

The discussion above takes a deliberately broad view of risk-based governance so that a firm can best explain its strategic objectives through a framework of corporate social responsibility. This responds to the expanding interests of more groups, and provides more information on more topics. Inevitably this provides a much richer picture of the firm, and encourages external parties to contribute to the development of its strategy. Whether this style of governance is embraced cynically and for the wrong reasons, or through altruism matters little: the result is to meet broader social interests and enhance shareholder value.

CHAPTER 11
National Risk Strategy

Our country: when right to be kept right; when wrong to be put right.
Carl Schurz (1829–1906) US General, Senator and Secretary of Interior

Analysis in Chapter 2 showed that strategic-level corporate risks have risen several fold in recent decades, largely due to the greater complexity and tighter interlinkages of modern business processes. For similar reasons there has been a parallel growth in the frequency and intensity of social and political risks at the national level, whether they be obesity, pandemics, terrorism or global warming. The range and potential severity of national risks gained new urgency after a number of countries were hit by major, seemingly avoidable, crises such as Bovine Spongiform Encephalopathy (BSE, or mad cow disease) and foot and mouth disease in the UK, and terrorist attacks in the US. This, of course, overlays the recurrence of disasters from natural causes (such as Hurricane Katrina in the US and the Boxing Day 2004 tsunami in east Asia) and catastrophic man-made incidents (such as explosion of a chemical plant in Toulouse, France in 2001 that killed 29 people).

Although such risks may appear qualitatively different, they arise in a complex national governance system and are proving to have linked systemic effects that can threaten the efficacy of government. Just as firms responded to growing risk by introducing enterprise-wide risk management, governments have become alert to the emerging need for a national approach to risk management. For instance, Secretary of Australia's Department of Prime Minister and Cabinet Dr Peter Shergold (2003) said:

> *We need to embrace risk management at all levels of decision making ... [We should not] treat risk management simply as a checklist of hazards to be avoided or insured against ... The big public policy issues which presently face government ... necessarily comprise interlocking problems in which the management of risks involved is extraordinarily difficult .. It is essential to have that culture of risk management supported by a robust risk management framework that underpins the systematic and explicit consideration of risks in the wide range of decision making that our agencies undertake.*

Several countries have responded aggressively to growing national risk, with effective strategic risk programmes in Canada, New Zealand, the UK and the US, often including some version of a department of Homeland Security.

This chapter summarizes the new field of national risk strategy by building a conceptual framework for national risk assessment; identifying the strengths and weaknesses of national programmes; and synthesizing best practices. It starts by developing a generic framework for evaluating and strategically managing risks at the national level that would provide a blueprint for national organizations – both public and private sector – to implement their own programmes to address key risks. Whilst recognizing that each country faces a unique set of risks to economic prosperity and welfare, this chapter draws upon contemporary perspectives on risk management across multiple disciplines to establish a process to identify and manage strategic risks, particularly those that could impact national security, major systems and key institutions. The example used is that of Australia, which is a mid-level developed country that does not have a national risk strategy.

Nature of National Risks

This section discusses the various types of national risk, and reports the limited data on their frequency and causes.

National risk lacks a definition, but can be usefully thought of in terms of the nature and quantum of its impact. Thus a national risk will incorporate a major threat to the security, economic health or welfare of the nation; or could bring crisis to a national institution which could result in damage to assets, reputation or performance of such magnitude that its viability is threatened. National risks also include events with such serious consequences that response is beyond the capability of local and State authorities.

Examples of recent incidents that would rank as 'national risks' are listed in Table 11.1.

Table 11.1 Examples of national risks

Country	Category	Event
Britain	Technology	BSE contamination of meat supplies
		Delays in passport processing following new computer system in 1999
France	Governance	Uncontrolled rioting in multiple cities in November 2005
Ireland	Governance	Conspiracy to cover up criminal activity of paedophile priests
Thailand	Economic	1997 currency collapse
	Governance	Weeks-long airports blockade in 2008
	Natural event	Boxing Day 2004 tsunami
United States	Economic	2007–8 stock market collapse and credit crisis
	Governance	Threatened impeachment of President Clinton
		Collapse of Enron
		Revelation of market abuses by fund managers
	Natural event	Destruction of New Orleans by Hurricane Katrina
	Technology	Electricity blackouts in August 2003
	Terrorism	9-11 attacks on New York and Washington

Although there are many types of national risks, it is convenient to think of them as falling into three broad categories involving risks to national security, critical systems and major institutions.

Most countries face obvious threats to national security. This is true even of an isolated, island continent such as Australia which has experienced military assaults on its major city, Sydney, as recently as 1942; and saw 90 citizens killed in the 2002 Bali bombing that targeted Westerners. Virtually all of Australia's near neighbours save New Zealand have characteristics that make them potentially unstable. Australia sits in a region that Dibb (2001) refers to an 'arc of instability' which runs from Indonesia through into Polynesia, and forms an extension of the 'arc of crisis' that runs around the Indian Ocean from the Horn of Africa to the Indian subcontinent. In the future, credible risks to national security will be broader than conventional or terrorist attacks, because national security can be impacted by factors as diverse as technology, meteorology, disease and other nations' policies. Thus any strategy to avoid security risks needs a broad-ranging perspective on exposures.

A second group of national risks relates to critical systems. An important contributor to doubling of the standard of living in developed countries since 1960 has been greater productivity and efficiency from integrating infrastructure, systems, plants and communications networks. There is a cost, though, as this closer coupling of inherently risky systems brings the possibility of contagion when one part fails: the impacts can quickly spread – perhaps in quite unexpected ways – throughout the network.

The vulnerability of critical systems was shown in the near simultaneous failure of three previously reliable utilities in Australasia during 1998: Sydney water, Melbourne gas and Auckland electricity. Each utility was out of operation for several weeks and caused such economic loss as to contribute to three of the region's largest class action law suits. This experience of severe infrastructure failure has been repeated elsewhere, including widespread blackouts in the US in the summer of 2003 and follows privatization and deregulation of utilities in the last 20 years. This pattern of infrastructure unreliability and congestion is true in virtually every country and points to systemic failure to maintain and expand capacity. Everyone's future prosperity relies upon continuous, efficient operation of critical systems such as infrastructure, financial payments, food production, communications networks and delivery of essential services: management of their systemic risks is an essential economic priority.

The third group of national risks relate to major institutions. Modern societies rely upon the integrity and efficiency of numerous institutions: the government and its officers and authorities; the police and judiciary; essential services such as fire brigade and hospitals; regulators in government, private sector and the professions; and organizations that supply utilities and essentials such as food and clean water. In addition there is a general expectation that goods and services will be provided at reasonable quality and price, and customers will be treated equitably and fairly. In short, reliable institutions are essential for economic prosperity and efficiency in government.

Chronic prosecution of politicians and active roles for corruption watchdogs show that government institutions are not immune from risk. As examples, in Australia during 2006 alone two former Federal Ministers made front-page news on charges of child molestation and tax fraud. One in every 5,000 US government officials is indicted each year for public corruption (US Census Bureau, 2006: table 327).

166 Risk Strategies

Unfortunately, many other institutions have proven vulnerable to systematic risks, following crises as varied as sexual predation inside Church bodies; contamination of Red Cross blood supplies; deceptive fundraising practices by charities; and the rapid collapse of respected companies. Every time an institution fails there is a material cost, not least to national reputation; so threats to their integrity are an important risk. The principal consequence of eroding faith in institutions is a demand for greater regulation, presumably on the assumption that risks of abuse or incompetence can be identified and eliminated by appropriate monitoring and sanctions.

Although it is convenient to compartmentalize national risks according to security, systems and institutions, they cannot be treated in isolation. A good example of the wide-ranging consequences from an isolated risk is the powerful earthquake that hit the Japanese city of Kobe in January 1995. Over 6,000 people died and damages exceeded $US80 billion (Swiss Re, 1996); the Japanese stock market fell by almost 10 per cent in the following week. At this time Barings Bank – through its trader Nick Leeson – had speculated on stability in the Japanese stock market and sustained such huge losses that it went into receivership a month later. Thus a natural disaster caused massive damage to Japan's physical and financial infrastructure, and had serious impacts on the UK banking system.

Linkages between the three objectives above mean that national strategy needs to comprehend factors such as the transfer of risks between and within government and private sectors; dialling up the right level of national risk propensity; the broad impacts on national reputation of an institutional or systemic failure; and the impacts on risks of government and private sector policies and strategies.

Possibly the most obvious gap in the literature on national risk strategies is a practical process that can assemble the 'facts' around each risk. Whilst it is easy to brainstorm a shopping list of potential hazards, many identified risks can be pretty much a black box which are hard to understand and quantify. However, this is essential to a correct response given the huge cost of prediction failures such as those in Table 11.2. Billions of dollars, for instance, have been wasted in responding to risks – such as Y2K in 1998–9, weapons of mass destruction in Iraq in 2004, and avian bird flu in 2005 – that proved non-existent. Other risks have been recognized but completely misjudged: in Australia, for

Table 11.2   Failures in prediction of national risks

False Positives		False Negatives	
Date	Event	Date	Event
1970s	Looming global crises on overpopulation and commodity shortages		Disasters following launches of space shuttles *Challenger* (1986) and *Columbia* (2003)
1995	Global *Ebola* virus pandemic	2001	Enron collapse
1998–9	Millennium Bug or Y2K	2002–4	Travel warnings on Bali
2003	WMD in Iraq	2007–8	Safety of credit derivatives
2005–6	Avian bird flu pandemic		

instance, cane toads were deliberately introduced in the 1930s and are now threatening the survival of native species across much of the country's north; and travel advisories issued by the government completely missed the Bali bombings in 2002 and 2004. On the other hand, billions of dollars in damages have followed crises that were not identified, ranging from corporate collapses such as Enron to natural disasters such as the Boxing Day 2004 tsunami in the Indian Ocean. With risks, false positives can be as expensive as false negatives!

It is essential, then, to be able to quantify the probability of an unwanted event (or sequence of events) and understand the consequences. This identifies the need for some mechanism of accountability in the risk evaluation and management process. But how can this be done when the probability of an event is unknowable (for example, what effect did all the anti-Y2K expenditures – especially in the US during 1998–9 – actually have? Was it none? Or did it completely eliminate the risks?). Moreover, the spectacle of 'duelling experts' is all too common, in which one says that a dire event is inevitable and another equally qualified expert dismisses it as remote. At the time of writing this is true of topics as diverse as climate change, global pandemics and Weapons of Mass Destruction (WMD) attacks on civilian targets.

There are population-based statistics available for many identified risk events that make it possible to provide specific assessments of their probability and impact. At a basic level, many authorities maintain disaster databases (http://slp.icheme.org/incidents.html), with good compilations of global disasters by insurance firms such as Munich Re (2005) and Swiss Re (2005a) and specialist bodies such as Center for Research on the Epidemiology of Disasters (CRED). Other listings are national such as that developed by Emergency Management Australia which lists natural and man-made disasters in Australia dating back to 1622 (available at www.ema.gov.au/ema).

These databases support national decision makers. For instance, in Canada, Etkin, Haque, Bellisario and Burton (2004) reported 'an alarming increase in natural disaster loss' that they expected to continue. Analysis of natural disasters in Australia by the Bureau of Transport Economics (2001: xvii) found 'some evidence that the number of disasters per year is increasing due partly to better reporting in recent years and possibly to increasing population in vulnerable areas'. Other studies provide more granularity on specific risks such as cyclones, floods, storms and other natural disasters, terrorist incidents and international safety. This makes it possible to validate site-specific risk evaluations, and thus provide an 'outside view' of risk that guards against what Lovallo and Kahneman (2003) termed 'outcome myopia' which involves over-reliance on the biased forecasts of those close to decisions who can have a vested interest in their outcome, irrespective of risks involved.

For many national risks, though, empirical validation is not practicable. They may have had such a low historical frequency that historical data are of little use. An example is global influenza pandemics which are rare, with only a few serious occurrences in recorded history. Other risks such as climate change or Y2K may not offer any comparable precedent, or the nature of the risks may be changing and hence their probability is dynamically indeterminate. Finally some risks are embedded in surrounding systems that are so complex that they cannot effectively be tested or even modelled.

Conversely there have been some far-sighted analyses that were able to make sense of complex data. For instance, Enders and Sandler (2000) argued well before 9-11 that terrorism changed in quality in late 1991: they concluded that despite a significant decline in incidents, there was more activity by 'religious groups and amateurs'.

Overlaying the difficulty in obtaining good estimates of the probability and consequences of credible risks is that such data are irrelevant to many national decision makers. Although theoretical descriptions of decision techniques invariably find that the intensity of risk management responses should reflect the product of risk's probability and consequences, 'many risk managers ... base their decisions on qualitative information' (The Presidential/Congressional Commission on Risk Assessment and Risk Management, 1997: 90). This is partly because many risks cannot be measured; they can only be estimated, and even then must be addressed in a much broader qualitative framework that encompasses behavioural biases and prejudices. It is also due to the tendency of many people to think of risk in affective terms that relate to its nature and emotional cues rather than as a probabilistic measure.

It seems that decision makers pay little heed to the content of a risky decision, but use their own unique perspective and the decision context to evaluate the future, virtually independently of the stated risk probabilities. This is why many studies of decision making show that executives pay minimal heed to facts and historical data in reaching conclusions. Similarly political leaders choose policies, goals and broad strategies in light of qualitative factors and expectations.

This suggests an alternative approach to resolving national risks which is to move away from worrying about potential crises with uncertain natures and focus on the range of consequences and response requirements that would follow a range of possible events. Rather than developing specific responses to each low-probability high-consequence risk, acknowledge that there are so many that at least one will occur. Thus put in place an effective plan that can respond to the effects of a range of generic risk types. Exactly this, of course, is the role of emergency departments in industrial and residential settings.

The discussion above can be extended to develop a model of national risk as shown in Table 11.3. This adopts the conventional approach to risk management of observe-rationalize-respond: first set out the broad categories of risk; identify their sources; then establish parameters to measure their frequency and impact; and finally understand their drivers so that appropriate management strategies can be put in place.

The risks are divided into four categories comprising those impacting national security, critical systems and major institutions and those sourced in individual behaviours. In each case the resulting risks have a locus or source, whether insecurity, disaster or social breakdown, and have quantifiable indicators such as frequency of occurrence. The risks can be traced to fundamental drivers and these in turn can be controlled or mitigated. This process is very similar to that of Enterprise Risk Management (ERM) described in Chapter 6 whose steps include establishing the framework and developing tools to manage risks.

Review of Existing National Risk Strategies

This section reviews national risk strategies that have been implemented in Canada, New Zealand, the UK and the US. The aim is to summarize the key features of each programme, and identify their particular strengths. With several years of experience of national risk strategies in these four countries, their learnings and experience are becoming more widely available, including 'Special Issue on Terrorism and Security' in *Risk Analysis*

Table 11.3 Model of national risk management

Category	Locus	Indicators	Fundamental Drivers[1]	Controls/Response[2]
National security	Regional insecurity	Failed states	• Political weakness • Slow economic growth	• Administrative support, investment • Adequate defence
	Domestic unrest Terrorism	Political volatility Riots	• International factors • Unequal opportunities	• Adequate forward defence • Group-specific support
	Natural disasters	Extreme weather Earthquakes Volcanic eruptions	• Climate modifiers • More vulnerable assets	• Understand science • Disaster-proof social fabric
	Disease	Outbreaks	• International factors	• Monitor emergence
	Competitiveness	Terms of trade Import demand	• International factors • Declining commodity prices	• Diversify investment base
Critical systems	Infrastructure overload or failure	Unreliability of systems Congestion and collapse	• Population and prosperity • Inadequate investment • Close coupling of systems	• Precautionary principle • Reduce system demand • Develop alternatives
	Industrial disasters	Events	• Inherently risky technologies	• Isolate risky facilities • Precautionary principle
	Food chain contamination	Events	• Terrorism • New high-risk technologies	• Watchdog vigilance • Precautionary principle
Major institutions	Corporate failures	Crises and collapses Operational incidents	• Market failure	• Watchdog vigilance • Improved accountability
	Bureaucratic failures	Incidents of incompetence	• Weak monitoring and reporting	
	Regulatory failures	Incidents of incompetence Market abuses		• Watchdog vigilance • Integrate monitoring systems

Table 11.3 *Concluded*

Category	Locus	Indicators	Fundamental Drivers[1]	Controls/Response[2]
Individual behaviours	Horrendous violence	Massacres Serial crimes	• Psychopaths	• Restrict weapons • Constrain potential offenders
	Social breakdown	Riots	• Race • Socio-economic inequity	• Promote integration
	Lifestyle diseases	Diabetes, obesity, cancer	• Poor lifestyle choices • Socio-economic inequity	• Increase personal accountability • Promote better lifestyles

[1] Most also include weak governance, poor ethics and lack of accountability.
[2] Most include improved intelligence; better crisis management; enhanced stakeholder expectations; and improved generic response capabilities.

(Zilinskas, Hope and North, 2004) and 'Democratic Governance in the Aftermath of September 11, 2001' in *Public Administration Review* (Terry and Stivers, 2002). The performance of specific bodies has also been evaluated, particularly the Department of Homeland Security (for example, Kettl, 2004)

During the late 1990s, the Government in Canada came under criticism that its practices needed modernization 'to be more citizen-focused and better prepared to meet Canadians' changing needs and priorities' (Treasury Board of Canada, 2001: 2). It responded by introducing a systematic approach to managing national risks called the *Integrated Risk Framework* that was located in the Treasury, and extended ERM throughout government as described in a companion *Implementation Guide*.

The Framework supports national governance by understanding risks associated with government policies and programmes and addressing unwanted impacts; improving decision making and accountability within and outside government; and strengthening the ability of government bodies to safeguard their own and the public's resources. This has four principal limbs:

1. develop a profile of each organization's risks through a broad understanding of its operating environment, identifying threats and opportunities, and matching management to this risk profile and risk tolerance;
2. establish an infrastructure for risk management through integrating risk into decision processes, appropriately reporting outcomes and developing a learning organization;
3. ensure management remains committed to the risk management process by identifying, assessing, ranking and responding to risks;
4. continually improve the process through stakeholder involvement.

Factors that have proven critical in successful implementation of the Framework include senior-level political and management support, executive awareness of the needs for risk management and a realistic strategy for implementation.

New Zealand was another country to recognize that it faced unmanaged exposures, primarily geological and meteorological risks. These arise because New Zealand straddles two tectonic plates which are chronic causes of earthquakes and volcanic eruptions; is on the fringes of a cyclonic region; is exposed to tsunamis formed in the Pacific Ocean; and is subject to severe droughts and floods.

Although these natural disasters are chronic, they only emerged as poorly managed national risks after a 1990s review of domestic and foreign disasters found systemic weaknesses in the country's emergency services capabilities. A particular concern was the gap between assistance that the public expected to be forthcoming and the capability of governments to respond. According to Britton and Clark (2000: 146):

The [Emergency Services Review Task Force] recommended to the government a new structure comprising a ministry with policy, purchase and audit functions, and an operational structure to deal with emergency response that would integrate local and central government emergency service providers.

The review also called for a more strategic perspective on these high-consequence risks and more professional development of emergency services personnel.

As a result, the Ministry of Civil Defence and Emergency Management was established and – according to its website (www.civildefence.govt.nz) – 'Work[s] with its stakeholders to create a new way of thinking about civil defence and emergency management to build on existing civil defence practice [and preserve] New Zealand as a world leader in developing a risk-based approach that will increase the capability of communities and individuals to prepare for, respond to and recover from disasters.' The Ministry's role is to:

Provide strategic policy advice on New Zealand's capability to manage and be resilient to the social and economic costs of disasters; ensure the establishment of structures to provide the capability to manage and respond to disasters in New Zealand; provide support to sector stakeholders in their delivery of civil defence emergency management; ensure a co-ordinated approach, at both national and community level to planning for reduction, readiness, response, and recovery; and manage central government response and recovery functions for large scale events that are beyond the capacity of local authorities.

Canada and New Zealand adopted a comprehensive approach to national risk strategies following reviews that identified gaps between vulnerabilities and response capabilities. By contrast, the UK and US introduced national risk strategies following dramatic trigger events.

A string of crises impacted the United Kingdom in 2000–2001, especially the serious flooding and fuel crises of 2000 and outbreak of foot and mouth disease in 2001. These revealed the inability of UK authorities to predict, prevent and handle emergencies, and prompted the government to commission the Cabinet's Strategy Group to study how to better handle UK risks. The concept was that risk management was proving so central to the business of good government that it should become a core function of decisions across the public sector. In particular, government policies and decisions should strike the right balance between seeking benefits from innovation and change whilst avoiding unwanted shocks and crises.

In July 2001 the Civil Contingencies Secretariat was established to:

Improve the UK's resilience against disruptive challenges through working with others to anticipate, assess, prevent, prepare, respond and recover. We define resilience as the ability at every level – national, regional and local – to detect, prevent and if necessary handle disruptive challenges. These could range from floods, through outbreaks of human or animal disease, to terrorist attacks.

The programme has been implemented within the UK Treasury (Risk Support Team, 2004).

The UK's initial proposal was set out in a white paper prepared by the Strategy Unit (2002) that provided 'a comprehensive programme of change to improve risk management across government …[with] a two year timetable' (page 104). I attended the 2004 Society of Risk Analysts Conference where the UK strategy was described by UK Treasury official Mr. Brian Glicksman. Summarized below is my paraphrasing of the key points he made in an engrossing presentation:

An increased focus on quality in Britain's public service has brought stretch targets and a focus on outcomes. This in turn has lifted the actual and apparent risk of projects, which have always been prone to failure. Today's pace of change negates open, balanced consideration of every issue; global connectivity is another overlay; and people are better educated, informed and demanding about risk. Trust in institutions is low, and this sits ill with public demand for certainty. There is now a lower willingness to accept risky innovation, and greater demand for regulation.

Such general concerns were given immediacy by a series of crises from natural disasters and failure of services delivery (for example, delays in the Passport Office) and led to a determination to improve government capability by addressing risks in operations (which are endemic to doing business) from external threats, and those which are 'self-imposed' by stretch goals. The Government established a number of principles to build public trust and understanding. These include: openness and transparency; handling risks through third party bodies independent of government; and attention to evidence, responsibility and choice.

The UK now has developed an impressive set of documents setting out a national risk strategy. Amongst their major attributes, the plans are ambitious, draw upon public opinion, incorporate the large body of risk knowledge in existence, and explicitly depict decision strategy.

This new approach did, however, require numerous trade-offs, especially between risks and outcomes. Estimating risk is hard. This is a taxing issue as governments are being asked to deal with risks that have uncertain causality, probability and outcomes: this brings demands for precautionary measures, which can be hard to define as there is little guidance on their implementation.

Risk management is about choices. In particular, it is about choices between which: risks to consider, remedies to entertain and trade-offs to accept.

Although the public – and experts – all too often focus on just the risks and choices, good strategies explicitly consider technical, economic, social and political aspects of risk. Quantitative analytical tools are used as aids by incorporating technical analyses for transparency. This frames the problem more broadly, and allows a balance between science and judgement, which is particularly important in the face of uncertainty.

Perhaps the best known national risk strategy is in the US. Following the 11 September 2001 terrorist attacks, the US Congress established The 9-11 Commission (2004) that provided a comprehensive evaluation of possible improvements in national risk management. This led to establishment of a Department of Homeland Security (DHS) and *The National Response Plan* that:

Establishes a comprehensive all-hazards approach to enhance the ability of the United States to manage domestic incidents. The plan incorporates best practices and procedures from incident management disciplines – homeland security, emergency management, law enforcement, fire fighting, public works, public health, responder and recovery worker health and safety, emergency medical services, and the private sector – and integrates them into a unified structure. It forms the basis of how the federal government coordinates with state, local, and tribal governments and the private sector during incidents.

The DHS became the third largest cabinet department after bringing together 22 previously existing bodies, to give it a total of 184,000 employees and an annual budget of $US43 billion. DHS executes a multiplicity of functions with 15 different 'department components' covering everything from preparedness and emergency management, through transportation security and border protection, to the Coast Guard and Secret Service. An important issue is how well the apparently disjointed organization structure can achieve efficiency of operations. DHS strategic goals, for instance, are unusually vague with a mission to 'lead the unified national effort to secure America'. Moreover, since being established, it has been subjected to reorganizations and – like bodies that are cobbled together – seems to respond as a group of unruly fiefdoms.

Management of National Crises

When a catastrophe strikes, individuals at the scene – especially trained emergency personnel in the public and private sectors, but also untrained bystanders – usually respond well, whether it be to a plant explosion, widespread natural disaster or 9-11 scale attack (Scanlon, 2001). These people look around, identify specific tasks and take action. Even untrained participants in a crisis do not conform to the assumed stereotype and panic; rather they respond efficiently and often at considerable peril to themselves (Shaw, 2001). In a typical post-audit of a major disaster, the Inquiry into devastating bushfires in Canberra in 2003 directed much praise at the efforts of the fire fighters, police and other emergency workers and the volunteers. On-scene response is generally well managed.

This is in marked contrast to paralysis and myopia that seem to grip officials charged with high-level response to major crises who prove relatively ineffective in crisis management for two reasons. The first is that they treat disasters as scaled-up incidents, which means they tend to work within an irrelevant paradigm. A second contributor to failure of emergency coordination is that disasters frequently knock out communications, transport and key infrastructure across a wide area, and this compounds the inherent difficulties in obtaining information about what is happening. Good examples include the failure to immediately deploy a military response to the 9-11 attacks; and France's inability to control riots for 10 days in November 2005. One of the most glaring examples of inaction involved FEMA in the face of Hurricane Katrina's devastation of New Orleans in 2005. Unfortunately FEMA has been the subject of chronic criticism except for a short period during the late 1990s (see, for example, the review of its performance by Schneider, 1998).

Chronic weakness at the strategic and command levels of major crises is not a trivial issue and is recognized by emergency managers. A New York Fire Department Deputy Assistant Chief wrote: 'The vast majority of [emergency response] plans work well during routine operations but often fail in a crisis, since a crisis often eliminates the relevance of standard assumptions made during planning' (Sawyer and Pfeifer, 2006: 249). This reflection from tough experiences goes on to argue that plans are prepared to meet compliance requirements, rather than to provide realistic guidance; have limited circulation; and are quickly out of date. The plans are tested in unrealistic scenarios and static settings that fail to 'force decision makers into uncomfortable territory ... Lead us to overestimate our capabilities to respond to an extended crisis ... and allow complacency to emerge'.

Retrospectives of national crises point to three deficiencies in their management. The first is that crisis managers are either not briefed well or do not listen to their briefs, and even well after the incident do not appear to have a grasp on their magnitude. For example, a week after Hurricane Katrina hit New Orleans in September 2005, the city's mayor put the death toll at more than 10,000, whereas the final toll was about 2,500 including missing people.

The second deficiency is for national crisis managers to overdramatize the incident. New Orleans Mayor Ray Nagin told Oprah Winfrey: 'They have people standing out there, have been in that frickin' Superdome for five days watching dead bodies, watching hooligans killing people, raping people' (Carr, 2005). Although similar wild reports were common, each proved unfounded. This is consistent with the perspective of Parachini (2006: 31) who argued that politicians are rewarded for decisiveness, their 'instinctive route is to play it safe and extrapolate worst-case conclusions from imperfect information, even if serious consequences for government resource allocation result'.

The third point is that Government will needlessly withhold information from the public. A good example came in the wake of the London bombings on 7 July 2005 when Australia's Foreign Minister Downer told a doorstop interview: 'We've had very good briefings from the British Government ... They've given us figures on casualties and so on but we'd leave them to make those announcements.' At this time London's police chief Sir Ian Blair was being interviewed on BBC television and refused to answer any questions about casualties.

An exception to the pattern of weak crisis management was the archetypal response by Mayor Giuliani's team following 9 September 2001. In a thorough review of his actions after the attacks, Cohen, Eimicke and Horan (2002) drew a number of important conclusions. Response planning is essential and they pointed to the $US13 million 4,500 square metre watch command that had been established downtown and constant insistence on preparedness that avoided complacency setting in. Unfortunately this emergency operations post could not be used as it was in the World Trade Center, but catastrophe-ready procedures quickly shifted control to the library at the Police Academy. Pre-arrangement of emergency plans and responses allowed for decentralized decision making which became vital when communications failed due to damage and overload and the formal chain of command broke down. Despite this, transportation control over buses, trains, ferries and traffic lights operated independently to evacuate the city. One omission was that communications systems were not redundant, and emergency workers failed to collect all their equipment before responding. Certainly cynical observers might dismiss such positive evaluations as unduly favourable, but they do point towards what is best practice.

Looking ahead the poor record of management of national crises is a significant risk in every country. Certainly the first critical response to most disasters is provided by people on the spot: commuters, local policemen, off-duty firemen and so on. Whether this has involved a house fire or tragedy on the scale of 9-11, victims are generally well served by their fellow citizens. This is the best protection for those who suffer disaster.

But politicians and senior officials who manage national crises have a much greater strategic role. Their first duty, of course, is to prevent disasters. The media have reported that numerous major terrorist incidents have been thwarted since 9-11, but provided only sketchy details, and ran the government line uncritically. I personally would be comforted by some in-depth coverage. Those whose plans were ruined know all the details, so it is hardly a matter of national security to withhold the information. The public who are at risk from incidents have a right to know the nature and scale of these threats; it is up to them to judge what response to take, including – if they deem it appropriate – make changes in their lifestyle to minimize risk.

A second duty of crisis managers is to have in place a mechanism that enables speedy and efficient response. The evidence suggests that facts are not assembled and analyzed: most governments desperately need a working crisis room where experienced people can assess a situation, develop responses and monitor progress.

The third responsibility is to entrust management of a crisis only to people who have appropriate skills and can cope with pressures and uncertainties. These are not necessarily possessed even by the most capable and senior politicians and bureaucrats. Crisis managers need to be appointed for their ability, not status. Sawyer and Pfeifer (2006: 256) propose military training as an appropriate model as it delivers 'targeted training ... [which] exposes individuals (and organizations) to high stress training in completely unfamiliar scenarios, and then rigorously reviewing with trainees the ways they gathered information to help them recognise threats, identify central problems and make correct decisions'. This is the type of exposure needed by all crisis managers.

Conclusions

Although risk management is a well-studied topic, national risk strategies are very much in their infancy. Part of this is due to the complexity of the issue. Part is due to the natural tendency to break big problems into components that can be directly addressed. Unfortunately, the reductionist approach prevents a holistic perspective on national issues.

Looking ahead there are a growing number of credible risks that could impact at a national level and/or require a national-level response. Some are international in nature, such as: global environmental and health threats; regional economic and market contagion; backlashes from marginalized or threatened nations and social groups; and risks to physical links and commerce between nations. Other risks are domestic and are sourced in government and non-government institutions; critical infrastructure; and provision of essential goods and services. These national risks can be natural or man-made; slow or fast to emerge; new and old (although predictions of the occurrence of new risks is far less likely to prove well-founded than claimed by their sponsors).

Today's risk environment is different to that of earlier times because of the greater complexity of many technologies and systems, tighter linkages that cause shocks to cascade unpredictably and concentration of processes that prevents individuals from monitoring their efficacy. Thus risks have proliferated and become more diffuse; they are difficult to understand, detect and control. The stresses of contemporary risks require coordinated response at the national level that has sufficient strategic capability to identify emerging and longer-term exposures. This is easily said, but can only be achieved by meeting complex technical, social and managerial challenges. History shows that complacency will inevitably have high cost in lives and damaged resources. It is time for most countries to take a more comprehensive and integrated perspective on national risks.

CHAPTER 12 Management of Corporate Crises

To avoid all mistakes in the conduct of great enterprises is beyond man's powers.
Plutarch (46–127), *Lives: Fabius*

Things usually improve for the better.
John Wayne in his title role of *Chisum* (1970)

This chapter diverges from the book's theme as – rather than introducing strategies that proactively manage risk – it outlines techniques for corporates and governments to respond to unexpectedly elevated risks, or crises. The focus is largely on man-made disasters.

The crisis management literature is extensive and growing. However, it is dominated by case studies which assume crises impacting organizations are infrequent, often unique events. Thus the emphasis is on avoidance through sound risk management, and flexible response through robust crisis management plans. These are concerned with the mechanics of crises: they tend to report best practices in crisis management teams, and summarize learnings from well-publicized crises. My approach, however, is to profile techniques and tools that will be required by executives and Boards of companies in crisis.

This chapter starts by defining a corporate crisis and then discusses the experience of corporate crises in Australia; this background is used to develop a natural history of corporate crises, and a framework for their management.

What Constitutes a 'Crisis'?

A *crisis* involves a single incident or issue which escalates uncontrollably and causes such serious damage to the assets, reputation and performance of an organization that its viability is threatened. Crises are characterised by abrupt emergence or unexpected escalation, and sweeping potential damage. They are serious, threatening events outside the organization's normal experience.

The incidents and issues leading to a corporate crisis may have natural causes or be man-made; can have their genesis inside or outside the company; impact the firm at a single location or be diffused and even virtual; damage either tangible or intangible assets; involve a legislative breach or not; and be confined to the firm or extend to other firms or even envelop whole industries. Table 12.1 gives some examples of recent Australian crises to show their breadth.

Table 12.1 Examples of corporate crises in Australia

Attribute	Category	Example
Cause	Natural event	Sudden death of Qantas passenger with DVT in 2000
	Man-made	Macquarie Bank employee charged with insider trading in 1997
Source	Inside firm	National Bank board room dispute following unauthorized trading losses in 2004
	Outside firm	Cyclone Larry destroyed banana crop in 2006
Location in firm	Confined	Legionnaire's disease killed patrons at Melbourne Aquarium in 2000
	Widespread/virtual	Contamination of Mobil-supplied avgas in 1999
Assets damaged	Tangible	Pasminco collapse in 2001 following trading losses
	Intangible	Cash-for-comment in 1999 after radio broadcasters promoted bank activities
Behaviour	Legislative breach	Recall of Panadol tablets in 2000 following deliberate strychnine contamination
	Legal activities	Criticism of BHP in 1994 over environmental damage at Ok Tedi mine
Extent of impact	Confined to firm	LPG tank at Boral's Sydney facility exploded in 1990
	Industry wide	Breast implant class actions around the world after late 1980s

This leads to a typology of crisis types based on their source (inside or outside the firm) and whether their impact is tangible (largely operational failures) or intangible (impacting reputation, ethics).

An important implication of my definition of corporate crisis is that serious incidents and issues can occur without escalating into crises. For instance, defective or contaminated products have become relatively common. In Australia, product recalls have doubled in frequency since the late 1990s to average around 750 voluntary each year. Very few, however, become crises, perhaps no more than 1 per cent.

A source of crisis that rarely escalates is white collar crime and employee theft: anecdotal evidence is that serious examples – such as deliberate falsification of financial and operating reports – are relatively common, but most are handled quietly and rarely make the news. Another good example of an incident with generally stillborn crisis potential is failure of containment of radioactive material. Although there have been at least six serious leaks of radioactive material from Australia's operating uranium mines since 1994, none escalated into a crisis. Other examples of incidents that did not become crises include industrial fatalities under questionable circumstances, financial scandals such as insider trading and botched medical procedures.

	Tangible (Operations)	**Intangible**
Internal	Sabotage Supplier/utility failure Natural disaster	Regulation Takeover Theft
	Product defect Fire, explosion Systems failure	Labour dispute Ethical breach Theft

Figure 12.1 Taxonomy of crisis types

Given that there are many incidents that could become crises but do not, it is interesting to examine factors which trigger escalation to a crisis.

The first contributor to emergence of a corporate crisis is a big target, preferably one that is already prepped for censure. Typically a company that becomes embroiled in a crisis already ranks low in the opinion of the media and public. With minimal trust, doubt and malicious interpretations become a natural response. In addition, large organizations are expected to respond efficiently and sympathetically to any perceived shortcomings, and their failure to perform is not forgiven as it might be in a firm with fewer resources. McDonald and Härtel (2000a) catalogue other factors that influence the escalation of a serious incident: amount and intensity of media coverage; familiarity of the company's name and its reputation; severity of the incident and injuries; regulatory attention; consumer involvement; and the company's response.

The second pointer to crisis is location of the incident. Crises tend to arise in population clusters such as the Sydney-Canberra-Melbourne axis in Australia, or the north-east and south-west coasts of the US. They are especially likely to escalate when the incident has a simple, graphic cause-and-effect that makes it telegenic. A truism is that the intensity of community reaction is directly related to individuals' personal links: a peripheral problem will be catalogued with remote humanitarian crises; but something close to home which taps people's worst fears evokes emotion. Thus crises arise out of situations in which many observers believe that they are, or could have been, affected. 'Hey! That could be me!'

The third key to development of a crisis is a champion to keep the issue alive. This can be an activist individual or group; and it will be ensured by any hint of cover-up, stonewalling or bunker mentality by the company involved. One certain trigger is to refuse comment – even for the initial few hours – as it shows the company is not in control of the events, or fears exposure. That is why swift acceptance of responsibility, delivered plainly with an assurance of restitution (and ideally an honest apology) can so often defuse a situation: it stops a chain reaction which villianizes the company. From the perspective of consumer audiences, the most satisfying corporate responses to crises are in decreasing order of merit: confession and apology; excuse and justification; and denial and silence (McDonald and Härtel, 2000a). This explains why most incidents quickly disappear from public attention unless the company shows signs of mismanaging the response.

Unfortunately, too many organizations think about crises in their own terms, and lose sight of the fact that other people may not share the same paradigm. Putting it bluntly, there is no point in providing a coldly logical response to an emotional concern. Perhaps that is why so many poorly managed crises involve companies with an inward-looking culture that are run by technocrats.

The final contributor to escalation of a crisis is judgement by the media and other observers (who are often not knowledgeable, much less expert, in the topic) that it *should* have been preventable (Smith, 1992). Thus recurring, expected mishaps – white collar crime, road trauma and isolated accidents – which form the staple of 'bad news' stories are covered in brief by the media and then dismissed as routine foibles. Similarly an earthquake or wildfire will be excused as beyond anyone's control, and reporting is limited to costs and injuries. But spectacular industrial disasters, sloppy responses to crisis and uncaring officials can be stereotyped to symbolize all that is wrong with technology and modern organizations. Thus a plant explosion should have been avoided by technology and skill; bodies charged with emergency response should function flawlessly; and executives should smoothly manage great uncertainty. The media report these incidents as unique events caused by a clearly errant party, rather than just another episode in a complex, ever-changing industrial environment. Although the media is often said to have a short attention span, it and the public will follow a juicy crisis for 2 weeks or more, which can seem a lifetime to those impacted.

Frequency of Corporate Crises

An important gap in the literature of corporate crises is that data on their frequency is very limited, and little has been compiled with academic rigour. In their survey of 114 *Fortune* 1,000 companies, Mitroff, Pauchant and Shrivastava (1989) estimated that large American corporations face ten crises a year. The Institute of Crisis Management (ICM, 2005) found the frequency of crises in the US stayed roughly constant during the 1990s at around 7,000 per year (it defines 'crisis' as 'any problem or disruption which triggers negative stakeholder reactions and results in extensive public scrutiny'). There was an increase in crises resulting from class actions, product recalls and workplace violence, whilst those arising from environmental damage, corporate mismanagement and white collar crime diminished. According to one UK survey of disasters, companies suffered a major Information Technology event every 6 years (Price, 2000).

The balance of this section reports results from my study of crises in Australia (Coleman, 2004), as a guide to their frequency in developed economies.

Australia is generally a low-risk continent: the frequency of man-made disasters is only a quarter of that expected if the world's crises were distributed according to population or GDP; even the frequency of natural disasters is under half the expected value (Swiss Re, 2006 and earlier years).

Using the earlier definition, there have been six types of corporate crises in Australia:

- product defect or contamination;
- operational failure, mostly fires and explosions;
- financial, including trading losses and unwanted takeovers;

- organizational, including labour disputes and whistle blowing;
- regulatory and legal, including action by government authorities;
- threat and extortion, including blockades.

Between 1990 and 2001, 55 such crises occurred and their details are summarized in Table 12.2. Some of these are the subject of published case studies, including: extortion threats against Herron and GlaxoSmithKline (*CEO Forum* at www.ceoforum.com.au/200109_ceodialogue.cfm); Kraft's contaminated peanut butter incident (McDonald and Härtel, 2000b); an outbreak of legionnaires' disease in Sydney in 1992 (Lupton, 1995); and an oil spill in Sydney Harbour (Lipscombe, 2000).

A number of interesting conclusions come from this data:

- Corporate crises were infrequent until 1992–3 brought a wave of product recalls, extortion threats and operating disasters. Since then, their frequency has been roughly constant at around five each year.

Table 12.2 Australian corporate crises 1990 to 2001

	1990–1992	1993–1995	1996–1998	1999–2001	TOTAL
Type of Crisis					
Product Defect	1				1
Operational	2	7	9	11	29
Financial		1	1	2	4
Organizational		2	2	2	6
Regulatory/Legal	1	2	2	1	6
Threat/Extortion	2	2	2	3	9
Industry Involved					
Agriculture		1	2		3
Mining & Resources		4	1	2	7
Manufacturing	4	5	7	5	21
Wholesale & Retail		1			1
Transport	1			5	6
Banking & Finance		1	1	2	4
Services	1	2	5	5	13
TOTAL	6	14	16	19	55

182 Risk Strategies

- Over half of all crises are operational when some aspect of plant or process fails and leads to an incident or product defect. The annual frequency is increasing.
- Most years saw an extortion threat serious enough to reach the media. This is probably somewhat less than the total given that there were 13 cases of extortion or threats in Australia between 1990 and 1993 (Burbury, 1993), but only four were reported by the media. Although irritating for researchers, this is understandable given industry's determination to play down such incidents because extortion attempts tend to spawn copy cat imitators.
- Many crises are extortion attempts and product defects which directly impact wholesalers and/or retailers, and make this sector the most prone to crisis with a cost to consumers of $A10 million each year (Crittle, 2000).
- No industry is immune from crisis; and they can occur well outside normal activities. Canberra Hospital, for instance, was embroiled in an operational crisis when its demolition went wrong and a spectator was killed by flying debris.
- Crises tend to cluster, with sequential impacts within companies and industries. Their frequency has fallen in the resources sector, but grown in transport and services.
- Almost half the crises involved large companies (defined as members of the Business Council of Australia).
- At least 14 of the 51 companies involved in crises have gone out of business through liquidation, sale or takeover; or else lost their identity in a merger. In Australia, 27 per cent of companies did not survive a crisis.
- Of the 37 companies that survived, four faced years of rolling crises.

The key conclusion from this data is that crises tend to have traits in common and can be categorized. This suggests that much can be learned from their patterns.

Lifecycle of a Crisis

A complication in seeking to describe the natural history of crises is that they follow a chaotic course: these complex, shocking events do not have a roadmap, nor is there a track that they habitually follow. Some incidents never become crises; but in identical cases, minor actions (analogous to the flap of a butterfly's wings) precipitate huge consequences. Because crises are susceptible to external nudges, allowing them to develop unfettered is irresponsible. This is why crises can – and must – be managed.

Share prices are directly impacted by crises which typically trigger an immediate drop of up to 10 per cent (Hooker and Salin, 1999). After that – in testimony to Nietzsche's observation: 'What doesn't kill me makes me stronger' – the share price of companies whose management demonstrates talent in responding to the crisis rises to be about 10 per cent above the pre-crisis price at the end of 2 months; conversely the share price of firms where management responds poorly lose an average of about 15 per cent (Knight and Pretty, 1997). Viscusi (1993) reported that fatalities in major incidents such as airline crashes and hotel fires were valued by stock markets at a current day equivalent of around $US100 million per death, presumably because disasters raise doubts about other potential exposures and bring into question management's ability, particularly to avoid further loss.

Experience around the world shows that crises can roll on and on when their root causes are systemic. This typically occurs in high-risk conditions such as those created by financial pressures which push resources and people to their limits; external shifts such as deregulation which promote moral hazard and distract management; and restructuring, takeover or change which weaken expertise and continuity. Moreover crises attract unprecedented attention which can identify parallel problems or magnify otherwise minor incidents. And inevitably the distraction of a crisis and its stresses on people and resources exacerbate other smouldering problems. Crises are no respecters of geography, and the internationalization of companies brings crises offshore following political turmoil, environmental incidents and illegal activities.

Thus it is not surprising that crises can become endemic. For instance BHP was considered one of Australia's best corporate performers until the mid 1990s when everything started to go wrong: 20 workers were killed in 2 years; a debilitating class action commenced over environmental damage caused by its Ok Tedi mine in Papua New Guinea; and the company suffered Australia's worst oil spill (Howarth, 1995). A similar fate had enveloped Pacific Dunlop a few years earlier after its strategies were routinely doubted amidst a string of embarrassing product recalls (Shoebridge, 1995). And Qantas experienced a series of maintenance problems after one of its 747s overshot the runway in Bangkok in late 1999 (Mercer, 2000); it again underwent the same wide questioning of its maintenance efficiency after yet another string of incidents in 2008, including explosion of an oxygen cylinder in flight.

Similar sequential crises befall whole industries, too, largely when chronic shortcomings emerge and attract intense scrutiny. Travails across an industry (as with a firm) are often preceded by hubris. For instance, in January 1995 a young girl died and several hundred others were poisoned by *mettwurst*, a form of fermented meat, made by Garibaldi Smallgoods in South Australia. Just before this crisis, Australia's food monitors bragged about their achievements (de Silva, 1994):

> In Australia food is now so safe that the scientists who regularly test it for contaminants are finding it difficult to plot their results. The latest survey of foods by the National Food Authority – the 1992 Australian Market Basket Survey – shows that Australian food is safer than ever ... Levels of contaminants were now so low or non-existent that the authority was having great problems presenting the survey results.

Perhaps the most interesting industry-wide series of crises in the Australian region occurred during 1998 with disastrous failures at three utilities: bacterial contamination of Sydney's water supply; an explosion at Esso's Longford plant which cut natural gas supplies to Melbourne; and failure of Mercury Energy's electricity network to Auckland. Each had been previously reliable but suffered process failures that lasted weeks and paralyzed a major city. At the time of writing, industry-wide crises which have emerged or could emerge involve financial planners, security guards, broadband services and water utilities.

No matter what the cause of chronic crises, it is hard not to conclude that a shared system of the wrong values within an organization or industry predisposes it to multiple defects that precede serious failures.

Psychic Aspects of Crises

For many people impacted by a crisis, it is a paradigm shattering event: how could this happen? The shock can be huge because 'disasters destroy not only lives, but also reputations, resources, legitimacy and trust' (Farjoun and Starbuck, 2005: 3).

Crises typically occur suddenly, or – even if recognized and smouldering – were not expected to cause trouble. Because of their shock, crises can unfold along the lines of a classic grieving process. The first response is denial and anger: how can this happen given all our work on risk management, quality control, and so on? An unfortunate consequence is that this can mire the company in denial and leave it slow to implement crisis management plans and react appropriately to urgent issues.

Anyone who has participated in a crisis knows they have a life, and – like all living beings – pass through stages. Table 12.3 shows reactions to be expected in those close to the crisis, and those who are more remote with an organizational perspective.

Table 12.3 Chaotic sequencing of crises

Stage	Personal Reactions	Organizational Reactions
Trigger/Incident	Not acknowledged or remedied	Recognition
Build-up	Denial, isolation, stress	Emotional response builds
Crisis	Grief, anger	Anger and outrage
Post-crisis	Recrimination, reaction	Litigation, regulation
Recovery	Radical change or collapse	Reputation fallout

Dealing with grief is a learned response, so individuals and organizations that have been through one crisis generally handle the next one(s) better. This means that there is always room to learn and improve the way crises are handled. This has encouraged growing interest in providing crisis teams with guidance on what psychologists term naturalistic decision making, which is the style required under time pressure in ill structured, dynamic and risky environments. However, there is still little guidance on the shattering personal consequences and pressures which are typical of most crises, and few crisis management teams are trained to expect and handle the stress of crisis trauma, and the affects it has on performance.

There is considerable coverage of the psychic aspects of crises in the medical and psychology literature, particularly of natural disasters. Krug et al. (1998) evaluated the scale of psychic disruption as measured by suicide rates after major natural disasters in the US between 1982 and 1989. When compared to national figures, the suicide rate in affected counties was 63 per cent higher in the year after an earthquake, 31 per cent higher in the 2 years after a hurricane, and 14 per cent higher in the 4 years after a flood. Steinglass and Gerrity (1990) studied families relocated after natural disasters in the US and found significant short-term symptoms which only abated after about 18 months.

Another characteristic of crises that can unsettle those involved is their uncertainty. Even in the case of a discrete, one-time event – fire, accident, structural failure – the full extent of the impact can take time to unravel as knock-on effects emerge. And, of course, there are many other crises – especially those with less tangible impacts on quality, health, reputation and financial capability – which can become quite drawn out because their evolution depends on time or the judgement and actions of others.

The significance of people issues and the depth of uncertainty make leadership critical. This requires the core competencies of being able to lift the fog surrounding the crisis, clarify its issues and lay down a framework that can shape the response of those with good technical skills, but less foresight or perspective. A crisis is an unplanned – but time critical – event, often involving significant expenditures and many rapid decisions. For people used to schedules, well-laid plans and clear budgets, it can be unsettling. Leaders help with adaptation to more fluid processes. They also preserve sufficient integrity in *all* systems to ensure they withstand close scrutiny, even well after the event.

A final psychic aspect of crises is the need for 'closure': participants tend to want or expect some formal recognition that signals an end to the crisis and provides catharsis so they can put the experience behind them and move on. Crisis leaders will be alert to the need for closure, but will resist acting too early only to face a flare-up. Thus they set clear measures which signal the end of crisis and wait until they are met: as these milestones pass by, they send their own powerful signal.

Crises are replete with behavioural biases. One is an unwillingness to crystallize losses or accept an error, so acknowledging a crisis exists – (say) by convening a crisis management team, or even using the word 'crisis' – means admitting a serious deficiency and can be avoided. A second common behavioural bias is the high discount rate that is applied to risk, expenditure and the negative aspects of a decision: this can also lead decision makers to defer consideration of a crisis. Overlaying this, too, is the instinctive reaction to shock which is denial. Taken together, these biases can make firms in a crisis appear to procrastinate, dither and refuse to acknowledge what might appear quite obvious to dispassionate observers. Leaders in a crisis need to push ahead more assertively than is required in normal business settings.

In summary the intensely human aspects of a crisis are only rarely captured in training or commentaries, but they need to be specifically comprehended in crisis response.

Crisis Planning

Military planners assume that 'on any day there could be a crisis. And the chances are great that it would happen at night at a point exactly between the borders of two outdated maps' (Cohen, 2006: 29). The old adage, then, is right that 'you can never be prepared for a crisis, but you must always be ready for one,' and demands a comprehensive crisis plan and training.

Risk-alert organizations recognize they can usually intervene somewhere along the chain of events to stop crises. Thus Enterprise Risk Management (ERM) and Key Risk Indicators (KRIs) are important tools in crisis planning and response. Finance organizations are good examples of best-practice in avoidance as everyone is continually alert to risks. Recruiting and training emphasize responsibility and integrity; auditing is internalized and continual; monitoring and reporting are open and thoughtful; there are early warning systems to detect problems in operations or quality; and management agrees with Thomas Jefferson that the price of operational integrity is eternal vigilance.

But with our limited foresight, even the best risk management cannot guarantee a crisis will never occur. By the time a firm is embroiled in a crisis, which is a significant probability no matter how good risk management processes are this, it is too late to plan. All firms must have a shelf strategy available that sets out generic responses, resources, policies and responsibilities to recover from crises. Some of these elements are set out in the description of Plan B in the accompanying box.

Table 12.4 Plan B

Critical Question: Is Plan B in Place?

Is there a mechanism to independently monitor operational performance (including customer feedback) for defects and lead indicators of crisis?

Are there adequate resources to identify and fix problems before they escalate?

Are resources pre-positioned to cope with generic crises? This includes nominated staff and identified facilities.

Who is the 'Red Adair'* of each potential crisis?

What is our crisis strategy?

* Paul N. 'Red' Adair (1915–2004) helped pioneer the technology of extinguishing oil well fires and fought major blazes including those following a 1968 Bass Strait blowout, the Piper Alpha North Sea platform explosion in 1988 and the 1991 Kuwaiti oil well fires. His exploits were immortalised in the movie *Hellfighters* starring John Wayne.

The Crisis Plan should clearly set out resources and responsibilities in the event of a crisis. But it should also detail key principles that will be used to guide participants. These could include safety, preservation of the environment, customer interests, stakeholder need to know and protection of reputation.

Good crisis management plans will map out key strategy issues: 'this is what we promise'. These principles cover safety, costs, reliability and compensation. They include a customer charter and dedicated call centre; an insistence on ethical, honest and equitable behaviours; and a clear statement that nothing will be contemplated which could damage brand or reputation. Plans recognize that crises demand communications with third parties on an abnormal scale and provide adequate skilled resources. Every company should have up-to-date electronic mailing lists of all its shareholders, employees and customers so that it can quickly communicate with these key stakeholders.

Crisis planning needs to incorporate criteria that enable quick acknowledgement of serious incidents and initiates early intervention. Recurring findings of crisis post audits are that they are not isolated acts-of-god but the culmination of a series of incidents, often with enough warnings to have enabled pre-emption. Thus in a scathing review of Boeing's practices after a crash, the *Washington Post* said: '... we know that most disasters have early warning signals that responsible people fail to detect' (Ignatius, 1999). Many disaster post-audits will attribute the occurrence of a disaster to a culture of denial (Hopkins, 2002).

Given repeated delays in crisis responses, the Crisis Plan's bias should be towards prudent over-reaction. It costs nothing to pull together a crisis team: do it as soon as a potential crisis emerges so that real horsepower is turned on to an issue when it is still controllable. Bring in skilled outside resources (which should have been pre-identified) early for their expertise in unfamiliar areas, and the immediate boost to scanty resources in specialist groups such as public affairs, response planning and insurance. Good outsiders are also detached from events and provide a much-needed independent reality test of plans. This supports an outward-looking perspective for crisis response.

In fact it is desirable to aggressively over-resource every area. Time becomes a precious commodity: everyone wants information immediately; everyone wants every task completed fast. At the same time everyone is at the bottom of the learning curve and under great pressure. A good example of useful specialist skills is provided by the disaster in 2006 at the Beaconsfield Mine in Tasmania where two miners were trapped underground for 2 weeks. Management brought in experts on nutrition and psychology who had been involved in a similar incident in Thredbo in 1997 where a man was trapped under a mudslide for 3 days (Wright, 2006).

Ensure there is a regular presence of highly visible senior executives in affected areas. Set up a toll-free number and ensure it is staffed during extended hours. Publish bulletins, press releases and other briefs on the company's website. Be seen. Conduct face-to-face briefings with government and key interest groups. Identify and brief vocal opponents.

Watch out for people involved in the crisis response. Go overboard on hygiene (food, drinks); insist on taxis to and from work for anyone working long hours. Make space for all participants. Enforce rest breaks, prevent pointless meetings, dedicate weekends to strategy. Tired people make mistakes, and – unless there is time for reflection – errors can be serious. Force people to physically get away at least every 2 weeks. If the crisis is likely to prove prolonged, set up A and B crisis management teams that rotate in and out.

By definition, every crisis results in major costs, and it is natural for those affected to seek compensation through litigation, including class actions. So even though claims processes are oft neglected in crisis preparations, they are a powerful tool in a well-developed strategy to respond quickly and equitably to damages from a crisis. This area is discussed in some detail in a following section.

Management of a Crisis

Without writing a manual, what lessons can be learned from crises?

By definition a crisis takes its managers outside their historical experience, and it demands rarely used skills and competencies. The logistics of a product recall, for instance, are not the mirror image of product delivery as recall involves simultaneous return and resupply, storage and disposal of large quantities of defective inventory, extensive testing of product quality and rework of faulty products.

Crises also tend to isolate the participants so that they lose their normal frames of reference, which places a premium on good communications to and from the crisis managers. The intensity and duration of effort required of crisis managers can be high. Crises move faster than expected, in unanticipated directions. This makes it hard to distinguish overreaction from prudent anticipation and no-regrets actions. Moreover stress levels can be very high.

These factors combine so that managers of crises face four challenging paradoxes:

- stakes are high, but control is impracticable;
- knowledge gaps are huge, but action is essential;
- the causes of the crisis may be systemic, but response must be flawless;
- insiders must manage the response, but they can lack independent credibility.

Crises are typically plagued by inadequate resources, as their onset is often traced to a lack of adequate physical, financial or managerial resources. The shortage(s) that brought on the crisis need to be immediately redressed, and additional resources brought in to handle the surge in crisis response activity. Not surprisingly, the most common strategic blunder when crises emerge is to be slow in deploying adequate equipment, personnel and other supports to respond and accelerate early recovery. For instance, a victims' perspective of the response of the Federal Emergency Management Agency (FEMA) following the destruction of New Orleans by Hurricane Katrina in 2005 was that: 'most of [FEMA's failings] reflected simple ineptitude in the art of mustering available resources' (Horne, 2006: 89). Similarly the major criticism of the response by Exxon Corporation's management to the 1989 oil spill in Alaska from its tanker the *Valdez* was that they seemed slow to take the matter seriously, and to deploy adequate clean up resources.

Crisis managers need to have a strong bias towards aggressive proaction, but must also recognize numerous barriers, most obviously because it is invariably hard to fully comprehend the impact of a crisis as it unfolds: even when the effects are geographically concentrated, assets are damaged, observers are distracted and communications are disrupted. Thus crisis managers can face lengthy delays in gaining a full appreciation of what needs to be done.

Once the decision is taken to deploy resources, the process of getting them in place can prove unexpectedly complicated because crises disrupt normal supply lines through their direct effects and also because they induce heavy congestion from respondents and observers. For instance a plant explosion will close nearby streets; see others blocked by fire trucks, ambulances and emergency vehicles; and attract sightseers. This makes access difficult. Communications can be disrupted, too, by physical damage to power and telecommunications equipment; and by congestion on the system.

Thus a crisis manager who is determined to act prudently and avoid overreaction will take so long to gain complete certainty and respond appropriately that the effort will be clearly inadequate: unfortunately this outcome is common. Crisis managers must, therefore, act without certainty. In fact uncertainty is the defining characteristic of a crisis, and it can be very broad ranging. Just some of the uncertain aspects include: what happened and why; the extent of damage and its implications; what immediate dangers and risks exist; what resources and skills are required for response, and their availability; who is entitled to what (if any) compensation; and when and how will 'normal operations' be resumed. These are pressing concerns to those impacted by a crisis who include owners, employees, suppliers and customers of the affected entity; each will seek to understand their position and protect their rights. Crisis managers require considerable judgement in seeking timely response. They can do worse than mimic Nelson's advice to his captains on the eve of the Battle of Trafalgar: 'No captain can do very wrong if he places his ship alongside that of an enemy.'

Given the importance of the psychological aspects of a crisis, 'soft' issues are critical in planning the best response. Although every crisis is different, good technical solutions are but half of best practice management: the balance is ensuring acceptable perception of the response. It does not take long for the wrong attitude to make employees, customers and shareholders lose faith; regulators and analysts feel exposed; industry groups and unions feel let down; and everybody with a grudge seek revenge. A significant portion of the response to any crisis needs to be directed at its broad-ranging human consequences.

When communicating about crises, start with an explanation and expression of sympathy; never say anything that is wrong, incomplete or undeliverable; and continually emphasize the importance of solutions, safety and equitable treatment for everyone affected. Let those interested understand what happened, how, and why it will not happen again: provide clear briefs in lay and technical language.

Outside the company, crises produce victims and perpetrators, spectators and bystanders; and they attract a gallery. None can be ignored. A good response is to quickly establish a hardship fund which gives modest, but credible, ex gratia amounts to anybody who is impacted by the crisis; and to cover their out of pocket expenses such as accommodation and travel.

The other half of every optimal response will be to manage a set of interests, concerns and stakeholder needs which are unfamiliar in their character, volume and geography. Even application of technical skills is usually in unaccustomed fashion. An example discussed above is that a distribution group instructed to implement a product recall must efficiently carry out tasks that are quite different to its normal work.

Thus, although it seems logical to select a crisis manager from amongst senior executives with detailed operating knowledge of the area impacted, it can be better to deploy a skilled individual with experience in crises and the proven ability to withstand their pressures. The pool of potential crisis managers should only include those who answer a firm 'Yes' when asked: 'Do the following statements accurately describe your behaviour?':

- I find it easy to stay cool under pressure;
- I rarely suffer from hurt feelings;
- I remain cheerful when things go wrong;
- I evaluate situations quickly and accurately;
- I can make many quick decisions.

Because the lessons of successful crisis management can best be learned experientially, the ideal crisis manager will have already been involved in a crisis, and will be biased towards promoting favourable public judgement. No matter what the textbooks say, there is no way to train for a crisis. In fact my experience is that simulations are so different to a real crisis that they can instil a false sense of confidence. Thus first hand experience is a vital component of any crisis management team.

One of the delegates at a conference where I presented on risk management came up to me afterwards and introduced himself. He was a senior Army officer and believed that much military training was in fact preparation for crisis management. That makes it relevant to see the qualities that Sir Basil Liddell Hart (1943), the doyen of military strategy analysts, said were required of a general: mental initiative, a strong and positive personality; understanding of human nature; capacity for ruthless determination; an ability to communicate clearly; the power to quickly assess complex situations; and both exceptional ability and commonsense. These are the attributes required of a crisis manager, too.

Once a company is in a crisis, four initial decisions seem crucial.

The first is whether or not to pre-empt possibilities. Prudent anticipation, no-regrets actions and the like acknowledge that events move so fast that waiting for certainty will leave crisis managers too far behind. Thus low-cost activities like pre-positioning resources or planning major efforts such as product recalls can give a jump start if needed. Moreover a bias in favour of employees, safety and customers will help accelerate desirable responses.

A valuable no-regrets initiative is to call on support from suppliers – everyone from banks to security services – and assistance from local authorities and even competitors. This clearly establishes a willingness to accept help in reaching a solution, and can also speed the recovery process. Similarly quickly engaging experts provides an outside view, experienced input and additional scarce assistance. Moreover everyone in a crisis is time poor, so it is wise to activate support resources, including administrators, secretarial support and so on.

The second decision relates to communications, particularly in relation to pre-emption which can be considered at two levels. The first is in deciding how to announce a potential crisis: management change, product or strategy failure, profit reversal and the like. There can be a temptation to downplay issues and assume (or hope) that no one will notice. But if there is a void and the company does not fill it, then someone else will; and this may be with rumour, innuendo or speculation that can be both wrong and damaging.[1] Seizing the initiative secures some control over the process.

The other area of pre-emptive communications arises because crisis teams become so focussed on their tasks that they lose normal contact. They need to guard against failure to hear stakeholder disquiet. Crisis teams need to establish formal and informal mechanisms to monitor the voice of the customer and other key stakeholders. This can be achieved through media reports, summaries of telephone contacts and the like.

A related step is to select the public face of the company during the crisis. There is a natural tendency to stall until 'all' the facts are known, and use public relations professionals to deal with the media. Conversely, the Jack Welch view is that when companies are confronted with a crisis, the chief executive needs to face the public with self-confidence. Best practice companies issue a statement within a few hours of an incident, and update it continuously.

The question of an apology inevitably surfaces during a crisis. It is quite practical to act responsibly without accepting (or even expecting) liability. This is common, for instance, with mutual aid where an organization will contribute assistance even though it had no part in causing the crisis or incident. But on other occasions swift acceptance of responsibility, assurance of restitution and an honest apology will demonstrate control and defuse a situation (McDonald and Härtel, 2000a).

Communicate early and earnestly with customers, employees and other important groups. Even if it is hard to say 'sorry', apologizing for any inconvenience is a nice touch. Similarly it is good to commit to act responsibly, even without accepting any responsibility.

---

[1] Winston Churchill: 'A rumour can be half way round the world before truth has time to get its trousers on.'; Alexander Pope: 'All who told it added something new; and all who heard it made enlargements too.'

Appoint a clear thinking, resilient 'conscience' who independently monitors and reports all feedback whether it be by phone, letter or media.

Build 'responsibility' into crisis management. Make sure accountants, safety officers, engineers and marketers are in every loop. Designate explicit 'voices' of the customer, employees and community. Have dedicated facilities in place for the crisis management team(s). When any commitments are made, have a formal process to ensure compliance, such as an external auditor onsite.

Also important in a crisis is facing down vocal critics. Just as young army officers are taught to head for the sound of gunfire when in doubt, senior executives should personally visit influential stakeholders. They need to explain the situation and the company's response to the media, regulators and government, and to large customers and distributors, unions and interest groups, including lenders and ratings agencies; above all they should continually update employees who control important channels of communications. The corporate website can be a powerful ally in getting messages across.

The outcome of any communications strategy owes much to what behavioural scientists term 'framing', which – in a crisis – is the context and presentation of the company's position. The reader has quite different reactions to two communications strategies which are independently judged as: open, honest, apologetic and responsible; and slow, guarded, misleading and reactive. Framing also extends to the style of a response, particularly how well the company communicates what stakeholders want to hear, and whether it is done in a sympathetic and comprehensive style. A company has most success by framing its crisis response through obvious action to address and solve issues. The media, public and customers expect to see leaders out and about: they need to adopt a high profile and be seen as actively working to fix the problem and remedy any wrongs.

The third decision is how to separately manage public relations issues, operational recovery and compensation. Respectively, each has its own distinct: audience – media, employees and customers; core competencies – communication, operations and customer service; and geography – headquarters, site and service centre.

Although there can be pressures during a crisis to get the job done no matter what it takes, all decisions are open to extensive post-audit for their justification and probity; moreover all expenditures and commitments need to be approved and accurately recorded. So appropriate approvals, controls and reports must be an integral part of the crisis response. This is another reason to involve an external auditor full time who is charged with ensuring that processes are followed properly. The auditor can also provide reports on performance against mandated or public performance guidelines, such as compensation agreements.

The fourth, sensitive decision is whether lawyers on the crisis team are there to provide advice, or to manage the response. Recent years have seen increasingly hostile public reaction to any explanation beginning with the words: 'On legal advice, we …'. Conversely legal positioning is important for its impact on prioritizing responses between company needs and those of customers, community and employees. As this becomes a decision about whether the company is facing a legal, technical or public relations problem, the best position is to clearly establish the right objectives to meet each goal and stick to them.

A similar decision relates to marketing groups that can be acutely customer focussed and may seek to carve out narrow responses that help their most important customers or clients. They can tend to over-promise or overcommit and the inevitable disappointments cause trouble.

In a crisis, there is a natural desire to get back to normal as quickly as possible and to move from crisis mode to 'project status'. This can lead to short cuts (possibly accepting standards below normal), blindness to flare-ups (which are common because the impacts of crises roll out across stakeholders at different speeds), and reduction in resources or support. This needs to be avoided with clear guidelines on criteria that constitute recovery.

Another point is not so much a decision as a style: crises move fast, and can quickly get ahead of 'the facts'; they chaotically mutate into strange and illogical guises; and they challenge every organization's preconceptions. Responding adequately needs a dedicated team: usually small, perhaps only two or three people; but experienced, with credibility and the skill to think creatively and independently. Every crisis manager needs a brains trust to act as conscience and guide, and to develop strategy to stay ahead of the crisis. This should scan the environment, test planned responses for consequential problems (including failure), and – most importantly – try to anticipate what issues are emerging.

Finally a viable Business Continuity Plan (BCP) must be in place to ensure continued availability of mission critical resources. Importantly a BCP might be required when another organization experiences a crisis: this can be serious failure of a utility which cuts gas, electricity or telecommunications; or an incident which denies access to facilities. These points are summarized in the table of Crisis Management Rules (Table 12.5).

Compensation Strategy

Many crises contribute to loss or damage involving customers and third parties that does not arise out of a contractual breach. A key strategic decision is whether to resolve these claims through negotiation or litigation. This requires an evaluation of three important questions. Does the firm have a legal liability to pay compensation? Put differently: if claims go to court, is the firm likely to lose? The second key question relates to the criteria that would be applied by a court to assess the amount of compensation payments.

A third question that is germane to the decision on litigation as opposed to negotiation is the potential value of compensation claims. Obviously if the value of claims is small, it is tempting to simply make ex gratia payments and quickly resolve the issue.

The decision to negotiate claims should be made on the basis that it is practicable to achieve efficient, equitable and speedy resolution on terms that are no less favourable than the probable court judgement. The objective is to provide claimants with their expected payouts, but with considerable savings of time, money and angst to them and the firm. The latter also avoids distraction and reputation fallout from prolonged litigation, and may actually enhance its reputation through equitable settlement processes.

Whilst the expected cost of any crisis is probably minimized by negotiation, there can be circumstances where it is decided to litigate claims. Obviously claims for compensation amounts that are in excess of a likely court judgement would be resisted. Negotiated settlements can also appear unlikely when the claims involve significant subjective elements such as pain and suffering. There may also be circumstances where negotiation

Table 12.5 Rules of Crisis Management

Don't let lawyers run the show – they are defensive and focus on worst outcomes.
Don't let engineers run the show – they focus on the optimum solution.
Don't let marketers run the show – they focus on a minority of critical customers.
Prevent the possibility of any further damage.
Establish a strategy team to get ahead of the crisis.
Establish an operations team to oversee planning and execution.
Appoint an external auditor to monitor compliance against all commitments.
Ensure the voice of the customer, employee and shareholder (and other key stakeholders if appropriate) is heard.
Get outside help from experts in critical areas.
Ensure a high-profile firm presence in the field.
Recognize crises unfold slowly: implement no-regrets initiatives, cast action nets wide, suspect systematic problems, prudently overreact.
Clearly define what is meant by clean, safe, repaired or whatever and stick to it.
Aggressively protect reputation: do not say or do anything unethical, sloppy or untrue.
Plan for the long haul and over-resource everyone.
Emphasize the 'soft issues': make space for people; watch stress, morale and health. Insist on teamwork.
Over-communicate in a sympathetic and comprehensive style.
Identify opponents, stumbling blocks and trouble spots: tackle them soon and hard.
Pay special attention to telegenic impact sites.
Be extremely sensitive to any victims and their families.
Assure counterparties that they are being treated ethically.
Define stakeholders broadly (include analysts, rating agencies, lenders) and communicate regularly and openly.
Beware the 'distant fields syndrome': things you don't understand (which is most things in a crisis) are never simple.
Don't ignore the need for proper controls and procedures.
Keep good records, but resist the temptation to compile reports.
It is never too late in a crisis to start following these rules.

may establish an unwanted precedent. Thus litigation – possibly by encouraging a class action – will be preferred when there is no realistic chance of reaching an equitable settlement.

On balance, though, litigation usually has major shortcomings for all parties because processes are uncertain, take a long time (typically between 2 and 5 years elapse before payouts commence), and require extensive paperwork and involvement by claimants. An attractive alternative is for companies to identify which claims would be successful in court, and offer qualifying claimants an equivalent amount immediately on signing a release.

When it is decided to establish a negotiated compensation system, a number of issues need to be resolved:

- Is the problem fixed?
- What are the bases of compensation?
- How large is potential compensation?
- What is the most efficient way to process claims?
- What resources are required to manage claims?

Lawyers need to be involved in the design and operation of any compensation system. However, their naturally cautious advice needs to be balanced so that the small potential savings from avoiding hypothetical minor problems are not allowed to swamp the tangible immediate benefits of speedy resolution. The process also needs to be automated so that statistics can be reported to provide continuous analyses of issues, and evidence the pace of response.

In the absence of a breach of any contractual obligations, most claims for compensation arising out of a crisis event will be based on negligence by the firm. The test is that the firm failed in its duty to take reasonable care whilst carrying out its business, and this led to an actual loss. When determining what is appropriate in terms of duty of care, the standards that are applied exceed mere legal compliance and will be that expected of a reasonable operator. This performance will be established in light of industry norms, published guidelines and the like, and typically involves an expert witness who describes what is 'reasonable'.

Claims fall into three categories. The first involves damage or loss suffered as a result of use or consumption of the firm's products. The intuition here is that consumers have a right to expect that goods will be of merchantable quality and not defective, and that their use will not lead to any loss. Such provisions are often explicitly incorporated in consumer protection legislation. The second category of claim involves damage or loss suffered as a result of the firm's negligence, including failure to act reasonably or take reasonable care.

The third category involves indirect loss, which has arisen out of the crisis but involves third, or more remote, parties. For example, destruction of a plant may involve its closure and this will stop orders of goods and services. The owners and employees of the plant and those with service contracts suffer direct loss; but the loss to parties that are not contracted to supply the plant is indirect. These can include casual employees, suppliers who respond to irregular orders and firms that provide services such as casual transport and accommodation. Claims for compensation by these remote parties are qualitatively more tenuous than those who are directly impacted, and few are successful.

The fine details of equitable compensation vary between legal jurisdictions and cases. But payments will typically cover some combination of:

- Replacement or repair of any defective goods, or refund of the purchase price.

- Reimbursement of costs arising from the firm's negligence. These include cleaning or repair of damaged equipment; remediation or replacement of damaged property; and associated costs, including labour and personal expenses.
- Loss of income as a direct result of the negligence. This typically means net losses incurred through interruption to their normal business, and is calculated as gross revenue less variable costs, using an appropriate baseline such as same period in the prior year. For employees who lose work it is wages.

These payments will be reduced by any amounts received from other sources such as insurance.

Claims processing requires appropriate forms, supporting explanatory documentation and loss adjustment. The system should build in an identifier that makes each claim unique. When equipment is affected it may be a registration number; for premises it will be a business address and Business Number; and for individuals it might be a driver's license.

If the firm carries insurance, it will recover some or all of the compensation payments under its insurance policy. If the amounts of compensation are significant, it will be necessary to have payments pre-approved by the insurer and an appropriate process established. This typically involves negotiation between the firm and the insurer to establish that liability exists and why, agreement on the terms of compensation and implementation of procedures to validate claims and make the payments.

It can often be effective to outsource this work to a loss-adjusting firm with resources and expertise (especially if their costs are covered by insurance). In this case the firm may second one of its staff to work with the loss adjustor and explicitly protect its interests, especially reputation.

Governance During Crises

What is the role of the Board – particularly non-executive directors – during a crisis? In brief it is to ensure that senior executives who are managing the crisis have adequate support and resources, and are responding appropriately in terms of timing and effectiveness.

Non-executive directors occupy a unique position because they are at once knowledgeable about the firm and its operations, but have a measure of independence. They can be a valuable resource as wise counsellors and perceptive strategists.

The most important step is to ensure that the crisis is adequately understood and being properly managed. This might involve a meeting to brief the Board and cover items such as those set out in the checklist in Table 12.6. Non-executive directors can then meet independently of management to review the situation and establish their requirements in terms of involvement in the crisis and input on actions that executives should take.

A related step is to ensure that there are adequate resources on hand. In particular this means skills that have been brought in to fill gaps in unfamiliar areas such as media strategy or technical responses to the crisis. Naturally it goes without saying that the Board will ensure that the firm has an established crisis management plan and has mapped out generic responses to the most probable crisis scenarios.

Table 12.6 Crisis checklist: Key questions for any crisis manager

Details of the crisis

- What occurred; where; when?
- What damage has occurred: people (who, level of injuries), facilities?
- What third parties have been affected?
- Is the crisis contained; is the site secure?
- What are the medium- to longer-term consequences?
- How much confidence is there in these details?

Responsibility

- Who is responsible for the incident?
- What, if any, liability is involved?
- What has been said publicly?
- Is an immediate apology in order?

Notification

- External: government, regulators, stock exchange, financiers.
- Stakeholders: media, community.
- Internal: executives, employees, shareholders, customers, suppliers.

Response capability

- Are internal resources adequate: employees, managers, financial?
- What expert assistance is available: technical, media, support?
- Can additional resources be brought to bear?
- Is a 'hot line' required for people to call in?

Strategic outlook

- Are there any potential long-term health or other impacts?
- Are there any particularly sensitive features: environmental, process, location?
- What are the expected and likely worst-case scenarios?
- Is business continuity assured?
- What are supply chain impacts, including third parties?
- Is a briefing package available: site records, layouts, inspections, performance?
- Are other facilities open to a similar incident?
- Is the incident serious enough to concern ratings agencies and counterparties?

Response plan

- What is the recovery strategy?
- Who is responsible for crisis management: overall and key components?
- Who is onsite: is a senior executive visit required?
- Have crisis response centres been established and staffed?
- What are the response objectives: are capabilities matched?
- What is the communications strategy: spokesman, timetable, attitudes?
- What are the long-term objectives of the response: key messages?

Table 12.6 *Concluded*

> Response performance
>
> - Are adequate procedures and controls in place within the response team?
> - Is an independent third party monitoring compliance and equity?
> - How will brand and reputation be protected?
>
> Legal and liability issues
>
> - Is immediate baseline data required: drug/alcohol tests, air/water samples?
> - Are records, reports, logs and other documents securely retained?
> - Should any aspects of the response be recorded by minutes or video?
> - Does a compensation scheme need to be established?
> - Are third-party responses being monitored?
> - Will the incident lead to any contractual breaches?
>
> Insurance
>
> - Does insurance cover apply: has the insurer been notified?
> - Is a loss adjuster or onsite insurance expert required?

Conclusion

Corporate crises are not uncommon, affecting at least one firm in every 500 each year. Their direct costs are measured in the tens of millions of dollars; and one in four organizations impacted by a crisis does not survive. Most companies could have (or did) see the crisis developing; but – as hubris is a common feature of crisis-prone organizations – the response was typically inadequate. It is common for management to defer commitment of resources (especially the time of senior personnel) in training and preparations for crises in favour of more immediate issues. Organizations should consciously avoid this trap.

Successfully managing a crisis involves tapping others' hard won experience; and depends upon delivering a response that meets stakeholder expectations, rather than providing a technically excellent solution. Although best practice organizations are continually alert to risks, even perfect risk management cannot prevent every crisis. Thus it is essential to maintain practical, up-to-date plans to manage crises and preserve business continuity.

Crises propel organizations into unfamiliar territory in an environment of high stress and totally inadequate information. They bring out the best and worst in people, and put real competencies and skills on public display. Firms which fail this test take up to a decade to recover.

Firms which handle crises well gain credibility which can actually strengthen them. They are characterised by a few over-riding responses where they:

- Adopt a policy of prudent over-reaction on the basis that information is permanently inadequate and crises usually move further than anticipated. They immediately take no-regrets and low-cost actions that could be useful; and retain a permanent bias towards pre-emptive responses, no matter how expensive.

- Recognize that the crisis has come from a major mistake, and so adopt zero tolerance for under-performance and further error. Excess resources are put in place; skills are contracted in from experts; external scrutiny is welcomed through procedural auditors; and senior management is intimately involved.
- Listen for the voice of the customer and ensure stakeholder needs – customer, community, employee and shareholder – receive respectful consideration.
- Pay great attention to communications:
    1. never make a statement that is not 100 per cent correct and completely comprehensive: do not shade the truth;
    2. never commit to anything that cannot be achieved, or which may be regretted later;
    3. provide an excess of information using all media including Internet sites, internal communications and background briefings;
    4. keep the firm's best advocates – customers, employees and shareholders – fully informed;
    5. ensure the top person is highly visible.
- Recognize that many of the human problems surrounding crises reflect the fact that it is in large measure a grieving process. Stakeholders in business crises need the equivalent of the counselling that therapists provide during personal crises.

Weak crisis management can be traced to a few key causes. One is the assumption that senior personnel with demonstrated operational capability are automatically competent to step straight into the role of incident commander. The few post-mortems on actual crises show that this often leaves managers facing situations and decisions for which they can be quite unprepared. Effective crisis response typically requires an early appreciation of the situation and appropriate instructions. However, this must often be done under conditions of great stress and uncertainty, in a totally unfamiliar environment. Thus a particular concern is to ensure that those given this responsibility possess attributes such as intelligence, tenacity and resilience.

CHAPTER 13 Lessons from the 'Great Risks'

Corporation, noun. An ingenious device for obtaining individual profit without individual responsibility.

Ambrose Bierce (1946), *The Devil's Dictionary*

In order to give real-world content to the discussion of risk, this chapter discusses a number of great risks, the most successful and less so decisions by major organizations in the face of significant uncertainty. Details are taken from secondary sources, both academic journals and popular accounts. They take the form of root cause analyses that use hindsight to clearly connect events that preceded a serious incident or crisis, but whose course was not then evident.

These studies form part of the rich literature of post audits of disasters which – despite its size – needs to be treated cautiously. First, most studies impose a framework around the environment or process that led the organization into crisis and this shapes every historical account. My favourite example of the difficulties inherent in unravelling the mechanics of steps leading up to a crisis was recounted by Tuchman (1962) and involves a German general who was asked how the First World War started, to which he replied, 'Ach, if we only knew!'. Case studies, perhaps more than most historical accounts, are actively structured according to the authors' judgements: this gives them strong retrospective biases and introduces the omitted variables problem where important information is consciously or unwittingly omitted. Typical paradigms are those of Perrow (1984) and Beck (1992) who – despite taking different perspectives – argue that major technological disasters are inherent in our industrial and social structures and hence unavoidable.

Second the case studies are retrospectives of highly complex events that tend to treat their subjects mechanically as arising from an obvious chain of contributing actions and inevitably 'correct history, altering the past to make it consistent with the present, implying that errors should have been anticipated' (Vaughan 1996: 393). Although irresistible to some authors, it is facile to conclude that complex and multi-faceted crises and disasters such as 9-11 and Enron were so obvious as to have been 'predictable'. Although Plutarch (100: 157) argued 'to avoid all mistakes in the conduct of great enterprises is beyond man's powers' there have been a number of great enterprises that have been executed near flawlessly and – like the dog that didn't bark[1] – tell as much about managing risk as the spectacular failures. They, too, deserve study.

Case studies need to be used cautiously. Although each may trace the trajectory and timeline of a crisis, few actually demonstrate that the events are linked, nor that they

---

[1] This alludes to Arthur Conan Doyle's short story *The Adventure of Silver Blaze* where Sherlock Holmes solved a case by noticing something that didn't happen.

200 Risk Strategies

directly contributed to the unwanted outcome. Cause and effect are only inferred, not proven. In the jargon, connecting the dots after an event does not prove that exactly this chain of events actually led up to the event, but only indicates one possible way that the event could have unfolded. Despite these and other shortcomings, historical accounts do show factors that could have promoted the favourable or unfavourable in the face of major risk, and thus suggest lessons to be learned.

Table 13.1 shows examples of great successes and great failures from recent times. A number of these will be covered in this chapter.

Table 13.1 Some recent 'Great Risks', successful and not so

Successful Risks	Unsuccessful Risks
Apollo 11 Lunar Landing	*Challenger* and *Columbia* shuttle launches
D-Day landings in Normandy	John de Lorean's gull wing sports car
Exxon-Mobil merger	RJR Nabisco buyout
Vanguard business model	Abu Ghraib prison
Explorations of Sir Ernest Shackleton	LTCM business model
Pearl Harbor attack by Japan	Enron
Virgin group of companies	Amateur climbs of Mt Everest
	Oil spill by *Exxon Valdez*

NASA

The National Aeronautics and Space Administration (NASA) is modern history's pre-eminent risk taker. It has pioneered technologies and geographies, and literally does have the mission 'To boldly go where no man has gone before'.

NASA was established in 1958, and its Apollo missions from 1969 to 1972 built an admired reputation for safety in high-risk areas. Even then, though, NASA had problems. Apollo I blew up on the launch pad during testing in 1967 with three deaths; and the Apollo 13 mission was aborted after an on-board explosion. Thus out of 12 manned Apollo missions, two failed; and the astronaut fatality rate was 8 per cent.

The immensely successful lunar landings overshadowed NASA's failures, but the organization continued to falter with a string of serious problems including the Hubble telescope which was launched in 1990 and immediately found to have a defective main mirror that slashed its capabilities until repaired 3 years later; two shuttle disasters involving *Challenger* in 1986 and *Columbia* in 2002 out of over 115 launches; and – after a record of 90 per cent successes with robotic planetary exploration vehicles during the 1990s – loss of two Mars probes in 1999. Although Heimann (1997: 163) says that prior to *Challenger*, NASA had a 'long history of reliable performance', the statistics paint a grim picture of NASA, with a failure rate of between 2 and 40 per cent for different projects. Moreover NASA had developed a parallel reputation for budget overruns, best evidenced by the blow out in costs of the International Space Station.

Perhaps the most closely examined of NASA's failures was the 1986 *Challenger* disaster when the shuttle exploded a minute after lift-off and killed seven astronauts, including teacher-in-space Christa McAuliffe. The proximate technical cause was failure of an O-ring that sealed a rocket motor; and the resultant escape of hot gases ignited the main fuel tanks. An inquiry quickly determined that NASA engineers had identified this risk in 1977, and that *Challenger* had been particularly prone to O-ring failure during its eight previous launches since commissioning in 1983.

Despite the obvious mechanical failure that led directly to the disaster, most studies blame organizational shortcomings. NASA was subject to strong budgetary pressures and continuously under threat of cutback, largely because it lacked a large, natural constituency: NASA's 'primary goal of putting humans in outer space remains inspiring, but it is not a social or economic national imperative' (Handberg 2003: 1). Exacerbating doubts ahead of the *Challenger* flight, the media had been mocking of chronic delays in shuttle launches. Just a day before the disaster, CBS anchor Dan Rather reported 'yet another costly, red-faced all-around space shuttle launch delay ... [a] high-tech low comedy'. There was also pressure to avoid delays to the shuttle launch because it might hold up other time-critical missions such as study of Halley's Comet.

This led to the conclusion that political and economic pressures over-rode NASA engineers and resulted in a serious error in judgement. In short, a core driver of the pattern of failures through NASA's history has been 'allowing its political environment, which has no technological expertise whatever, to determine its technological goals and schedules' (Farjoun and Starbuck, 2005: 4).

Similar interpretations were applied following the *Columbia* tragedy which also had a simple proximate technical cause: just after the shuttle's launch, a piece of insulating foam broke away from an external tank and damaged the left wing which failed 16 days later during re-entry. Despite this, the *Report* by the Columbia Accident Investigation Board (2003: volume I, page 9) reached a very broad conclusion:

> *The organizational causes of this accident are rooted in the space shuttle program's history and culture, including the original compromises that were required to gain approval for the shuttle, subsequent years of resource constraints, fluctuating priorities, schedule pressures, mischaracterization of the shuttle as operational rather than developmental, and lack of agreed national vision for human space flight.*

It seemed that – again and sadly – NASA's practices and culture had as much to do with a shuttle accident as the flying foam.

Two specific challenges have been raised about these conventional explanations, particularly in relation to the *Challenger* tragedy. Starbuck and Milliken (1988: 319) noted that failure followed 24 successful launches and concluded: 'organizations often interpret past successes as evidencing their competence' and will accept increasing risk. They suggested that NASA had simply relaxed its safety precautions until something failed.

A second challenge to the conventional thinking that the shuttle disasters occurred because external pressures over-ride managers' judgements (in NASA and elsewhere) is offered by Vaughan (1996) in a self-proclaimed 'revisionist history' of *Challenger* (page xiii). She argues that the disaster stemmed from a simple technical error: in deciding to launch after a night of record cold temperatures, the engineers relied upon incorrect assumptions and misjudged the magnitude of the risk. Her analysis poses the rhetorical question of whether such a massive tragedy could ever be due to something as basic as an error of professional judgement, or must it always involve an equally large cause such as total systemic failure.

NASA's experience epitomizes the limitations of many disaster post-audits, especially those that involve complex systems, risky technologies and large organizations. They are amenable to multiple explanations involving different perceptions of the roles of individuals and organizations, how critical decisions are framed and made, and what is knowable. In particular these studies find that external pressures on NASA's managers induced actions and inactions that brought repeated disasters, as if NASA alone of all large organizations suffered pressures. A more telling question is why so many high-reliability organizations in equally challenging settings (the military, research facilities, global firms) prove more resilient.

In hindsight, NASA's Apollo success and the huge boost it gave to the US psyche cowed potential critics and exempted the organization from normal oversight and procedural controls. NASA routinized huge risks, which made failure statistically inevitable. A simple example of NASA's hubris and unparalleled risk propensity is that it resumed shuttle operations after *Columbia's* loss without satisfying three of the 15 return-to-flight recommendations made by the accident investigators (Wilson, 2005).

Enron

Of all the corporate crises and collapses in recent decades, Enron's has been the most significant for the sheer havoc it wrecked in the boardrooms and internal processes of companies around the world. It shook the foundations of US financial markets by revealing systemic weaknesses in the country's corporate management, reporting and oversight. Given the blizzard of legislation and regulatory controls that followed Enron's collapse in 2001, casual observers could be forgiven for assuming that the failed firm's management did little that was illegal. Despite that, the former Chairman and CEO, Ken Lay, former CEO Jeff Skilling and 19 others were found guilty of various securities charges.

What exactly happened? The most colourful depiction is the bestseller by *Fortune* writers Bethany McLean and Peter Elkind (2004) entitled *The Smartest Guys in the Room*. Their judgement (pages v, xix and xxi): 'Ultimately ... [the company's Icarus-like fall] is a story about people ... The tale of Enron is a story of human weakness, of hubris and greed and rampant self-delusion; of ambition run amok; of a grand experiment in the deregulated world; of a business model that didn't work; and of smart people who believed their next gamble would cover their last disaster – and who couldn't admit they were wrong'.

As far back as 1987, an internal auditor had been contacted by a bank official concerned about unusual transactions in Enron's oil trading subsidiary, and the resulting investigation found that two employees had stolen money. Both were convicted of fraud and $US85 million was written-off in accumulated losses.

Within a few years, though, Enron was on a seemingly unstoppable upward trajectory. In the early 1990s, Jeff Skilling began building up natural gas trading and distribution in Enron Capital and Trade Resources (ECT) and by 1996 it was the source of almost a quarter of Enron's earnings. To finance this rapid growth, Skilling had introduced a number of techniques common in financial-services companies, particularly securitization and off balance sheet operations. The idea was 'to figure out ways to separate energy from the hard assets needed to produce it' (McLean and Elkind, page 70), and the schemes attracted blue chip investors including $US250 million in 1993 from CalPERS, the California Public Employees Retirement System, for a half interest in an energy investment business.

Skilling brought another financial technique to ECT in mark-to-market accounting which involved immediately booking the estimated financial impact of any investment, and then recording subsequent changes in value as they occurred. Thus all future profits from a sale, investment or strategy were reported in its first year: as a result, growth appeared phenomenal. However, each project or investment had only a one-time impact and so there was huge pressure to bring in new investments. Despite its shortcomings relative to conventional historical cost accounting that booked profits as they were made, the change was supported by Enron's auditor Arthur Anderson and approved in 1992 by the Securities and Exchange Commission. Not everyone was happy with these changes, however, and as the effects became clear in the company's accounts, they were frequently criticized by analysts.

Gradually ECT became increasingly creative in its use of the combination of mark-to-market accounting and off balance sheet operations. In one case Enron wished to sell some international operations, but could not dispose of the asset due to loan covenants. So it sold a minority interest for $US225 million after constructing the venture so it would be run independently by an oversight committee. Enron's accountants, Arthur Anderson, approved the structure, and – as ECT no longer controlled the assets – they went off balance sheet and a profit was recorded from their sale.

After he was appointed President and COO of Enron in December 1996, Jeff Skilling pushed the company more deeply into the newly deregulated electricity sector, paying a 40 per cent premium above market for electricity generator Portland General. By mid-1998 Enron was the biggest electricity and natural gas trader in North America.

At the time, the California electricity market had been only partially deregulated so that a variety of price caps and other controls remained. Enron exploited these using proprietary strategies with names such as Fat Boy (overstating demand projections), Death Star (overstating transmission requirements to create apparent supply congestion) and Get Shorty (selling reserve supplies short on the assumption they would never be required). By 2000 growth in electricity demand in California had overtaken supply so infrastructure was inadequate. Enron had taken a huge long position in electricity, and spiralling prices brought profits of over $US2 billion from trading in 2000.

As a firm, Enron was marked by senior executives who displayed outrageous behaviour. 'Few other American corporations would have tolerated [their] antics'. Many were 'old cronies [of Chairman Ken Lay and] … had ill-defined jobs and a line straight to the man who had hired them.' Former executive Mimi Swartz described Enron as a 'company enveloped in chaos' (Swartz and Watkins, 2003: 135). 'Morale was terrible … [Lay] cultivated a powerful sense of personal entitlement' to many Enron assets and used the corporate jets for family activities, pushed corporate travel through his sister's business and funnelled contracts to his children's firms (McLean and Elkind, 2004: 25 and 90).

Skilling accelerated development of this weak culture inside Enron. Profligate expenditure was encouraged. Destructive internal competition was institutionalized by the annual process of ranking staff in a 'seriatim' and publicly contesting attractive promotions. Most significantly, 'after he was named its President, Skilling turned [Enron] into a place where financial deception became almost inevitable'. Moreover, Enron had completely lost sight of its fundamentals: 'The word was out, says [former Enron executive Amanda] Martin: 'Don't do business with Enron. They'll steal your wallet when you aren't looking' ' (McLean and Elkind, 2004: 114 and 200–201).

Another important aspect of Enron culture was to tie managers' annual bonuses to reported income, or earnings per share. This encouraged mark-to-market accounting, and also encouraged any investment that yielded more than interest expense. A similarly misaligned set of drives came from paying bonuses on construction projects for their completion, rather than financial success. As a result investment for its own sake ballooned, and Enron's pre-tax return on assets was a paltry 7 per cent. According to Stewart (2006: 119):

The real reason Enron failed [is that] everything, and not just risk management, was directed to managing and manipulating accounting earnings rather than creating and sustaining real economic value. The wrong measures and wrong incentives overrode human judgement, overran normal business ethics and precipitated the largest bankruptcy in US history.

Cover for Enron's risks and weak internal processes was provided in 1998 by appointing a Chief Risk Officer, Rick Buy, who headed a 150-person group with a $US30 million budget entitled the Risk and Control Department (RAC). This was seen extremely positively by outsiders as an assurance that Enron's high-risk plays were under control. It lulled Wall Street and analysts as sophisticated as Standard and Poor's. According to DeLoach (2000: 187), 'we [have not] encountered an industrial organization further along in the journey towards [enterprise-wide risk management] than Enron'. The RAC, however, was a show piece with an ineffectual head who was constantly over-ridden. 'Much of the culture Skilling installed at Enron was just like RAC: it sounded great in theory, but the reality was something else entirely' (McLean and Elkind, 2004: 118).

Doubts about Enron's business model had been clear since the early 1990s, at least to several prominent Americans including former cabinet members Commerce Secretary Robert Mosbacher and Treasury Secretary Robert Rubin who refused invitations to join the Board. Similarly reporters at *Forbes*, *Fortune* and other magazines raised serious doubts about Enron practices. Few people, however, heeded these critics on the basis that Enron's performance spoke for itself.

Through the 1990s Enron's stock grew three times faster than the S&P 500 Index and the company was treated reverentially and uncritically by thought leaders such as the *Financial Times* and *The Economist*, Wall Street analysts, ratings agencies and reputable consultants such as Arthur Andersen and McKinsey (Skilling had been McKinsey's youngest partner). Enron CEO Ken Lay was hailed as a business visionary, with a typical laudatory article in *The Economist* of 1 June 2000 under the headline 'The energetic messiah': 'by bending all the rules of the energy business, Kenneth Lay has turned Enron from a stodgy gas concern into a soaring new-economy company … In sum, the Enron tale is every bit as remarkable as it seems.' The article reported that Lay was a friend of jailed Drexel Burnham Lambert junk bond trader Michael Milken and observed: 'the arrogant Drexel collapsed in a heap of bad debts and ignominy. For all of its arrogance, Enron is hardly likely to share that fate: but hubris can lead to nemesis, even so'[2].

A breathtaking example of Enron hubris and observer awe is a paper in the *Journal of Applied Corporate Finance* entitled 'Transforming Enron: The Value of Active Management' (Kaminski and Martin, 2001). Written, respectively, by Enron's Director of Research and a Baylor University finance professor, it details how 'Enron's management has turned a $200 million regulated natural gas pipeline owner into a $100 billion new economy trading powerhouse ... and competitive juggernaut'; and tabulates 'the firm's accomplishments [which] have gained the respect of Wall Street and high praise from a variety of sources in the financial press'.

Only when Enron seemed to falter did doubts became more strident. For instance, around 1995–7 when return to shareholders fell below that of the S&P 500 for the first time since 1989, an increasing number of analysts questioned the complexity of the firm's accounting processes, the opacity of its reports and the artificiality of its income. But this was only temporary, and Enron usually shrugged off bad news in favour of enthusiasm such as the single day during the January 2000 analysts' briefing when its stock price skyrocketed 26 per cent to $US67.

By the time Enron shares peaked at $US90 in August 2000, observers had been lulled into a false sense of security because of silence by reputable bodies that were close enough to Enron to sound warnings if any of its reputed problems were significant. Arthur Andersen and the SEC approved questionable aspects of its accounting. Standard & Poor's rated its debt at BBB+, and no ratings agency raised any doubts (by, for instance, putting Enron on negative credit watch or downgrading its rating) until just weeks before its bankruptcy. America's largest banks – Chase Manhattan and Citigroup – loaned it billions of dollars.

In late 1999 Andersen recognized that Enron was not only its biggest client, but one of its most risky. It directed Carl Benn, a highly experienced accounting partner in Andersen's Professional Standards Group, to scrutinize Enron's accounts. This highlighted a series of potential problems that triggered a formal review by Anderson in February 2001 on whether it should retain the $US100 million per year account. They decided 'yes', and – following pressure from Enron – reassigned Benn.

By this time Enron Chairman Lay and CEO Skilling had begun steadily selling their Enron stock, and scepticism re-emerged in the investment community, best evidenced by an article in *Fortune* entitled 'Is Enron overpriced?' [19 February 2001]. Enron had got into real problems after the US equity market peaked in March 2000 because mark-to-market accounting began to produce losses. Enron's stock price dropped, with a 10 per cent fall on 21 March 2001 to below $US56. Senior staff began to leave, culminating in the resignation of Skilling in August after just 6 months in the job. When the stock dropped further to $US40, *Wall Street Journal* reporters scented trouble and wrote a series of articles questioning Enron's accounting, particularly transactions with senior finance executives that appeared to

---

2 *The Economist* is known for howlers on its front covers, and a detailed list is provided by Sullivan (1999). The best-known recent example is the 1999 cover story entitled 'Drowning in Oil' which predicted that oil prices would head down just before they began to treble. Another glaring example of the magazine's uncanny ability to misread reality came with a piece in late 2000 under the heading: 'The invisible enemy – Has the threat of bioterrorism been overstated?' However, other well-regarded magazines are as bad. For instance, a cover story entitled 'The Crazy Things People say to Justify Stock Prices' appeared in *Forbes* in 1992 when the US S&P 500 was only a quarter of its March 2000 peak (Baldwin, 1992).

be serious conflicts of interest. The SEC launched an informal inquiry, the stock hit $US20 in late October 2001, and S&P warned Enron it was considering a credit downgrade. Investors then refused to buy Enron's commercial paper and it was forced to draw down on a $US3 billion back-up credit line. S&P announced a downgrade, the stock hit $US10 – down almost 90 per cent in 14 months – and the SEC demanded full disclosure of Enron's accounts. By the end of November a proposed merger with gas rival Dynergy unravelled, the share price hit $US0.61 and on 2 December Enron – which had been America's seventh largest company by revenues in 2000 – filed for chapter 11 bankruptcy owing $US38 billion.

In 2006 Lay and Skilling were tried on six and 28 counts, respectively, involving securities fraud. Lay was convicted on all counts but died shortly afterwards of a heart attack; Skilling was convicted on 19 counts. A total of 21 people charged with crimes involving Enron either pleaded guilty or were convicted.

Did any one action within Enron bring about its demise? Apparently not. 'The Enron scandal grew out of a steady accumulation of habits and values and actions that began years before and finally [in late 2001] spiralled out of control' (McLean and Elkind 2004: 132). Former Enron employee Brian Cruver (2002: 343–346) blames its independent directors who ignored three facts. The first is 'there are a lot of crooks out there' and he cited nearly half a million arrests in the US in 1999 for white collar crimes such as fraud and embezzlement and SEC charges against 500 companies each year. The second is that 'risk has gotten riskier' and Boards should take a much more active interest in the many potential risks that their firms face. And third that 'ethical behaviour = higher returns' because misleading people and cheating counterparties destroys value.

As the dust began to settle from the Enron collapse, measured analyses emerged. Healy and Palepu (2003) provide a detailed analysis of how poor governance and misaligned incentives led first to Enron's rise and then its equally spectacular fall. An ethnographic analysis by Boje, Gardner and Smith (2006) shows how Enron deliberately manipulated analysts' judgements about the firm so they would continue to support the stock despite obvious concerns. An article in *The New Yorker* by Malcolm Gladwell (2007) reports that a group of Cornell University business school students studied Enron as a term project in 1998 and concluded that the company was a 'Sell'. He says that the true state of Enron was then apparent, although it took skill, persistence and independence of thought to get to the truth. That, of course, is a Wall Street responsibility that it failed to accept.

Exxon Valdez

Shortly after midnight in the early morning of Good Friday 1989, Exxon Shipping's newest and most advanced tanker, the *Exxon Valdez*, hit Bligh Reef and spilled at least 11 million gallons of crude oil in what Keeble (1999: 17) called 'the most destructive spill in the history of the world'.

After the port of Valdez had opened in 1977, the safety of oil transport proved to be a continuous concern as tankers from the port experienced a growing frequency of near catastrophes: in 1980 the *Prince William Sound* lost its engines during a gale, and in 1985 *Arco Anchorage* ran aground off Washington State; in 1987 the tanker *Stuyvesant* ruptured twice, and *Glacier Bay* hit a submerged rock; and then *Thompson Pass* had a moderate spill in the harbour in early 1989. Despite the number of incidents, each was dismissed as 'minor', and precautions were steadily relaxed, including abolishing a permanent oil spill response team in 1981, reduced radar monitoring of vessels, lower crew requirements and less onerous requirements for navigation using pilots (Smith, 1992).

The *Exxon Valdez* had arrived in Valdez about 24 hours before the grounding, and – because it had fallen behind schedule – was hard pressed to quickly take on its cargo of crude oil. Whilst in port, a number of procedures imposed by Exxon and the Coast Guard were breached in what appeared to be routine failure to follow requirements. The vessel's captain Joseph Hazelwood had several drinks despite a ban on alcohol within 4 hours of duty; officers worked through the night whilst loading even though there was a requirement for them to have 6 hours off duty in the 12 hours prior to sailing; although two ship's officers were required on the bridge during departure, there was only one for most of the period leading up to the spill; the officer in charge during the grounding did not have the required endorsement for Prince William Sound; and a lookout was not continuously posted.

After the *Valdez* sailed, it dropped its pilot and was then authorized to change shipping lanes to avoid ice. Although this was a non-routine action close to the hazardous Bligh Reef, the captain had departed the bridge leaving the supertanker in charge of the unqualified third mate who – for a never adequately explained reason – did not take the appropriate course to avoid the Reef.

A criticism of management of the spill was poor response. Initial clean-up effort was expected to come from Alyeska Pipeline Service Company which operated the Valdez terminal on behalf of the oil producers (50 per cent BP, 21 per cent ARCO, 20 per cent Exxon, plus four other companies). Despite its responsibility, the operator's staff took 13 hours to reach the scene and then arrived with totally inadequate equipment and made only token effort. Not surprisingly, when President of Exxon Shipping Frank Iarossi arrived from Houston on the evening of the spill, Exxon took over the clean-up, but it, too, was slow to get resources on site.

To complicate the response, a dispute immediately emerged between Exxon and the State of Alaska and the Coast Guard over the use of dispersants to break up the oil. It was not resolved before bad weather intervened and halted clean-up operations. This dispute over an issue that is fundamental in tackling any oil spill was part of an apparent pattern of poor responses. 'The contingency plan in place at Alyeska was laughable … The oil companies had cut their costs and allowed procedures to become sloppy where they could get away with it' (Keeble, 1999: 174–175).

Exxon spent around $US3.5 billion on the clean-up and damages claims, and paid a further $US0.5 billion in punitive damages after litigating for almost 20 years. Despite this and actions such as taking out advertisements in newspapers and magazines across the US to apologize, Exxon clearly lost the PR battle. Significantly this contrasted sharply with the much more lenient treatment of local residents even though they responded to the inundation of Valdez by National Guardsmen and other respondents with extortion, charging $US100 in cash per night to sleep on lounge room floors.

The other principal focus of criticism fell on to Captain Hazelwood who had been with Exxon since 1968 and was one of its best mariners. However, he had drink driving arrests in 1985 and 1988, and a blood test 10 hours after the grounding showed a blood alcohol level of 0.061 per cent. He was charged with four counts relating to the grounding, and – after a 6-week trial in early 1990 – convicted of misdemeanour negligent discharge of oil. Exxon fired him.

Exxon was roundly criticized for putting a drunk captain in charge of its vessel. As part of a comprehensive response to the spill, Exxon implemented a confidential counselling programme for all employees who had concerns over excess drinking. When a deck officer on another of its tankers enrolled in the programme, Exxon faced a Hobson's choice which it resolved by transferring the officer to shore duties. Predictably it faced odium for breaching confidentiality.

Although Exxon's efforts to respond to the spill were reported positively at first, growing frustration at delay in achieving results brought criticism that made Exxon management defensive and unresponsive to the media, and further worsened relations. Fairly or not, the media held Exxon to 'an impossible expectation: that most of the mess could have been cleaned up if Alyeska and Exxon had responded more quickly' (Smith, 1992: 94). The media, however, did not do all the damage as Exxon was frequently inept, with a typical outcry triggered after its Chairman Lawrence Rawl – who claimed to have made an unannounced visit to the site soon after the spill – said the costs of settlements with the Alaska State and US Federal governments 'will not have a noticeable effect on our financial results … the customer always pays everything' (Keeble, 1999: 317–318).

D-Day, Normandy, June 1944

Seaborne invasions are hideously complicated undertakings, with few successes against anything larger than atolls. Britain, for instance, has not been invaded since 1066 despite myriad formidable enemies, including Napoleon and Hitler. The population-based probability of failure of a large-scale amphibious invasion is high. Well-resourced invasions that failed were launched by Chinese Emperor Kubla Khan against Japan in 1281, the Spanish against England in 1588, by the British in Crimea in 1854–5 and at Gallipoli in 1915, by emigrés against Cuba in 1961 and Allied forces in Dieppe in 1942. In World War II Allied forces under General Eisenhower made successful landings in North Africa, Sicily and Salerno but none of the coastlines was fortified or staunchly defended; and German airborne troops captured Crete in 1941 but suffered appalling losses. Most successful invasions are flanking operations executed rapidly over land, with obvious examples in 1938–1942 when German forces captured Poland, The Netherlands, France and other countries, and Japan occupied much of East Asia.

D-Day saw landings in Normandy by Allied (mainly US, Canadian and British) troops on 6 June 1944. It is by far the most successful invasion in history, and thus a prime example of triumph over high risks. The risks *from* (as opposed to of) failure were also formidable as it would inevitably mean massive loss of men and materials; and it would set back the Allied cause by giving Germany the front foot and time to leverage it using new weapons including larger rockets, long-range U boats and jet fighters. Given that Winston Churchill termed it 'the most difficult and complicated operation ever to take place', it is no surprise that Amazon.com lists over 400 books with 'D-Day' in their title. This section summarizes Ambrose (1994), and Gilbert (2004) to explain how General Eisenhower and his staff managed risk to execute such a successful enterprise.

Planning for D-Day started in December 1941, shortly after the Japanese attack on Pearl Harbor and Germany's declaration of war against the US mobilized the latter's strength and resources which were critical to an invasion. Germany independently recognized its exposure and started building a massive defence barrier called the Atlantic Wall on the western coastline of its occupied territories. Despite the benefit that a European front would provide to Russia, which was then locked in a bitter struggle on Germany's eastern front, sufficient forces to mount an invasion could not be assembled at a base in Britain until early

1944 because of limits on shipping and constraints on US resources which were siphoned off to the Pacific War. Even so, preparations continued apace and an Anglo-American planning group was established in early 1943 for Operation Overlord, the invasion's code name. An important early choice was the location for the landing. It had to be as close as possible to the ultimate target of the German Rhine region, accessible to English-based fighter aircraft, away from heavily defended strongpoints, with open beaches and protection from the Atlantic. By a process of elimination, Normandy became the landing site. The shortest timeline to deliver sufficient men and materials meant that D-Day would be in the summer of 1944.

Strategy and tactics developed along several fronts with an emphasis on innovation. New military units were set up such as the Airborne Division, and new weapons designed including floating tanks. An important engineering innovation was the floating harbour that could be sunk in place and avoided the need to capture heavily defended ports. A group was established to prepare detailed maps of the French coast, which were augmented by postcards, guide books and aerial photos. Beaches were surveyed by commandos in midget submarines, and French resistance members detailed the defences and obstacles to great detail that included soil samples and beach gradients. The resulting understanding of beach obstacles and mines meant that almost a quarter of the American troops in the initial landing were engineers. An interesting omission by the planners, though, was their failure to seek lessons from seaborne landings by American troops in the Pacific, which had started with Guadalcanal in mid-1942. Admittedly the latter were in a different hemisphere against forces with no hope of reinforcement, but it was a surprise that lessons were not exchanged between the two theatres.

General Dwight Eisenhower was appointed Commander of Overlord in December 1943. Although a soldier since entering West Point in 1911, he did not see action until North Africa in 1943 after which he commanded successful landings in Sicily and Italy. Eisenhower consciously adopted an optimistic demeanour with 'mannerisms and speech in public [that] would always reflect the cheerful certainty of victory.' On the battlefield he was cautious and calculating, best using his hand in the form of superior forces to overwhelm the enemy.

Eisenhower had a team approach and picked staff typified by Field Marshal Montgomery whom he described as 'careful and meticulous' who was able to secure admiration from his men. Eisenhower was convinced that 'before the battle is joined plans are everything' and set up an operation of great complexity, scoped down to the last detail by the responsible unit. This is a classic response of a risk-averse manager to a highly risky proposition. Eisenhower spent much of his time inspecting training, getting to know his men and letting them take his measure. There was continuous review of plans by British Prime Minister Churchill and staff groups. By contrast, US President Roosevelt, even though an ocean away, was much less involved, perhaps to distance himself from the operation or from Churchill with whom he did not have a close rapport.

Training was intense over a minimum of 6 months. It was as realistic as possible, conducted using live fire on terrain in Britain similar to that of the landing beaches. It covered all aspects of the invasion from boarding landing craft on the high seas to fighting in hedgerows. As plans unfolded, troop numbers grew until 175,000 men would land on D-Day, along an 80 kilometre coastline (about 1/12th of the Spain to Denmark littoral that Germany defended).

In parallel with physical operations, an intelligence strategy was established to mislead Germany over the timing and objective of the cross-Channel invasion, and then delay defensive response after the invasion began by convincing them it was a feint.

General Patton – one of America's best – was put in charge of the huge, but spurious, First US Army Group and convinced German spies that he was planning a landing at the Pas de Calais, which was the closest point in Europe to England and intuitively the most logical invasion point. A similar British unit was established with the objective of a Norwegian invasion. To protect the secrets of real and sham armies, the government used dictatorial powers to achieve unprecedented security, including a ban on all civilian visits to the south and east coasts. The deception plans extended to manipulating the prices of Norwegian stocks on the Stockholm exchange in the month before D-Day to give the impression that insiders in London believed Norway was the invasion target.

In the months prior to the invasion, bombers systematically attacked rail centres and repair shops in France to prevent mobilization of reinforcements after the invasion. Three weeks before D-Day, all diplomats in Britain (save those of the Soviet Union and US) were banned from sending or receiving uncensored written or radio communications. A double for Montgomery was sent to Gibraltar to sow further confusion about Allied plans.

The actual date of D-day was not decided until just a month beforehand when weather, moon and tides pointed to a window during 5–8 June, almost exactly 4 years after the Dunkirk rout. It was timed for around 6.30 am, which was low tide in daylight so beach obstacles could be identified. History showed that the invasion was a triumph.

Three features stand out as key attributes of D-Day's success. The first is the choice of Eisenhower as commander: he was skilled after proving successful in similar invasions; a team player, with strong people skills (he later became one of America's most successful Presidents); and optimistic and strongly committed to success. The second key to success was detailed planning that emphasized innovation, scheduling and clearly devolved responsibility. The third key was provision of excess resources which avoided the need for shortcuts that virtually always bring failure.

HIH Insurance

HIH floated on the Australian Stock Exchange in 1992, primarily as a workers' compensation insurer. Within a few years it embarked on an ambitious growth strategy, expanding offshore and into other classes of insurance, including several acquisitions. In late 1999, however, HIH reported a loss, and the company was placed into provisional liquidation in March 2001.

Troubles within HIH appeared as early as 1995 when the company struck a deal with Swiss-broker Winterthur to take a majority interest. Winterthur contracted Ernst & Young to conduct due diligence and their report 'stated that HIH had barely acceptable accounting practices or accounting methods which have been the subject of criticism or controversy for some time' (Westfield, 2003: 55).

Further concerns emerged the following year when Winterthur audited HIH's international operations based in London. The audit team 'found discrepancies everywhere. Numbers didn't match and the Swiss believed they had been fed inaccurate information. Their main concern, voiced in a damning report ... was the almost complete lack of management control' (Westfield, 2003: 46). The London office had increased its exposure by providing insurance to fringe activities such as Hollywood movies and football teams, and in high-risk fields such as aviation and pharmaceuticals. Whether unaware or blasé about these increased risks, it failed to manage the exposures. The auditors also raised concerns about conflicts of interest because senior London staff were organizing deals with Lloyd's syndicates in which HIH managers were members. The UK insurance regulator then took an interest, and told HIH in July 1997 that it had 'one of the worst compliance records of any company currently underwriting' (Westfield, 2003: 48).

The London situation seemed to typify HIH. The company was replete with fundamental conflicts as HIH's Chairman and CFO were both former employees of its auditor Arthur Anderson; and the CFO, Dominic Fodera, had been HIH's auditor when he was lured away from Andersen. In addition it seemed that the company's reporting and managerial controls were weak. In March 1999, the HIH Board Audit Committee heard from its external auditor that the firm's 'reserves are at the very low end of both the actuary's tolerable limits and ours' and that he may have to qualify the accounts. The auditor from Arthur Anderson subsequently told the Committee that 'board members generally were not receiving enough financial information' (Westfield, 2003: 131).

Another poor strategy was executed in January 1999 when HIH acquired FAI Insurance for $300 million without any due diligence. Almost immediately FAI operations revealed huge losses, and 6 months later HIH valued FAI at less than $50 million, with the balance shown in its accounts as goodwill. At financial year end in mid-2000, HIH had net assets of $928 million, but $476 million or 51 per cent, was goodwill; HIH suffered an operating cash outflow for the year of $678 million.

Perhaps one of the more interesting aspects of HIH's collapse is the apparent suddenness in the deterioration of its accounts (from net assets of around $1 billion in mid 2000 to bankruptcy and deficit of over $4 billion in March 2001). Signalling the foresight of the markets, an equally savage deterioration in its share price had begun 2 years earlier (see Figure 13.1).

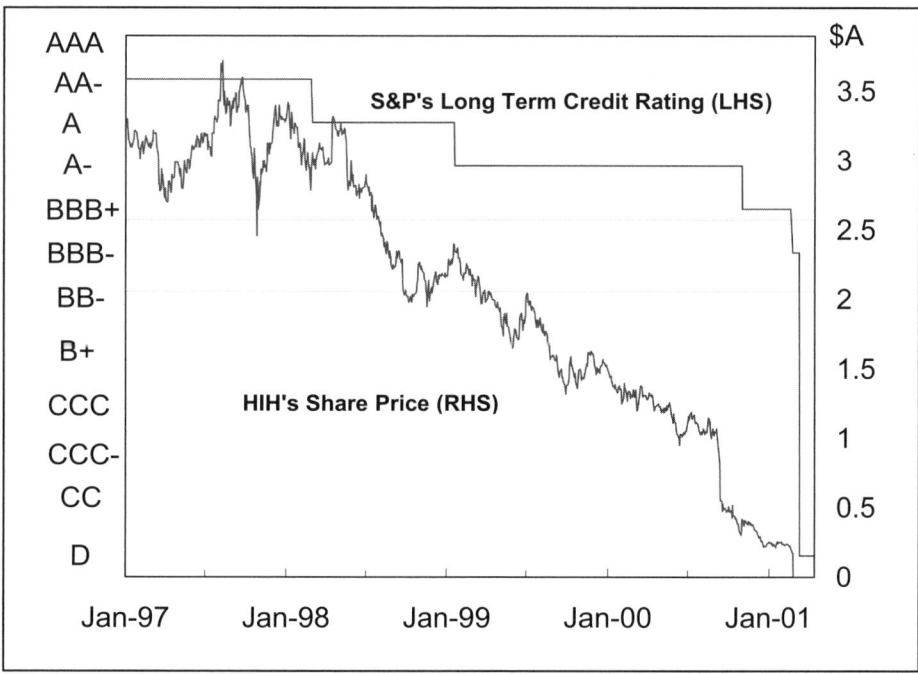

Figure 13.1 HIH Insurance Stock Price and S&P Rating

Of the HIH directors, Rodney Adler was sentenced to 4 years gaol on charges relating to making false statements to support HIH's share price; and CEO Ray Williams received a 3-year gaol term. Former Chairman Geoffrey Cohen was banned from being a director for failing to ensure that relevant materials were brought before the HIH Board, that the audit committee was independent, and that his own conflicts of interest were disclosed [APRA *Media Release* 6 October 2005]. CFO Fodera received 3-years gaol following six charges relating to falsification of accounts. Businessman Brad Cooper received an 8-year term for paying bribes to receive falsified payments from HIH; and several other HIH and FAI executives also received gaol terms.

Derivatives Disasters

When use of derivatives exploded during the 1980s, their counterparty and legal risks should have been obvious because they traded in over-the-counter markets. Even so, the appearance of each of a string of billion dollar plus trading debacles during a short space in the mid-1990s was greeted with shock. This section discusses two prominent 1995 examples: options trading by Barings Plc; and Daiwa Bank's US bond trading losses.

From a risk management perspective, the most interesting feature of the cases is that each was blamed on a single rogue trader who was able to hide huge accumulated losses over at least 3 years. Problems, though, appeared chronic and losses followed early warnings.

Nick Leeson, General Manager of Baring Futures Singapore, was responsible for trading and back office functions, and also had control of a settlement account after 1992. This lack of segregation of duties enabled Leeson to post fictitious trades which appeared to offset losses and covered them up. At Barings, the 'organizational structure was poorly articulated. It exhibited cloudy reporting lines and internal controls, failed to segregate control of trading and settlement, and embraced uninformative accounting standards' (Kane and DeTrask, 1999: 208). Although some of these weaknesses had been identified in a 1994 internal audit, Barings failed to complete basic checks which would have identified the growing losses such as reconciling settlement accounts by matching balances in its books with those reported by counterparties.

In January 1995 an external audit by Coopers and Lybrand identified accumulated losses of Yen 8 billion, and – although Leeson tried to dismiss them with forged bank records – concerns and internal scrutiny grew. On 16 January Leeson placed a short straddle on the Nikkei Index (selling both put and call options) betting that it would not move. Next day a magnitude 7.2 earthquake hit Kobe, and caused 6,000 deaths and $US80 billion in damages. The Japanese stock market fell 10 per cent, and Barings' losses exceeded $US1.4 billion within days. Late in January the Bank for International Settlements and journalists queried Barings losses, but these 'were treated only as public-relations problems' (p. 209). Next month Leeson fled to Thailand, and the truth emerged.

The loss at Daiwa Bank had many similarities with Barings as it, too, occurred remote from headquarters, and involved over $US1 billion arising from account falsification over several years by a trader – Toshihide Iguchi – who was also responsible for accounting. Losses from securities trading were covered up by the simple expedient of not recording the transfer of sold securities from custody so the accounts showed them still in inventory.

There was a significant difference in Daiwa's case, though: senior management in New York had colluded in covering up the loss. This resulted in a prison sentence for its general manager on a charge of conspiracy, and successful indictment of Daiwa on 24 counts that saw it expelled from the US. According to Kane and DeTrask (1999: 222), 'Daiwa's actions exhibit a dangerous cycle of failing to control its traders followed by accounting trickery and outright falsification and forgery to hide the losses and keep regulators in the dark'. The Daiwa loss only came to light when Iguchi wrote a confession to the bank's President in Japan and the situation was disclosed to regulators 2 months later.

Conclusion

Even though the incidents discussed above appear very diverse, they share four common features. The first is that they were preceded some years beforehand by serious procedural breaches – often covering each of failed operational processes, conflicts of interest and fraud – that were sufficiently obvious and serious as to be picked up and reported by auditors and counterparties (some also attracted criminal charges). These early warning signs are termed 'safety drift' in the organizational literature, but were dismissed as anomalies and any lessons that could have been learned were ignored. Even worse, the fact that no event led to any dread catastrophe induced a sense of complacency and reduction of precautions (even though these had presumably contributed to the absence of disaster in a high-risk activity). The organizations then went on to become highly regarded, often because they appeared to be so successful in taking large risks; and – in a form of moral hazard – were encouraged to take on major projects such as acquisitions that proved disastrous.

This typically led to the second feature of disaster-struck organizations which was development of an awe-like admiration by media and consultants. This extended, too, to senior management which tended to isolate itself from the apparently successful organization, either geographically or in competence, and allowed it to operate without hindrance. Thus many disasters involved foreign subsidiaries or occurred in remote locations.

Induced by hubris and over-confidence, internal processes and standards were further weakened and promoted the third feature which is neglect of the firm's key stakeholders, particularly customers, and inequitable treatment of counterparties in general. In some cases this was accelerated by the wrong incentives and goals for executives. This inevitably became apparent to informed observers outside the organization, and led to the fourth feature common to corporate disasters which is a significant and sustained decline in share price well ahead of the culminating failure. If employees, customers and suppliers of a firm hold it in poor regard, it is not long before this intelligence reaches the market and affects the stock price.

It is true that many corporate collapses appear to stem from failed decisions on strategy. Pasminco and Sons of Gwalia failed following errors in their hedging strategy; Manville Corporation filed for bankruptcy over asbestos litigation; and assorted airlines entered bankruptcy due to competitive pressures. But by far the largest contributor to bankruptcy has been overconfidence. A classic example of unwarranted overconfidence was Long Term Capital Management whose Nobel laureates sneered at mere journalists who could not understand their processes.

This argument is supported by the frog framework of Richardson, Nwankwo and Richardson (1994) which sees leading indicators of corporate collapse in symptoms of overconfidence such as complacency, hyperactivity or hubris. In the 'boiled frog' failure, successful organizations drift complacently whilst their surrounding environment heats up and they lag far behind competitors. This is analogous to an Argenti (1976) Type III failure where the performance of a mature firm plunges at intervals until it finally collapses. The 'drowned frog' failure stems from aggressive strategies that over-extend the firm, exhaust resources and bring collapse. These firms are ambitious, aggressive, arrogant and usually initially very successful. A variation is the 'bullfrog' which pursues flashy high-growth investments that provide poor returns. Its failure arises in agency problems where managers waste resources in building empires.

The corporate disasters discussed above exemplify these failure types. The *Exxon Valdez* – like many major environmental disasters – reflected a boiled frog's failure to identify exploding risk in operations. HIH successively slumped following its acquisitions until it reached bottom. Barings' Nick Leeson simply exhausted all resources like a drowning frog. Enron and NASA were successful, allowed arrogance to fuel their growth, and ultimately invested unwisely until they ran out of funding. Enron executives displayed unwarranted overconfidence when pressured to explain how they could sustain stellar earnings growth. Barings' Nick Leeson and HIH's Ray Williams had little in common except to punt major companies on their judgement.

This litany of linked disasters might suggest that firms rarely learn the lessons of history. If true, it is because history's lessons are so infrequently taught, and rarely well. This is a pity as they offer much of value, especially in such a critical area as avoiding disaster.

As a source of motivation and a model for risk management, the headline disasters discussed above point to a few critical factors for Boards:

- understand the business environment;
- bundle risks into self-controlling groups;
- establish 'no-go' zones and report breaches;
- watch moves in cash;
- report meaningful measures;
- send clear messages;
- reward desirable behaviours.

Steps such as these will help provide an environment where risk management is part of the culture. It is this latter point, though, that is critical in effective risk strategy. An organization bent on leveraging risk strategically must establish its attitude towards risk, codify this in a structure and detailed auditable guidelines, promote a culture that operationalizes the risk strategy and then continuously measure risk performance and adherence to guidelines. New strategies must be tested for their conformance to the strategy and implications for risk; each employee, contractor and supplier must be held accountable for meeting risk guidelines; and each operation must be regularly audited for compliance.

CHAPTER 14
Summary and Conclusions

Madam, the wings of opportunity are fledged with the feathers of death.
Sir Francis Drake (1540–1596) to Queen Elizabeth

This chapter draws together the many threads discussed into several simple themes to meet the needs of readers looking for a summary of the book.

The first theme is that firm risk has undergone a fundamental shakeout in the last few decades. Although firms were dangerous for employees, customers and the environment in the 1970s, legislation and stakeholder expectations have dramatically transformed this, so that products and processes are now up to an order of magnitude safer. These point-sourced risks have fallen under environmental, consumer and workplace legislation and the operations of regulators such as Environmental Protection Agency; Occupational Safety and Health Administration and Securities and Exchange Commission.

Other legislative changes, however, had quite different impacts and increased firm risk through moral hazard. Deregulation, privatization and savings incentives have transformed the competitive landscape and – by making the future less controllable and more uncertain – subjected firms to increasing pressures to perform. To survive they were forced into more frequent strategic initiatives, which – because at least half of such complex decisions do not succeed – have increased firm strategic risks several fold since the 1970s. Quite simply, government policies such as deregulation and privatization have made industries more competitive and forced firms to take risks that they would otherwise not have considered. Further moral hazard has been induced by the greater competition inherent in globalization, and by markets that have become more fickle as a growing portion of consumer expenditure became discretionary.

These strategic risks are the outcome of interplays between a firm's external environment – industry and competitor traits – and its internal decision environment. The latter is driven by Board objectives; organization structure and managerial traits; products, processes and markets; and strategic decisions including funding and investment.

The most striking feature of this shift in risk loci is that it has arisen because of a change in the boundaries of the firm. Prior to the 1970s firms could be introspective, and were criticized for considering external obligations. In a famous newspaper article, Nobel laureate Milton Friedman (1970) argued that firms had no social responsibilities, including that of avoiding pollution. But a string of very public examples made this view untenable: an oil well blow out off Santa Barbara in 1969 that despoiled 35 miles of beach; toxic waste pollution from Love Canal after 1978; 3,000 deaths at the Bhopal plant in 1984; and the *Exxon Valdez* oil spill in 1989. These incidents – and the intense publicity and public criticism that followed – sensitized at least the oil and chemical companies to the shattering fallout to be expected from badly judged risks.

Thus the closed economic systems preferred by engineers and accountants where firms operate solely to maximize return to shareholders gave way to acceptance that successful management of interfaces with stakeholders was increasingly important to financial success. Firms became open systems and the scope of their risks exploded in terms of both drivers and consequences (Hoffman, 2001). Strategic risks – which had barely existed in the 1960s – now loom ever larger, and their control is proving elusive.

Despite the range of risks we face, there is a need to retain perspective: for instance, the interest bill for most corporates is only a couple of per cent of total expenses, but it seems to consume a huge amount of time and effort through risk-limiting tools, including derivatives with exotic names such as Forward Rate Agreements (FRAs), futures, options and swaps. But all too rarely does anyone acknowledge that no tool can protect against a bad investment or financing decision; and it is in the latter area that most corporate disasters are sourced. For instance, a Booz Allen study of value lost in 1,200 large firms during 1998 to 2004 found that 60 per cent of losses were due to poor strategy. Business decisions rather than process lapses now cause the greatest loss of shareholder value.

In driving to retain perspective, it is sobering to recall that our most obvious modern technologies might have made marvellous improvements in many fields, but have not changed everything. Whilst finalizing this work, I had lunch in Melbourne with two colleagues. They were from London and Los Angeles, but with accents muted by travel and life overseas. Our restaurant overlooked a river where rowers took advantage of the early spring weather. The table was covered in linen, iron flatware, glasses and pottery; we drank wine and ate fresh cooked seafoods from far away. We spoke of commerce and trade, and of developments around the populated world. Literally everything – our lifestyles, clothes, outlook, food and conversation – would have been familiar to Phoenicians lunching a millennium before Christ's birth. Despite huge changes, much has stayed the same in our everyday lives.

Two paradoxes emerge as corollaries of changes that have occurred in corporate risk. The first is that the majority of risks facing firms are old. As expected by the general consensus that we live in more dangerous times, the frequency of industrial disasters grew exponentially during the twentieth century (Coleman, 2006a). Surprisingly, though, most of the increase in disaster frequency was due to explosions and fires; little of it came from new technologies such as chemicals and radiation. The second paradox is that the largest firm-level losses in value emerge from conscious decisions that have gone wrong. This leads to the sobering fact that most crises emerge in well-established processes where management had neglected the risk being run, which is typical with financial disasters, or from deliberate strategies that fail.

This poor control of strategic risks continues because traditional risk management has been focussed on individual sources of risk, where it has been immensely successful. But by pigeon holing risks, each has been tackled alone with little heed to systems and how they might form and interact. Risks are not managed strategically in light of firms' full exposures to markets, investments, operations and processes. This is an important motivation for this book which proposes a more integrated style of risk management that addresses firm-level strategic risks.

Poor management of strategic risks leads firms to make two types of error in decisions on risk as shown in Figure 14.1. The first is a Type I error which decides incorrectly that a risk is low: this leads to failed acquisitions, crashed space shuttles and plant explosions. Failure is incorrectly rejected as improbable. The second, Type II error involves deciding

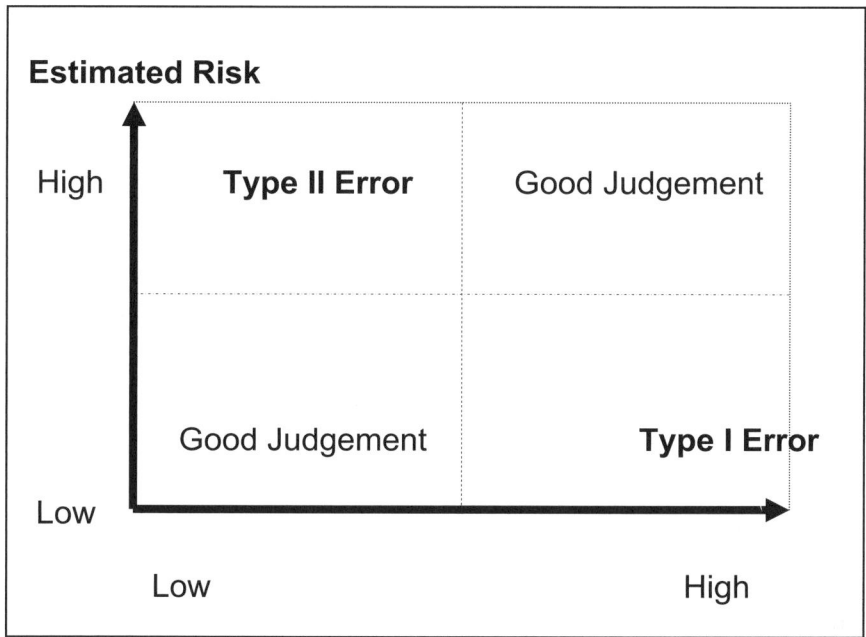

Figure 14.1 Type I and II errors in risk judgements

incorrectly that a risk is too high: this leads to refusal to accept reasonable risks and brings the opportunity costs from foregoing good investments and strategies.

Traditional risk management is designed to avoid Type I errors through a logical process that identifies hazards, quantifies their probability and eliminates or contains them through avoidance, elimination or insurance. As a result, there can be little doubt that people are much safer now in most aspects of their lives than a few decades ago. Some improvements have been spectacular, with technologies such as commercial aviation and nuclear energy an order of magnitude safer than in the 1970s.

Although modern risk management techniques have had great success, this has usually been achieved by recognizing specific, potential risks and managing them through some combination of avoidance, reduction, transfer, retention and sharing. This perspective means that current risk management practices are reductionist and very mechanical, relying heavily on checklists and products, including market-based instruments. Thus a recurring feature of contemporary risk management is that it inevitably reaches a point of diminishing returns where further risk reduction stalls. An excellent example can be seen in efforts over 30 years to reduce the road toll: the benefits of each initiative (compulsory seat belts, bans on drink driving, reduced speed limits and so on) have been repeatedly exhausted; thus further reduction in risk continually requires new approaches.

Not surprisingly, a good deal of risk management involves looking backwards both to learn from past events and to justify future actions, much as the military is sometimes accused of training for the last war. This can leave risk management blind to emerging risks, even those that in hindsight appear quite obvious. A difficulty for risk managers in taking pre-emptive action and using resources in anticipation of an unwanted event that has not yet occurred is that it can be hard to justify, particularly when it will bring unwanted disruption.

A second concern over traditional management of Type I risks is that – whilst point sources of risk have proved amenable to reductionist management and dropped – the frequency of systemic risks seems to have risen. In particular, firm-level strategic risks have grown rapidly. For instance, the incidence of man-made disasters grew exponentially last century, so that the current rate is about five times that before the mid-1970s. Share price volatility or risk to shareholder returns has increased three-fold since 1979, largely due to increasingly common shocks to firm value from higher strategic risk. The rates of increase in these two risk indicators – 5 and 4 per cent per year, respectively – are matched by other indicators. For instance, the corporate default rate has roughly trebled in the last 25 years; the mean tenure of chief executives has fallen by a third in the last decade; and the frequency of corporate crises in the US has increased by a quarter in the last decade.

A third concern is that firms which limit Type I errors also suffer more Type II failures (Heimann, 1997). Obviously, then, an important aspect of risk strategy is striking the right balance between risk taking and returns. In combination, the increase in strategic risks and growing business uncertainty make it necessary to develop a new approach to risk management.

Few managers or investors can doubt that better risk management reduces costs, improves competitive position and rewards stakeholders. Arguably this is *the* core managerial competence. Even more so given the obvious fact that the most important decisions involve risk. Choosing correctly when there is little to lose or gain adds no value; choosing badly in the face of potential losses (including opportunity costs) destroys value.

Decision making balances anticipated benefits against costs, including adverse outcomes. This is risk management pure and simple. Even the cheery aphorism 'You make your own luck' is true because events which befall us reflect the outcomes of our risk management strategies. In management little matters except making the correct decision in the face of risk.

The risk attitudes of managers and firms follow predictable patterns. Each, for instance, tends to react more strongly to losses than gains, and – when confronted by a large loss – will either take a large risk with the hope of recovering, or freeze and do nothing. Managers who tend to take more risks are younger, better educated, male and adopt multiple risky behaviours such as smoking and adventure sports. Firms that take more risks are smaller, with fewer slack resources and decentralized decision making, and measure performance and reward success.

The importance of success in strategic decision making is clear from the different fortunes of firms which started off with the same products, opportunities and potential benefits: Apple and Microsoft; the inventors of Beta and VHS video recorders; the various American, British, Japanese and Korean motor vehicle manufacturers; Montgomery Ward and WalMart (the same is true, too, of countries with all but identical resources where differences in strategy led to quite different outcomes: North and South Korea, East and West Germany; Greece and Turkey).

Although Michael Porter and other authors have built impressive reputations around the assumption that it is possible to bring together a competitive set of resources without heed to the possibility of error, experience tells us that well-motivated and well-advised individuals and firms regularly make horrendous misjudgements. The results are buried whenever practicable. But even when they emerge, sanctions are not automatic because most of us recognize how difficult it is to get things right. One of Mark Twain's many laconic characters quipped: 'There is nothing more difficult to predict than the future.' Risk managers know the truth of it!

Given the shortcomings in management of risks, the performance of current techniques should be rated poorly. A striking indication of this comes from the study by management consultant McKinsey that concluded: 'scandals and environmental mishaps seem as inevitable as the likelihood that these incidents will be subsequently blown out of proportion, thereby fuelling resentment and creating a political and regulatory backlash' (Davis and Stephenson, 2006: 4). Surely a principal concern of governance should be to avoid scandals and environmental mishaps? Moreover this is quite realistic given that the feasibility of low-risk operations has been successfully demonstrated by a number of global companies operating in high-risk industries and environments.

My conclusion is that risk management as currently practiced by corporates around the world focuses too much on minimizing variations in income, and on the blindingly obvious, conventional, high-frequency risks. It is too little concerned over the low-probability, high-cost disasters which could threaten firms' viability. It virtually ignores complex exposures embedded deep in technologies, and has proven blind to their linkages. Perhaps this is the key message for all of us involved in managing risk, along with the fact that it remains more art than science. Above all, risk management should *always* be the preserve of strategically focussed senior managers, not junior engineers and accountants.

This leads to the second error in decisions on risk which is Type II, or deciding incorrectly that a risk is too high: the result is refusal to accept reasonable risks. Readers with a resource-based view of firms and investment will recognize that these misjudgements of risk impose potentially large opportunity costs from foregoing good investments and strategies. How, then, to balance risk and return?

A recurring theme has been to question conventional thinking across many disciplines that return has a linear relationship with risk. This implies that risk-adjusted returns are constant, and – providing risks are well judged – risk management is merely a strategic judgement on what risks an organization should accept.

Intuitively investors and managers think otherwise and recognize the benefits of good risk management. Surveys of investors show they consider 'risk' is the possibility of loss, and rate this as 'highly important' in investment selection. Managers hold similar views and spend considerable effort on managing risks. This makes sense for a number of reasons. First managers are in the best position to identify and manage risks. Even with a purely financial risk that shareholders could manage such as interest rate on debt, managers know far more about the actual debt levels, cash flows and natural hedges. In the case of operational and strategic risks, shareholders have little idea of what is involved and cannot directly manage them. Thus managers can most effectively manage risks.

A second reason for risk management is that there is a 'sweet spot' for organizations where a particular level of risk maximizes their return. Although conventional thinking is that return has a linear relationship with risk, it seems far more likely that the relationship is concave or -shaped. That is, return rises with risk until it reaches the optimum or sweet spot, after which further risk leads to declining returns. This is confirmed by the poor returns that are common with high-risk management strategies such as mineral exploration, IT projects and acquisitions. Investors know it, too, in the poor returns from developing markets, venture capital and the like. When gamblers follow high-risk strategies despite their low expected return it is called the longshot bias; when firms and managers pursue ambitious objectives whose success is improbable they, too, are gambling. Without exception, gambling has a negative expected return.

In short, firms will optimize their financial performance by selecting a level of risk that is neither too low nor too high. An important Type II error, therefore, is to fail to dial risk up or down to the firm's sweet spot, and so forego the benefits from well-judged, appropriate risks.

Extending the resource-based view of firms, risk strategy can be leveraged to generate value in three ways. One involves action by managers to proactively manage risk to improve their firms' risk-adjusted return to shareholders. The second relates to investment selection that identifies positive risk-adjusted returns. The third way to generate value is for other stakeholders – ranging from creditors to regulators – to better calibrate firms' risks and hence anticipate exposures (in the case of creditors) or minimize them.

Given that firms have an optimum risk level, managers can maximize the risk-adjusted return to shareholders by proactively managing their risk propensity. Reliable management of risky processes and systems requires: commitment to make safety paramount; redundancy between and within each process or system; a 'culture of reliability' in operations; and monitoring and learning from experience. This has three core elements: cost effectively eliminating downside risks; establishing a risk-effective operational and strategic environment; and selecting investments and projects to secure the target risk.

Enterprise Risk Management (ERM) is the process used to manage risks and a good outline of its techniques is provided in the internationally acclaimed *Australian Standard on Risk Management* which is designed as 'A generic guide for managing risk ... [that] may be applied to a wide variety of activities, decisions or operations.' The Standard sets out a set of logical steps: consult with those involved; establish the context; identify, analyze and evaluate the risks; put in place management plans; and continually monitor and review the process.

A number of finance techniques can be useful in optimizing ERM. One is asset-liability management in which corporations integrate their assets and liabilities, off balance sheet exposures and revenue streams in order to optimize risk through the business cycle. A second useful concept is that of real options where risk management is used to limit a firm's downside exposures. Thus the firm's expected value has the same structure as that of a call option with uncapped upside and limited downside.

An extended risk application of real options is to think of insurance as a put option: that is, if an insured event occurs, the firm can put the damaged assets to the insurer and recover their loss. Considering insurance as a put option resolves the puzzle of why firms take out insurance given that it has a negative expected value.

As risk-related regulations and reporting requirements become more onerous and risk management techniques become increasingly sophisticated, the process across a firm is often centralized with responsibility given to a Chief Risk Officer (CRO). This function has responsibility for compliance, traditional risk management functions such as audit and occupational safety, and for adding value by integrating risk into key decisions.

A powerful technique that can be applied by the CRO is introduction of Key Risk Indicators (KRIs) that monitor risks and their leading indicators. This firm-wide view of risk and giving responsibility for it to a senior manager introduces a new perspective at Board level that is termed 'risk governance'. This recognizes that taking the right risk is key to corporate success and poorly judged risks are the most common cause of value destruction. Thus Boards become more involved in ensuring risk levels are optimized. In particular they promote ethical treatment of counterparties that have been proven to add value; and encourage sustainability in decision processes to protect the long-term viability of the firm and its physical, economic and financial environment.

Just as firms have recognized the increasingly urgent need for a more holistic approach to risk management and the benefits it can bring, so have governments. Some – such as those in the UK and US – have been forced by external events to take national risks more seriously; others – such as Canada and New Zealand – have introduced it as part of modern governance. National risk strategies are a response to the stretch targets and risks of contemporary policies and programmes and share many of the features of ERM.

In closing it is useful to acknowledge the common features of many of the great corporate disasters, which constitute examples of poor risk judgements. The first is that they were preceded some years beforehand by serious procedural breaches – often attracting criminal charges – which were early warning signs of 'safety drift'. Second, most disaster-struck organizations had secured an awe-like admiration by media and consultants. Senior management became complacent about the apparently successful organization and relaxed scrutiny. Induced by hubris and over-confidence, internal processes and standards were further weakened and promoted neglect of the firm's key stakeholders, particularly customers, and inequitable treatment of counterparties in general. In some cases this was accelerated by the wrong incentives and goals for executives.

Thus meeting the modern day challenge of taking and managing greater strategic risks has deep-seated roots that arise from structural weaknesses in contemporary risk management. The loci of modern risks are spread across many legacy systems: thus risks are path-dependent and arise from historical decisions. Dire risks based on 'catastrophe science' generally prove welcome for their shock value, and because many groups expect them to catalyze their desired changes. There is a general tendency towards decentralization that has militated against central analysis and monitoring, and hence tended to miss systemic risks.

Chief Financial Officer Action Plan

Given the many conflicts and uncertainties inherent in effective risk management, what can a CFO – to whom this book is directed – do to proactively implement an appropriate risk framework?

The first step is to codify the firm's risk strategy. This is not merely a statement of philosophy, but should comprise a comprehensive Board paper that clearly establishes the firm's *actual* risk environment and record. The nature of the risk environment is a function of industry factors such as regulation, structure and competition; the firm's products, processes and markets; and its strategies, including recruiting and training, organization design and investments. The firm's risk record needs to be comprehensively quantified in terms of risk indicators and outcomes. It should also include a post-audit of the nature and results of previous risks, including capital projects and investments, and major strategic initiatives such as product or organizational changes. In each case results should be compared with those of other firms, especially competitors.

The second step is to evaluate risk propensity of the firm's physical assets, processes and managers. This is partly innate such as managers' psychodemographics or how often a process fails; and part is actual performance using risk indicators and outcomes.

These two steps set out where risks could arise and where they have already arisen; and show the firm's performance against that of competitors. The next step is to test this actual risk performance against the desired level. The Board should decide whether the firm's risk propensity and record are appropriate and optimized.

This leads to the fourth step which is preparation of a *Risk Policy* that sets out expectations in terms of the quantum and nature of risks a firm will run, and how they will be managed. This should match the detail of other policies so that it can provide guidance in decision making and can be audited for compliance. As a minimum, the risk policy should cover staffing and organization, investment criteria, risk reporting and risk audits. It should embrace all risk-related activities, including ERM, treasury, credit, audit and occupational safety.

The final step is to cascade this new policy throughout the organization. The Board should have risk as a permanent agenda item, reviewing performance and ensuring that all proposals incorporate an assessment of the risk impact. The CEO and CFO performance contracts should include meeting risk objectives; and these should cascade through the performance evaluations of other managers. All investments and strategic initiatives should specifically examine risk impacts using standardized criteria and qualitative assessments; their risk attributes should be signed off by a CRO, or equivalent.

Although these steps will establish and dial up the appropriate strategic risk, executives must also be alert to operational risks. The latter are embedded in processes and hard to observe. The only effective control is to set out the correct procedures in writing, and monitor activities for compliance. A valuable intermediate step is to implement an internal controls system and self-audit process so that committed managers can regularly test the effectiveness of their key processes. Unfortunately, though, self-regulation rarely works. As noted by Comer (1998: 7): 'People steal because they see an opportunity and believe they can get away with it. They are prevented by good controls, the fear of detection and punishment.'

Even if avoiding risk – rather than theft – is the goal, the same approach is required. It is well recognized that to engage broad participation in a framework as comprehensive as ERM, everybody impacted needs to accept that there is a real issue that needs resolution and that they can contribute to the solution. In the case of risk management, this requires a compelling empirical case that strategic risks are rising and an education campaign that demonstrates good practices by individuals – which have slashed point-sourced risks – can achieve the same with escalating strategic risks.

Thus managers need to be made accountable for controls and procedural compliance, given adequate training and resources, and then audited thoroughly and regularly. Senior executives should continually stress the advantages and need for controls, quality and equity to ensure these guideline resonate through the organization. Proactively establishing an appropriate risk framework can be achieved through an enterprise risk strategy using the conventional formula of hazard identification and evaluation, and subsequent design of appropriate risk management processes. The latter will indicate procedures and controls that need to be in place. After these have been comprehensively set out, employees can be trained and their performance audited. Obviously these steps need to be regularly repeated to revise and refine the strategy. Key is to continually evaluate performance by reporting appropriate risk measures and conducting environmental assessments.

As risk is a chaotic process, accidents, thefts and other unwanted losses do not occur randomly, but recur and repeatedly affect the same manager, group or process. Experience has shown that many disasters have been preceded by similar, if much less consequential, breaches that can be identified by adequate reporting; and disasters often arise in areas where fundamentals such as quality and ethics, safety and customer service have become neglected. Regularly re-audit every person, group and activity that has a poor risk record. Heed warnings.

In summary, the contribution of this book is to help develop a methodology to identify the sources and magnitude of strategic risks in firms, and point to techniques for their management and control. Recognizing the value of a new perspective on risk, this integrates existing practices through a holistic approach and broad perspective. The aim is to shift focus on to systemic risks, and identify trends and scenarios that themselves are not a danger, but could trigger loss.

Sadly the subject of 'risk' lacks a body of theory, largely because it has not been subjected to the scientific process of collecting data, developing hypotheses and testing them to build theories. This book is driven by the conviction that 'risk management' requires a large amount of effort and evolution before it can claim to be a formal intellectual discipline. Ideally it makes a start on building an effective body of risk theory.

Selected Reading List

This section sets out a selection of readings that support the discussion and analysis in each chapter.

Accessible general introductions to the topic are available in the following:

Coleman, L. (2006). *Why Managers and Companies Take Risks*. Springer, Heidelberg.
Crouhy, M (2006). *The Essentials of Risk Management*. McGraw Hill, New York.
Culp, C. L (2001). *The Risk Management Process*. John Wiley, New York.
Doherty, N. A (2000). *Integrated Risk Management*. McGraw Hill, New York.
Frame, J. D. (2003). *Managing Risk in Organizations*. Jossey-Bass, San Francisco.
Young, P. C and Tippins S. C. (2001). *Managing Business Risk: An Organization-wide Approach to Risk Management*. Amacom, New York.

Chapter 1 Introduction

Bartram, S. M (2000). Corporate Risk Management as a Lever for Shareholder Value Creation. *Financial Markets, Institutions and Instruments* 9 (5): 279–324.
Bernstein, P. L. (1996). *Against the Gods*. John Wiley & Son, New York.
British Royal Society (1992). Risk: Analysis, Perception and Management.
Clarke, C. J. and Varma, S. (1999). Strategic Risk Management: The New Competitive Edge. *Long Range Planning* 32 (4): 414–424.
Culp, C. L (2002). The Revolution in Corporate Risk Management. *Journal of Applied Corporate Finance* vol 14 (4) 8–26.
Deloach, J. (2000). *Enterprise-wide Risk Management: Strategies for Linking Risk and Opportunity*. Arthur Andersen, Houston.
Gallagher, R. B. (1956). Risk Management: A New Phase of Cost Control. *Harvard Business Review* 34 (5): 75–86.
Jensen, M. C. (1993). The Modern Industrial Revolution, Exit, and the Failure of Internal Control Systems. *The Journal of Finance* 48 (3): 831–880.
Kendall, R. A. H. (1998). *Risk Management for Executives*. Pitman Publishing, London.
Lo, A. W (1999). The Three Ps of Total Risk Management. *Financial Analysts Journal* 55 (1) 13–26.
March, J. G. and Shapira, Z. (1987). Managerial Perspectives on Risk and Risk Taking. *Management Science* 33 (11): 1404–1418.
Rawls, S. W. and Smithson, C. W. (1990). Strategic Risk Management. *Journal of Applied Corporate Finance* 2 (4): 6–18.
Sharpe, W. F. (1964). Capital Asset Prices: A Theory of Market Equilibrium under Conditions of Risk. *Journal of Finance* 19: 424–442.
Vedpuriswar, A. V. (2003). A Strategic Approach to Managing Risks: The CFO's role. *ICFAI Reader*: 42–45.

Chapter 2 Nature and Sources of Corporate Risk

Camerer C (1998). Prospect Theory in the Wild. Working Paper. California Institute of Technology
Perrow, C. (1984). *Normal Accidents*. New York, Basic Books Inc.
Raith, M. (2003). Competition, Risk, and Managerial Incentives. *American Economic Review* 93 (4).
Simons, R. (1999). How Risky is Your Company? *Harvard Business Review* 77 (3): 85–94.
Singh, J. V. (1986). Performance, Slack, and Risk taking in Organisational Decision Making. *Academy of Management Journal* 29 (3): 526–585.
Sykes, T. (1994). *The Bold Riders: Behind Australia's Corporate Collapses*. Allen & Unwin, Sydney.

Chapter 3 Why Organizations Take Risks

Dess, G. G. and Beard, D. W. (1984). Dimensions of Organizational Task Environments. *Administrative Science Quarterly* 29 (1): 52–73.
Hofstede, G. (1997). *Cultures and Organisations: Software of the Mind*. London: McGraw Hill.
Lovallo, D. and Kahneman, D. (2003). Delusions of Success: How Optimism Undermines Executives' Decisions. *Harvard Business Review* 81 (7): 56–63.
McDermott, R. (1992). Prospect Theory in International Relations: The Iranian Hostage Rescue Mission. *Political Psychology* 13: 237–263.
Simon, H. A. (1959). Theories of Decision-making in Economics and Behavioural Science. *American Economic Review* 49: 253–283.
Slovic, P. (2000). *The Perception of Risk*. Earthscan Publications, London.
Smallwood, P. D. (1996). An Introduction to Risk Sensitivity. *American Zoologist* 36: 392–401.
Trimpop RM (1994). The Psychology of Risk Taking Behavior. Elsevier Science, Amsterdam.

SURVEYS OF RISK AND DECISION ANOMALIES

Camerer, C. (1995). Chapter 8 – Individual Decision Making. Published in J. H. Kagel and A. E. Roth (ed). *The Handbook of Experimental Economics*. Princeton University Press, Princeton.
Rabin M (1998). Psychology and Economics. *Journal of Economic Literature* 36: 11–46.
Ricciardi, V. (2004). A Risk Perception Primer: A Narrative Research Review of the Risk Perception Literature in Behavioral Accounting and Behavioral Finance. Accessed: 17 February 2005. http://ssrn.com/abstract=566802.
Slovic, P. (1972). Psychological Study of Human Judgment: Implications for Investment Decision Making. *The Journal of Finance* 27 (4): 779–799

Chapter 4 Decision Making and Risk

Aspesi, C. and Yardhan, D. (1999). Brilliant Strategy, But Can You Execute? *The McKinsey Quarterly* (1): 89–99.
Bremer, M., McKibben, B. and McCarty, T. (2006). *Six Sigma Financial Tracking and Reporting*. McGraw-Hill, New York.
Coleman, L. and Casselman, R. M. (2004). *What You Don't Know Can Hurt You: Towards an Integrated Theory of Knowledge and Corporate Risk*. Department of Management Working Paper. The University of Melbourne, Melbourne.

Knight, F. (1921). *Risk, Uncertainty and Profit*. Houghton-Mifflin, Boston.
Koestler, A. (1972). *The Roots of Coincidence*. Hutchinson and Co, London.
Kouradi, J. (1999). *Decisionmaking*. Orion, London.
Lindley, D. V. (1985). *Making Decisions* Wiley, New York.
Lovallo, D. and Kahneman, D. (2003). Delusions of Success: How Optimism Undermines Executives' Decisions. *Harvard Business Review* 81 (7): 56–63.
Marsh, N., McAllum, M. and Purcell, D. (2002). *Strategic Foresight*. Crown Content, Melbourne.
Miller, K. D. and Chen, W.-R. 2004. Variable Organizational Risk Preferences: Tests of the March-Shapira model. *Academy of Management Journal* 47(1): 105–115.
Nohria, N, Joyce, W. and Roberson, B. (2003). What Really Works *Harvard Business Review* July: 43–52.
Nutt, P. C. (1999). Surprising but True: Half the Decisions in Organizations Fail. *Academy of Management Executive* 13 (4): 75–90.
Schnaars, S. P. (1989). *Megamistakes: Forecasting and the Myth of Rapid Technological Change*. The Free Press, New York.

REAL OPTIONS

Arnold, T. and Shockley, R. L. (2002). Real Options, Corporate Finance and the Foundations of Value Maximization. *Journal of Applied Corporate Finance* 15 (2): 82–88.
Botteron, P. (2001). On the Practical Application of the Real Options Theory. *Thunderbird International Business Review* 43 (3): 469–479.
Chorn, L. G. and Shokhor, S. (2006). Real Options for Risk Management in Petroleum Development Investments. *Energy Economics* 28 (4): 489–505.
Copeland, T. and Antikarov, V. (2001). *Real Options*. Texere, New York.
Dixit, A. K. and Pindyck, R. S. P. (1995). The Options Approach to Capital Investment. *Harvard Business Review* 73 (3): 105–116.
Leslie, K. and Michaels, M. (1997). The Real Power of Real Options. *The McKinsey Quarterly* 3.
Paddock, J. L., Siegel, D. R. and Smith, J. L. (1988). Option Valuation of Claims on Real Assets: The Case of Offshore Petroleum Leases. *The Quarterly Journal of Economics* 103 (3): 479–508.
Triantis, A. J. (2000). Real Options and Corporate Risk Management. *Journal of Applied Corporate Finance* 13 (2): 64–73.

Chapter 5   Impact of Risk on Shareholder Value

Aaker, D. A. and Jacobson, R. (1987). The Role of Risk in Explaining Differences in Profitability. *Academy of Management Journal* 30 (2): 277–296.
Bartram, S. M. (2000). Corporate Risk Management as a Lever for Shareholder Value Creation. *Financial Markets, Institutions and Instruments* 9 (5): 279–324.
Benston, G. J., Hunter, W. C. and Wall, L. D. (1995). Motivations for Bank Mergers and Acquisitions. *Journal of Money, Credit and Banking* 27 (3): 777–788.
Campbell, J. Y., Lettau, M., Malkiel, B. G. and Xu, Y. (2001). Have Individual Stocks become more Volatile? *Journal of Finance* 56 (1): 1–43.
Chew, D.H. (ed) (2001). *The New Corporate Finance: Where Theory Meets Practice*. McGraw Hill-Irwin, Boston.

Fama, E. F. and French, K. R. (1995). Size and Book-to-Market Factors in Earnings and Returns. *The Journal of Finance* 50 (1): 131–155.

Lins, K. and Servaes, H. (1999). International Evidence on the Value of Corporate Diversification. *The Journal of Finance* 54 (6): 2215–2239.

Myers, S.C. (ed) (1976). *Modern Developments in Financial Management*. Praeger Publishers, New York.

Nichols, N. A. (1994). Scientific Management at Merck: An Interview with CFO Judy Lewent. *Harvard Business Review* 72 (1): 88–99.

Olsen, R. A. and Troughton, G. H. (2000). Are Risk Premium Anomalies Caused by Ambiguity? *Financial Analysts Journal* 56 (2): 24–31.

Smith, C. W. and Stulz, R. M. (1985). The Determinants of Firms' Hedging Policies. *Journal of Financial and Quantitative Analysis* 20 (4): 391–405.

Smithson, C. and Simkins, B. J. (2005). Does Risk Management Add Value? A Survey of the Evidence. *Journal of Applied Corporate Finance* 17 (3): 8–17.

Chapter 6   Enterprise Risk Management

Deloach, J. (2000). *Enterprise-wide Risk Management: Strategies for Linking Risk and Opportunity*. Arthur Andersen, Houston.

Gallagher, R. B. (1956). Risk Management: A New Phase of Cost Control. *Harvard Business Review* 34 (5): 75–86.

Harrington, S., Niehaus, G. and Risko, K. (2002). Enterprise Risk Management: The Case of United Grain Growers. *Journal of Applied Corporate Finance* 14 (4): 71–81.

IBM (2005). *The Clairvoyant CRO*. IBM Business Consulting Services, Somers NY.

Lam, J. (2003). *Enterprise Risk Management: From Incentives to Controls*. Wiley, Hoboken, NJ.

Meulbroek, L. K. (2002). *Integrated Risk Management for the Firm: A Senior Manager's Guide*. Harvard Business School, Boston MA.

Power, M. (2003). *The Invention of Operational Risk*. Working Paper. London School of Economics, London.

Chapter 7   Financing Risk: Insurance and Asset-liability management

INSURANCE

Cummins, J. D. (2006). Should the Government Provide Insurance for Catastrophes? *Federal Reserve Bank of St Louis Review* 88 (4): 337–379.

Doherty, N. A. and Smith, C. W. (1993). Corporate Insurance Strategy: The Case of British Petroleum. *Journal of Applied Corporate Finance* 6 (3): 4–15.

MacMinn, R. D. (1987). Insurance and Corporate Risk Management. *Journal of Risk & Insurance* 54 (4): 658–677.

Trieschmann, J. S., Hoyt, R. E. and Sommer, D. W. (2005). *Risk Management and Insurance*. Thomson, Mason OH.

ASSET LIABILITY MANAGEMENT

Harris, T. S., Melumad, N. D. and Shibano, T. (1996). An Argument Against Hedging by Matching the Currencies of Costs and Revenues. *Journal of Applied Corporate Finance* 9: 90.

Lhabitant, F.-S. and Tinguely, O. (2001). Financial Risk Management: An Introduction. *Thunderbird International Business Review* 43 (3): 343–363.

Treynor, J. L. and Black, F. (1976). Corporate Investment Decisions. Published in S. C. Myers (ed). *Modern Developments in Financial Management*. Praeger Publishers, New York.

Chapter 8 Managing Risks in Financial Operations

Altman, E. I. and Saunders, A. (1998). Credit Risk Measurement: Developments Over the Last 20 Years. *Journal of Banking & Finance* 21: 1721–1742.

Beck, T. and Levine, R. (2004). Stock Markets, Banks and Growth: Panel Evidence. *Journal of Banking and Finance* 28 (3): 423–442.

Koch, T. W. and MacDonald, S. S. (2006). *Bank Management (6th Edition)*. Thomson, Mason OH.

Oldfield, G. S. and Santomero, A. M. (1997). *The Place of Risk Management in Financial Institutions*. Working Paper. Wharton Financial Institutions Center, Philadelphia PA.

Chapter 9 The New Function of Chief Risk Officer

Aabo, T., Fraser, J. R. S. and Simkins, B. J. (2005). The Rise and Evolution of the Chief Risk Officer: Enterprise Risk Management at Hydro One. *Journal of Applied Corporate Finance* 17 (3): 62–75.

Clarke, C. J. and Varma, S. (1999). Strategic Risk Management: The New Competitive Edge. *Long Range Planning* 32 (4): 414–424.

Economist Intelligence Unit (2005). *The Evolving Role of the CRO*. London.

Financial Services Roundtable (1999). *Guiding Principles in Risk Management for US Commercial Banks*. The Financial Services Roundtable, Washington DC.

Liebenberg, A. P. and Hoyt, R. E. (2003). The Determinants of Enterprise Risk Management: Evidence from the Appointment of Chief Risk Offficers. *Risk Management and Insurance Review* 6 (1): 37–52.

Meulbroek, L. K. (2002). *Integrated Risk Management for the Firm: A Senior Manager's Guide*. Harvard Business School, Boston MA.

Chapter 10 Governance and Ethics

Coles, J. L., Daniel, N. D. and Naveen, L. (2006). Managerial Incentives and Risk-taking. *Journal of Financial Economics* 79 (2): 431–468.

Colley, J. L. J. (2003). *Corporate Governance*. McGraw-Hill, New York.

Jensen, M. C. (2001). Value Maximization, Stakeholder Theory and the Corporate Objective Function. *Journal of Applied Corporate Finance* 14 (3): 8–21.

Morgan, A. G. and Poulsen, A. B. (2001). Linking Pay to Performance – Compensation Proposals in the S&P 500. *Journal of Financial Economics* 62: 489–523.

Orlitzky, M., Schmidt, F. L. and Rynes, S. L. (2003). Corporate Social and Financial Performance: A Meta-Analysis, *Organization Studies*. 24 (3): 403–441.

Scandizzo, S. (2005). Risk Mapping and Key Risk Indicators in Operational Risk Management. *Economic Notes* 34 (2): 231–256.

Scholtens, B. (2006) Finance as a Driver of Corporate Social Responsibility, *Journal of Business Ethics* 68, 19–33.

Sheridan, G. (2006). Did AWB Really Do Something Wrong? *The Australian*. Sydney. 9 February 2006.

Soppe, A. (2004). Sustainable Corporate Finance, *Journal of Business Ethics* 53: 213–224.

Starbuck, W. H. and Milliken, F. J. (1988). Challenger: Fine-tuning the Odds until Something Breaks. *Journal of Management Studies* 25 (4): 319–339.

Zegart, A. (1999). *Flawed by Design: The Evolution of the CIA, JCS, and NSC*. Stanford University Press, Stanford CA.

Chapter 11 National Risk Strategy

Britton, N. R. and Clark, G. J. (2000). From Response to Resilience: Emergency Management Reform in New Zealand. *Natural Hazards Review* 1 (3): 145–150.

Cohen, S., Eimicke, W. and Horan, J. (2002). Catastrophe and Public Service: A Case Study of the Government Response to the Destruction of the World Trade Center. *Public Administration Review* 62 (Special): 24–32.

Coleman, L. (2006). It's time for a national risk strategy. *Quadrant* 50 (1): 40–44.

Commonwealth of Australia. (2004). *Protecting Australia Against Terrorism*. Department of Prime Minister and Cabinet, Canberra.

Emergency Management Australia. (1996). *Australian Emergency Manual – Disaster Recovery*. Emergency Management Australia, Canberra.

McLeod, R. (2003). *Inquiry into the Operational Response to the January 2003 Bushfires in the ACT*. Australian Capital Territory, Canberra.

Risk Support Team. (2004). *The Risk Programme: Improving Government's Risk Handling – Final Report to the Prime Minister*. HM Treasury, London.

Scanlon, J. (2001). *Lessons Learned or Lessons Forgotten: The Canadian Disaster Experience*. Institute for Catastrophic Loss Reduction, Toronto.

Schneider, S. K. (1998). Reinventing Public Administration: A Case Study of the Federal Emergency Management Agency. *Public Administration Quarterly* 22 (1): 35–57.

Treasury Board of Canada. (2001). *Integrated Risk Management Framework*. Treasury Board, Ottawa.

Zilinskas, R. A., Hope, B. and North, D. W. (2004). A Discussion of Findings and their Possible Implications from a Workshop on Bioterrorism Threat Assessment and Risk Management. *Risk Analysis* 24 (4): 901–908

Chapter 12 Management of Corporate Crises

Cohen, S., Eimicke, W. and Horan, J. (2002). Catastrophe and Public Service: A Case Study of the Government Response to the Destruction of the World Trade Center. *Public Administration Review* 62 (Special): 24–32.

Knight, R. F. and Pretty, D. J. (1997). *The Impact of Catastrophes on Shareholder Value*. The Oxford Executive Research Briefings. University of Oxford, Oxford.

Mitroff, I. I. and Anagnos, G. (2001). *Managing Crises Before They Happen: What Every Executive and Manager Needs to Know about Crises Management*. AMACOM, New York.

Mitroff, I. I. and Alpaslan, M. C. (2003). Preparing for Evil. *Harvard Business Review*: 109–115.

Quarantelli, E. L. (1995). The Future is Not the Past Repeated: Projecting Disasters of the 21st Century from Present Trends [http://dspace.udel.edu:8080/dspace/handle/19716/637].

Viscusi, W. K. (1993). The Value of Risks to Life and Health. *Journal of Economic Literature* 31 (4): 1912–1946.

Weick, K. (1996). Prepare Your Organization to Fight Fires. *Harvard Business Review* 74 (3): 143–148.

Chapter 13 Lessons from the 'Great Risks'

Boje, D. M., Gardner, C. L. and Smith, W. L. (2006). (Mis)Using Numbers in the Enron Story. *Organizational Research Methods* 9 (4): 456–474.

Kuprianov, A. (1995). Derivatives Debacles: Case Studies of Large Losses in Derivatives Markets, *Federal Reserve Bank of Richmond Economic Quarterly* 81, 1–39.

McLean, B. and Elkind, P. (2004). *The Smartest Guys in the Room: The Amazing Rise and Scandalous Fall of Enron*. Portfolio, New York.

Chapter 14 Summary and Conclusions

Davis, I. and Stephenson, E. (2006). Ten Trends to Watch in 2006. *The McKinsey Quarterly*. Accessed: 25 October 2006. www.mckinseyquarterly.com/links/22698.

References

Akerlof, G. A. (1970). The Market for Lemons: Quality Uncertainty and the Market Mechanism. *Quarterly Journal of Economics* 84 (3): 488–500.
Alexander, C. (ed) (2003). *Operational Risk*. FT Prentice Hall, London.
Allayannis, G. and Weston, J. P. (2001). The Use of Foreign Currency Derivatives and Firm Market Value. *The Review of Financial Studies* 14 (1): 243–276.
Allison, G. T. (1971). *Essence of Decision: Explaining the Cuban Missile Crisis*. Harper Collins, New York.
Ambrose, S. E. (1994). *D-Day*. Simon & Schuster, New York.
American Meteorological Society. (1991). Weather Forecasting: A Policy Statement of the American Meteorological Society. *Bulletin American Meteorological Society* 72 (8).
Angell, N. (1912). *The Great Illusion*. William Heinemann, London.
Argenti, J. (1976). *Corporate Collapse: The Causes and Symptoms*. McGraw-Hill, London.
Arnold, T. and Shockley, R. L. (2002). Real Options, Corporate Finance and the Foundations of Value Maximization. *Journal of Applied Corporate Finance* 15 (2): 82–88.
Austin, E. J., Deary, I. J. and Willock, J. (2001). Personality and Intelligence as Predictors of Economic Behavior in Scottish Farmers. *European Journal of Personality* 15 (S1): S123–S137.
Baldwin, W. (1992). The Crazy Things People Say to Justify Stock Prices. *Forbes*. 27 April 1992
Barberis, N. and Thaler, R. (2003). A Survey of Behavioral Finance. Published in G. M. Constantinides, M. Harris and R. M. Stulz (ed). *Handbook of the Economics of Finance*. Elsevier/North-Holland, Boston.
Bartram, S. M., Brown, G. W. and Fehle, F. R. (2004). International Evidence on Financial Derivative Usage. Accessed: 9 May 2006. http://ssrn.com/abstract=471245.
Basel Committee on Banking Supervision. (2001). *Consultative Document: The New Basel Capital Accord*. Bank for International Settlements, Basel.
Basel Committee on Banking Supervision. (2002). *The Quantitative Impact Study for Operational Risk: Overview of Individual Loss Data and Lessons Learned*. Basel Committee, Basel.
Basel Committee on Banking Supervision. (2003a). *The 2002 Loss Data Collection Exercise for Operational Risk: Summary of the Data Collected*. Basel Committee, Basel.
Basel Committee on Banking Supervision. (2003b). *Sound Practices for the Management and Supervision of Operational Risk*. Bank for International Settlements, Basel.
Bazerman, M. H. (2006). *Judgment in Managerial Decision Making*. John Wiley, Hoboken NJ.
Bazerman, M. H. and Watkins, M. D. (2004). *Predictable Surprises: The Disasters you Should have Seen Coming, and How to Prevent Them*. Harvard Business School Press, Boston MA.
Beach, L. R. (1997). *The Psychology of Decision Making*. Sage Publications, Thousand Oaks CA.
Beaty, J. and Gwynne, S. C. (1993). *The Outlaw Bank: A Wild Ride into the Secret Heart of BCCI*. Random House, New York NY.
Beck, U. (1992). *Risk Society, Towards a New Modernity*. Sage Publications, London.
Bernstein, P. L. (1996). *Against the Gods*. John Wiley & Sons, New York.
Bernstein, W. J. (2000). *The Intelligent Asset Allocator*. McGraw Hill, New York.
Bessis, J. (1998). *Risk Management in Banking*. John Wiley & Sons, Chichester.
Bierce, A. (1946). *The Collected Writings of Ambrose Bierce*. The Citadel Press, New York.

Bloom, N. and Van Reenen, J. (2002). Patents, Real Options and Firm Performance. *The Economic Journal* 112 (478): C97–C116.

Board of Governors of Federal Reserve System. (1997). *Branch and Agency Examination Manual*. United States Federal Reserve, Washington DC.

Board of Governors of Federal Reserve System. (2006). *Flow of Funds Accounts of the United States*. US Federal Reserve, Washington DC.

Boari, B., Salmi, R., Gallerani, G., Malagoni, A. M., Manfredi, F. and Manfredini, R. (2007). Acute Myocardial Infarction: Circadian, Weekly, and Seasonal Patterns of Occurrence. *Biological Rhythm Research* 38 (3): 155–167.

Boje, D. M., Gardner, C. L. and Smith, W. L. (2006). (Mis)Using Numbers in the Enron Story. *Organizational Research Methods* 9 (4): 456–474.

Bolger, F. A. and Wright, G. (1994). Assessing the Quality of Expert Judgement. *Decision Support Systems* 11 (1): 1–24.

Bosch, H. (1995). *The Director at Risk*. Pitman Publishing, South Melbourne.

Bottomley, S. (1997). From Contractualism to Constitutionalism: A Framework for Corporate Governance. *Sydney Law Review* 19 (3): 277–313.

Bowman, E. H. (1980). A Risk-Return Paradox for Strategic Management. *Sloan Management Review* 21: 17–33.

Britton, N. R. and Clark, G. J. (2000). From Response to Resilience: Emergency Management Reform in New Zealand. *Natural Hazards Review* 1 (3): 145–150.

Buckley, R. (1991). *Precision in Environmental Impact Prediction*. Resource and Environmental Studies. Australian National University CRES, Canberra.

Budner, S. (1962). Intolerance of Ambiguity as a Personality Variable. *Journal of Personality* 30 (3): 29–50.

Burbury, R. (1993). Extortion: Avoiding a Lingering Shelf Life. *Sydney Morning Herald*. Sydney. 2 December 1993.

Bureau of Economic Analysis. (2006). National Income and Product Accounts Table. Washington DC. Accessed: 2 March 2006. www.bea.gov/bea/dn/nipaweb/TableView.asp#Mid.

Bureau of Justice Statistics. (2006). Key Crime and Justice Facts at a Glance. Washington DC. Accessed: 27 February 2006. www.ojp.usdoj.gov/bjs/glance.htm#Crime.

Bureau of Transport Economics. (2001). *Economic Costs of Natural Disasters in Australia*. Bureau of Transport Economics, Canberra.

Bureau of Transportation Statistics. (2005). *National Transportation Statistics 2004*. US Department of Transportation, Washington DC.

Burrough, B. and Helyar, J. (1990). *Barbarians at the Gate: The Fall of RJR Nabisco*. Harper & Row, New York.

Byrnes, J. P., Miller, D. C. and Schafer, W. D. (1999). Gender Differences in Risk Taking: A Meta-analysis. *Psychological Bulletin* 125 (3): 367–383.

Camerer, C. (1995). Chapter 8 – Individual Decision Making. Published in J. H. Kagel and A. E. Roth (ed). *The Handbook of Experimental Economics*. Princeton University Press, Princeton.

Camerer, C. and Lovallo, D. (1999). Overconfidence and Excess Entry: An Experimental Approach. *American Economic Review* 89 (1): 306–318.

Campbell-Hunt, C. (2000). What Have We Learned About Generic Competitive Strategy? A Meta-analysis. *Strategic Management Journal* 21 (2): 127–154.

Campbell, J. Y., Lettau, M., Malkiel, B. G. and Xu, Y. (2001). Have Individual Stocks Become More Volatile? *The Journal of Finance* 56 (1): 1–43.

Caraco, T., Blanckenhorn, W., Gregory, G., Newman, J., Recer, G. and Zwicker, S. (1990). Risk-Sensitivity: Ambient Temperature Affects Foraging Choice. *Animal Behaviour* 39: 338–345.
Carr, D. (2005). More Horrible Than Truth: News reports. *New York Times*. New York. 19 September 2005.
Carson, R. (1962). *Silent Spring*. Houghton Mifflin, Boston.
Carter DA, Rogers DA, Simkins BJ. (2006). Does Fuel Hedging Make Economic Sense? The Case of the US Airline Industry. *Financial Management* 35 (1): 53–86.
Casssidy, T. and Lynn, R. (1989). A Multifactorial Approach to Achievement Motivation: The Development of a Comprehensive Measure. *Journal of Occupational Psychology* 62: 301–312.
Cecil, L. G. (1921). *Life of Robert Marquis of Salisbury*. Hodder and Stoughton, London.
Chami, R., Cosimano, T. F. and Fullenkamp, C. (2002). Managing Ethical Risk: How Investing in Ethics Adds Value. *Journal of Banking and Finance* 26 (9): 1697–1718.
Chekhov, A. P. (1978). *The Cherry Orchard*. Eyre Methuen, London.
Ciampa, D. and Watkins, M. (1999). *Right from the Start*. Harvard Business School Press, Boston MA.
Clancy, T. (1994). *Debt of Honor*. Putnam, New York.
Clarke, C. J. and Varma, S. (1999). Strategic Risk Management: The New Competitive Edge. *Long Range Planning* 32 (4): 414–424.
Cochrane, J. H. (1999). *New Facts in Finance*. Working Paper. Working Paper. National Bureau of Economic Research, Washington DC.
Cohen, S., Eimicke, W. and Horan, J. (2002). Catastrophe and Public Service: A Case Study of the Government Response to the Destruction of the World Trade Center. *Public Administration Review* 62 (Special): 24–32.
Cohen, W. S. (2006). *Dragon Fire*. Forge, New York.
Coleman, L. (1998). The Age of Inexpertise. *Quadrant* 42 (5): 63–66.
Coleman, L. (2004). The Frequency and Cost of Corporate Crises. *Journal of Contingencies and Crisis Management* 12 (1): 2–13.
Coleman, L. (2006a). Frequency of Man-Made Disasters in the 20th Century. *Journal of Contingencies and Crisis Management* 14 (1): 3–11.
Coleman, L. (2006b). *Why Managers and Companies Take Risks*. Springer, Heidelberg.
Coleman, L. and Casselman, R. M. (2004). *What You Don't Know Can Hurt You: Towards an Integrated Theory of Knowledge and Corporate Risk*. Department of Management Working Paper. The University of Melbourne, Melbourne.
Columbia Accident Investigation Board. (2003). *CAIB Report*. National Aeronautics and Space Administration, Arlington, VA.
Comer, M. J. (1998). *Corporate Fraud*. Gower, Brookfield VT.
Coombes, P. and Watson, M. (2002). *Global Investor Opinion Survey 2002*. McKinsey & Co.
COSO. (2004). *Enterprise Risk Management – Integrated Framework*. Committee of Sponsoring Organizations of the Treadway Commission.
Crittle, S. (2000). Corporate Terrorism Spreads its Poison. *Sun Herald*. Sydney. 18 June 2000.
Cruver, B. (2002). *Anatomy of Greed*. Carroll & Graf, New York.
Culp, C. L. (2002). The Revolution in Corporate Risk Management. *Journal of Applied Corporate Finance* 14 (4): 8–26.
Cummins, J. D., Doherty, N. A. and Lo, A. (1999). *Can Insurers Pay for the `Big One'?* Working Paper Series. The Wharton School.
D'Aveni, R. A. (1994). *Hypercompetition: Managing the Dynamics of Strategic Maneuvering*. The Free Press, New York.

Damodaran, A. (2001). *Corporate Finance*. John Wiley & Sons, Hoboken NJ.
Daniell, M. H. (2000). *World of Risk*. John Wiley & Sons, Singapore.
Darwin, C. (1871). *The Descent of Man*. John Murray, London.
Dauphinais, G. W. (2000). *Wisdom of the CEO: 29 Global Leaders Tackle Today's Most Pressing Business Challenges*. Wiley, New York.
Davis, D. (1985). New Projects: Beware of False Economies. *Harvard Business Review* 63 (2): 95–101.
Davis, I. and Stephenson, E. (2006). Ten Trends to Watch in 2006. The McKinsey Quarterly. Accessed: 25 October 2006. www.mckinseyquarterly.com/links/22698.
de Geus, A. (1997). *The Living Company*. Harvard Business School Press, Boston MA.
de Silva, J. (1994). Survey Finds Australian Food is Safer than Ever. *The Age*. Melbourne. 25 May 1994.
DeLoach, J. (2000). *Enterprise-wide Risk Management: Strategies for Linking Risk and Opportunity*. Arthur Andersen, Houston.
Dibb, P. (2001). Asia at a Crossroads. *Naval War College Review* 54 (1).
Dimson, E., Marsh, P. and Staunton, M. (2006). The Worldwide Equity Premium: A Smaller Puzzle. Accessed: www.fma.org/Stockholm/Papers/TheWorldwideEquityPremium_1Dec05.pdf.
Doherty, N. A. (2000). *Integrated Risk Management*. McGraw-Hill, New York.
Dolan, S. L. and Garcia, S. (2002). Managing by Values: Cultural Redesign for Strategic Organizational Change at the Dawn of the Twenty-first Century. *Journal of Management Development* 21 (2): 101–117.
Dow, S. C. (1996). Why the Banking System Should be Regulated. *The Economic Journal* 106 (436): 698–707.
Drucker, P. F. (1967). *Managing for Results: Economic Tasks and Risk-taking Decisions*. Pan Books, London.
Drucker, P. F. (1979). *Management*. Pan, New York.
Economist Intelligence Unit. (2005a). *The Evolving Role of the CRO*. The Economist Intelligence Unit, London.
Economist Intelligence Unit. (2005b). *Regulatory Risk*. The Economist Intelligence Unit, London.
Elkington, J. (1998). Stakeholders and Bottom Lines. Published in J. Mitchell (ed). *Companies in a World of Conflict*. Royal Institute of International Affairs, London.
EM-DAT. (2005). The OFDA/CRED International Disaster Database. Accessed: 16 December 2005. www.cred.be/emdat/intro.html.
Enders, W. and Sandler, T. (2000). Is Transnational Terrorism Becoming More Threatening? *The Journal of Conflict Resolution* 44 (3): 307–332.
Etkin, D., Haque, E., Bellisario, L. and Burton, I. (2004). *Natural Hazards and Disasters in Canada*. Canadian Natural Hazards Assessment Project, Ottowa.
Fair, R. C. (2002). Events that Shook the Market. *Journal of Business* 75 (4): 713–731.
Fama, E. F. and French, K. R. (2003). *New Lists: Fundamentals and Survival Rates*. Working Paper No. 03-15. Amos Tuck School of Business at Dartmouth College, Hanover, NH.
Fama, E. F. and MacBeth, J. D. (1973). Risk, Return, and Equilibrium: Empirical Tests. *The Journal of Political Economy* 81 (3): 607–636.
Farjoun, M. and Starbuck, W. H. (2005). Introduction. Published in W. H. Starbuck and M. Farjoun (ed). *Organization at the Limit*. Blackwell, Malden MA.
Fernandez, L. and Piron, R. (1999). Should She Switch? A Game-theoretic Analysis of the Monty Hall Problem. *Mathematics Magazine* 72: 214–218.
Fiegenbaum, A. and Thomas, H. (1988). Attitudes Toward Risk and the Risk-return Paradox: Prospect Theory explanations. *Academy of Management Journal* 31 (1): 85–106.

Flyvbjerg, B., Holm, M. S. and Buhl, S. (2002). Underestimating Costs in Public Works Projects: Error or Lie? *Journal of the American Planning Association* 68 (3): 279–295.

Folkard, S., Lombardi, D. A. and Spencer, M. B. (2006). Estimating the Circadian Rhythm in the Risk of Occupational Injuries and Accidents. *Chronobiology International* 23 (6): 1181–1192.

Foster, R. N. and Kaplan, S. (2001). *Creative Destruction*. Financial Times, London.

Friedman, M. (1970). The Social Responsibility of Business is to Increase its Profits. *The New York Times Magazine*. New York NY. 13 September 1970.

Froot, K. A. (2001). The Market for Catastrophe Risk: A Clinical Examination. *Journal of Financial Economics* 60: 529–571.

Froot, K. A. and Posner, S. (2000). *Issues in the Pricing of Catastrophe Risk*. Marsh & McLennan Securities Corporation, New York.

Gallagher, R. B. (1956). Risk Management: A New Phase of Cost Control. *Harvard Business Review* 34 (5): 75–86.

Geiss, S. (2006). Stochastic Processes. Accessed: 22 July 2007. http://www.math.jyu.fi/~geiss/scripts/stochastic-processes.pdf#search=%22%22gamblers%20ruin%22%22.

Georgiev, G., Gupta, B. and Kunkel, T. (2003). *The Benefits of Real Estate Investment*. Working Paper. Center for International Securities and Derivatives Markets, University of Massachusetts, Boston.

Gigerenzer, G. (2002). *Reckoning with Risk*. Allen Lane, London.

Gilbert, M. (2004). *D-Day*. John Wiley & Sons Inc, Hoboken NJ.

Gladwell, M. (2007). Open Secrets. *The New Yorker*. 8 January 2007.

Grable, J. E. (2000). Financial Risk Tolerance and Additional Factors that Affect Risk Taking in Everyday Money Matters. *Journal of Business and Psychology* 14 (4): 625–630.

Griffin-Pierson, S. (1990). The Competitiveness Questionnaire: A Measure of Two Components of Competitiveness. *Measurement and Evaluation in Counselling and Development* 23 (3): 108–115.

Gruber, M. J. (1996). Another Puzzle: The Growth in Actively Managed Mutual Funds. *Journal of Finance* 51 (3): 783–810.

Handberg, R. (2003). *Reinventing NASA*. Praeger, Westport CT.

Harari, O. (1993). Ten Reasons Why TQM Doesn't Work. *Management Review* 82 (1): 33–38.

Harvey, C. R. (1995). Predictable Risk and Returns in Emerging Markets. *The Review of Financial Studies* 8 (3): 773–816.

Healy, P. M. and Palepu, K. G. (2003). The Fall of Enron. *The Journal of Economic Perspectives* 17 (2): 3–26.

Heimann, C. F. L. (1997). *Acceptable Risks*. The University of Michigan Press, Ann Arbor MI.

Heinrich, H. W. (1959). *Industrial Accident Prevention: A Scientific Approach*. McGraw-Hill, New York.

Henry, D. (2002). Why Most Big Deals Don't Pay Off. *Business Week*. 14 October 2002.

Hicks, J. R. (1935). Annual Survey of Economic Theory: The Theory of Monopoly. *Econometrica* 3 (1): 1–20.

Higgs, H. (ed). (1926). *Palgrave's Dictionary of Political Economy*. Macmillan and Co, London.

Hoffman, A. J. (2001). *From Heresy to Dogma: An Institutional History of Corporate Environmentalism*. Stanford University Press, Stanford CA.

Hooker, N. H. and Salin, V. (1999). Stock Market Reaction to Food Recalls. Accessed: 11 November 2003. http://agecon.tamu.edu/faculty/salin/research/nafs.pdf.

Hopkins, A. (2002). *Lessons from Longford: The Trial*. CCH Australia, North Ryde, N.S.W.

Horne, J. (2006). *Breach of Faith: Hurricane Katrina and the Near Death of a Great American City*. Random House, New York.

Howarth, I. (1995). Good Results will not Mask BHP's Bad Image. *Australian Financial Review*. Sydney. 21 September 1995.

Huntington, S. P. (1993). The Clash of Civilizations? *Foreign Affairs* 72 (3): 22–49.

Ignatius, D. (1999). *Washington Post*. Washington DC.

Institute for Crisis Management. (2005). Annual ICM Crisis Report. Accessed: 22 February 2006. www.crisisexperts.com/pub.htm.

International Federation of Accountants. (2003). *Enterprise Governance: Getting the Balance Right*. International Federation of Accountants, New York.

Jackofsky, E. F., Slocum, J. W. J. and McQuaid, S. J. (1988). Cultural Values and the CEO: Alluring Companions? *Academy of Management Executive* 2 (1): 39–49.

Jensen, M. C. (2001). Value Maximization, Stakeholder Theory and the Corporate Objective Function. *Journal of Applied Corporate Finance* 14 (3): 8–21.

Jin Y, Jorion P. (2006). Firm Value and Hedging: Evidence from U.S. Oil and Gas Producers. *The Journal of Finance* 61 (2): 893–919.

Kaen, F. R. (2003). *A Blueprint for Corporate Governance*. American Management Association, New York.

Kahneman, D. (2003). Maps of Bounded Rationality: Psychology for Behavioral Economics. *The American Economic Review* 93 (5): 1449–1475.

Kahneman, D. and Tversky, A. (1979). Prospect Theory: An Analysis of Decision Under Risk. *Econometrica* 47 (2): 263–291.

Kaminski, V. and Martin, J. (2001). Transforming Enron: The Value of Active Management. *Journal of Applied Corporate Finance* 13 (4): 39–49.

Kane, E. J. and DeTrask, K. (1999). Breakdown of Accounting Controls at Barings and Daiwa. *Pacific-Basin Finance Journal* 7 (2): 203–228.

Karter, M. J. J. (2003). *Fire Loss in the United States During 2002*. National Fire Protection Association, Quincy MA.

Keeble, J. (1999). *Out of the Channel*. EWU Press, Spokane WA.

Keeley, M. C. (1990). Deposit Insurance, Risk, and Market Power in Banking. *The American Economic Review* 80 (5): 1183–1200.

Keinan, G. (1984). Measurement of Risk Takers' Personality. *Psychological Reports* 55: 163–167.

Kendall, R. A. H. (1998). *Risk Management for Executives*. Pitman Publishing, London.

Kessler, R. (2003). *The CIA at War*. St. Martin's Press, New York.

Kettl, D. F. (ed). (2004). *The Department of Homeland Security's First Year – A Report Card*. The Century Foundation Press, New York.

Kleindorfer, P. R., Kunreuther, H. C. and Schoemaker, P. J. H. (1993). *Decision Sciences: An Integrative Perspective*. Cambridge University Press, Cambridge, England.

Knight, F. (1921). *Risk, Uncertainty and Profit*. Houghton-Mifflin, Boston.

Knight, R. F. and Pretty, D. J. (1997). *The Impact of Catastrophes on Shareholder Value*. The Oxford Executive Research Briefings. White Paper. University of Oxford, Oxford.

Koch, T. W. and MacDonald, S. S. (2006). *Bank Management (6th Edition)*. Thomson, Mason OH.

Kocourek, P. and Newfrock, J. (2006). Are Boards Worrying About The Wrong Risks? *Corporate Board* 27 (157): 6–11.

Koerner, R. J. (1993). The Behaviour of Pacific Metallurgical Coal Markets: The Impact of Japan's Acquisition Strategy on Market Price. *Resources Policy* 19 (1): 66–79.

Koestler, A. (1972). *The Roots of Coincidence*. Hutchinson and Co, London.

Kouradi, J. (1999). *Decisionmaking*. Orion, London.

KPMG. (1999). Unlocking Shareholder Value: The Keys to Success [Mergers and Acquisitions: Global Research Report 1999]. London. Accessed: 12 September 2002. www.kpmg.fi/attachment.asp?Section=176&Item=352.

KRIeX.org. (2005). *Report on a Survey of KRI Programs*. The Risk Management Association, Philadelphia PA.

Krug, E. G., Kresnow, M.-J., Peddicord, J. P., Dahlberg, L. L., Powell, K. E., Crosby, A. E. and Annest, J. L. (1998). Suicide after Natural Disasters. *The New England Journal of Medicine* 338 (6): 373–379.

Kruger, J. and Dunning, D. (1999). Unskilled and Unaware of It: How Difficulties in Recognizing One's Own Incompetence Lead to Inflated Self-assessments. *Journal of Personality and Social Psychology* 77 (6): 1121–1134.

Kuhn, T. S. (1970, 2nd edition). *The Structure of Scientific Revolutions*. University of Chicago Press, Chicago.

La Porte, T. R. (1996). High Reliability Organizations: Unlikely, Demanding and at Risk. *Journal of Contingencies and Crisis Management* 4 (2): 60–71.

Lanham, B. and Maxson-Cooper, P. (2003). Is Six Sigma the Answer for Nursing to Reduce Medical Errors and Enhance Patient Safety? *Nursing Economics* 21 (1): 39–42.

Levenson, H. (1974). Activism and Powerful Others. *Journal of Personality Assessment* 38 (4): 377–383.

Lewis, G. and Zalan, T. (2004). *The CEO-Advisors Nexus: Toward an Explanation of Merger Preference in Mergers and Acquisitions*. MBS Working Papers. University of Melbourne, Melbourne.

Liddell Hart, S. B. H. (1943). *Thoughts on War*. Faber, London.

Liebenberg, A. P. and Hoyt, R. E. (2003). The Determinants of Enterprise Risk Management: Evidence from the Appointment of Chief Risk Officers. *Risk Management and Insurance Review* 6 (1): 37–52.

Linsmeier, T. J. and Pearson, N. D. (2000). Value at Risk. *Financial Analysts Journal* 56 (2): 47–67.

Livingstone, C. (2002). *Managing Risks in Innovation*. "Living with Risk in Our Society" Conference, Sydney, Australian Academy of Technological Sciences and Engineering. NSW Division.

Lipscombe, R. (2000). Australia's Tyranny of Distance in Oil Spill Response. *Spill Science & Technology Bulletin* 6 (1): 13–25.

Lomborg, B. (2001). *The Skeptical Environmentalist: Measuring the Real State of the World*. Cambridge University Press, New York.

Loosemore, M. (1999). A Grounded Theory of Construction Crisis Management. *Construction Management and Economics* 17 (1): 9–19

Lopes, L. L. (1987). Between Hope and Fear: The Psychology of Risk. Published in L. Berkowitz (ed). *Experimental Social Psychology*. Academic Press, San Diego. 20.

Lovallo, D. and Kahneman, D. (2003). Delusions of Success: How Optimism Undermines Executives' Decisions. *Harvard Business Review* 81 (7): 56–63.

Lubatkin, M. and O'Neill, H. M. (1987). Merger Strategies and Capital Market Risk. *Academy of Management Journal* 30 (4): 665–684.

Lucier, C., Schuyt, R. and Tse, E. (2005). The World's Most Prominent Temp Workers. *strategy+business* 34.

Lupton, D. (1995). Anatomy of an Epidemic: Press Reporting of an Outbreak of Legionnaires' Disease. *Media Information Australia* 76 (2): 92–99.

Lupton, D. L. and Tulloch, J. (2002). Risk is Part of Your Life: Risk Epistemologies Among a Group of Australians. *Sociology* 36 (2): 317–334.

Mackenzie, B. W. (1981). Looking for the Improbable Needle in the Haystack: The Economics of Base Metal Exploration in Canada. *CIM Bulletin* 74: 115–123.

Mackenzie, B. W. and Doggett, M. D. (1992). *Economics of Mineral Exploration in Australia*. Australian Mineral Foundation, Glenelg SA.

MacLeod, D. (2004). Pillinger Plans Second Mission to Mars. *Guardian*. 6 July 2004.

MacMinn, R. D. (1987). Insurance and Corporate Risk Management. *Journal of Risk & Insurance* 54 (4): 658–677.

Malkiel, B. G. and Xu, Y. (1997). Risk and Return Revisited. *Journal of Portfolio Management* 23 (3): 9–14.

March, J. G. and Shapira, Z. (1987). Managerial Perspectives on Risk and Risk Taking. *Management Science* 33 (11): 1404–1418.

Marsh, N., McAllum, M. and Purcell, D. (2002). *Strategic Foresight*. Crown Content, Melbourne.

Maslow, A. H. (1954). *Motivation and Personality*. Harper, New York.

Maturi, R. J. (1993). *Divining the Dow*. Probus Publishing Company, Chicago IL.

Mayers, D. and Smith, C. W. (1982). On the Corporate Demand for Insurance. *Journal of Business* 55 (2): 281–296.

Mayo, E. (1933). *The Human Problems of an Industrial Civilization*. Macmillan, New York.

McClelland, D. C. (1961). *The Achieving Society*. The Free Press, New York.

McDonald, L. and Härtel, C. E. J. (2000a). *Consumer-preferred Company Responses Following a Crisis*. Working Paper. 85-00. Monash University Faculty of Business and Economics, Melbourne.

McDonald, L. and Härtel, C. E. J. (2000b). Peanut Butter, Salmonella Poisoning and Children: On Becoming 'Involved' and Angry Following a Company Crisis. *Queensland Review* 7 (1): 69–76.

McLean, B. and Elkind, P. (2004). *The Smartest Guys in the Room: The Amazing Rise and Scandalous Fall of Enron*. Portfolio, New York.

Meadows, D. H., Meadows, D. L., Randers, J. and Behrens, W. W. (1974). *The Limits to Growth: A Report for the Club of Rome's Project on the Predicament of Mankind*. Universe Books, New York.

Mehr, R. I. and Hedges, B. A. (1963). *Risk Management in the Business Enterprise*. Richard D. Irwin, Inc., Homewood, IL.

Mercer, I. (2000). In a Flap. *Sydney Morning Herald*. Sydney. 20 May 2000.

Merrow, E. W., Phillips, K. E. and Myers, C. W. (1981). *Understanding Cost Growth and Performance Shortfalls in Pioneer Process Plants*. Report R-2569-DOE. Rand Corporation, Santa Monica CA.

Merton, R. C. (1977). An Analytic Derivation of the Cost of Deposit Insurance and Loan Guarantees: An Application of Modern Option Pricing Theory. *Journal of Banking and Finance* 1 (1): 3–11.

Meulbroek, L. K. (2002). *Integrated Risk Management for the Firm: A Senior Manager's Guide*. Harvard Business School, Boston MA.

Meyer, J. R. and Kuh, E. (1957). *The Investment Decision*. Harvard University Press, Cambridge MA.

Micklethwait, J. and Wooldridge, A. (2003). *The Company: A Short History of a Revolutionary Idea*. Modern Library, New York.

Middlebrook, M. and Mahoney, P. (1977). *Battleship*. Allen Lane, London.

Miller, G. A. (1956). The Magical Number Seven. *Psychological Review* 63: 81–97.

Miller, K. D. and Bromiley, P. (1990). Strategic Risk and Corporate Performance. *Academy of Management Journal* 33 (4): 756–779.

Mitroff I, Pauchant T, Shrivastava P. (1989). Crises, Disasters, Catastrophe: Are you ready? *Security Management* 33 (2): 101–108.

Modigilani, F. and Miller, M. H. (1958). The Cost of Capital, Corporation Finance and the Theory of Investment. *American Economic Review* 48 (3): 261–297.

Moody's Investors Service. (2004). *Risk Management Assessments*. New York.

Munich Re. (2005). Annual Review: Natural Catastrophes 2004. Accessed: 10 January 2006. www.w.munichre.com/pdf/topics_2002_e.pdf.

Myers, R. (1995). Trust Betrayed. *Treasury and Risk Management*.

Myers, S. C. (1977). Determinants of Corporate Borrowing. *Journal of Financial Economics* 5 (2): 147–175.

Nader, R. (1973). *Unsafe at Any Speed*. Bantam, London.

Nichols, N. A. (1994). Scientific Management at Merck: An interview with CFO Judy Lewent. *Harvard Business Review* 72 (1): 88–99.

Noronha, G. and Singal, V. (2004). Financial Health and Airline Safety. *Managerial and Decision Economics* 25 (1): 1–26.

Nutt, P. C. (1999). Surprising but True: Half the Decisions in Organizations Fail. *Academy of Management Executive* 13 (4): 75–90.

NYSE. (2002). *Corporate Governance Rule Proposals*. NYSE Corporate Accountability and Listing Standards Committee, New York NY.

Oldfield, G. S. and Santomero, A. M. (1997). *The Place of Risk Management in Financial Institutions*. Working Paper. Wharton Financial Institutions Center, Philadelphia PA.

Olsen, R. A. and Troughton, G. H. (2000). Are Risk Premium Anomalies Caused by Ambiguity? *Financial Analysts Journal* 56 (2): 24–31.

Osborn, R. N. and Jackson, D. H. (1988). Leaders, Riverboat Gamblers, or Purposeful Unintended Consequences in the Management of Complex, Dangerous Technologies. *Academy of Management Journal* 31 (4): 924–948.

Pablo, A. L., Sitkin, S. B. and Jemison, D. B. (1996). Acquisition Decision-making Processes: The Central Role of Risk. *Journal of Management* 22 (5): 723–746.

Paddock, J. L., Siegel, D. R. and Smith, J. L. (1988). Option Valuation of Claims on Real Assets: The Case of Offshore Petroleum Leases. *The Quarterly Journal of Economics* 103 (3): 479–508.

Palmer, T. B. and Wiseman, R. M. (1999). Decoupling Risk Taking from Income Stream Uncertainty: A Holistic Approach. *Strategic Management Journal* 20 (11): 1037–1062.

Parachini, J. (2006). Putting WMD Terrorism into Perspective. Published in R. Howard, J. Forest and J. Moore (ed). *Homeland Security and Terrorism*. McGraw-Hill, New York.

Park, S. H. and Ungson, G. R. (1997). The Effect of National Culture, Organizational Complementarity and Economic Motivation on Joint Venture Dissolution. *Academy of Management Journal* 40 (2): 279–307.

Pascale, R. (1990). *Managing on the Edge: How the Smartest Companies use Conflict to Stay Ahead*. Simon and Schuster, New York.

Pennings, J. M. E. (2002). Pulling the Trigger or not: Factors Affecting Behavior of Initiating a Position in Derivatives Markets. *Journal of Economic Psychology* 23: 263–278.

Perrow, C. (1984). *Normal Accidents*. Basic Books Inc, New York.

Peters, T. J. and Waterman, R. H. (1982). *In Search of Excellence: Lessons from America's Best-run Companies*. Harper & Row, 1982.

Pillar, P. R. (2006). Intelligence, Policy and the War in Iraq. *Foreign Affairs* 85 (2): 15.

Plutarch. (100). *Plutarch Lives – Pericles and Fabius Maximus. Nicias and Crassus*. Loeb, London.

Porter, M. E. (1980). *Competitive Strategy: Techniques for Analysing Industries and Competitors*. Free Press, New York.

Porter, M. E. (1985). *Competitive Advantage*. Free Press, New York.

Price, R. (2000). Do You Feel Lucky? *International Journal of Business Continuity Management* 1 (2): 1–4.

Quinn, L. R. (2004). The CRO: A species at Risk. *Risk & Insurance*. 1 September 2004

Rabin, M. (1996). Psychology and Economics. Accessed: 4 May 2003. http.://elsa.berkeley.edu/~rabin/peboth7.pdf.

Raiffa, H. (1968). *Decision Analysis – Introductory Lectures on Choices under Uncertainty*. Addison-Wesley, Reading MA.

Rajgopal, S. and Shevlin, T. (2002). Empirical Evidence on the Relation between Stock Option Compensation and Risk Taking. *Journal of Accounting and Economics* 33 (2): 145–171.

Real, L. (1991). Animal Choice Behaviour and the Evolution of Cognitive Architecture. *Science* 253: 980–986.

Reeve, S. (2000). *One Day in September*. Faber and Faber, London.

Reuer, J. J. and Leiblein, M. J. (2000). Downside Risk Implications of Multinationality and International Joint Ventures. *Academy of Management Journal* 43 (2): 203–214.

Ricciardi, V. (2004). A Risk Perception Primer: A Narrative Research Review of the Risk Perception Literature in Behavioral Accounting and Behavioral Finance. Accessed: 17 February 2005. http://ssrn.com/abstract=566802.

Richardson, B., Nwankwo, S. and Richardson, S. (1994). Understanding the Causes of Business Failure Crises. *Management Decision* 32 (4): 9–22.

Ringland, G. (1998). *Scenario Planning: Managing for the Future*. John Wiley, New York.

Risk Support Team. (2004). *The Risk Programme: Improving Government's risk handling – Final Report to the Prime Minister*. HM Treasury, London.

Robinson, J. P., Shaver, P. R. and Wrightsman, L. (1991). *Measures of Personality and Social Psychological Attitudes*. Academic Press, San Diego.

Rohrmann, B. (1997). Risk Orientation Questionnaire: Attitudes Towards Risk Decisions. University of Melbourne, Melbourne.

Roll, R. (1986). The Hubris Hypothesis of Corporate Takeovers. *Journal of Business* 59 (2): 197–216.

Roskelly, N. (2002). If I Ran Your Company. *New Products Magazine* (November).

Royal Society. (1992). *Risk: Analysis, Perception and Management*. The Royal Society, London.

Ruefli, T. W., Collins, J. M. and Lacugna, J. R. (1999). Risk Measures in Strategic Management Research: Auld Lang Syne? *Strategic Management Journal* 20 (2): 167–194.

Rumelt, R. P. (1991). How Much Does Industry Matter? *Strategic Management Journal* 12 (3): 167–185.

Ryan, M. K. and Haslam, S. A. (2005). The Glass Cliff: Evidence that Women are Over-Represented in Precarious Leadership Positions. *British Journal of Management* 16 (2): 81–90.

Sagristano, M. D., Trope, Y. and Liberman, N. (2002). Time-Dependent Gambling: Odds Now, Money Later. *Journal of Experimental Psychology* 131 (3): 364–371.

Sawyer, R. and Pfeifer, J. (2006). Strategic Planning for First Responders: Lessons Learned from the NY Fire Department. Published in R. Howard, J. Forest and J. Moore (ed). *Homeland Security and Terrorism*. McGraw-Hill, New York.

Scandizzo, S. (2005). Risk Mapping and Key Risk Indicators in Operational Risk Management. *Economic Notes* 34 (2): 231–256.

Scanlon, J. (2001). *Lessons Learned or Lessons Forgotten: The Canadian Disaster Experience*. Institute for Catastrophic Loss Reduction, Toronto.

Schnaars, S. P. (1989). *Megamistakes: Forecasting and the Myth of Rapid Technological Change*. The Free Press, New York.

Schneider, S. K. (1998). Reinventing Public Administration: A Case Study of the Federal Emergency Management Agency. *Public Administration Quarterly* 22 (1): 35–57.

Schneider, S. L. and Lopes, L. L. (1986). Reflection in Preferences Under Risk: Who and When May Suggest Why. *Journal of Experimental Psychology: Human Perception and Performance* 12 (4): 535–548.

Schultz, J. V. (1997). *A Framework for Military Decision Making under Risks*. Thesis submitted for degree of in School of Advanced Airpower Studies at Maxwell Air Force Base Maxwell AL.

Scruggs, J. T. (1998). Resolving the Puzzling Intertemporal Relation Between the Market Risk Premium and Conditional Market Variance: A Two-factor Approach. *The Journal of Finance* 53 (2): 575–603.

Sharpe, W. F. (1964). Capital Asset Prices: A Theory of Market Equilibrium under Conditions of Risk. *Journal of Finance* 19: 424–442.

Shaw, R. (2001). Don't Panic: Behaviour in Major Incidents. *Disaster Prevention and Management* 10 (1): 5–9.

Shefrin, H. (ed). (2001). *Behavioral Finance*. Edward Elgar Publishing, Cheltenham UK.

Shergold, P. (2003). *Presentation to Comcover CEO Breakfast Forum*. Canberra.

Shimpi, P. (2003). Asset/liability Management as a Corporate Finance Function. Published in L. M. Tilman (ed). *Asset/Liability Management of Financial Institutions*. Euromoney Institutional Investor, London UK.

Shleifer, A. and Vishny, R. W. (1997). A Survey of Corporate Governance. *The Journal of Finance* 52 (2): 737–783.

Shoebridge, N. (1995). How PacDun Bit Off more than it can Chew. *Business Review Weekly*. 2 April 1995

Singh, J. V. (1986). Performance, Slack, and Risk Taking in Organizational Decision Making. *Academy of Management Journal* 29 (3): 526–585.

Slovic, P. (1972). Psychological Study of Human Judgment: Implications for Investment Decision Making. *The Journal of Finance* 27 (4): 779–799.

Smallwood, P. D. (1996). An Introduction to Risk Sensitivity. *American Zoologist* 36: 392–401.

Smith, C. (1992). *Media and Apocalypse*. Greenwood Press, Westport CT.

Smith, C. S., Lonsdale, W. M. and Fortune, J. (1999). When to Ignore Advice: Invasion Predictions and Decision Theory. *Biological Invasions* 1 (1): 89–96.

Social Investment Forum. (2006). *2005 Report on Socially Responsible Investing Trends in the United States*. Washington DC.

Soll, J. B. (1996). Determinants of Overconfidence and Miscalibration. *Organizational Behavior and Human Decision Processes* 65 (2): 117–137.

Soros, G. (1994). The Theory of Reflexivity. Speech to the MIT Department of Economics World Economy Laboratory Conference, Washington DC. Accessed: 12 November 2003. w.ww.soros.org/textfiles/speeches/042694_Theory_of_Reflexivity.txt.

Standard & Poor's. (2004). Ratings Performance 2003. Accessed: 22 February 2005. www.creditmodel.com/csa/DefaultStudy2003.pdf.

Starbuck, W. H. and Milliken, F. J. (1988). Challenger: Fine-tuning the Odds until Something Breaks. *Journal of Management Studies* 25 (4): 319–339.

Statman, M. and Tyebjee, T. T. (1985). Optimistic Capital Budgeting Forecasts: An Experiment. *Financial Management* 14: 27–33.

Steinglass, P. and Gerrity, E. (1990). Natural Disasters and Post-traumatic Stress Disorder: Short-term Versus Long-term Recovery in Two Disaster-affected Communities. *Journal of Applied Social Psychology* 20 (1): 1746–1766.

Sternberg, E. (2004). *Corporate Governance: Accountability in the Marketplace*. The Institute of Economic Affairs, London.

Stewart, B. (2006). The Real Reasons Enron Failed. *Journal of Applied Corporate Finance* 18 (2): 116–119.

Strategy Unit. (2002). *Risk: Improving Government's Capability to Handle Risk and Uncertainty.* UK Cabinet Office, London.

Sullivan, A. (1999). London Fog. *The New Republic.* 14 June 1999.

Sunstein, C. R. (2005). Moral Heuristics. *Behavioral and Brain Sciences* 28 (4): 531–573.

Svenson, O. (1981). Are We All Less Risky and More Skillful than our Fellow Drivers? *Acta Psychologica* 47 (2): 143–148.

Swartz, M. and Watkins, S. (2003). *Power Failure.* Aurom Press, London.

Swiss Re. (1996). *1995 Record Losses due to Catastrophes.* Swiss Re Insurance, Zurich.

Swiss Re. (2004). The Risk Landscape of the Future. Accessed: 20 May 2005. www.swissre.com.

Swiss Re. (2005a). Natural Catastrophes and Man-made Disasters in 2004. Accessed: 22 January 2006. ww.w.swissre.com.

Swiss Re. (2005b). *World Insurance in 2004.* Sigma. Swiss Reinsurance Company, Zurich.

Swiss Re. (2006). Natural Catastrophes and Man-made Disasters in 2005. Accessed: 22 June 2006. www.swissre.com.

Sykes, T. (1994). *The Bold Riders: Behind Australia's Corporate Collapses.* Allen & Unwin, Sydney.

Taylor, F. W. (1967). *The Principles of Scientific Management.* Norton, New York.

Terry, L. D. and Stivers, C. (2002). Democratic Governance in the Aftermath of September 11, 2001. *Public Administration Review* 62 (Supplement 1): 16–17.

Tetlock, P. E. (1999). Theory-driven Reasoning about Possible Pasts and Probable Futures: Are We Prisoners of our Preconceptions? *American Journal of Political Science* 43: 335–366.

Thaler, R. (1985). Mental Accounting and Consumer Choice. *Marketing Science* 4 (3): 199–214.

The 9/11 Commission. (2004). *Final Report of the National Commission on Terrorist Attacks Upon the United States.* W. W. Norton & Company, New York.

The Presidential/Congressional Commission on Risk Assessment and Risk Management. (1997). *Risk Assessment and Risk Management in Regulatory Decision-Making.* US EPA, Washington DC.

The Standish Group. (1995). Chaos. Accessed: 26 August 2002. www.scs.carleton.ca/~beau/PM/Standish-Report.html.

Thurow, L. C. (1981). *The Zero-Sum Society.* Penguin Books, New York.

Treasury Board of Canada. (2001). *Integrated Risk Management Framework.* Treasury Board, Ottawa.

Treynor, J. L. and Black, F. (1976). Corporate Investment Decisions. Published in S. C. Myers (ed). *Modern Developments in Financial Management.* Praeger Publishers, New York.

Triantis, A. J. (2000). Real Options and Corporate Risk Management. *Journal of Applied Corporate Finance* 13 (2): 64–73.

Trimpop, R. M. (1994). *The Psychology of Risk Taking Behavior.* Elsevier Science, Amsterdam.

Tuchman, B. W. (1962). *The Guns of August (also August 1914).* Constable, London.

Tufano, P. (1996). Who Manages Risks? An Empirical Examination of Risk Management Practices in the Gold Mining Industry. *The Journal of Finance* 51 (4): 1097–1137.

Tufano, P. (1998). The Determinants of Stock Price Exposure: Financial Engineering and the Gold Mining Industry. *The Journal of Finance* 53 (3): 1015–1052.

Tunaru, R., Clark, E. and Viney, H. (2005). An Option Pricing Framework for Valuation of Football Players. *Review of Financial Economics* 14 (3-4): 281–295.

Tversky, A. and Kahneman, D. (1971). Belief in the Law of Small Numbers. *Psychological Bulletin* 76 (2): 105–110.

Tversky, A. and Kahneman, D. (1992). Advances in Prospect Theory. *Journal of Risk and Uncertainty* 5: 297–323.

Unsworth, B. (1999). *Losing Nelson.* Penguin Books, London.

US Census Bureau. (2005). *Statistical Abstract of the United States*. United States Department of Commerce, Washington DC.
US Census Bureau. (2006). *Statistical Abstract of the United States*. United States Department of Commerce: Washington DC.
Vaughan, D. (1996). *The Challenger Launch Decision*. The University of Chicago Press, Chicago IL.
Vaughan, E. J. (1997). *Risk Management*. John Wiley & Sons, New York.
Viscusi, W. K. (1993). The Value of Risks to Life and Health. *Journal of Economic Literature* 31 (4): 1912–1946.
Viscusi, W. K. (2000). Corporate Risk Analysis: A Reckless Act? *Stanford Law Review* 52 (3): 547–597.
Walker, S. M. (2001). *Operational Risk Management*. Conley Walker, Melbourne.
Walls, M. R. and Dyer, J. S. (1996). Risk Propensity and Firm Performance: A Study of the Petroleum Exploration Industry. *Management Science* 42 (7): 1004–1021.
Westfield, M. (2003). *HIH: The Inside Story of Australia's Biggest Corporate Collapse*. John Wiley & Sons, Milton Queensland.
Whiting, R. (1998). Development in Disarray. *Software Magazine* 18 (12): 20.
Williams, S. and Narendran, S. (1999). Determinants of Managerial Risk: Exploring Personality and Cultural Influences. *The Journal of Social Psychology* 139 (1): 102–125.
Wilson, J. (2005). NASA Accused of Breaking Safety Rules in Rush to Launch Discovery. *The Guardian*. London. 19 August 2005.
Wright, T. (2006). *Bad Ground: Inside the Beaconsfield Mine Rescue*. Murdoch Books, Sydney.
Yates, J. F. (1990). *Judgment and Decision Making*. Prentice Hall, New Jersey.
Young, P. C. and Tippins, S. C. (2001). *Managing Business Risk*. American Management Association, New York.
Zaleskiewicz, T. (2001). Beyond Risk Seeking and Risk Aversion: Personality and the dual nature of economic risk taking. *European Journal of Personality* 46: S105–S122.
Zeckhauser, R. (1995). Insurance and Catastrophes. *The Geneva Papers on Risk and Insurance Theory* 20 (2): 157–175.
Zegart, A. (1999). *Flawed by Design: The Evolution of the CIA, JCS, and NSC*. Stanford University Press, Stanford CA.
Zilinskas, R. A., Hope, B. and North, D. W. (2004). A Discussion of Findings and Their Possible Implications from a Workshop on Bioterrorism Threat Assessment and Risk Management. *Risk Analysis* 24 (4): 901–908.

Index

Adverse selection 81, 91, 102–103, 107, 119, 161
Against the Gods (Peter Bernstein) 7
Agency costs 80, 102, 139
Andretti, Mario 129
Angell, Sir Norman 9
Asset-liability management 12, 13, 101, 111–118, 220
Aviation 20–22, 36, 62, 217
  Safety 8–10, 20

Barings Bank 2, 95, 129, 166, 212, 214
Base rate effect: *see* probabilities
Bayes: *see* decision making
Behavioral finance 4, 30, 31
  see also: decision making, risk propensity
BHP Billiton 5, 73, 146–147, 178, 183
Boeing Inc 60, 61, 186
Bond, James 82

Capital Asset Pricing Model 15, 116
Central Intelligence Agency (CIA) 36, 39, 44, 143
Chaos Theory 39–40, 62, 182, 223
Chief Executive Officer (CEO) 5, 18, 34, 40, 70, 91, 134, 140, 142
  Recruiting 148–152
Chief Financial Officer (CFO) xi, 221–223
Chief Risk Officer (CRO) 13, 78, 129–137, 142, 220, 222
Churchill, Sir Winston 139, 190, 208–209
Clarke, Sir Arthur C 58, 60, 154
Company directors 145
Confluential events 9
Corporate crises 177–182
  Circadian rhythms 91
  Compensation strategy 192–195
  Frequency 19–22, 181–182
  Management 174, 177–198
  Predictable surprises 9, 10–11, 98
  Psychic aspects 184–185
Corporate Social Responsibility 156–157, 161
Counterparty risk 111, 124–125, 128, 212
Cultural lock in 60
Crisis: *see* corporate crises, natural disasters

D-Day (1944 Normandy Invasion) 200, 208–210
Daiwa Bank 212–213
Decision making
  Bayesian 45, 51
  Biases 31–38
    Affect heuristic 33, 168
    Bounding 32, 33, 46
    Competitor neglect 90
    Gamblers fallacy 35, 49
    Gender based 32
    Illusion of control 32
    Immediate gratification 37
    Longshot bias 35, 77
    Loss aversion 31, 35, 77, 219
    Managerial failures 25
    Mental accounting 31, 34, 35, 51
    Overconfidence: *see* longshot bias
    Performance 38
    Risk aversion 209
    Self-serving 70
  Facts 35, 44, 168
  Models 45
  Real options 54–56
    see also: options
  Reference levels 29, 34, 38, 51
  Weaknesses 35

Debt of Honor (Tom Clancy) 10
Dell Inc 5–6, 60
Domino theory 8

Drake, Sir Francis 215
Drucker, Peter 7, 43

Enron 8, 60, 129, 130, 164–167, 199, 202–206, 214
Enterprise Risk Management (ERM) 3, 4, 79–99, 112, 129, 131, 136, 143, 168, 170, 185, 220, 221
Equator Principles 158–160
Ethics 13, 17, 47, 62, 69, 70, 83, 90, 144–145, 158, 160–161, 170
  see also: corporate social responsibility governance
Experts 4, 34, 44, 47, 71, 154, 167, 190, 198, 158
  Management of 68–70
  see also: forecasts
ExxonMobil Corp 17, 57, 178, 200
  Exxon Valdez 84, 188, 200, 206–208, 214, 215

Federal Bureau of Investigation (FBI) 39, 136
Financial distress 75, 80, 102
Firm 1
  Culture 80, 86, 136, 145, 148–149, 154, 163, 180, 186, 201, 203, 214
  Exogenous forces 2, 18, 25, 39, 41, 45, 62, 64, 124, 126, 130, 150
  Return
    Link to risk 26, 38, 76–77, 116, 219
    Reliability xi, 18, 86, 202, 213, 220
Firm Risk
  Definition 3, 15, 16, 20
  Drivers 16
    Deregulation 5, 23–26, 62, 128, 165, 183, 215
    Legislation 4, 17, 18, 23, 24, 84, 215
    Technology 24, 155
  Frequency 74, 218
  Linkages between measures 17
  Models 2, 16
  Optimum level 77, 78, 93, 112, 146–148, 219–220
  Point-source risk 17, 20, 21, 23, 41
  Strategic risk 4–6, 12, 16–17, 21–24, 26, 41, 43, 75, 77, 112, 139, 215–217

  see also: counterparty risk, Treasury operations
Fisher, Irving 33
Forecasts 17, 34, 37, 47–48, 58–59, 62–65, 68–70, 88, 98, 146, 158, 166
Framing 2, 33, 37–38, 44, 47, 95, 149, 191
  see also: decision biases
Frog framework 214

Governance 2, 16–18, 26, 40, 41, 76, 97, 102, 130, 139–161, 170, 206
  Crises 195–197
  Definition 140–141
  Risk governance 13, 141–142, 145–146, 219–221
  Stock exchange requirements 144
  see also: company directors
Graham, James 1
Giuliani, Mayor Rudy 174

Hedging 4, 12, 55, 57, 74–76, 79–80, 114–117
  Natural hedging 55, 74, 82, 93–94, 114–117
Herodotus 73, 76
Hicks, Sir John 24
HIH Insurance 5, 38, 107, 143, 210–212, 214
Hindsight effect 43, 71, 84, 98, 99
Hurricane Katrina 33, 108, 163, 173–174, 188

Insurance 4, 11–13, 55, 75, 79–81, 101–111, 115, 167, 195, 197
  As a real option 11, 52, 54, 108–110, 220
  Catastrophe insurance 107–108
Insurance companies 110–111

Johnson, President Lyndon 7, 69
Jones, John Paul 27

Kennedy, President John F 43, 71
Key Risk Indicators (KRI) 97, 131, 133–134, 142, 146, 185, 220
Knowledge risk 88

Lam, James 130
Let's Make a Deal (Monty Hall) 50
Liddell Hart, Sir Basil 43, 189

Mars missions 37, 200
Merck 57, 119
Mobil Corporation: *see* ExxonMobil
Moral hazard 2, 9, 13, 26, 81, 91, 102–104, 126, 139, 149, 183, 213, 215
NASA 10, 55, 84, 95, 200–202, 214
National Australia Bank 36, 40, 123
National risk strategy 163–176
    Canada 170
    New Zealand 171
    United Kingdom 171–172
    United States 164, 173
Natural disasters
    Frequency 19–20, 167
Nehru, Jawaharlal 73, 93
Nelson, Admiral Lord Horatio 151, 188
Nike 61
Nine-eleven (9-11) 8, 9, 10, 136, 167, 173, 174–175, 199
Normal Accidents (Charles Perrow) 10, 26, 41, 199
Nuclear energy 17–18, 77, 80, 81, 89, 217

Oil crisis 23, 116
Olympic Games 39, 63
Options 75
    Theory 11
    Real options 5, 44, 52–57, 75, 110, 155, 220
Outside view 19, 167, 190

Pearl Harbor 10, 90, 200, 208
PEST, PESTLE, etc *see* Firm: exogenous forces
Phoenicia 58, 216
Plutarch 177, 199
Porter (Michael) Model 4, 16, 62, 218
Princess Diana 9
Probabilities 47
    Base rate effect 47, 51, 98
Prospect Theory 27–29

Qantas 115, 178, 183

Risk
    Compliance risk 85, 130–132, 134, 140
    Definition
    Frequency 74, 122–123
    Indicators of risky environments 66–67
    Liquidity risk 117, 120, 125, 130
    Pure risk 75, 79, 102
    Speculative risk 102
    see also: corporate crises, firm risk
Risk budget 116, 127–128
Risk chain 93
Risk communications 155–156
Risk policy 222–223
Risk management
    Approaches 4
    Banking 119–124
        CAMELS 120–121
        see also: counterparty risk, Treasury operations
    Benefits 74
    Checklists 3
    Confluence with finance 11
    Definition 7, 16
    Passive 57, 78, 81, 95
    Techniques
        Avoid 4, 12, 20, 76, 79, 99, 101, 177, 217
        Reduce 4, 12, 55, 74, 82, 217
        Retain 4, 12, 79–81, 101, 217
        Transfer 4, 12, 80
    Type I and II errors 216–219
    see also: Chief Risk Officer, ERM, hedging, insurance, risk policy
Risk maps 96, 121–122, 133
Risk propensity 27, 134, 145
    Definition 11, 16
    Firm 27, 38–41, 75, 147–151, 202, 220
    Managerial 25, 27, 30–32, 34–35, 44–45, 68, 80, 124, 222
    National 166
Risk sensitive foraging 27, 30–31, 34, 38
Risk paradox 143
Risk Society (Ulrich Beck) 7, 26, 199
Root cause analysis 8, 9, 41, 84, 97, 199

Safety drift 213, 221
    see also: firm reliability

Saint Paul 101

Sarbanes Oxley Act of 2002 129, 131, 139, 143, 144, 155
Scenario planning 64–68, 71, 154
Share prices
    Volatility of returns 7, 22–23, 74, 110, 218
Sharpe, William 1, 3
Sheedy, Kevin 39
Six Sigma 47, 131
Sophocles 80
Strategic foresight 44, 58–59, 62
Sun Tzu xi
Sustainability 140, 145, 149, 157, 160, 221
    Sustainability reports 143, 160
Swiss Re 1, 19, 111, 167

Technology
    Managing risks of 155
Treasury operations 112, 119, 136
    Risk management 84, 126–127

Value-at-risk 116, 127–128, 147

Wayne, John 177, 186
Welch, Jack 190
Workplace safety 17, 20
World War I 9, 52, 199

Y2K 64, 91, 99, 129, 166, 167

Zero Sum Society (Lester Thurow) 10

If you have found this book useful you may be interested in other titles from Gower

Understanding and Managing Risk Attitude
David Hillson and Ruth Murray-Webster
208 pages; 978-0-566-08798-1

Estimating Risk: A Management Approach
Andy Garlick
264 pages; 978-0-566-08776-9

Brand Risk:
Adding Risk Literacy to Brand Management
David Abrahams
224 pages; 978-0-566-08724-0

Intelligent Internal Control and Risk Management
Designing High-Performance Risk Control Systems
Matthew Leitch
272 pages; 978-0-566-08799-8

Managing Group Risk Attitude
Ruth Murray-Webster and David Hillson
192 pages; 978-0-566-08787-5

Hacking the Human:
Social Engineering Techniques and Security Countermeasures
Ian Mann
272 pages; 978-0-566-08773-8

GOWER